Remoting Patterns

Remoting Patterns

Foundations of Enterprise, Internet and Realtime Distributed Object Middleware

Markus Völter, voelter - ingenieurbüro für softwaretechnologie, Heidenheim, Germany

Michael Kircher, Siemens AG Corporate Technology, Munich, Germany

Uwe Zdun, Vienna University of Economics and Business Administration, Vienna, Austria

John Wiley & Sons, Ltd

Copyright © 2005 John Wiley & Sons Ltd, The Atrium, Southern Gate, Chichester,
West Sussex PO19 8SQ, England
Telephone   (+44) 1243 779777

Email (for orders and customer service enquiries): cs-books@wiley.co.uk

Visit our Home Page on www.wileyeurope.com or www.wiley.com

All Rights Reserved. No part of this publication may be reproduced, stored in a retrieval system or transmitted in any form or by any means, electronic, mechanical, photocopying, recording, scanning or otherwise, except under the terms of the Copyright, Designs and Patents Act 1988 or under the terms of a licence issued by the Copyright Licensing Agency Ltd, 90 Tottenham Court Road, London W1T 4LP, UK, without the permission in writing of the Publisher, with the exception of any material supplied specifically for the purpose of being entered and executed on a computer system for exclusive use by the purchaser of the publication.Requests to the Publisher should be addressed to the Permissions Department, John Wiley & Sons Ltd, The Atrium, Southern Gate, Chichester, West Sussex PO19 8SQ, England, or emailed to permreq@wiley.co.uk, or faxed to (+44) 1243 770620.

This publication is designed to provide accurate and authoritative information in regard to the subject matter covered. It is sold on the understanding that the Publisher is not engaged in rendering professional services. If professional advice or other expert assistance is required, the services of a competent professional should be sought.

Other Wiley Editorial Offices

John Wiley & Sons Inc., 111 River Street, Hoboken, NJ 07030, USA

Jossey-Bass, 989 Market Street, San Francisco, CA 94103-1741, USA

Wiley-VCH Verlag GmbH, Boschstr. 12, D-69469 Weinheim, Germany

John Wiley & Sons Australia Ltd, 33 Park Road, Milton, Queensland 4064, Australia

John Wiley & Sons (Asia) Pte Ltd, 2 Clementi Loop #02-01, Jin Xing Distripark, Singapore 129809

John Wiley & Sons Canada Ltd, 22 Worcester Road, Etobicoke, Ontario, Canada M9W 1L1

Wiley also publishes its books in a variety of electronic formats. Some content that appears in print may not be available in electronic books.

Library of Congress Cataloging-in-Publication Data

Völter, Markus.
  Remoting patterns: foundations of enterprise, internet and realtime distributed object middleware / Markus Völter, Michael Kircher, Uwe Zdun.
     p. cm.
  Includes bibliographical references and index.
  ISBN 0-470-85662-9 (cloth : alk. paper)
 1. Computer software—Development. 2. Software patterns. 3. Electronic data processing—Distributed processing. 4. Middleware. I. Kircher, Michael. II. Zdun, Uwe. III. Title.
  QA76.76.D47V65 2004
  005.1—dc22
                                                              2004018713

British Library Cataloguing in Publication Data

A catalogue record for this book is available from the British Library

ISBN 0-470-85662-9

Typeset in 10.7/13.7 pt Book Antiqua by Laserwords Private Limited, Chennai, India
from files produced by the authors
Printed and bound in Great Britain by Biddles Ltd, King's Lynn
This book is printed on acid-free paper responsibly manufactured from sustainable forestry in which at least two trees are planted for each one used for paper production.

Contents

Foreword   ix

Series Foreword   xiii

Preface   xvii

   How to read this book   xvii
   Goals of the book   xix
   About the authors   xx
   Acknowledgments   xxii
   Patterns and Pattern Languages   xxiii
   Our Pattern form   xxviii
   Key to the illustrations   xxxi

1 Introduction To Distributed Systems   1

   Distributed Systems: reasons and challenges   1
   Communication middleware   7
   Remoting styles   9

2 Pattern Language Overview   19

   Broker   20
   Overview of the Pattern chapters   27

3 Basic Remoting Patterns   35

   Requestor   37
   Client Proxy   40
   Invoker   43
   Client Request Handler   48
   Server Request Handler   51
   Marshaller   55
   Interface Description   59
   Remoting Error   63
   Interactions among the patterns   66

4 Identification Patterns — 73

Object ID — 74
Absolute Object Reference — 77
Lookup — 81
Interactions among the patterns — 85

5 Lifecycle Management Patterns — 87

Basic lifecycle patterns — 88
Static Instance — 90
Per-Request Instance — 93
Client-Dependent Instance — 96
General resource management patterns — 99
Lazy Acquisition — 100
Pooling — 103
Leasing — 106
Passivation — 109
Interactions among the patterns — 111

6 Extension Patterns — 127

Invocation Interceptor — 130
Invocation Context — 133
Protocol Plug-In — 135
Interactions among the patterns — 138

7 Extended Infrastructure Patterns — 141

Lifecycle Manager — 143
Configuration Group — 146
Local Object — 149
QoS Observer — 151
Location Forwarder — 154
Interactions among the patterns — 158

8 Invocation Asynchrony Patterns — 163

Fire and Forget — 165
Sync with Server — 168
Poll Object — 170
Result Callback — 173
Interactions among the patterns — 176

9 Technology Projections — 185

10 .NET Remoting Technology Projection — 187

A brief history of .NET Remoting — 187
.NET concepts – a brief introduction — 188
A pattern map for Remoting Patterns — 189
A simple .NET Remoting example — 190
Remoting boundaries — 195
Basic internals of .NET Remoting — 197
Error handling in .NET — 198
Server-activated instances — 199
Client-dependent instances and Leasing — 208
More advanced lifecycle management — 215
Internals of .NET Remoting — 217
Extensibility of .NET Remoting — 221
Asynchronous communication — 228
Outlook for the next generation — 235

11 Web Services Technology Projection — 239

A brief history of Web Services — 239
A pattern map for Remoting Patterns — 244
SOAP messages — 244
Message processing in Web Services — 256
Protocol integration in Web Services — 264
Marshaling using SOAP XML encoding — 266
Lifecycle management in Web Services — 269
Client-Side asynchrony — 270
Web Services and QoS — 276
Web Services security — 278
Lookup of Web Services: UDDI — 279
Other Web Services frameworks — 280
Consequences of the pattern variants used in Web Services — 289

12 CORBA Technology Projection — 293

A brief history of CORBA — 293
A pattern map for Remoting Patterns — 294
An initial example in CORBA — 296
CORBA basics — 298
Messaging in CORBA — 318
Real-Time CORBA — 323

13 Related Concepts, Technologies, and Patterns **333**

Related patterns 335
Distribution infrastructures 338
Quality attributes 347
Aspect-orientation and Remoting 353

Appendix A Extending AOP Frameworks for Remoting **355**

References **363**

Index **377**

Foreword

Many of today's enterprise computing systems are powered by distributed object middleware. Such systems, which are common in industries such as telecommunications, finance, manufacturing, and government, often support applications that are critical to particular business operations. Because of this, distributed object middleware is often held to stringent performance, reliability, and availability requirements. Fortunately, modern approaches have no problem meeting or exceeding these requirements. Today, successful distributed object systems are essentially taken for granted.

There was a time, however, when making such claims about the possibilities of distributed objects would have met with disbelief and derision. In their early days, distributed object approaches were often viewed as mere academic fluff with no practical utility. Fortunately, the creators of visionary distributed objects systems such as Eden, Argus, Emerald, COMANDOS, and others were undeterred by such opinion. Despite the fact that the experimental distributed object systems of the 1980s were generally impractical – too big, too slow, or based on features available only from particular specialized platforms or programming languages – the exploration and experimentation required to put them together collectively paved the way for the practical distributed objects systems that followed.

The 1990s saw the rise of several commercially successful and popular distributed object approaches, notably the Common Object Request Broker Architecture (CORBA) promoted by the Object Management Group (OMG) and Microsoft's Common Object Model (COM). CORBA was specifically designed to address the inherent heterogeneity of business computing networks, where mixtures of machine types, operating systems, programming languages, and application styles are the norm and must co-exist and cooperate. COM, on the other hand, was built specifically to support component-oriented applications running on the Microsoft Windows operating system.

Today, COM has been largely subsumed by its successor, .NET, while CORBA remains in wide use as a well-proven architecture for building and deploying significant enterprise-scale heterogeneous systems, as well as real-time and embedded systems.

As this book so lucidly explains, despite the fact that CORBA and COM were designed for fundamentally different purposes, they share a number of similarities. These similarities range from basic notions, including remote objects, client and server applications, proxies, marshalers, synchronous and asynchronous communications, and interface descriptions, to more advanced areas, including object identification and lookup, infrastructure extension, and lifecycle management. Not surprisingly, though, these similarities do not end at CORBA and COM. They can also be found in newer technologies and approaches, including .NET, the Java 2 Enterprise Edition (J2EE), and even in Web Services (which, strictly speaking, is not a pure distributed object technology, but nevertheless has inherited many of its characteristics).

Such similarities are of course better known as 'patterns'. Patterns are generally not so much created as discovered, much as a miner finds a diamond or a gold nugget buried in the earth. Successful patterns result from the study of successful systems, and the remoting patterns presented here are no exception. Our authors, Markus, Michael, and Uwe, who are each well versed in both the theory and practice of distributed objects, have worked extensively with each of the technologies I've mentioned. Applying their pattern-mining talents and efforts, they have captured for the rest of us the critical essence of a number of successful solutions and approaches found in a number of similar distributed objects technologies.

Given my own long history with CORBA, I am not surprised to find that several of the patterns that Markus, Michael, and Uwe document here are among my personal favorites. For example, topping my list is the Invocation Interceptor pattern, which I have found to be critical for creating distributed objects middleware that provides extensibility and modularity without sacrificing performance. Another favorite of mine is the Leasing pattern, which can be extremely effective for managing object lifecycles.

This book does not just describe a few remoting patterns, however. While many patterns books comprise only a loose collection of patterns, this book also provides a series of technology projections that tie the patterns directly back to the technologies that employ them. These projections clearly show how the patterns are used within .NET, CORBA, and Web Services, effectively recreating these architectures from the patterns mined from within them. With technology projections like these, it has never been easier to see the relationships and roles of different patterns with respect to each other within an entire architecture. These technology projections clearly link the patterns, which are already invaluable by themselves, into a comprehensive, harmonious, and rich distributed objects pattern language. In doing so, they conspicuously reveal the similarities among these different distributed object technologies. Indeed, we might have avoided the overzealous and tiresome 'CORBA vs. COM' arguments of the mid-1990s had we had these technology projections and patterns at the time.

Distributed objects technologies continue to evolve and grow. These patterns have essentially provided the building blocks for the experimental systems of the 1980s, for the continued commercial success and wide deployment of distributed objects that began in the 1990s, and for today's Web Services integration approaches. Due to the never-ending march of technology, you can be sure that before too long new technologies will appear to displace Web Services. You can also be sure that the remoting patterns that Markus, Michael, and Uwe have so expertly provided for us here will be at the heart of those new technologies as well.

Steve Vinoski
Chief Engineer, Product Innovation
IONA Technologies

March 2004

Series Foreword

At first glance writing and publishing a remoting pattern language book might appear surprising. Who is its audience? From a naïve perspective, it could only be distributed object middleware developers – a rather small community. Application developers merely *use* such middleware – why should they bother with the details of how it is designed? We see confirmation of this view from the sales personnel and product 'blurbs' of middleware vendors: remote communication should be transparent to application developers, and it is the job of the middleware to deal with it. So why spend so much time on writing – and reading – a pattern language that only a few software developers actually need?

From a realistic perspective, however, the world looks rather different. Despite all advances in distributed object middleware, building distributed systems and applications is still a challenging, non-trivial task. This applies not only to application-specific concerns, such as how to split and distribute an application's functionality across a computer network. Surprisingly, many challenges in building distributed software relate to an appropriate use of the underlying middleware. I do not mean issues such as using APIs correctly, but fundamental concerns. For example, the type of communication between remote objects has a direct impact on the performance of the system, its scalability, its reliability, and so on and so forth. It has an even stronger impact on how remote objects must be designed, and how their functionality must be decomposed, to really benefit from a specific communication style.

It is therefore a myth to believe that remote communication is transparent to a distributed application. The many failures and problems of software development projects that did so speak very clearly! Failures occur due to the misconception that 'fire and forget' invocations are reliable, that remote objects are always readily available at their clients' fingertips, or problems due to a lack of awareness that message-based remote communication decouples operation invocation from operation execution not only in space, but also in time, and so on.

But how do I know what is 'right' for my distributed system? How do I know what the critical issues are in remote communication and what options exist to deal with them? How do I know what design guidelines I must follow in my application to be able to use a specific middleware or remote communication style correctly and effectively? The answer is simple: understanding both how it works, and why it works the way it works. Speaking pictorially, we must open the black box called 'middleware', sweeping the 'shade' of communication-transparency aside, and take a look inside. Fundamental concepts of remoting and modern distributed object middleware must be known to, and understood by, application developers if they are to build distributed systems that work! There is no way around this.

But how can we gain this important knowledge and understanding? Correct: by reading and digesting a pattern language that describes remoting, and mapping its concepts onto the middleware used in our own distributed systems! So in reality the audience for a remoting pattern language is quite large, as it comprises every developer of distributed software.

This book contributes to the understanding of distributed object middleware in two ways. First it presents a comprehensive pattern language that addresses all the important aspects in distributed object middleware – from remoting fundamentals, through object identification and lifecycle management, to advanced aspects such as application-specific extensions and asynchronous communication. Second, and of immense value for practical work, this book provides three technology projections that illustrate how the patterns that make up the language are applied in popular object-oriented middleware technologies: .NET, Web Services, and CORBA. Together, these two parts form a powerful package that provides you with all the conceptual knowledge and various viewpoints necessary to understand and use modern communication environments correctly and effectively. This book thus complements and completes books that describe the 'nuts and bolts' – such as the APIs – of specific distributed object middlewares by adding the 'big picture' and architectural framework in which they live.

Accept what this book offers and explore the secrets of distributed object middleware. I am sure you will enjoy the journey as much as I did.

Frank Buschmann
Siemens AG, Corporate Technology

Preface

Today distributed object middleware belongs among the basic elements in the toolbox of software developer, designers, and architects who are developing distributed systems. Popular examples of such distributed object middleware systems are CORBA, Web Services, DCOM, Java RMI, and .NET Remoting. There are many other books that explain how a particular distributed object middleware works. If you just want to use one specific distributed object middleware, many of these books are highly valuable. However, as a professional software developer, designer, or architect working with distributed systems, you will also experience situations in which just understanding how to use one particular middleware is not enough. You are required to gain a deeper understanding of the inner workings of the middleware, so that you can customize or extend it to meet your needs. Or you might be forced to migrate your system to a new kind of middleware as a consequence of business requirements, or to integrate systems that use different middleware products.

This book is intended to help you in these and similar situations: it explains the inner workings of successful approaches and technologies in the field of distributed object middleware in a practical manner. To achieve this we use a pattern language that describes the essential building blocks of distributed object middleware, based on a number of compact, Alexandrian-style [AIS+77] patterns. We supplement the pattern language with three technology projections that explain how the patterns are realized in different real-world examples of distributed object middleware systems: .NET Remoting, Web Services, and CORBA.

How to read this book

This book is aimed primarily at software developers, designers, and architects who have at least a basic understanding of software development and design concepts.

For readers who are new to patterns, we introduce patterns and pattern languages to some extend in this section. Readers familiar with patterns might want to skip this. We also briefly explain the pattern form and the diagrams used in this book. You might find it useful to scan this information and use it as a reference when reading the later chapters of the book.

In the pattern chapters and the technology projections we assume some knowledge of distributed system development. In Chapter 1, *Introduction To Distributed Systems*, we introduce the basic terminology and concepts used in this book. Readers who are familiar with the terminology and concepts may skip that chapter. If you are completely new to this field, you might want to read a more detailed introduction such as Tanenbaum and van Steen's *Distributed Systems: Principles and Paradigms* [TS02].

For all readers, we recommend reading the pattern language chapters as a whole. This should give you a fairly good picture of how distributed object middleware systems work. When working with the pattern language, you can usually go directly to particular patterns of interest, and use the pattern relationships described in the pattern descriptions to find related patterns.

Details of the interactions between the patterns can be found at the end of each pattern chapter, depicted in a number of sequence diagrams. We have not included these interactions in the individual pattern descriptions for two reasons. First, it would make the pattern chapters less readable. Second, the patterns in each chapter have strong interactions, so it makes sense to illustrate them with integrated examples, instead of scattering the examples across the individual pattern descriptions.

We recommend that you look closely at the sequence diagram examples, especially if you want to implement your own distributed object middleware system or extend an existing one. This will give you further insight into how the pattern language can be implemented. As the next step, you might want to read the technology projections to see a couple of well-established real-world examples of how the pattern language is implemented by vendors.

If you want to understand the commonalities and differences between some of the mainstream distributed object middleware systems, you should read the technology projections. You can do this in any order you prefer. They are completely independent of each other.

Goals of the book

Numerous projects use, extend, integrate, customize, and build distributed object middleware. The major goal of the pattern language in this book is to provide knowledge about the general, recurring architecture of successful distributed object middleware, as well as more concrete design and implementation strategies. You can benefit from reading and understanding this pattern language in several ways:

- If you want to *use* distributed object middleware, you will benefit from better understanding the concepts of your middleware implementation. This in turn helps you to make better use of the middleware. If you know how to use one middleware system and need to switch to another, understanding the patterns of distributed object middleware helps you to see the commonalities, in spite of different remoting abstractions, terminologies, implementation language concepts, and so forth.
- Sometimes you need to *extend* the middleware with additional functionality. For example, suppose you are developing a Web Services application. Because Web Services are relatively new, your chosen Web Services framework might not implement specific security or transaction features that you need for your application. You must then implement these features on your own. Our patterns help you to find the best hooks for extending the Web Services framework. The patterns show you several alternative successful implementations of such extensions. The book also helps you to you find similar solutions in other middleware implementations, so that you avoid reinventing the wheel.

  Another typical extension is the introduction of 'new' remoting styles, implemented on top of existing middleware. Consider server-side component architectures, such as CORBA Components, COM+, or Enterprise Java Beans (EJB). These use distributed object middleware implementations as a foundation for remote communication [VSW02]. They extend the middleware with new concepts. Again, as a developer of a component architecture, you have to understand the patterns of the distributed object

- middleware, for example to integrate the lifecycle models of the components and remote objects.
- While distributed object middleware is used to integrate heterogeneous systems, you might encounter situations in which you need to *integrate* the various middleware systems themselves. Consider a situation in which your employer takes over another company that uses a different middleware product from that used in your company. You need to integrate the two middleware solutions to let the information systems of the two companies work in concert. Our patterns can help you find integration points and identify promising solutions.
- In rarer cases you might need to *customize* distributed object middleware, or even *build* it from scratch. Consider for example an embedded system with tight constraints on memory consumption, performance, and real-time communication [Aut04]. If no suitable middleware product exists, or all available products turn out to be inappropriate and/or have a footprint that is to large, the developers must develop their own solution. As an alternative, you could look at existing open-source solutions and try to customize them for your needs. Here our patterns can help you to identify critical components of the middleware and assess the effort required in customizing them. If customizing an existing middleware does not seem to be feasible, you can use the patterns to build a new distributed object middleware for your application.

The list above consists of only a few examples. We hope they illustrate the broad variety of situations in which you might want to get a deeper understanding of distributed object middleware. As these situations occur repeatedly, we hope these examples illustrate why we think the time is ready for a book that explains such issues in a way that is accessible to practitioners.

About the authors

Markus Völter

Markus Völter works as an independent consultant on software technology and engineering based in Heidenheim, Germany. His primary focus is software architecture and patterns, middleware and model-driven software development. Markus has consulted and coached in many different domains, such as banking, health care, e-business, telematics, astronomy, and automotive embedded systems, in projects ranging from 5 to 150 developers.

Markus is also a regular speaker at international conferences on software technology and object orientation. Among others, he has given talks and tutorials at ECOOP, OOPSLA, OOP, OT, JAOO and GPCE. Markus has published patterns at various PLoP conferences and writes articles for various magazines on topics that he finds interesting. He is also co-author of the book *Server Component Patterns*, which is - just like the book you are currently reading - part of the Wiley series in Software Design Patterns.

When not dealing with software, Markus enjoys cross-country flying in the skies over southern Germany in his glider.

Markus can be reached at voelter@acm.org or via www.voelter.de

Michael Kircher

Michael Kircher is working currently as Senior Software Engineer at Siemens AG Corporate Technology in Munich, Germany. His main fields of interest include distributed object computing, software architecture, patterns, agile methodologies, and management of knowledge workers in innovative environments. He has been involved in many projects as a consultant and developer within various Siemens business areas, building software for distributed systems. Among these were the development of software for UMTS base stations, toll systems, postal automation systems, and operation and maintenance software for industry and telecommunication systems.

In recent years Michael has published papers at numerous conferences on topics such as patterns, software architecture for distributed systems, and eXtreme Programming, and has organized several workshops at conferences such as OOPSLA and EuroPLoP. He is also co-author of the book *Pattern-Oriented Software Architecture, Volume 3: Patterns for Resource Management*.

In his spare time Michael likes to combine family life with enjoying nature, engaging in sports, or just watching wildlife.

Michael can be reached at michael@kircher-schwanninger.de or via www.kircher-schwanninger.de

Uwe Zdun

Uwe Zdun is working currently as an assistant professor in the Department of Information Systems at the Vienna University of Economics and Business Administration. He received his Doctoral degree from the University of Essen in 2002, where he worked from 1999 to 2002 as research assistant in the software specification group. His research interests include software patterns, scripting, object-orientation, software architecture, and Web engineering. Uwe has been involved as a consultant and developer in many software projects. He is author of a number of open-source software systems, including Extended Object Tcl (XOTcl), ActiWeb, Frag, and Leela, as well as many other open-source and industrial software systems.

In recent years he has published in numerous conferences and journals, and co-organized a number of workshops at conferences such as EuroPLoP, CHI, and OOPSLA.

He enjoys hiking, biking, pool, and guitar playing.

Uwe can be reached at zdun@acm.org or via wi.wu-wien.ac.at/~uzdun

Acknowledgments

A book such as this would be impossible without the support of many other people. For their support in discussing the contents of the book and for providing their feedback, we express our gratitude.

First of all, we want to thank our shepherd, Steve Vinoski, and the pattern series editor, Frank Buschmann. They have read the book several times and provided in-depth comments on technical content, as well as on the structure and coherence of the pattern language.

We also want to thank the following people who have provided comments on various versions of the manuscript, as well as on extracted papers that have been workshopped at VikingPLoP 2002 and EuroPLoP 2003: Mikio Aoyama, Steve Berczuk, Valter Cazzalo, Anniruddha Gokhale, Lars Grunske, Klaus Jank, Kevlin Henney, Wolfgang Herzner, Don Hinton, Klaus Marquardt, Jan Mendling, Roy Oberhauser, Joe Oberleitner, Juha Pärsinen, Michael Pont, Alexander Schmid, Kristijan Elof Sorenson (thanks for playing shepherd and proxy), Michael Stal, Mark Strembeck, Oliver Vogel, Johnny Willemsen, and Eberhard Wolff.

Finally, we thank those that have been involved with the production of the book: our copy-editor Steve Rickaby and editors Gaynor Redvers-Mutton and Juliet Booker. It is a pleasure working with such proficient people.

Patterns and Pattern Languages

Over the past couple of years patterns have become part of the mainstream of software development. They appear in different types and forms.

The most popular patterns are those for software design, pioneered by the Gang-of-Four (GoF) book [GHJV95] and continued by many other pattern authors. Design patterns can be applied very broadly, because they focus on everyday design problems. In addition to design patterns, the patterns community has created patterns for software architecture [BMR+96, SSRB00], analysis [Fow96], and even non-IT topics such as organizational or pedagogical patterns [Ped04, FV00]. There are many other kinds of patterns, and some are specific for a particular domain.

What is a Pattern?

A pattern, according to the original definition of Alexander[1] [AIS+77], is:

> ...a three-part rule, which expresses a relation between a certain context, a problem, and a solution.

This is a very general definition of a pattern. It is probably a bad idea to cite Alexander in this way, because he explains this definition

---

1. In his book, *A Pattern Language – Towns • Buildings • Construction* [AIS+77] Christopher Alexander presents a pattern language consisting of 253 patterns about architecture. He describes patterns that guide the creation of space for people to live, including cities, houses, rooms, and so on. The notion of patterns in software builds on this early work by Alexander.

extensively. In particular, how can we distinguish a pattern from a simple recipe? Consider the following example:

Context	You are driving a car.
Problem	The traffic lights in front of you are red. You must not run over them. What should you do?
Solution	Brake.

Is this a pattern? Certainly not. It is just a simple, plain if-then rule. So, again, what is a pattern? Jim Coplien, on the Hillside Web site [Cop04], proposes another, slightly longer definition that summarizes the discussion in Alexander's book:

> *Each pattern is a three-part rule, which expresses a relation between a certain context, a certain system of forces which occurs repeatedly in that context, and a certain software configuration which allows these forces to resolve themselves.*

Coplien mentions *forces*. Forces are considerations that somehow constrain or influence the solution proposed by the pattern. The set of forces builds up *tension*, usually formulated concisely as a problem statement. A solution for the given problem has to balance the forces somehow, because the forces cannot usually all be resolved optimally – a compromise has to be found.

To be understandable by the reader, a pattern should describe *how* the forces are balanced in the proposed solution, and *why* they have been balanced in the proposed way. In addition, the advantages and disadvantages of such a solution should be explained, to allow the reader to understand the *consequences* of using the pattern.

Patterns are solutions to recurring problems. They therefore need to be quite general, so that they can be applied to more than one concrete problem. However, the solution should be sufficiently concrete to be practically useful, and it should include a description of a specific software configuration. Such a configuration consists of the participants of the pattern, their responsibilities, and their interactions. The level of detail of this description can vary, but after reading the pattern, the reader should know what he has to do to implement the pattern's solution. As the above discussion highlights, a pattern is not merely a set of UML diagrams or code fragments.

Patterns are never 'new ideas'. Patterns are *proven* solutions to recurring problems. So *known uses* for a pattern must always exist. A good rule of thumb is that something that does not have at least three known uses is not a pattern. In software patterns, this means that systems must exist that are implemented according to the pattern. The usual approach to writing patterns is not to invent them from scratch – instead they are discovered in, and then extracted from, real-life systems. These systems then serve as known uses for the pattern. To find patterns in software systems, the pattern author has to abstract the problem/solution pair from the concrete instances found in the systems at hand. Abstracting the pattern while preserving comprehensibility and practicality is the major challenge of pattern writing.

There is another aspect to what makes a good pattern, the *quality without a name* (QWAN) [AIS+77]. The quality without a name cannot easily be described: the best approximation is *universally-recognizable aesthetic beauty and order*. So a pattern's solution must somehow appeal to the aesthetic sense of the pattern reader – in our case, to the software developer, designer, or architect. While there is no universal definition of beauty, there certainly are some guidelines as to what is a good solution and what is not. For example, a software system, while addressing a complex problem, should be efficient, flexible and easily understandable. The principle of beauty is an important – and often underestimated – guide for judging whether a technological design is good or bad. David Gelernter details this in his book *Machine Beauty* [Gel99].

Classifications of Patterns in this book

The patterns in this book are *software patterns*. They can further be seen as *architectural* patterns or *design* patterns. It is not easy to draw the line between architecture and design, and often the distinction depends on your situation and viewpoint. For a rough distinction, let's refer to the definition of software architecture from Bass, Clements, and Kazman [BCK03]:

> *The software architecture of a program or computing system is the structure or structures of the system, which comprise software components, the externally-visible properties of those components and the relationships among them.*

What we can see here is that whether a specific pattern is categorized as an architectural pattern or a design pattern depends heavily on the viewpoint of the designer or architect. Consider for example the *Interpreter* pattern [GHJV95]. The description in the Gang-of-Four book describes it as a concrete design guideline. Yet according to the software architecture definition above, instances of the pattern are often seen as a central elements in the architecture of software systems, because an *Interpreter* is a central component of the system that is externally visible.

Most of the patterns in this book can be seen as falling into both categories – design patterns and architectural patterns. From the viewpoint of the designer, they provide concrete guidelines for the design of a part of the distributed object middleware. Yet they also comprise larger, visible structures of the distributed object middleware and focus on the most important components and their relationships. Thus, according to the above definition, they are architectural foundations of the distributed object middleware as well.

From patterns to pattern languages

A single pattern describes one solution to a particular, recurring problem. However, 'really big problems' usually cannot be described in one pattern without compromising readability.

The pattern community has therefore come up with several ways to combine patterns to solve a more complex problem or a set of related problems:

- *Compound patterns* are patterns that are assembled from other, smaller patterns. These smaller patterns are usually already well known in the community. Often, for a number of related smaller patterns, known uses exist in which these patterns are always used together in the same software configuration. Such situations are good candidates for description as a compound pattern. It is essential that the compound pattern actually solves a distinct problem, and not just a combination of the problems of its contained patterns. A compound pattern also resolves its own set of forces. An example of a compound pattern is *Bureaucracy* by Dirk Riehle [Rie97], which combines *Composite, Mediator, Chain of Responsibility,* and *Observer* (all from the GoF book, [GHJV95]).

- A *family of patterns* is a collection of patterns that solves the same general problem. Each pattern either defines the problem more specifically, or resolves the common forces in a different way. For example, different solutions could focus on flexibility, performance or simplicity. Usually each of the patterns has different consequences. A family therefore describes a problem and *several* proven solutions. It is up to the reader to select the appropriate solution, taking into account how he wants to resolve the common forces in his particular context. A good example is James Noble's *Basic Relationship Patterns* [Nob97], which describes several alternatives ways in which logical relationships between objects can be realized in software.

- A *collection,* or *system of patterns* comprises several patterns from the same domain or problem area. Each pattern stands on its own, sometimes referring to other patterns in the collection in its implementation. The patterns form a system because they can be used by a developer working in a specific domain, each pattern resolving a distinct problem the developer might come across during his work. A good example is *Pattern Oriented Software Architecture* by Buschmann, Meunier, Rohnert, Sommerlad, and Stal (also known as POSA 1 [BMR+96]).

The most powerful way of combining patterns is a *pattern language*. Pattern languages have several characteristics:

- A pattern language has a language-wide goal. The purpose of the language is to guide the user step by step to reach this goal. The patterns in a pattern language are not necessarily useful in isolation. The patterns in this book, for example, form a pattern language in the domain of distributed object middleware.

- A pattern language is *generative* in nature. Applying the pattern language generates a *whole*. This generated whole should be 'beautiful' in the sense of QWAN. The whole is 'generated' by applying the patterns in the pattern language one after another in an incremental process of refinement. The basic idea is that each refinement step makes the whole successively more coherent.

- To generate the whole, the pattern language has to be applied in a specific order. This order is defined by one or more sequences. Depending on the context in which the pattern language is applied, or which aspects of the whole are actually required, there can be several sequences through a pattern language.

- Because the patterns must be applied in a specific sequence, each pattern must define its place in the sequence. To achieve this, each pattern has a section called its *context*, which mentions earlier patterns that must be implemented before the current pattern can be implemented successfully. Each pattern can also feature a *resulting context* that describes how to continue. This contains references to the patterns that can be used to help in the implementation of the current pattern, or explains how to proceed in the incremental refinement process of the whole.

Pattern languages – in contrast to the other forms of combining patterns discussed above – not only specify solutions to specific problems, but also describe a way to create the whole, the overall goal of the pattern language. Note that a particular pattern can play a role in more than one pattern language. For example, we integrate some patterns from other sources in our pattern language, such as the *Broker* pattern [BMR+96], which we use to motivate the overall problem and context of the pattern language in this book.

Our Pattern form

In this section we provide a brief introduction to the pattern form used in this book. The form of our patterns is similar to the Alexandrian [AIS+77] format, but omits examples in the pattern description and photographs used to visualize the pattern. This book contains many example applications of the patterns, but instead of presenting an example for each individual pattern, the example applications appear separately in the form of UML sequence diagrams at the end of each pattern chapter, and as *Technology Projections*.

The individual pattern descriptions are structured as follows: each pattern starts with a *name*. The name is an important part of a pattern in a pattern language, because it is used throughout the language to refer to the particular pattern. When referencing pattern names from our pattern language, we always write them in SMALLCAPS font. External patterns from the literature are highlighted in *Italics*.

The next section is the *context* of the pattern in the pattern language. The context is separated by three stars from the main body of the pattern. The main body starts with a *problem* section written in bold face font. The problem, addressed by the pattern, is then illustrated in more detail in the *problem detail* section plain font. The system of forces leading to the pattern's solution is discussed here. The section is written in two different styles:

- In structural patterns this section contains problem details and a short discussion of forces.
- In behavioral patterns, found in Chapter 5, *Lifecycle Management Patterns* and Chapter 8, *Invocation Asynchrony Patterns*, this section contains an example application scenario that motivates the need for the pattern's solution. We feel that such an example illustrates the forces for those patterns much better than an abstract discussion.

Following the problem discussion, the *solution* of the pattern is provided using bold face, illustrated by a figure. Three stars separate the main body of the pattern from the *solution details* that follow. The solution details discuss variants of the pattern, related patterns (in the pattern language and from literature), as well as the consequences of applying the pattern.

Examples and known uses are provided in the *Technology Projections* chapter, which projects the patterns onto a specific technology. We present technology projections for .NET Remoting, Web Services, and CORBA. Other known uses of the patterns are discussed in Chapter 13, *Related*

Concepts, Technologies, and Patterns. Below, the pattern format layout is illustrated by an example, with some side-headings for explanation.

Pattern Name	**Invocation Interceptor**
Context	Applications need to transparently integrate add-on services.

❄ ❄ ❄

Problem	In addition to hosting remote objects, the server application often has to provide a number of add-on services, such as transactions, logging, or security. The clients and remote objects themselves should be independent of those services.
Problem Detail and Forces - or - Motivating Example	Consider the typical concern of security in distributed object middleware: remote objects need to be protected from unauthorized access. The remote objects themselves should not have to worry about authorization – they should be accessible with or without authorization enabled. When the server application needs to enforce security, the client must add the relevant credentials, such as user name and password, to the request.

Therefore:

Solution	Provide hooks in the invocation path, for example in the INVOKER and REQUESTOR, to plug in INVOCATION INTERCEPTORS. INVOCATION INTERCEPTORS are invoked before and after request and reply messages pass the hook. Provide the interceptor with all the necessary information to allow it to provide meaningful add-on services, such as operation name, parameters, OBJECT ID, and, if used, the INVOCATION CONTEXT.

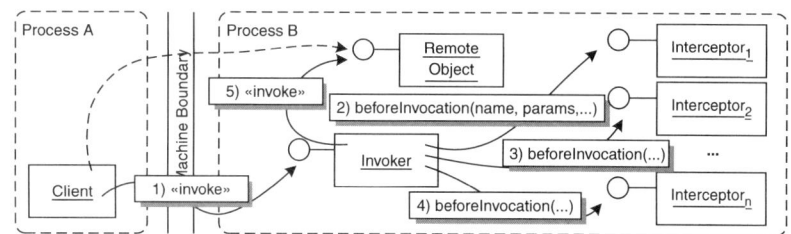

Scenario Illustration and Explanation	The INVOKER receives an invocation and checks whether INVOCATION INTERCEPTORS are registered for the remote object. If so, the interceptor is invoked before and after the actual invocation.

❄ ❄ ❄

Solution Details and Related Patterns	INVOCATION INTERCEPTORS allow for the transparent integration of additional orthogonal services. These additional services are independent of the individual clients and remote objects.
Consequences	If more than one INVOCATION INTERCEPTOR is applicable to an invocation, the interceptors are often interdependent. In most cases, therefore, they are arranged in a chain of interceptors. Each INVOCATION INTERCEPTOR forwards the invocation to the next interceptor in the chain. Alternatively, the components that provide the hooks, such as REQUESTOR and INVOKER, can manage the passing of information between elements of the chain.
References to Patterns from the Literature	The INVOCATION INTERCEPTOR is a specialization of *Interceptor* [SSRB00] for distributed object middleware.

Structure of the Pattern chapters

The pattern chapters have a specific structure. Some of the chapters provide additional sections, but the following three sections are common to each chapter:

- Each chapter starts with an introduction to the general topic of the chapter. Each pattern in the chapter is introduced with one or two sentences. An overview diagram that shows the relationship between the different patterns is provided. This diagram also connects the patterns to patterns in other chapters – the patterns from other chapters are rendered in gray in these figures.
- The second part of each pattern chapter introduces the patterns themselves. Each pattern – using the structure shown above – covers a couple of pages.
- A third section, called *Interactions among the Patterns*, shows how the patterns interact. The interactions show example usage scenarios only, and are therefore incomplete. The scenarios are illustrated with UML sequence diagrams and described in the associated text. The *Technology Projection* chapters provide more detailed example applications that focus on the pattern language as a whole.

Key to the illustrations

Most of the illustrations in this book use UML, with some slight variations. We explain the UML subset we use in the following sections. The collaboration diagrams used in the pattern descriptions are not true UML.

Collaborations

Each pattern is illustrated with a 'collaboration diagram'. In addition to the dynamic collaboration semantics known from the respective UML diagrams, we also display containment structures in these diagrams, so they are not formal UML diagrams. The following figure provides an example illustration, annotated with comments to serve as a key.

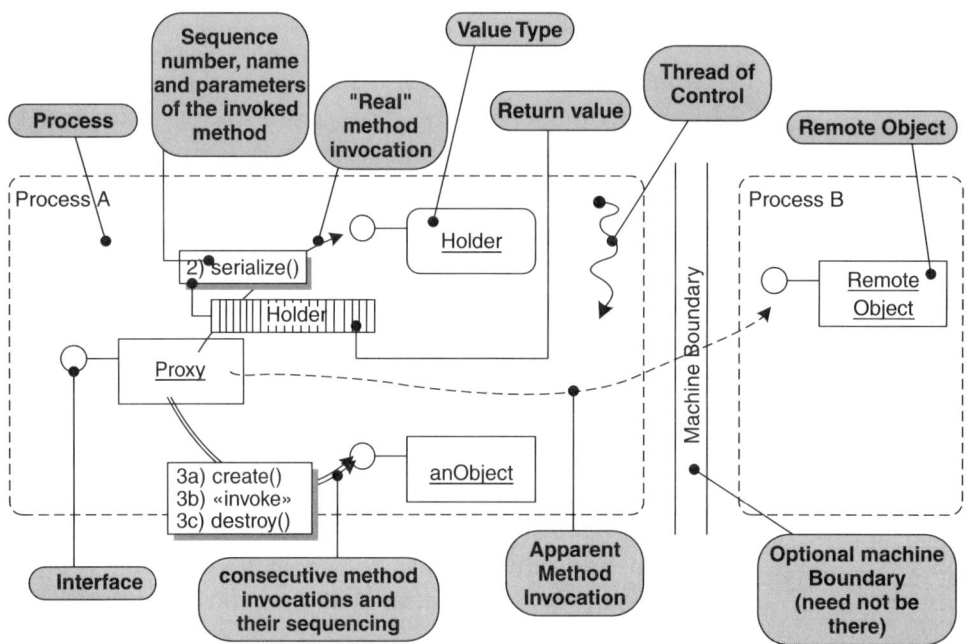

Here are some more details of our notation:

- Although remoting is used typically to communicate between one machine and another, that's not necessarily always the case – it can also be used for communication between two processes on the same machine. This is the reason why the *Machine Boundary* is optional.

- An *apparent method invocation* means that the denoted operation is logically executed directly by the invoking entity, but in reality other intermediate steps might be involved, such as a proxy.

- The «*stereotype*» notation used in some methods denotes the fact that we don't actually invoke an operation, but influence the target conceptually. For example, «create» does not mean that the create operation is called, but instead that the client *creates* the target object.

- The double-arrow does not mean that there are exactly two operations invoked, but instead, that a sequence of operations – those mentioned in the attached box – are executed directly after one another.

Class diagrams

Class diagrams are standard UML, except for the dependency arrow, which we draw as a solid arrow instead of a lined arrow. This is purely for aesthetic reasons.

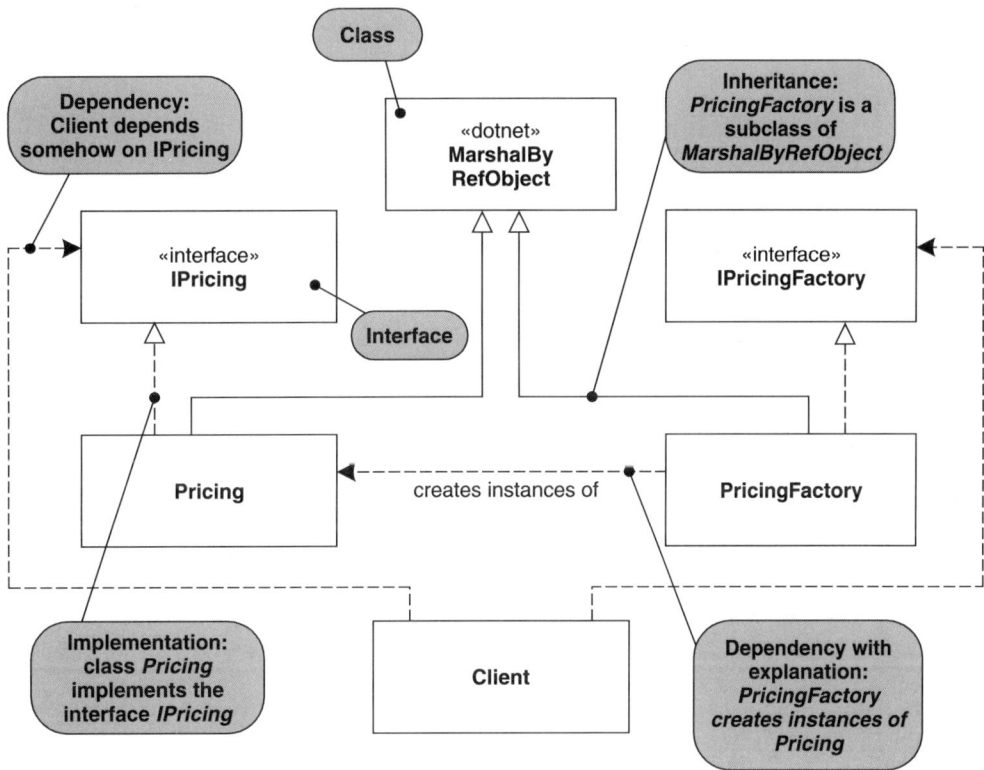

Interactions

At the end of each pattern chapter we illustrate the patterns, their use, and their collaborations with a set of sequence diagrams. These are mostly standard UML and thus require no specific explanation. However, we use some non-standard but intuitive notations, which the following example illustrates. For example, a multi-threaded object has two lifelines, and we use a *stereotype «create»* to denote the creation of other objects.

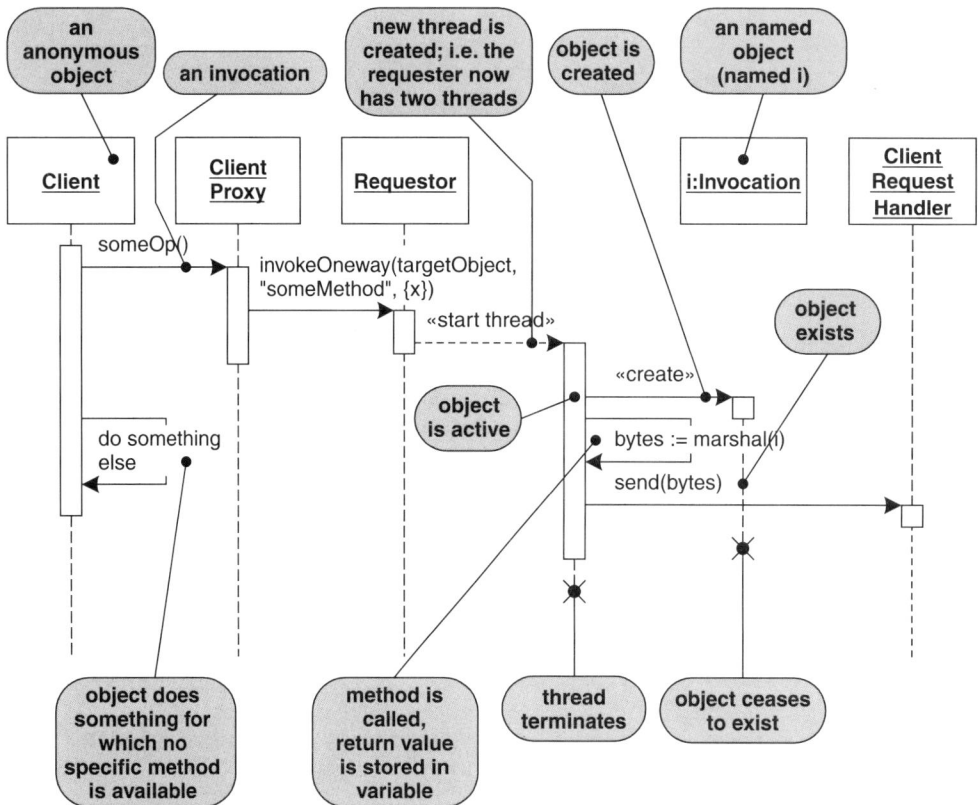

1 Introduction To Distributed Systems

In this chapter we introduce distributed systems briefly. In particular, we describe the fundamental challenges addressed by the patterns in this book, and introduce important terminologies and concepts. This chapter, however, cannot provide a complete introduction to the broad field of distributed systems. More extensive introductions to these topics can be found in other books, such as Tanenbaum and van Steen's *Distributed Systems: Principles and Paradigms* [TS02].

Distributed Systems: reasons and challenges

This section provides an introduction to distributed systems, the reasons why they exist, and the challenges in their design.

Application areas for distributed systems

The application areas for distributed systems are diverse and broad. Many major large and complex systems in use today are distributed systems. Below we provide examples to illustrate this.

The *Internet* can be seen as a large distributed system with a huge number of servers, providing services via a set of communication protocols such as HTTP, FTP, Telnet, and SMTP, to an even larger number of clients. The protocols used in the Internet are simple, rugged, and proven.

Telecommunication networks use digital switches that run software to provide communication facilities. That is, telecommunications networks depend heavily on distributed communication. As development cycles in this domain become shorter, the use of low-level programming and communication is replaced by object-oriented programming languages and corresponding distributed object middleware technologies. Those allow for higher programming efficiency, though often at the cost of memory overhead and somewhat reduced execution performance.

Business-to-business (B2B) collaboration systems, conducting electronic commerce among businesses, are an important application area for distributed systems. Today Electronic Data Interchange (EDI) [Ans04] is heavily used for electronic commerce, but Web-based technologies such as XML-based Web Services will probably be used in the future in this area (see for example [CFH+02]).

International financial transactions are executed via a distributed system provided by SWIFT (Society of Worldwide Interbank Financial Telecommunication). SWIFT is an industry-owned cooperative supplying secure, standardized messaging services and interface software to financial institutions. In 2002 more than 7,500 financial institutions in 200 countries were connected to SWIFT, processing about 7 million messages daily [Swi02]. The system was originally established to simplify the execution of international payments. Several financial and infrastructure services have been added to its portfolio recently.

Embedded systems, such as in-vehicle software, elevator control systems, household appliances, mobile devices, and many others, have crucial requirements for distributed communication. For example, modern cars contain a complex network of electronic control units (ECU). These ECUs run software that controls a particular aspect of the car. The features of a car typically are interrelated: for example, you should not be able to switch critical ECUs into diagnostic mode while the car is in use. The ECUs must therefore communicate with each other. As for other embedded systems, strict timing requirements have to be obeyed. More and more embedded systems are becoming network-aware, and therefore require efficient programmability of distributed communication. The upcoming AUTOSAR middleware standard [Aut04] addresses these concerns in the context of in-vehicle software.

Many *scientific applications*, such as DNA analysis, extraterrestrial signal interpretation, or cancer research, need massive amounts of computational power and thus cannot easily be run on a single machine. Clusters, Grids, or distributed peer-to-peer systems are commonly used to solve these types of problem collaboratively.

These are only a few examples of distributed systems – many other fields use distributed systems as well. We hope this incomplete list of examples nevertheless gives you an idea of the diversity and complexity of distributed systems.

Reasons for using distributed systems

Why do we use distributed systems? There are many reasons why distributed systems are used today. In general, we can distinguish *problem-related* reasons and *property-related* reasons, which often occur together.

Problem-related reasons for distributed systems occur when we face problems that are inherently distributed. For instance, if a computer user in Europe wants to read a Web page that is located on a server in the USA, the Web page has to be transported to the remote user – there is no way around that, it is simply the purpose of the system.

There are also property-related reasons for using distributed systems – that is, reasons that are motivated by a particular system property that should be improved by distributing the system. Examples of such system properties are:

- *Performance and Scalability.* If a system has to cope with sufficiently heavy loads that a single machine cannot cost-effectively solve the problem, the problem is divided and assigned to several machines to share the load. To allow these to efficiently handle the computing load, the machines have to be coordinated in some way. This process is called 'load balancing', and results in a distributed system. For example, most Web sites with very high hit rates are served by more than one machine. Another example is the area of super-computing: Grids of smaller machines are assembled to provide a performance unattainable by any single machine. We discuss availability and scalability patterns in Chapter 13, *Related Concepts, Technologies, and Patterns*.

- *Fault Tolerance.* Another reason for using distributed systems is fault tolerance. All hardware devices have some Mean Time Between Failure (MTBF) that is smaller than infinity. Software can also fail: a program might have a bug or some non-deterministic behavior that results in a failure, or in strange behavior that may happen only occasionally. As a consequence, every machine, or a part of it, will fail at some time. If the overall system should continue working in such an event, it must be designed so that the system does not fail completely when a partial failure occurs. One approach to this is to distribute the software system over many machines, and ensure that its clients do not notice when a specific machine fails. The coordination between different software components running on individual machines results in a distributed system. Note that there are ways to provide fault tolerance other than hardware redundancy. For more details, refer to Chapter 13, *Related Concepts, Technologies, and Patterns*.

- *Service and Client Location Independence*. In many systems the location of clients and services is not known in advance. In contrast to classical mainframe or client/server systems, services can be transparently executed on remote hosts equipped with more storage or computing power. For example, in a peer-to-peer system, new distributed or local peers providing additional services might join and leave the system at any time.

- *Maintainability and Deployment*. Deployment of software to a large number of machines is a maintenance nightmare that increases the total cost of ownership (TCO) of a system. An alternative solution is to provide *thin clients* that only accept user input and present output, and locate the business logic remotely on central servers. Changes to the business logic thus do not affect clients. Enterprise systems use this thin client approach, keeping the system functionality and the data on one or more central machines.

- *Security*. Another reason for using a distributed system is security. Security information, such as user credentials, might be consistently kept at a central site and accessed from many remote locations. Alternatively, for security reasons, some information or functionality might not be kept at a single site only, but instead distributed over a number of nodes, perhaps administered by different people and organizations. Some machines that store critical data might be located in specially secured computing centers, for example a restricted area that requires a special key for access and is monitored with security cameras. Such secured machines often need to be accessed by other nodes of the system. To coordinate the nodes, remote communication is again necessary.

- *Business Integration*. In the past business was mainly achieved by people interacting with each other, either directly, by surface mail, or by phone. When e-mail started to appear, some business was carried out via e-mail, but orders were still entered by people using personal computers. In recent years the term *Enterprise Application Integration* (EAI) has been introduced. EAI is about integrating the different systems in enterprises into one coherent, collaborating 'system of systems'. This integration involves communication between the various systems using different remoting styles, as well as data mapping and conversions, without human intervention.

Challenges in distributed system design

Compared to traditional, non-distributed systems, additional challenges arise when engineering distributed systems, such as:

- *Network Latency.* A remote invocation in a distributed system takes considerably more time than an invocation in a non-distributed system. If a certain performance level is required from the distributed system, or when strict deadlines have to be met, this additional time delay must be taken into account.

- *Predictability.* The time it takes to invoke an operation differs from invocation to invocation, because it depends on the network load and other parameters, such as the location of the remote process, how fast the invocation travels across the network, and how fast it is processed by the remote process. The network can even fail. Lacking end-to-end predictability of remote invocations is especially problematic for systems with hard real-time requirements that mandate specified deadlines that must not be missed, which would constitute a system failure. Guaranteeing real-time requirements is a major challenge in many distributed real-time embedded systems, such as aircraft flight control.

    Note that predictability cannot be assumed in non-distributed systems either. An operation's invocation time is influenced by many factors, such as processor load or the status of a garbage collector. However for many systems these times can be assumed to be very small and constant, and thus can be neglected in practice. Such assumptions cannot be made in a distributed system. Though, predictable transmission times in distributed systems can be provided by using time-triggered communication [Kop97], which is increasingly used in safety-critical real-time applications.

- *Concurrency.* Other problems arise from the fact that there is real concurrency in a distributed system. In contrast to multi-threaded or multi-process systems running on a single-processor machine, in distributed systems several processing steps can happen at the same time. Coordinating such systems is far from simple. Even basic coordination, such as providing a common time reference, requires sophisticated protocols. Concurrency can cause a number of problems, such as non-determinism, deadlocks, and race conditions.

- *Scalability.* Since different parts of a system, such as clients and servers, are distributed and therefore more or less independent systems themselves, it is not always possible to know in advance how many of these different systems are actually available, and how high the communication load is going to be at a certain time. For example, it is hard to determine the number of clients for a Web server: at certain peak times, many more clients than expected might want to access a Web site. The software, the hardware, and the network must be able to scale up to handle this additional load at any time – or at least fail gracefully.

- *Partial Failure.* In systems that run on a single machine, ideally in a single process, a failure such as a hardware problem or a fatal software bug usually has a simple consequence: the program stops running completely. It is not possible for only parts of the program to stop, which is what partial failure is all about. In distributed systems, this is different: it is quite possible for only a part of the overall system to fail.

    However, in many systems it can become very difficult to determine which part of the system has actually failed, and how to recover. For example, if a client communicates with a server and does not receive a reply, this can have many reasons: the server process may have crashed, or the server hardware may have gone down. Or maybe the process has not crashed, but is only overloaded, and may merely take longer to respond to the request. Finally, there might be no problem with the server at all, but the network itself might be broken, overloaded, or unreliable.

    Depending on how the system fails, different ways of recovery are necessary. Therefore the real problem is to determine the real cause of the failure. But it is sometimes impossible for clients to detect the causes of failures. There are many algorithms for detecting such problems [TS02], but none of them is simple, and all imply an additional performance overhead.

The 'bottom line' is that you should only distribute your system if distribution is really needed. Distribution adds complexity, concurrency, inefficiency, and other potential problems to your application that would not occur in a non-distributed context. We do not advocate avoiding the use of distributed systems, it's just important to carefully evaluate *when* and *what* to distribute. Check Fowler's *First law of distributed object design* in [Fow03], *Don't distribute your objects!*

Communication middleware

Distributed systems can be built directly on top of low-level network protocols. For example, communication can be based on TCP/IP sockets, which allow distributed processes to pass each other messages using *send* and *receive* operations directly [Ste98]. But this raises a number of problems, because developers have to deal with low-level networking details. In particular, such systems:

- Are usually not easy to *scale*
- Are typically rather *cumbersome* and *error prone* to use for developers
- Are hard to *maintain* and *change*
- Do not provide *transparency* of distributed communication

A common solution to these problems is to add an additional software layer, called *communication middleware*, or simply *middleware*, that hides the heterogeneity of the underlying platforms, and provides transparency of distributed communication for application developers. In this context, transparency aims to make remote invocations as similar as possible to local invocations. However, since remote invocations introduce new kinds of errors, latency, and so forth, complete transparency is not possible. This aspect will be addressed in more detail later in this book.

The figure below shows how the middleware hides the network services and other details of remote communication from clients and server applications.

The middleware is an additional software layer that sits between the network services offered by the operating system and the application layer hosting the client and server application. Due to the additional

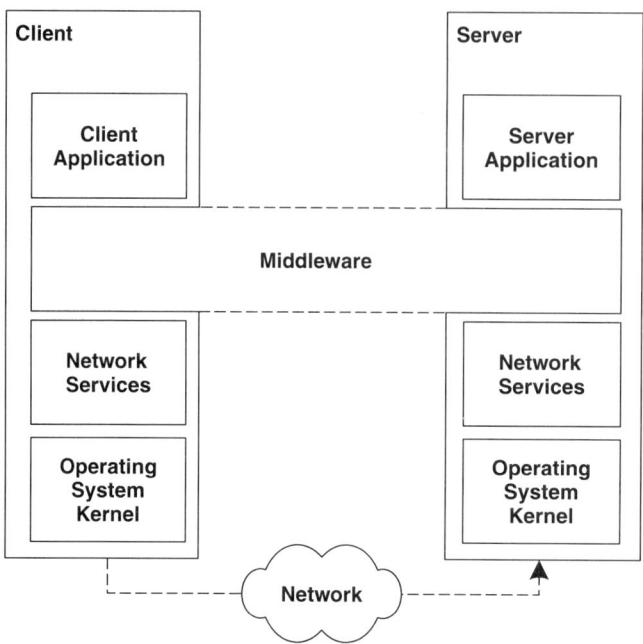

layer, the middleware hides the heterogeneity between the underlying platforms from application developers. Clients and server applications are usually not allowed to bypass the middleware layer and access low-level network services directly.

As the next section outlines, different middleware systems are based on different remoting styles, such as remote procedure calls or message passing. Whatever remoting styles are used in an application today, the application developer must be shielded from the details of how the respective middleware implementation actually communicates over the network. The middleware takes care of the specifics of realizing the remoting styles by using available lower-level services. Middleware provides a simple, high-level programming model to the developers, hiding all the nitty-gritty details if possible. For example, a middleware implementation might take care of connection handling, message passing, and serialization, but not try to hide the specific error conditions introduced by the fact that an invocation target is located remotely. Middleware specifications and products are available for all popular remoting styles. The technology projections we introduce later in the book show some examples of distributed objects middleware.

Remoting styles

A number of different remoting styles are used in today's middleware systems. In this section, we introduce some popular styles and explain a few prominent examples of middleware systems for each of the styles.

Historically, distributed computing is derived from simple *file transfers*. File transfer was the original means of program-to-program communication, and it is still the basis in many mainframe systems today.

The principle of file transfer is that each program works on a physical file. The programs accept files as its input and create new files, or modifies existing files, after which the files are exchanged with the next program. While file transfer has proven effective for solving many problems, the issues of latency and resource contention have made it unattractive for today's high-speed, high-volume systems.

In the following sections, we look briefly at the basic remoting styles that are used instead of file transfer today. There are systems that:

- Use the metaphor of a *remote procedure call* (RPC)
- Use the metaphor of posting and receiving *messages*
- Use a *shared repository*
- Use continuous *streams* of data

This book focusses mainly on object-oriented variants of the RPC style. However, any of these remoting styles can be used to implement the others. There are also combinations of the styles, such as a shared repositories accessed with RPC, or asynchronous RPC invocations sent as messages.

Because of these interrelations among remoting styles, it is important to understand their diversity in order to understand the pattern language contained in this book properly. It is also important to understand that there are many other remoting styles that are based on these basic remoting styles. Examples of such more advanced remoting styles are code mobility, peer-to-peer (P2P), remote evaluation, Grid computing, publish/subscribe systems, transaction processing, and many others. Note that these higher-level remoting styles are often implemented using the basic styles we list, or as variants of them. However, the internal realization of these styles is not made visible to their users. For example, the user of a P2P system based on RPC does not have to deal with the internal RPC mechanisms, nor with the naming service used for ad hoc lookup of peer services.

In Chapter 13, *Related Concepts, Technologies, and Patterns*, we discuss how some of these more advanced remoting styles can be realized using the pattern language presented in this book. When new remoting styles emerge, usually no complete, industry-level implementation is available. Thus parts of the system have to be built by hand using low-level remoting styles. Consider a small, custom publish/subscribe system built on top of an OO-RPC middleware. To build such a system, the internals of the OO-RPC middleware, as well as the possible ways to extend, customize, and integrate it, have to be well understood. The pattern language in this book provides a foundation for understanding distributed object middleware systems in such a way.

Remote procedure calls

Remote procedure calls extend the well-known procedure call abstraction to distributed systems. They aim at letting a remote procedure invocation behave as if it were a local invocation.

Use of low-level network protocols requires developers to invoke the *send* and *receive* operations of the respective network protocol implementations directly. Remote procedure call (RPC) systems [BN84] introduce a simple but powerful concept to avoid this problem: programs are allowed to invoke procedures (or operations) in a different process and/or on a remote machine.

In RPC, two different roles are distinguished: *clients* and *servers*. Clients invoke operations, servers accept operations. When a client process invokes an operation in a server process synchronously, the invoking client process is suspended, and the execution of the invocation in the server takes place. After, the server sends the result back to the client and the result is received, the client resumes its work.

A server provides a well-defined set of operations that the client can invoke. To the client developer, these operations look almost like local operations: typically they have an operation name, parameters, a return type, and a way to signal errors. One major difference from ordinary operations is that additional errors might occur during a remote invocation, for example because the network fails or the requested operation is not implemented by the server. These errors can be signaled to the client as specific types of exception.

As an extension to the RPC style, there are also many asynchronous RPC variants. In these, a client resumes its work after invoking a remote operation, without blocking until the result becomes available.

There are two different, popular flavours of remote procedure call systems:

- Those that purely use the procedure-based approach, in which a server application provides only the specified operations to clients
- Object-oriented remote procedure call systems (OO-RPC), in which a server application hosts a set of objects that provide the operations to clients as part of their public interface

The internal mechanisms are similar in both variants. However, in OO-RPC systems there is the notion of 'object identity' – meaning that clients can address objects separately. A distributed object can have its own state, whereas RPC-based systems often provide stateless services. In addition, the OO-RPC approach maps more naturally into today's object-oriented approach to software development, and is therefore used in new systems almost exclusively.

The figure below shows an example of an OO-RPC system. The OO-RPC middleware allows clients to access objects transparently within a server process.

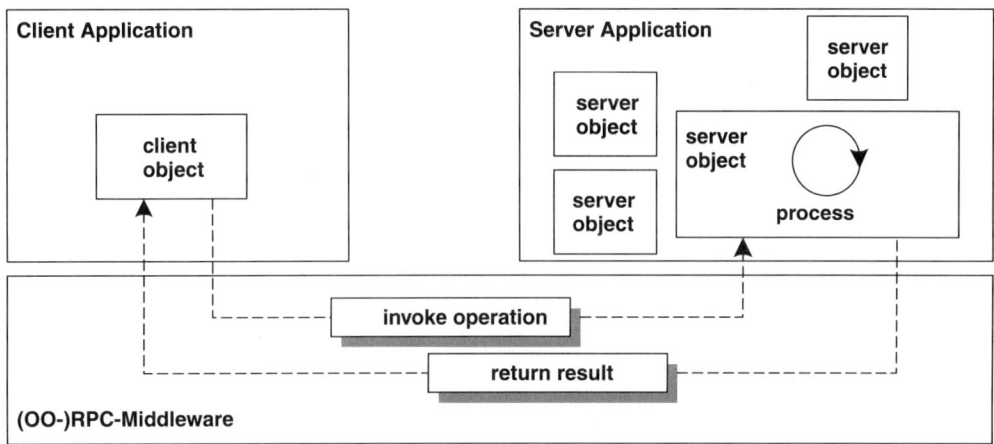

Popular procedure-based systems are the Distributed Computing Environment (DCE) [Ope91] and Sun RPC [Sun88]. DCE, for example, was developed by the Open Software Foundation. Originally designed as a RPC middleware for Unix platforms, it has later been ported to all major operating systems, including Windows variants and VMS.

DCE introduces a typical and straightforward way of performing RPC, which allows the server hosting the operations of interest to be located automatically (during a process called *binding*). The server first registers a procedure with the DCE daemon running within the server's machine as an endpoint, then it registers the service in a directory server, which might run on a different machine. When the client wants to access the remote procedure, it first looks up the server in the directory server. The server is then asked for the endpoint. This endpoint is then used to invoke the remote procedure.

Even though DCE is a procedure-based middleware, it also provides extensions for supporting remote objects. Nowadays there are many popular OO-RPC middleware systems specifically designed for distributed object communication. Examples are:

- Common Object Request Broker Architecture (CORBA) (see Chapter 12, *CORBA Technology Projection*)
- Microsoft's .NET Remoting (see Chapter 10, *.NET Remoting Technology Projection*)
- Web Services (see Chapter 11, *Web Services Technology Projection*)
- Microsoft's DCOM [Gri97]
- Sun's Java RMI [Gro01]

These middleware systems and their concepts are the primary focus of this book.

Message passing

While the (OO-)RPC middleware uses the metaphor of a procedure (or operation) invocation, the *message passing* metaphor is different. Messages are exchanged between peers, and the peers are free to consume the messages as and when they like. Message passing is inherently asynchronous.

Remoting styles

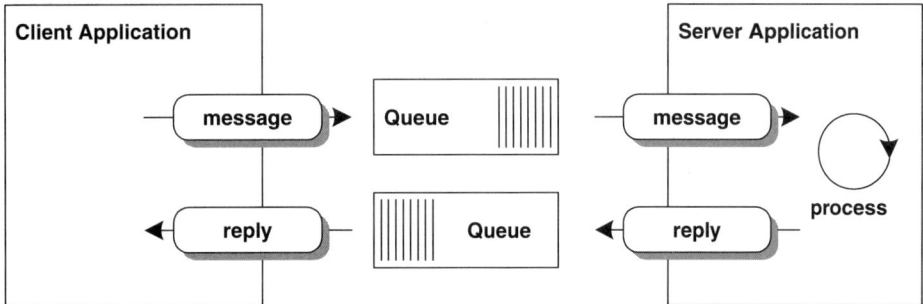

Messages are not passed from client to server application directly, but through intermediate message queues that store and forward the messages. This has a number of consequences: senders and receivers of messages are decoupled, so they do not need to know each other's identity. A sender just puts messages into a certain queue and does not necessarily know who consumes the messages. For example, a message might be consumed by more than one receiver. Receivers consume messages by monitoring queues.

The two peers of a remote communication exchange are decoupled chronologically – a sender can place a message in the message queue when there is no receiver running or connected. Receivers can later get the messages from the queue. The messaging style is thus inherently asynchronous. If applications require replies, they have to be modelled and sent as separate messages.

Many messaging protocols provide a reliable means of message delivery, such as an acknowledgement scheme. The ordering of messages is ensured, so that receivers process messages in the same order as they were sent, even if messages were retransmitted in the interim. Messaging therefore provides tolerance of temporal failures among peers. Many message passing systems also guarantee that once the message is placed in a queue, it will be delivered exactly once to the receiver. Consequently messaging systems can provide a high level of reliability to their users.

The message passing style allows for many variations in the implementations. Some systems distinguish between queues where there is one receiver and queues where there are several. In the latter case, each message is delivered to each receiver. This is often referred to as a 'publish/subscribe' system.

Typically messages are delivered asynchronously, as explained above. Some systems allow for synchronous delivery, blocking the sender until the message has been delivered successfully. Similarly to RPC invocations, the message is sent to the receiver and a reply is awaited. This mode is provided by messaging systems that support typical client/server transaction characteristics, for example. As a side effect, this technique can be used to coordinate concurrent systems.

The message passing style is conceptually different from remote procedure calls, for the reasons given above. Technically however, it is easily possible to implement RPC semantics with a message passing system, or to implement message passing using RPC.

A number of simple message passing systems exist, including Berkeley Sockets [Ste98] and the Message Passing Interface (MPI) [Qui03]. These allow mainly for asynchronous communication, although a number of message-queueing systems also allow for persistent messaging.

Message-Oriented Middleware (MOM) extends the concept of such simple message passing systems with support for inter-process messaging and persistent message queueing. That is, reliable communication is enabled: the MOM stores messages without having the sender or receiver actively participate in the network transfer. Once a message is put into a queue it remains there until it is removed. This model allows for loosely-coupled communication in which a receiver does not have to consume a message as soon as it arrives. This allows a server crash to be tolerated, for example. Popular MOM products are IBM's WebSphere MQ (formerly MQ Series) [Ibm04c], JMS [Sun04c], Microsoft's MSMQ [Mic04a], and Tibco [Tib04].

We discuss further details of messaging and how it relates to the pattern language presented in this book in Chapter 13, *Related Concepts, Technologies, and Patterns*.

Shared repository

A shared repository is based on the idea of shared data space read from and written to by independent clients.

There are two basic roles in the shared repository remoting style: the *shared repository* and its *clients*. The shared repository offers a small interface consisting of access primitives to the clients. Note that the data access in a remotely-shared repository is often implemented using RPC mechanisms.

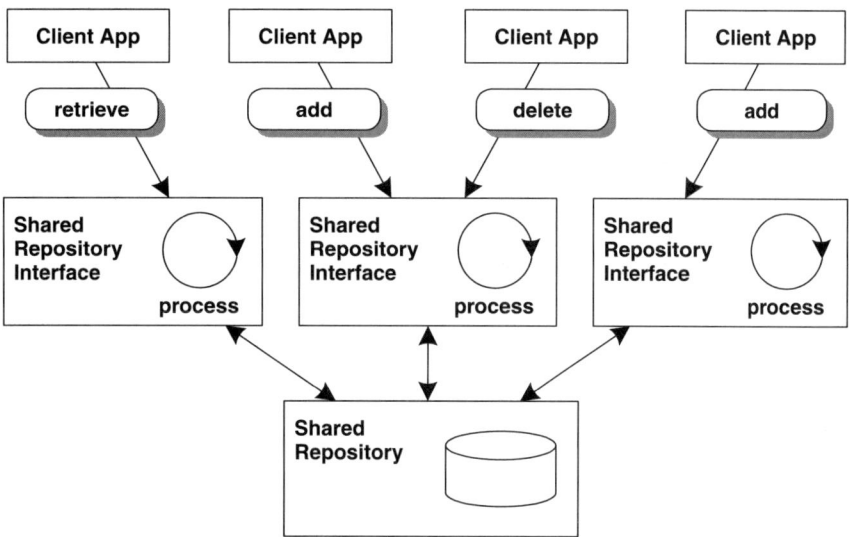

Systems for shared repositories exist in many different flavours. The simplest variant is a shared memory or file space with which different processes interact. When memory and file space are shared among different machines, a distributed system is created. In addition to simply sharing data, the following tasks generally have to be handled by a shared repository:

- Handle problems of resource contention, for example by locking accessed data
- Abstract from location of the shared data, the data storage, or the client
- Optimize performance and scalability
- Provide additional services, such as security

Some systems even introduce high-level access mechanisms, such as query languages or tuple spaces [GCCC85].

Databases provide one way to implement a shared repository. In a database, the database management system (DBMS) provides mechanisms for locking and unlocking the data, and standard mechanisms for creating, deleting, searching, and updating information. Most DBMSs provide query languages for high-level data access. Shared databases might use transaction processing monitors to support distributed transactions.

Some approaches to shared repositories, such as Linda [GCCC85] or PageSpace [CTV+98], are based on the concept of Virtual Shared Memory (VSM). VSM is a shared object repository that can be used to store shared data. It is virtual in the sense that no physically-shared memory is required. The underlying data structure of Linda is a tuple space: processes do not communicate directly, but rather by adding and removing tuples (ordered collections of data) to and from the tuple space. The tuples are then stored in shared memory. Tuple space-based systems typically provide only a very small set of operations on the shared tuple set. It has been demonstrated that many problems of distributed and concurrent applications can be solved very elegantly using this approach. Other examples of tuple-based systems include Sun's JavaSpaces [FHA99] and IBM's TSpaces [Ibm04a].

Streaming

While the remoting styles explained so far use discrete and complete units of data that are exchanged (such as invocation requests, messages, or data items), it is different in stream-based systems: here, information is exchanged as a continuously-flowing stream of data.

Two different roles need to be distinguished: *streaming servers* and *clients* who receive streams. There are also several different types of *streams* [TS02]:

- *Asynchronous streams* consist of data in which the sequence of packets is important, but not the timing. An example could be a file transmitted over a TCP/IP socket. It does not matter whether the transfer rate is slow or fast – a slower rate will result in a longer transfer time, but the file is nevertheless transferred correctly.
- *Synchronous streaming* is inherently time-dependent. The data packets have to be transferred at a certain minimum rate, otherwise the data may be useless to the receiver. Thus there is maximum permissible delay between two data packets. For example, measurements from a sensor might have to be transmitted at a specific rate to achieve the necessary accuracy in subsequent calculations.

- *Isochronous streaming* has even more rigid requirements for timing. Data items have to be transferred *on* time, not just *in* time. That is, there is a maximum *and* a minimum permissible delay between data packets. Typical examples are audio or video streams.

Stream-based systems can follow a one-to-one or one-to-many streaming concept. In the latter case, depending on the streaming technology, the stream might still have to be transported separately to each receiver.

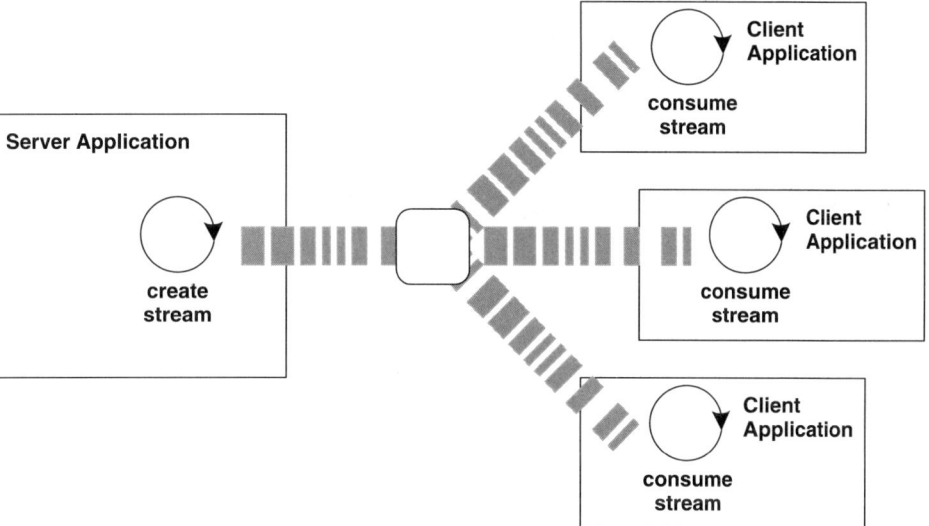

The figure above shows an example configuration in which a stream server application provides continuous streams of data to multiple clients. Streams often have to be received by several clients at a time. In a Web-based video or audio broadcast, for example, there is typically a single stream server and a relatively large number of clients. The necessary bandwidth must be ensured over the whole data path from the server to all the clients.

The primary challenge with stream-based systems, especially isochronous ones, is to ensure the necessary timing requirements. This is typically referred to as quality of service, or QoS.

Stream-based systems are not considered in this book.

2 Pattern Language Overview

This chapter provides an overview of the pattern language described in the following chapters. We start by recasting the *Broker* pattern from POSA1 [BMR+96] as the entry point into the pattern language. From our perspective, *Broker* is a compound pattern that is typically implemented using a number of patterns from our pattern language. The patterns in Chapter 3, *Basic Remoting Patterns*, especially, are used by almost any *Broker* architecture.

Next, we introduce two important participants of *Broker*-based systems in detail: the remote object and the server application. This is important because these two participants are used in almost any distributed object application, and thus are ever-present throughout our pattern language.

Broker

You are designing a distributed software system.

❊ ❊ ❊

Distributed software system developers face many challenges that do not arise in single-process software. One is the communication across unreliable networks. Others are the integration of heterogeneous components into coherent applications, as well as the efficient use of networking resources. If developers of distributed systems must overcome all these challenges within their application code, they may loose their primary focus: to develop applications that resolve their domain-specific responsibilities well.

Communication across networks is more complex than local communication, because connections need to be established, invocation parameters have to be transmitted, and a new set of possible errors has to be coped with. This requires handling invocations to local objects differently than invocations to remote objects. Additionally, allowing remote communication concerns to become entangled with the overall application structure complicates the application logic. From an object-oriented programming perspective, it would be ideal if remote objects could be invoked as if they were local objects.

In addition, the location of the remote objects should not be hard-wired into client applications. It should be possible to host remote objects on different machines without having to adapt the client's program code.

Therefore:

Separate the communication functionality of a distributed system from its application functionality by isolating all communication related concerns in a BROKER. The BROKER hides and mediates all communication between the objects or components of a system. A BROKER consists of a client-side REQUESTOR to construct and forward invocations, as well as a server-side INVOKER that is responsible for invoking the operations of the target remote object. A MARSHALLER on each side of the communication path handles the transformation of requests and replies from programming-language native data

types into a byte array that can be sent over the transmission medium.

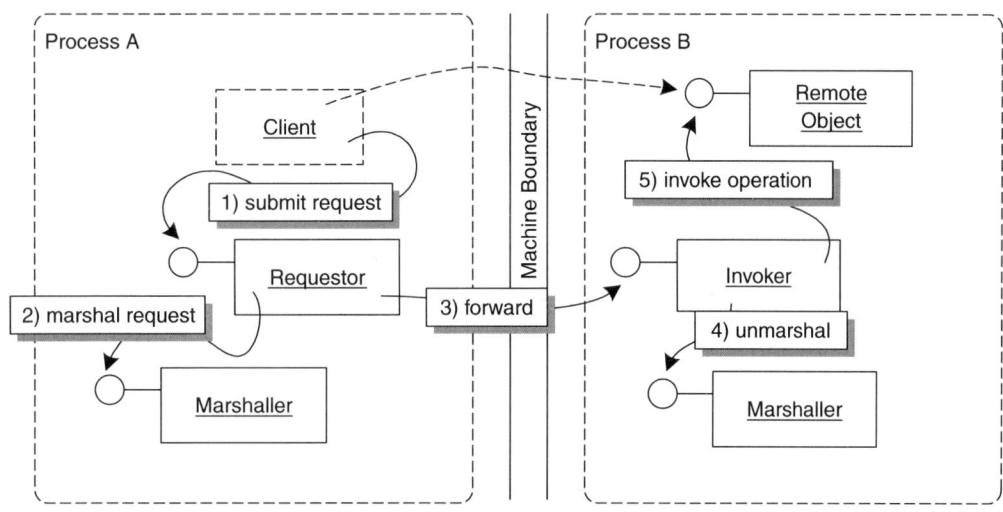

The client submits a request to the REQUESTOR, which marshals the request and transmits it across the network. The server-side INVOKER receives the invocation request and invokes the remote object.

❋ ❋ ❋

Local BROKER components on client and server sides enable the exchange of requests and replies between the client and the remote object. In addition to the core patterns consisting of REQUESTOR, INVOKER, and MARSHALLER, the BROKER typically relies on the following patterns:

- A CLIENT PROXY represents the remote object in the client process. This proxy has the same interface as the remote object it represents. The CLIENT PROXY transforms invocations of its operations into invocations of the REQUESTOR that, in turn, is responsible for constructing the request and forwarding it to the target remote object. A CLIENT PROXY is thus used to let remote operation invocations look like local operation invocations from a client's perspective. An INTERFACE DESCRIPTION is used to make the remote object's interface known to the clients. The client makes use of the INTERFACE DESCRIPTION in the form of a CLIENT PROXY.

- LOOKUP allows clients to discover remote objects. This ensures that the location of remote objects does not need to be hard-wired into the system. Remote objects can be moved to other hosts without compromising system integrity, and the location of remote objects is under the control of the server developers.
- The CLIENT REQUEST HANDLER and SERVER REQUEST HANDLER handle efficient sending, receiving, and dispatching of requests. Their responsibility is to forward and receive request and reply messages to and from the REQUESTOR and the INVOKER respectively.
- REMOTING ERRORS are used to signal problems of remote communication to the client side. REMOTING ERRORS are caused either by technical failures in the network communication infrastructure or by problems within the server infrastructure. The REQUESTOR and INVOKER are responsible for forwarding REMOTING ERRORS to the client if they cannot handle the REMOTING ERROR if there is no sensible way to react to the error on the server side.

In the following section we take a closer look at two important, additional participants of the BROKER-based applications: remote objects and the server application. Note that these are not participants of the BROKER pattern itself, they are merely necessary in applications that use a BROKER as their communications backbone.

Remote objects

Consider you are using or building distributed object middleware that is used to access objects remotely. Clients need to access functionality provided by remote application objects. In many respects, accessing an object over a network is different than accessing a local object. An invocation has to cross process and machine boundaries. Network latency, network unreliability, and many other distinctive properties of network environments play an important role and need to be 'managed' for the developer. In particular:

- For a remote invocation, machine and process boundaries have to be crossed. An ordinary, local operation invocation is not sufficient, because the operation invocation has to be transferred from the local process to the remote process running on the remote machine.

- Using memory addresses to define object identity will not work any more. While unique in the address space of one process, they are not necessarily unique across process boundaries, and especially not across machine boundaries.
- Compared to local invocations, invocations across a network involve unpredictable latency. Because networks must be considered to be unreliable, clients must deal with new kinds of errors.

The distributed object middleware provides solutions for these fundamental issues of accessing objects remotely using a BROKER architecture. The application logic implemented by server developers is provided in the form of *remote objects*. These remote objects are important conceptual building blocks for distributed applications. Each remote object provides a well-defined interface to be accessed remotely: that is, the remote client can address the remote object across the network and invoke its operations. The BROKER transfers local invocations from the client side to a remote object running within the server.

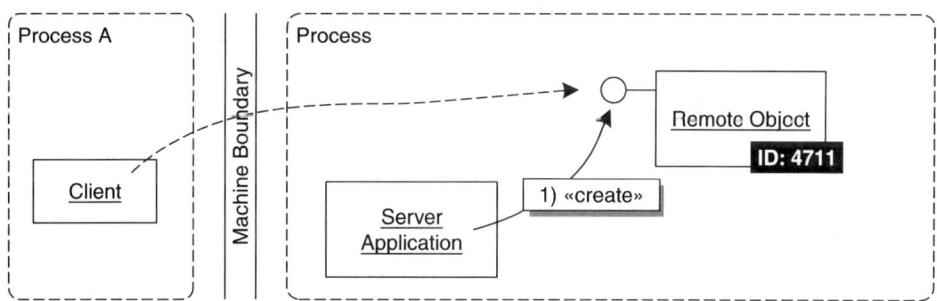

The server application instantiates a remote object. Clients can then access the remote object using the functionality provided by the distributed object middleware.

Remote objects have a unique OBJECT ID in their local address space, as well as a means to construct an ABSOLUTE OBJECT REFERENCE. The ABSOLUTE OBJECT REFERENCE is used to reference and subsequently access a remote object across the network.

A remote object is primarily a logical entity in the scope of the distributed object middleware. It can be realized by different programming language entities. Usually in an object-oriented language a remote object is realized as an object of the programming language. However, that does not mean that each remote object is realized by exactly one programming language object, or that all requests to one remote object are served by the same programming language object. For example, the resource optimization pattern POOLING lets a pool of multiple objects handle requests for a remote object. In non-object-oriented programming languages, other structures than objects are used to implement the remote object. To distinguish the runtime entity from the remote object as a logical entity, we call the entity that represents a remote object at runtime the *servant*. In cases, where there is exactly one servant for one remote object, we simply use the term *remote object* as a synonym for both the remote object and its servant.

Clients need to know the remotely-accessible interface of a remote object. A simple solution is to let remote clients access any operation of the servant. However, sometimes some local operations should be inaccessible for remote clients, such as operations used to access the distributed object middleware. Thus each remote object type defines or declares its remotely-accessible interface.

Remote objects are used to extend the object-oriented paradigm across process and machine boundaries. However, accessing objects remotely always implies a set of inherent problems, such as network latency and network unreliability, that cannot be completely hidden from developers. Different distributed object middleware systems hide these issues to different degrees. When designing distributed object middleware, there is always a trade-off between possible control and ease of use.

These problems can be avoided to a certain extent by following the principle 'Don't distribute your objects' [Fow03]. However, this only works as long as the application problem is not inherently distributed in nature. If distribution is necessary, make sure you co-locate objects that require a lot of communication, and design your interfaces in ways that allow for exchanging as much data as possible within one remote call, thus reducing the number of remote invocations to the minimum (see the *Data Transfer Object* and *Remoting Facade* patterns in [Fow03]). In the case of errors that are related to the remote nature of a remote object, make sure there is a way to signal these REMOTING ERRORS to the client in a well-defined manner.

Server applications

Remote objects need a *server application* that has to perform the following tasks:

- The constituents of the distributed object middleware have to be created and configured.
- The remote objects need to be instantiated and configured, if not done by the distributed object middleware constituents.
- Remote objects need to be advertised to interested clients.
- Individual remote objects need to be connected to distributed applications.
- If no longer needed, remote objects need to be destroyed or recycled.

To resolve these issues, use a server application as a building block that connects all parts of the distributed application. The server application instantiates and configures the distributed object middleware, as well as the remote objects. On shut-down the server application has to ensure used resources are freed by destroying remote objects, announcing their unavailability, and destroying the distributed object middleware instance.

Depending on how sophisticated the distributed object middleware is, the server application might delegate many of the remote object life-cycle management tasks to the distributed object middleware.

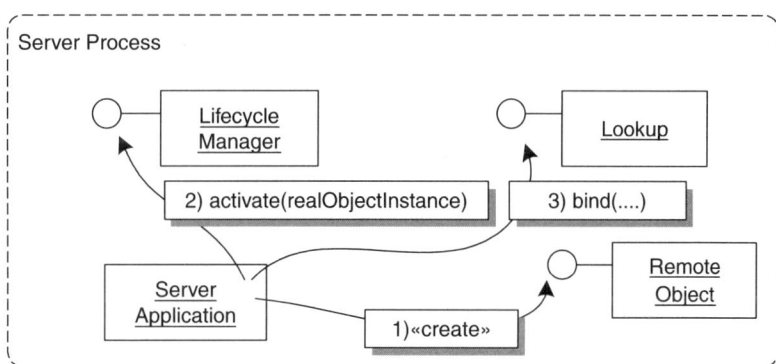

The server application creates an instance of a remote object, hands it over to the lifecycle manager of the distributed object middleware, and finally announces the availability of the remote object by registering it with a lookup service.

The server application bundles remote objects that conceptually belong together, and handles all object management tasks on behalf of the distributed object middleware.

Overview of the Pattern chapters

The patterns mentioned so far detail the BROKER pattern and will be described in Chapter 3, *Basic Remoting Patterns*. The following illustration shows the typical dependencies among the patterns.

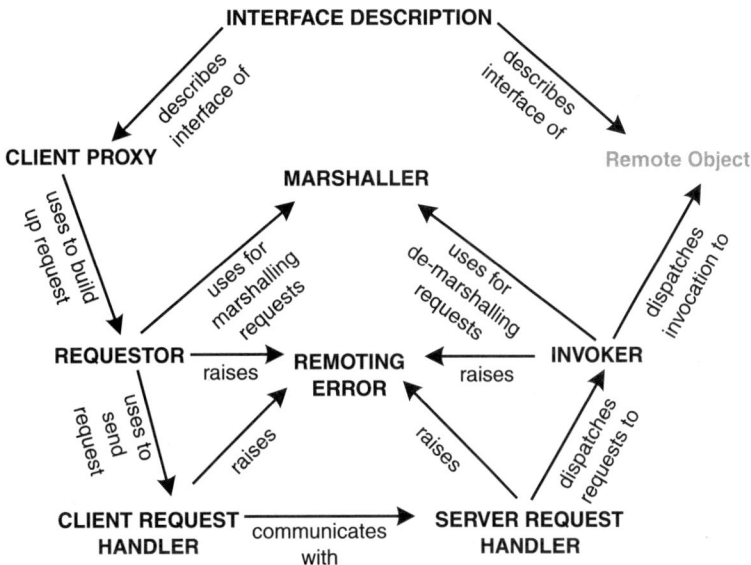

We use such dependency diagrams at the beginning of each pattern chapter. Pattern names are presented in small caps font. Participants, like remote object, are displayed in plain font. The patterns explained in a particular chapter are displayed in black font, while all other pattern and participant names are displayed in gray. The chapters after Chapter 3 present patterns that extend the elementary patterns. The remainder of this section provides an brief overview of them.

The patterns in Chapter 4, *Identification Patterns*, deal with issues of identification, addressing, and lookup of remote objects. It is important for clients to find the correct remote object within the server application. This is done by the assignment of logical OBJECT IDS for each remote object instance. The client embeds these OBJECT IDS in invocations, so that the INVOKER can find the correct remote object. However, this assumes that we are able to deliver the message to the correct server application – in two different server applications, two different objects with the same OBJECT ID might exist. An ABSOLUTE OBJECT REFERENCE extends the concept of OBJECT IDS with location information. Typical elements of an ABSOLUTE OBJECT REFERENCE are, for example, the hostname, the port, and the OBJECT ID of a remote object.

LOOKUP is used to associate remote objects with human-readable names and other properties. The server application typically associates properties with the remote object on registration. The client only needs to know the ABSOLUTE OBJECT REFERENCE of the lookup service, instead of the potentially huge number of ABSOLUTE OBJECT REFERENCES of the remote objects it wants to communicate with. The LOOKUP pattern simplifies the management and configuration of distributed systems, as clients can easily find remote objects, while avoiding tight coupling between them.

The dependencies among the patterns are illustrated in the following diagram.

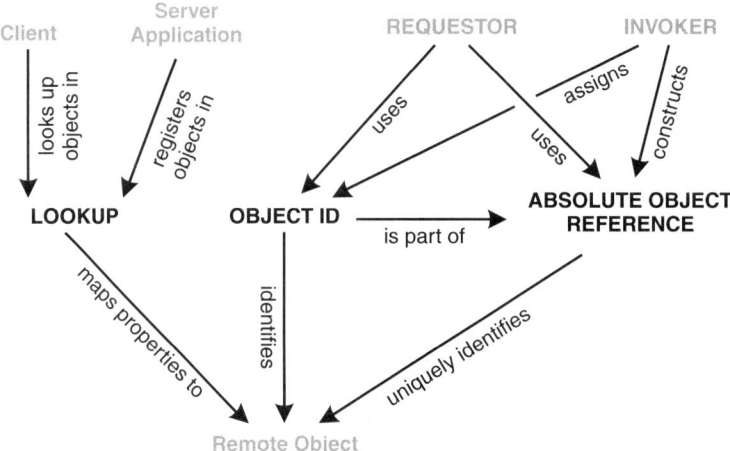

Chapter 5, *Lifecycle Management Patterns*, deals with the management of the lifecycle of remote objects. While some remote objects need to exist all the time, others need only be available for a limited period. The activation and deactivation of remote objects might also be coupled with additional tasks.

Lifecycle management strategies are used to adapt to the specifics of the lifecycle of remote objects and their use. These strategies have a strong influence on the overall resource consumption of the distributed application. Chapter 5 describes some of the most common strategies used in today's distributed object middleware.

Overview of the Pattern chapters

The three basic lifecycle strategy patterns have the following focus:

- STATIC INSTANCES are used to represent fixed functionality in the system. Their lifetime is typically identical to the lifetime of their server application.
- PER-REQUEST INSTANCES are used for highly concurrent environments. They are created for each new request and destroyed after the request.
- CLIENT-DEPENDENT INSTANCES are used to represent client state in the server. They rely on the client to instantiate them explicitly.

The lifecycle strategies patterns make use of a set of specific resource management patterns internally:

- LEASING is used to properly release CLIENT-DEPENDENT INSTANCES when they are no longer used.
- LAZY ACQUISITION describes how to activate remote objects on demand.
- POOLING manages unused remote object instances in a pool, to optimize reuse.

For state management, PASSIVATION takes care of removing unused instances temporarily from memory and storing them in persistent storage. Upon request, the instances are restored again.

The patterns and their relationships are shown in the following figure.

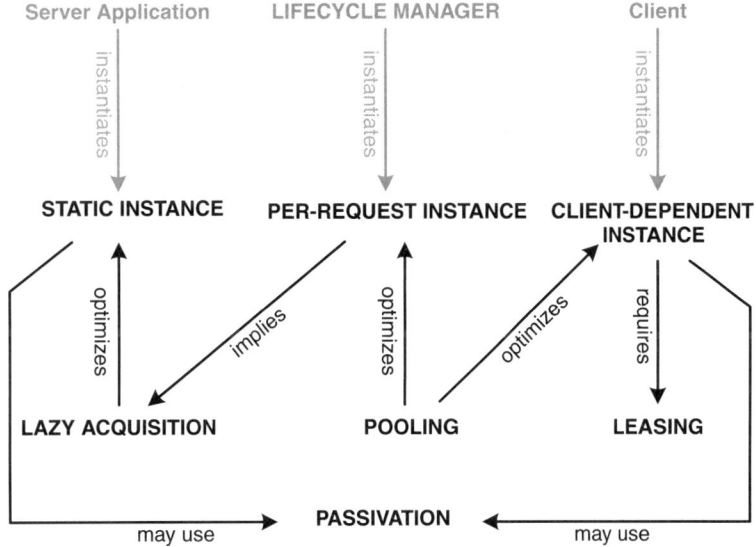

Chapter 6, *Extension Patterns*, deals with patterns that are used to extend distributed object middleware. Examples of such extensions are the support for security, transactions, or even the exchange of communication protocols.

To handle aspects such as security or transactions, remote invocations need to contain more information than just the operation name and its parameters – some kind of transaction ID or security credentials need to be transported between client and server. For that purpose INVOCATION CONTEXTS are used: these are typically added to the invocation on client side transparently and read on server side by the REQUESTOR, CLIENT/SERVER REQUEST HANDLERS, and INVOKER, respectively.

When the invocation process needs to be extended with behavior, for example when evaluating security credentials in the client and the server, INVOCATION INTERCEPTORS can be used. For passing information between clients and servers, INVOCATION INTERCEPTORS use the INVOCATION CONTEXTS we have already mentioned.

Another important extension is the introduction and exchange of different communication protocols. Consider again the example of a secure protocol that might be needed to encrypt the invocation data before it is sent and received using the CLIENT or SERVER REQUEST HANDLER respectively. While simple request handlers use a fixed communication protocol, PROTOCOL PLUG-INS make the request handlers extensible to support different, or even multiple, communication protocols.

Overview of the Pattern chapters

The relationships of the patterns are illustrated in the following figure.

```
                        Client
                         │ uses
                         ▼                                    Remote Object
      CLIENT                                                        │
      PROXY        │            INVOCATION                          │ uses
         │         │ uses       INTERCEPTOR                         │
         │ uses    │       provides         provides                │
         ▼         │       hooks for        hooks for               ▼
      REQUESTOR                                                  INVOKER
         │                    creates/
         │                     uses
         │                       ▼
         │              INVOCATION CONTEXT
         │ uses      transports      transports        │ uses
         ▼                                             ▼
      CLIENT REQUEST ──── communicates with ──── SERVER REQUEST
         HANDLER                                      HANDLER
              plugged into              plugged into
                     ▼                     ▼
                         PROTOCOL
                         PLUG-IN
```

Chapter 7, *Extended Infrastructure Patterns*, deals with specific implementation aspects of the server-side BROKER architecture.

The LIFECYCLE MANAGER is responsible for managing activation and deactivation of remote objects by implementing the lifecycle management strategies described in Chapter 5, typically as part of the INVOKER.

To be able to configure groups of remote objects – instead of configuring each object separately – with regard to lifecycle, extensions, and other options, CONFIGURATION GROUPS are used.

For monitoring the performance of various parts of the system, such as the INVOKER, the SERVER REQUEST HANDLER, or even the remote objects themselves, QOS OBSERVERS can be used. These help to ensure specific quality of service constraints of the system.

To make infrastructure objects in the distributed object middleware follow the same programming conventions as remote objects, while making them inaccessible from remote sites, LOCAL OBJECTS can be used. Typical LOCAL OBJECTS are LIFECYCLE MANAGERS, PROTOCOL PLUG-INS, CONFIGURATION GROUPS, and INVOCATION INTERCEPTORS.

ABSOLUTE OBJECT REFERENCES identify a remote object in a server. If the remote object instances are to be decoupled from the ABSOLUTE OBJECT REFERENCE, an additional level of indirection is needed. LOCATION FORWARDERS allow this: they can forward invocations between different server applications. This allows load balancing, fault tolerance, and remote object migration to be implemented.

The following figure shows the Extended Infrastructure Patterns and their relationships.

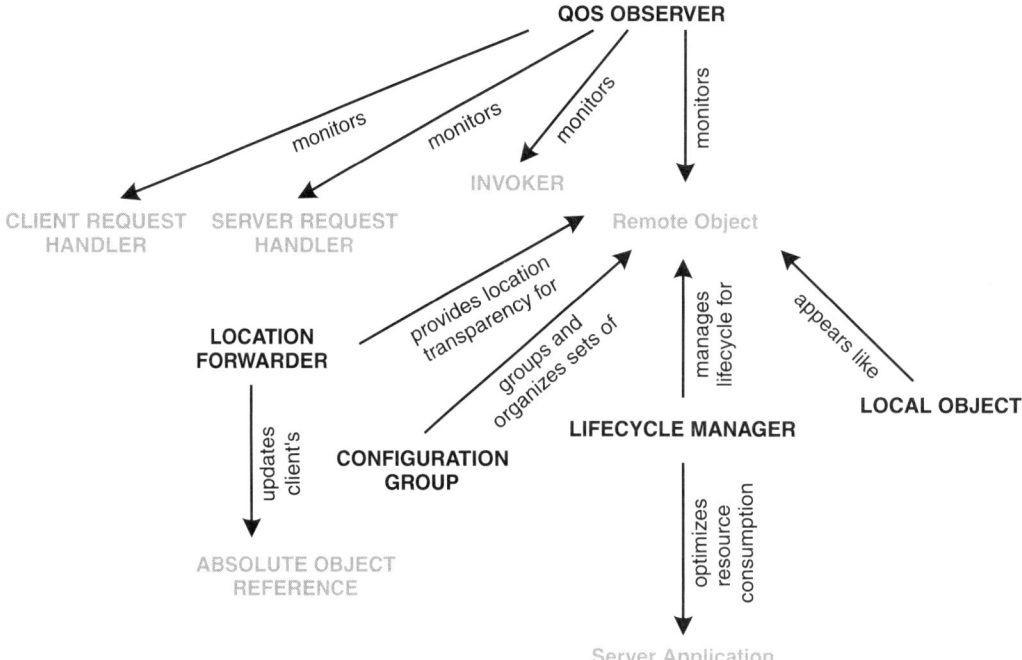

The last patterns chapter in the book, Chapter 8, describes *Invocation Asynchrony Patterns*, and deals with handling asynchronous invocations. It presents four alternative patterns that extend ordinary synchronous invocations:

- FIRE AND FORGET describes best-effort delivery semantics for asynchronous operations that have void return types.

- SYNC WITH SERVER sends an acknowledgement back to the client once the operation has arrived on the server-side, in addition to the semantics of FIRE AND FORGET.
- POLL OBJECTS allow clients to query the distributed object middleware for replies to asynchronous requests.
- RESULT CALLBACK actively notifies the requesting client of asynchronously-arriving replies.

The following figure illustrates the patterns and their interactions.

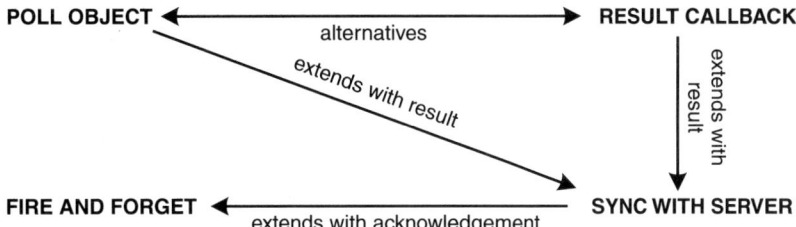

3 Basic Remoting Patterns

This chapter presents patterns that constitute the basic building blocks of distributed object middleware. These patterns are used in almost every middleware implementation. Before presenting the patterns themselves, we give an overview of the patterns and their interdependencies. At the end of this chapter, we show how the participants of the patterns interact with each other.

Distributed object middleware provides an infrastructure for clients to communicate with remote objects on a remote server. Remote objects are implemented as ordinary objects on the server side. The client invokes an operation of a local object and expects it to be forwarded to the remote object.

To make this happen, the invocation has to cross the machine boundary. A REQUESTOR constructs a remote invocation on the client side from parameters such as remote object location, remote object type, operation name, and arguments. A client can either use a REQUESTOR directly or use a CLIENT PROXY. The CLIENT PROXY is a local object within the client process that offers the same interface as the remote object. This interface is defined using an INTERFACE DESCRIPTION. Internally, the CLIENT PROXY uses the REQUESTOR to construct remote invocations.

The REQUESTOR on the client side uses a CLIENT REQUEST HANDLER to handle network communication. On the server side, the remote invocations are received by a SERVER REQUEST HANDLER. The SERVER REQUEST HANDLER handles message reception in an efficient and scalable way, and forwards invocations to the INVOKER once the message has been received completely. The INVOKER dispatches remote invocations to the relevant remote object using the received invocation information.

The parameters passed between client and server are serialized and deserialized using a MARSHALLER. If the client experiences technical problems in communicating with the server, or if the server has internal technical problems, this fact is returned to the CLIENT REQUEST HANDLER and signalled to the client using a REMOTING ERROR. The figure below shows the dependencies of the basic remoting patterns.

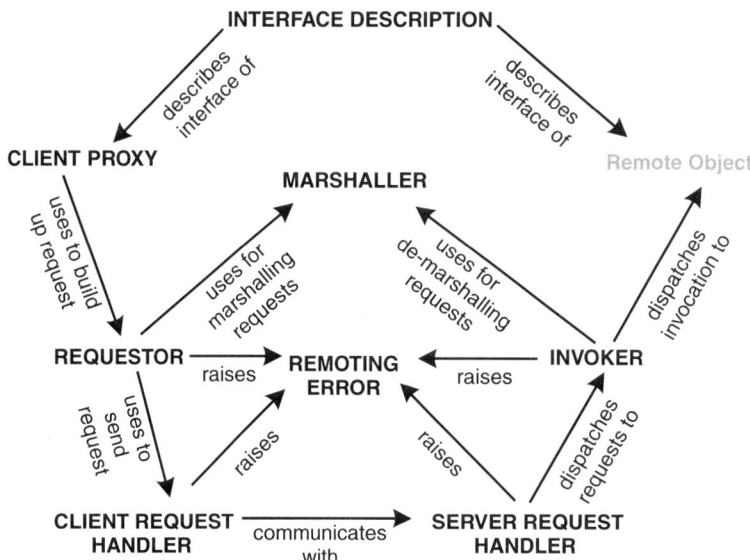

Requestor

A client needs to access one or more remote objects on a remote server.

❋ ❋ ❋

Invocation of remote objects requires that operation parameters are collected and marshaled into a byte stream, since networks only allow byte streams to be sent. A connection also needs to be established and the request information sent to the target remote object. These tasks have to be performed for every remote object accessed by the client, and can therefore become tedious for client developers.

Clients have to perform many recurring operations for every invocation. These include marshaling of invocation information, network connection management, the actual transmission of remote invocations across the network, handling the result of an invocation, as well as error handling.

It is unsatisfactory to require the client developer to remember and perform these tasks over and over again. Further, optimizations of single cases are lost in the common case, where they might also be applicable. Developers creating application software should be able to focus on the application logic, and not have to deal with these low-level details.

Therefore:

In the client application, use a REQUESTOR for accessing the remote object. The REQUESTOR is supplied with the ABSOLUTE OBJECT REFERENCE of the remote object, the operation name, and its arguments. It constructs a remote invocation from these parameters and sends the

invocation to the remote object. The REQUESTOR hides the details of the client side distributed object communication from clients.

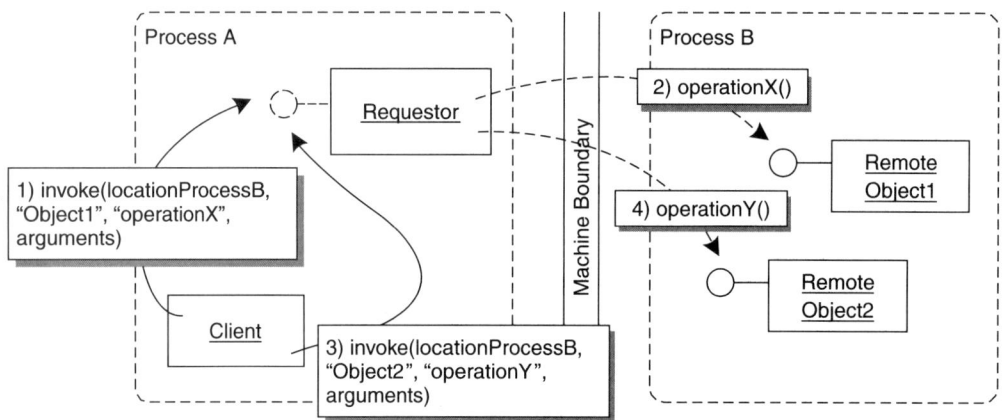

To invoke an operation on a remote object, the client passes the data necessary to invoke the operation to the REQUESTOR, who then sends this invocation across the network to the remote object. It handles the details of crossing the process and/or machine boundary. Note that the illustration does not explicitly show how return values are handled.

❈ ❈ ❈

The REQUESTOR accepts parameters passed to it by the client. It then delegates the tasks of marshaling and de-marshaling of parameters to the MARSHALLER. Next, it starts sending the request and receiving the reply using the CLIENT REQUEST HANDLER. If necessary, it triggers INVOCATION INTERCEPTORS.

Remote communication is inherently unreliable, and the invocation process is more complex than in case of local invocations. New kinds of error can result as a consequence. REMOTING ERRORS are used to communicate such exceptions to clients. Client developers cannot assume that the remote object is reachable all the time, for example because of network delays, network failures, or server crashes. The REQUESTOR abstracts these remoting details for clients by raising REMOTING ERRORS if necessary.

The REQUESTOR is independent of the specific remote object details, such as the type of the remote object or the signature of the operation, as defined by the INTERFACE DESCRIPTION. It constructs invocations dynamically from the information received from the client. To ensure type safety, statically-typed abstractions such as those provided by CLIENT PROXIES are used. Internally, they use the dynamic invocation construction provided by the REQUESTOR. Since the remote object's interface can change without the CLIENT PROXIES noticing, type safety problems are only minimized, not completely avoided. Type mismatches and dispatch failures on the server side are communicated to clients by the REQUESTOR using REMOTING ERRORS.

The REQUESTOR can be deployed in various ways. For a specific client, there might be one REQUESTOR that handles invocations for all objects in all server applications. In this case invocations to the REQUESTOR need to be synchronized, for example by using the *Monitor Object* pattern [SSRB00]. Alternatively, the REQUESTOR can be instantiated more than once, and synchronization of common resources, such as connections, is handled internally. In either case the REQUESTOR needs to be supplied with the complete ABSOLUTE OBJECT REFERENCE, or all necessary information to construct it, as well as all the data describing an invocation. If a REQUESTOR is only dedicated to a specific remote object, you can pre-initialize that REQUESTOR, which saves resources at runtime.

Client Proxy

A REQUESTOR is provided by the distributed object middleware to access remote objects.

✽ ✽ ✽

One of the primary goals of using remote objects is to support a programming model for accessing objects in distributed applications that is similar to that for accessing local objects. A REQUESTOR solves part of this problem by hiding many network details. However, using the REQUESTOR is cumbersome, since the methods to be invoked on the remote object, their arguments, as well as location and identification information for the remote object, have to be passed by the client in a format defined by the REQUESTOR for each invocation. The REQUESTOR also does not provide static type checking, which further complicates client development.

The main purpose of distributed object middleware is to ease development of distributed applications. Developers should not be forced to give up their accustomed way of programming. In the ideal case, they simply invoke operations on remote objects as if they were local objects – taking into account the additional error modes described in the REQUESTOR pattern.

The advantage of the REQUESTOR being generic and type-independent has to be paid for with a complex interface, which makes it cumbersome for client developers to perform remote invocations.

Using only a REQUESTOR carries the risk that invocations might not be understood by the target remote object. Simple typing errors in the name of the operation, or slight differences in the operation arguments, can lead to REMOTING ERRORS, since no compile-time type checking is possible.

Therefore:

Provide a CLIENT PROXY to the client developer that supports the same interface as the remote object. For remote invocations, clients only interact with the local CLIENT PROXY. The CLIENT PROXY translates the local invocation into parameters for the REQUESTOR, and triggers the invocation. The CLIENT PROXY receives the result from

the REQUESTOR, and hands it over to the client using an ordinary return value.

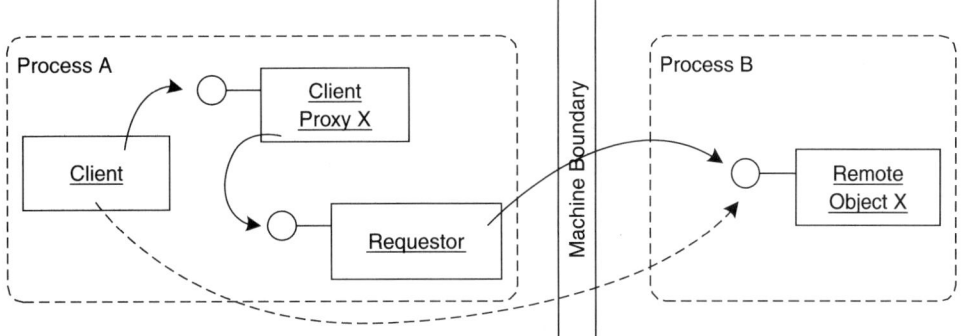

The client interacts with the CLIENT PROXY, which supports the same interface as the remote object. The CLIENT PROXY uses the REQUESTOR, as part of the distributed object middleware, to construct and send the remote invocation.

The CLIENT PROXY uses a REQUESTOR to construct and send invocations across the network. As the CLIENT PROXY is specific to the type of a remote object, it is typically generated from the remote object's INTERFACE DESCRIPTION.

To be available on the client side, the CLIENT PROXY has to be deployed to the client somehow. In the simplest case, the source code of the CLIENT PROXY is compiled with the client application. This has the obvious drawback that on every change of the CLIENT PROXY'S implementation, the client would need to be recompiled as well. The client should not have to necessarily change because of any CLIENT PROXY changes.

Alternatively CLIENT PROXIES can be bound late, for example during loading, linking, or at runtime. That is, the CLIENT PROXY implementation class is designed to be exchangeable in the client. The client uses a stable CLIENT PROXY interface, but the implementation of this interface is provided by the server application, which usually happens during start-up of the client.

The distribution of CLIENT PROXIES can also be done as part of a LOOKUP process. This has the advantage that CLIENT PROXIES can be exchanged transparently. Sometimes this is necessary in cases where the CLIENT PROXY takes part in failover or load-balancing policies. On the downside, this approach incurs the liability of sending CLIENT PROXY implementations across the network. This can be avoided by downloading or sending only the INTERFACE DESCRIPTION to the client, the client generating the late-bound CLIENT PROXY from this interface at runtime.

In some rare cases, even the remote object interfaces change during runtime. Such changes can be handled on the server side only, for example in the INVOKER. However, if this is not possible and the client needs to align with the interface change, the use of CLIENT PROXY should be avoided, and clients should use the REQUESTOR directly to construct remote invocations dynamically. To help the client do this, it needs runtime access to the INTERFACE DESCRIPTION, for example by looking it up in an interface repository, by querying the remote object, or by using reflection. Of course, the client's application logic has to be changed in any case if it wants to make use of the new interface provided by the remote object.

By directly providing the remote object's interface and by representing a specific remote object directly in the client process, a CLIENT PROXY is typically easier to use than a REQUESTOR, especially for inexperienced developers. Its look-and-feel is more aligned with non-distributed applications, and it provides a higher level of transparency.

However, a consequence is that a CLIENT PROXY is less flexible than a REQUESTOR. Because a CLIENT PROXY uses a REQUESTOR internally, the solution is (slightly) slower and consumes more memory than a pure REQUESTOR solution. After all, we need a dedicated CLIENT PROXY instance for each remote object we want to talk access.

The CLIENT PROXY applies the *Proxy* pattern from GoF [GHJV95] and POSA1 [BMR+96] to hide remote communication. POSA1 introduced a variant called *Remoting Proxy*. The CLIENT PROXY pattern is more specific than *Remoting Proxy*, as it hides the REQUESTOR but does not handle the remote communication itself.

Invoker

A REQUESTOR sends a remote invocation for a remote object to a server.

❊ ❊ ❊

When a client sends invocation data across the machine boundary to the server side, the targeted remote object has to be reached somehow. The simplest solution is to let every remote object be addressed over the network directly. But this solution does not work for large numbers of remote objects, as there may not be enough network endpoints for all the remote objects. Also, the remote object would have to deal with handling network connections, receiving and demarshaling messages, and so on. This is cumbersome and over-complex.

If a large number of remote objects were addressed directly over the network, the system would quickly run out of resources such as connection ports, handles, or other system resources, for example the threads used to listen for incoming connections on the communication endpoints.

Even if there are only a limited number of associations between clients and remote objects, there are still issues. Client developers would have to be aware of all network addresses of the required remote objects. The mapping of addresses to remote objects would be tedious to establish and maintain.

Instead, a client should only have to provide the information necessary to select the appropriate remote object and have the server application deal with dispatching and invoking that object.

The remote object implementation should be independent of any communication details, such as listening for incoming invocation messages, as well as demarshaling/marshaling of invocation parameters. Keeping this responsibility in the remote object itself is not a good example of the practice of *separation of concerns*. Additionally, in some cases the remote object might not be available all the time and only be activated on demand, which requires some part of the system to accept invocations and trigger the (re-)activation of the target remote object.

Therefore:

Provide an INVOKER that accepts client invocations from REQUESTORS. REQUESTORS send requests across the network, containing the ID of the remote object, operation name, operation parameters, as well as additional contextual information. The INVOKER reads the request and demarshals it to obtain the OBJECT ID and the name of the operation. It then dispatches the invocation with demarshaled invocation parameters to the targeted remote object. That is, it looks up the correct local object and its operation implementation, as described by the remote invocation, and invokes it.

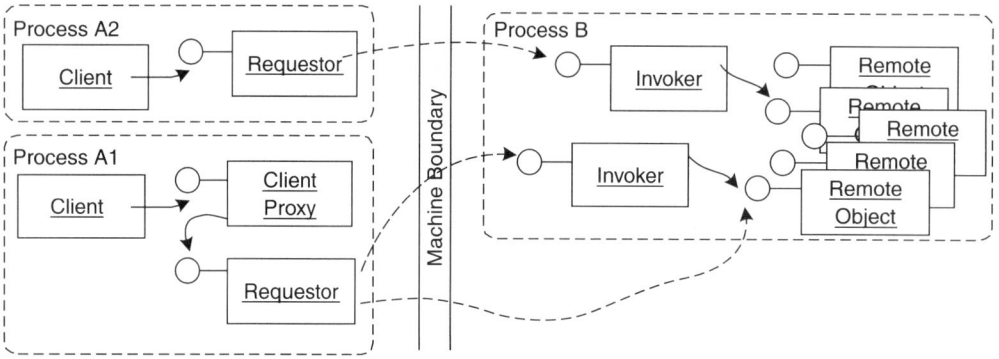

The requestor sends a request to the INVOKER. The INVOKER demarshals the request and dispatches it to the remote object implementation. Results are returned as replies in the reverse direction.

❄ ❄ ❄

The INVOKER is located on the server side within the process of the server application. Depending on the configured CONFIGURATION GROUPS, one or several INVOKER instances exist, since both concepts are closely related. An associated SERVER REQUEST HANDLER handles lower-level network communication. This includes receiving remote messages, management of threads, pooling of connections, as well as sending of replies.

When a request message has been received completely by the SERVER REQUEST HANDLER, the SERVER REQUEST HANDLER hands the invocation, contained in the message, over to the INVOKER. In the case of multiple INVOKERS, the message must contain enough information to allow the

SERVER REQUEST HANDLER to contact the correct INVOKER. The message therefore must contain information about the INVOKER, such as an INVOKER name or ID. If necessary, the INVOKER ID must be part of the ABSOLUTE OBJECT REFERENCE, as explained later in this book. Note that for the SERVER REQUEST HANDLER to be able to hand the message to the correct INVOKER, it has partially to demarshal the request message.

If not already done, the INVOKER demarshals the request message further to identify the target remote object, the operation name and the invocation parameters. The real de-marshaling is handled by a separate pattern, the MARSHALLER.

In the event that a target remote object cannot be found by the INVOKER, the INVOKER can delegate dispatching to a LOCATION FORWARDER. The LOCATION FORWARDER might be able to delegate to a remote object in another server application. Such approaches are used in cases where remote objects have been moved, or when the load is balanced between multiple remote objects.

More than one servant might be used to implement a single remote object at runtime. For example, when using POOLING, a remote object is realized by multiple servants managed in a pool. The INVOKER has to select one of these servant, or trigger the selection of a servant. The servant of a remote object might also have been evicted temporarily, to reduce the resource consumption. Here, the INVOKER requests the LIFECYCLE MANAGER to make the remote object's servant available again.

The INVOKER can trigger functionality, such as lifecycle management or other tasks orthogonal to invoking remote objects, by using INVOCATION INTERCEPTORS. INVOCATION INTERCEPTORS can generally be used to extend dispatching in the SERVER REQUEST HANDLER and INVOKER with custom functionality.

Determining and invoking the target object and operation can be performed dynamically or statically:

- *Static dispatch*. Static dispatching is done in so-called 'server stubs', sometimes also called 'skeletons'. These are part of the INVOKER, and are generated from INTERFACE DESCRIPTIONS. A separate server stub is generated for each remote object type. Thus the INVOKER *knows* the remote object type, including its operations and operation signatures, in advance. With this type information, the INVOKER can directly invoke the target operation, and it does not have to find the operation implementation dynamically.

- *Dynamic dispatch.* When it is undesirable or impossible to use server stubs, for example because remote object interfaces are not known at compile time, dynamic dispatch is advisable. The INVOKER has to decide at runtime which operation of which remote object be invoked. From the information in the demarshaled request message, the INVOKER finds the corresponding remote object and operation implementation in the local process, for example using runtime dispatch mechanisms such as *Reflection* [Mae87, BMR+96], or a dynamic lookup in a table.

  Using dynamic dispatch, an invocation can potentially contain a non-existent operation or use an incorrect signature. In this case, a special REMOTING ERROR has to be returned to the REQUESTOR at the client. Finally, the INVOKER invokes the operation on the target remote object. This form of dispatch is called 'dynamic dispatch', as the INVOKER dispatches each invocation by resolving the actual operation dynamically at runtime. For more details of this implementation variant, see the pattern *Message Redirector* [GNZ01].

Comparing dynamic dispatch with static dispatch, static dispatch is typically faster, as the overhead of looking up operation implementations at runtime is avoided. Dynamic dispatch, however, is more flexible. Dynamic dispatch is – in contrast to static dispatch – not type-safe, which is the reason why it introduces a new kind of REMOTING ERROR.

The INVOKER on the server side and the REQUESTOR on the client side have to be compatible with respect to the messages they exchange. The REQUESTOR has to put all the information required by the INVOKER into an request message, and the INVOKER has to send well-formed reply messages.

For extension and integration of application-specific functionality during dispatching, INVOCATION INTERCEPTORS can be used in combination with INVOCATION CONTEXTS. To configure dispatching constraints, the remote objects in a server application are typically partitioned into CONFIGURATION GROUPS, which encapsulate behavior specific to a group of objects. In cases where the remote objects have non-trivial lifecycles, the use of a LIFECYCLE MANAGER is advisable.

Using an INVOKER instead of direct network connections to remote objects reduces the number of network addressable entities required. It also allows the SERVER REQUEST HANDLER efficiently to share connections to servers hosting several remote objects.

Client Request Handler

The REQUESTOR has to send requests to, and receive replies from, the network.

❋ ❋ ❋

To send requests from the client to the server application, several tasks have to be performed: connection establishment and configuration, result handling, timeout handling, and error detection. In the case of timeouts or errors the REQUESTOR, and subsequently the CLIENT PROXY, have to be informed. Client-side connection management, threading, and result dispatching need to managed in a coordinated and optimized fashion.

CLIENT PROXIES support a proper abstraction of remote object access, and REQUESTORS support proper invocation construction. However, connection management, threading, and result dispatching are not handled efficiently by these patterns. For simple, single-threaded clients with only a few requests, these networking issues can be handled on a per-CLIENT PROXY or per-REQUESTOR basis. In more complex clients, it is possible that a large number of requests must be sent simultaneously. In such cases, the network access needs to be optimized across multiple CLIENT PROXIES and REQUESTORS. For example, network connections could be kept open and subsequently reused for additional requests to the same server application.

Therefore:

Provide a common CLIENT REQUEST HANDLER for all REQUESTORS within a client. The CLIENT REQUEST HANDLER is responsible for opening and closing the network connections to server applications, sending requests, receiving replies, and dispatching them back to the appropriate REQUESTOR. Additionally, the CLIENT REQUEST HANDLER copes with timeouts, threading issues, and invocation errors.

Client Request Handler

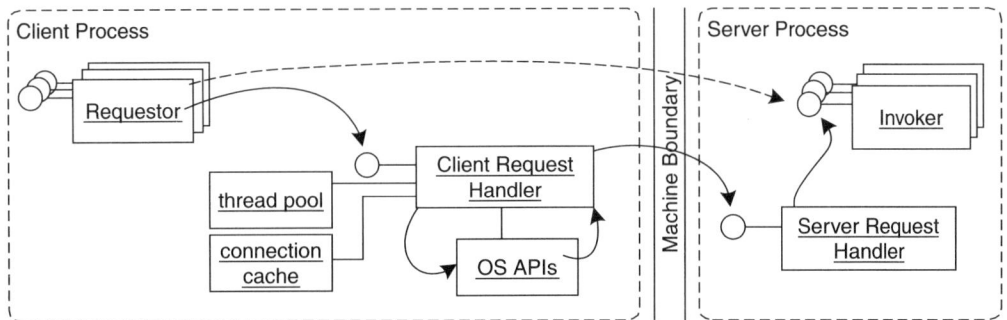

When a client issues a request using a REQUESTOR, the client REQUEST HANDLER establishes the connection, sends the request, receives the reply, and returns it to the requestor.

The CLIENT REQUEST HANDLER is responsible for handling network communication inside client applications. The internally-used *Connector* [SSRB00] establishes and configures connections to the remote server. A connection handle is used to identify connections and associate a handler. Typically a connection to a particular server and server port can be shared with other invocations sent to the same server application. The actual task of sending invocation data, especially in the context of several available transport protocols, is done using a PROTOCOL PLUG-IN.

It is the job of the CLIENT REQUEST HANDLER to ensure scalability. That is, it has to be designed in such a way that it handles concurrent requests efficiently. To do this, the *Reactor* [SSRB00] pattern is used to demultiplex and dispatch reply messages. A reactor uses the connection handle to notify the responsible handler about available results. The result can be handled in various ways in the client:

- In the case of synchronous invocations, after an invocation is sent across the network, the CLIENT REQUEST HANDLER has to wait for the result of the invocation. That is, it blocks until the result has arrived.

- For asynchronous invocations the REQUESTOR and CLIENT REQUEST HANDLER have to follow one of the client asynchrony patterns, described in Chapter 8. In the case of RESULT CALLBACK or POLL OBJECT, it dispatches the result to a callback object POLL OBJECT respectively, instead of handing the result back to the client invocation on the callstack.

When timeouts must be supported, the CLIENT REQUEST HANDLER informs the REQUESTOR about timeout events. For this purpose the CLIENT REQUEST HANDLER registers for a timeout when the invocation is sent to the remote object. If the reply does not arrive within the timeout period, the CLIENT REQUEST HANDLER receives the timeout event and informs the REQUESTOR. Depending on the configuration, it might also retry, sending an invocation several times before raising the REMOTING ERROR. The CLIENT REQUEST HANDLER must also detect other error conditions, such as an unavailable network or server application. In this case, it has to raise a REMOTING ERROR and forward it to the REQUESTOR.

For thread management the CLIENT REQUEST HANDLER makes use of the same patterns as the SERVER REQUEST HANDLER: *Half-sync/Half-async* [SSRB00] and/or *Leader/Followers* [SSRB00]. Further, *Caching* [KJ04] can be used to reuse connections to the same server application. *Pooling* [KJ04] can be used to create thread pools to reduce the overhead of creating threads repeatedly.

For many tasks, CLIENT and SERVER REQUEST HANDLER have to work in concert, especially for extensions of request handling such as INVOCATION INTERCEPTORS, INVOCATION CONTEXTS, PROTOCOL PLUG-INS, or other add-on services.

The CLIENT REQUEST HANDLER is typically shared between multiple REQUESTORS. CLIENT REQUEST HANDLERS hide connection and message handling complexity from the REQUESTORS. For very simple clients, the indirection and required resource management complexity in the CLIENT REQUEST HANDLER might be an overhead in some scenarios, for example if a high invocation performance is required. In such cases it might make sense to avoid this overhead by implementing REQUESTORS that connect to the network directly.

The role of the CLIENT REQUEST HANDLER is analogous to the *Forwarder* in the *Forwarder-Receiver* pattern in POSA1 [BMR+96].

Server Request Handler

You are providing remote objects in a server application, and INVOKERS are used for message dispatching.

❄ ❄ ❄

Before a request can be dispatched by an INVOKER, the server application has to receive the request message from the network. Managing communication channels efficiently and effectively is essential, since typically many requests may have to be handled, possibly even concurrently. Network communication needs to be managed in a coordinated and optimized way.

Simple implementations of the server-side parts of distributed object middleware would have each INVOKER listening to the network and receiving request messages. This solution does not scale if multiple INVOKERS are used. If a client uses remote objects from several of those INVOKERS, separate resources, for example connections, would be required. Further, how many INVOKERS the server application uses should be transparent to the client.

Managing request and reply messages can be complex, as it involves the management of several – typically scarce – system resources, such as connections, threads, synchronization primitives, and memory. For reasons of performance, scalability, and stability, it is crucial that these aspects are handled effectively and efficiently.

Therefore:

Provide a SERVER REQUEST HANDLER that deals with all the communication issues of a server application. Let the SERVER REQUEST HANDLER receive messages from the network, combine the message fragments to complete messages, and dispatch the messages to the correct INVOKER for further processing. The SERVER REQUEST HANDLER will manage all the required resources, such as connections and threads.

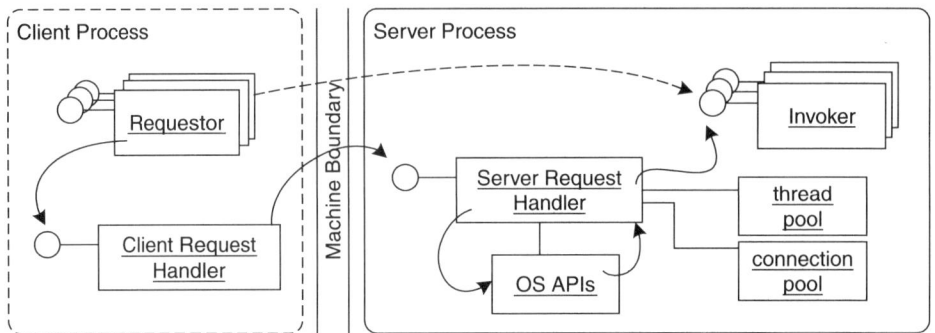

Incoming messages are received by the SERVER REQUEST HANDLER on the server side using suitable operating system APIs. The messages are then dispatched to the responsible INVOKERS using threads acquired from a thread pool.

The SERVER REQUEST HANDLER deals with *messages* and how they are sent and received over the network, whereas the INVOKER deals with *requests* and how they are dispatched and invoked. When multiple INVOKERS are present, the SERVER REQUEST HANDLER demarshals the message at least to the point where it can decide to which INVOKER to dispatch the message. The rest of the message is demarshaled later by the INVOKER.

The SERVER REQUEST HANDLER has to be designed in such a way that it handles concurrent requests efficiently. In many cases, efficient request handling requires a number of concurrent instances that can handle requests simultaneously. Several patterns in POSA2 [SSRB00] support such efficient SERVER REQUEST HANDLER designs.

The SERVER REQUEST HANDLER listens for connection requests on a network port, and, if a connection is established, for incoming messages. A *Reactor* [SSRB00] is typically used for demultiplexing and dispatching those connection requests and messages to the SERVER REQUEST HANDLER, which handles them accordingly.

Connection management is typically implemented by the SERVER REQUEST HANDLER using an *Acceptor* [SSRB00]. Connection requests are accepted asynchronously, and connection handles, identifying individual connections, are created.

For integrated thread and connection management the SERVER REQUEST HANDLER uses the patterns *Half-sync/Half-async* [SSRB00], which describes how to split common functionality between two objects, or *Leader/Followers* [SSRB00], which describes how to manage threads and their access to shared resources efficiently.

To optimize resource allocation for connections, the connections can be shared in a pool, as described by *Pooling* [KJ04]. Whether one thread per connection or an connection-independent thread pool performs better depends on the number of connections. Some SERVER REQUEST HANDLERS allow for connection establishment policies, typically implemented as *Strategies* [GHJV95]. Such a strategy could allow a server to start up using a thread-per-connection strategy and then transition to connection-independent thread pooling in the case where many connections are used. In cases where request priorities need to be obeyed, different threads might have different SERVER REQUEST HANDLERS associated with them.

In some application scenarios it can be expected that a client might communicate repeatedly with remote objects in the same server application, while in other scenarios this might not be the case. There are thus different strategies for connection establishment. For example, a new connection can be opened and closed for each message sent across the network. Alternatively, the connection can be held open for a specific time and then reused for subsequent invocations. The latter has the advantage of avoiding the overhead of establishing and destroying connections for repeated client requests. However, connections that are held open consume resources. The connection establishment strategy of the server application is implemented by the SERVER REQUEST HANDLER.

For the actual network communication, the SERVER REQUEST HANDLER uses PROTOCOL PLUG-INS. Since the client and server request handler have to work in concert when changing data, they have to use compatible PROTOCOL PLUG-INS.

An important consequence of using a SERVER REQUEST HANDLER is that low-level networking issues are centralized in a single system component. Connection pools and thread pools allow the SERVER REQUEST HANDLER to be highly concurrent, avoiding the risk of bottlenecks.

Note that there are some application areas in which multiple SERVER REQUEST HANDLER instances are useful, such as the case of direct binding of remote objects to network ports. For example, if there are only a few remote objects, but they require high performance, this result in different communication channel configurations and concurrency settings per remote object. It is hard to cope with this scenario in a centralized fashion by using only one SERVER REQUEST HANDLER.

The role of the SERVER REQUEST HANDLER pattern is analogous to the *Receiver* in the *Forwarder-Receiver* pattern in POSA1 [BMR+96].

Marshaller

Request and reply messages have to be transported over the network between REQUESTOR and INVOKER.

❄ ❄ ❄

For remote invocations to work, invocation information has to be transported over the network. The data required to describe invocations consists of the target remote object's OBJECT ID, the operation name, the parameters, the return value, and possibly other INVOCATION CONTEXT information. Only byte streams are suitable as a data format for transporting this information over the network.

To send invocation data across the network, there has to be some concept for transforming invocations of remote operations into a byte stream. For simple data, such as an integer value, this is trivial, but there are additional cases that make this task complicated. For example:

- Complex, user-defined types typically have references to other instances, possibly forming a complex hierarchy of objects. Such hierarchies might even contain multiple references to the same instance, and in such cases, logical identities must be preserved after the transport to the server.
- Local objects might have to be transmitted with an invocation. The object identity and attributes of these local objects need to be transported across the network.

Generating and interpreting a byte stream representation should not require additional programming efforts per instance, so it should only be defined once per type. The generation and interpretation of transport formats, as well as the data formats, should be extensible by developers to allow for customization and optimization.

A simple solution to the problem of transporting an object or data structure across the network is to send its memory representation. If different platforms have to be supported, however, this might lead to platform incompatibilities, such as 'big endian' versus 'little endian' byte ordering. Similar problems arise if different programming languages are involved, as these often use different in-memory representations of the data types, or even support completely different data types.

Therefore:

Require each non-primitive type used within remote object invocations to be serializable into a transport format that can be transported over a network as a byte stream. Use compatible MARSHALLERS on the client and server side that serialize invocation information. Depending on the environment, the serialization may be provided by the data types themselves. References to remote objects are serialized as ABSOLUTE OBJECT REFERENCES.

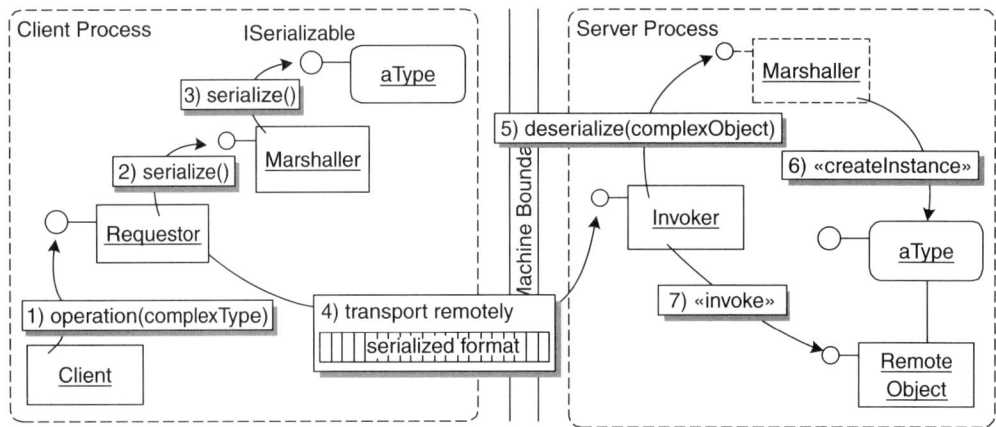

The client invokes an operation with a local object as its parameter. The REQUESTOR uses the relevant MARSHALLER to serialize the object into a byte stream. The serialized object is then transported across the network as a byte stream together with other invocation information. On the server side, the stream is deserialized by the MARSHALLER, and an instance of the object is recreated before operation invocation. Finally, the remote object is invoked using the recreated object as a parameter.

❊ ❊ ❊

A MARSHALLER converts remote invocations into byte streams. The MARSHALLER provides a generic mechanism that is not specific to any particular remote object type.

The REQUESTOR, INVOKER, and REQUEST HANDLERS use the MARSHALLER to retrieve the invocation information contained in the message byte stream. For complex data types the MARSHALLER recursively parses their type hierarchy. Object identities are handled as special data types, but are marshaled in a similar way to complex data types.

References to other remote objects are translated into ABSOLUTE OBJECT REFERENCES.

Local objects containing many data elements used by the invoked remote object should not be referenced remotely, but marshaled by value, because querying the data in these objects remotely would likely require a number of subsequent remote invocations, wasting network bandwidth and degrading performance. A generic transport format is required to transport such a data type across the network. The serialization of a complex type can be done in several ways:

- The programming language might provide a generic, built-in facility for serialization. This is often the case in interpreted languages such as Java or .NET, which can use *Reflection* [Mae87, BMR+96] to introspect the type's structure.
- Tools can be used to generate serialization code directly from the INTERFACE DESCRIPTION, assuming that the structure of such types is expressed in the INTERFACE DESCRIPTION (for example structs in CORBA).
- Developers may have to provide serialization functionality. In this case, the developer usually has to implement a suitable interface that declares operations for serialization and deserialization.

The concrete format of the data inside a byte stream depends on the distributed object middleware used. Everything is a byte stream when it is transported across the network. To represent complex data structures, it is advisable to use a structured format such as XML, CDR (CORBA's marshaling format), or ASN.1 (a marshaling format used mainly in telecommunications systems [Dub00]).

The distributed object middleware might support a hook to let developers provide a custom MARSHALLER, to allow for the cases in which generic marshaling may be too complex or inefficient for marshaling complex data structure graphs. A generic marshaling format can never be optimal for all data structures or scenarios. Depending on the use case, some serialization formats are better than others. XML is human-readable, but too inefficient with respect to bandwidth use for some domains, such as the embedded systems domain. CDR is a binary format and standardized, which means many tools are available for its use. For real-time and embedded applications it is often optimized further. Other binary formats are either similar to CDR or specifically optimized for compactness, reliability, or other non-functional requirements.

Exchanging a MARSHALLER is not necessarily transparent for the applications using the distributed object middleware. A custom MARSHALLER might, for instance, transport all attributes of an object, it might only transport the public ones, or it might just ignore those it cannot serialize, instead of throwing an exception.

If the MASHALLER has to serialize and de-serialize complete objects, the *Serializer* [RSB+97] pattern describes generically how to stream objects into data structures efficiently. The MASHALLER uses *Serializers* for object parameters and results that have to be sent across the network in call-by-value style.

Interface Description

A client wants to invoke an operation of a remote object using a CLIENT PROXY.

❈ ❈ ❈

The interfaces of a CLIENT PROXY and remote object need to be aligned to ensure that an INVOKER can properly dispatch invocations. To ensure that messages arrive properly at the INVOKER, marshaling and de-marshaling need to be aligned. Client developers need to be able to access the interfaces of the remote objects the client application may use.

A CLIENT PROXY, used as a local representative of a remote object, needs to expose the same interface as provided by the remote object. The CLIENT PROXY is responsible for ensuring that the remote object is used correctly with regard to operations and their signature.

On the server side, the INVOKER dispatches the operation invoked on the remote object. For static dispatch, the INVOKER has to know the operations and their signature before an invocation request arrives. In the case of dynamic dispatch, this information will be retrieved at run-time.

To summarize, CLIENT PROXY and INVOKER have to work together to ensure that no violation of the remote object's interfaces occurs. Client developers and remote object developers should not have to deal with ensuring compliance of remote object interfaces or propagating them manually. Instead, the distributed object middleware should provide suitable means for automating these issues as much as feasible.

In addition to these problems, the client and server application might be written in different programming languages. The two languages might expose different data types, operation types, invocation styles, and other interface elements. Developers should not have to deal with converting these elements from one language context to another.

Therefore:

Provide an INTERFACE DESCRIPTION in which you describe the interface of remote objects. The INTERFACE DESCRIPTION serves as the

contract between CLIENT PROXY and INVOKER. CLIENT PROXY and INVOKER use either code generation or runtime configuration techniques to adhere to that contract.

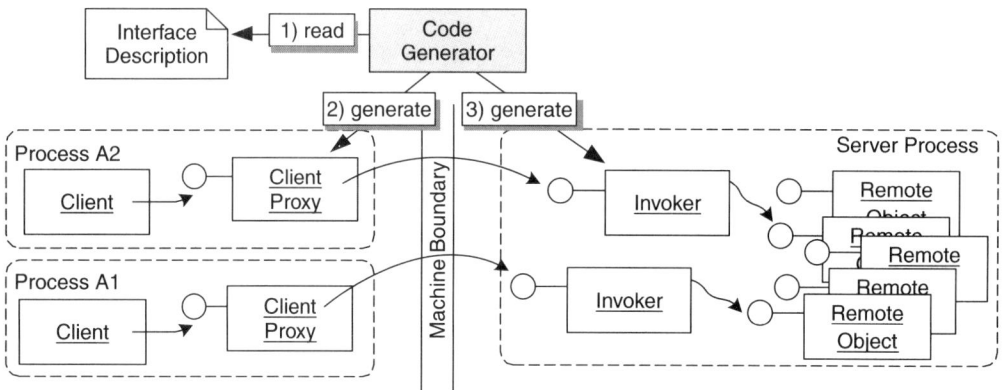

Using an INTERFACE DESCRIPTION in a separate file, a code generator generates code for CLIENT PROXY and INVOKER. The CLIENT PROXY used by the client adheres to the same contract as the IN-VOKER, which dispatches the invocation to the remote object. In this way the details required to ensure type safety are hidden from client and remote object developers. All they have to be concerned about is the INTERFACE DESCRIPTION and their own implementation based on that interface.

❊ ❊ ❊

Usually an INTERFACE DESCRIPTION contains interface specifications that include their operations and signatures, as well as the definition of user-defined complex types. The INTERFACE DESCRIPTION itself can exist in various forms:

- *Interface description language.* The INTERFACE DESCRIPTION is separated from the program text, for example in a file provided by the remote object developer. An interface description language defines the syntax and semantics of the declarations. A code generator generates the remote object type specific parts of CLIENT PROXY and INVOKER. This allows interface violations to be detected automatically when compiling client and CLIENT PROXY. Note that this will only work if mechanisms exist that ensure that the isolated INTERFACE DESCRIPTION really conforms to the current version of the remote object interface.

- *Interface repository.* The INTERFACE DESCRIPTION is provided to clients at runtime using an interface repository exposed by the server application, or some other entity. The interface repository is used for building CLIENT PROXIES at compile time, just as in the interface description language variant above. In addition, an interface repository can be used for dynamically-constructed invocations, to provide remotely-accessible interface information at runtime. The INVOKER has similar options.

- *Reflective interfaces.* The INTERFACE DESCRIPTION is provided by means of reflection [Mae87], either offered through the server-side programming language or using the *Reflection* pattern [BMR+96]. For clients to make use of reflection, the server application has to provide some means to allow this information to be queried remotely.

Note that the different variants of INTERFACE DESCRIPTION correspond to the implementation variants of CLIENT PROXY and INVOKER. Static variants of CLIENT PROXY and INVOKER use code generation techniques and thus primarily use interface description languages directly. Dynamic variants require INTERFACE DESCRIPTIONS, either on the client or on server side at runtime, so reflective interfaces or interface repositories are used. In many distributed object middleware solutions, more than one INTERFACE DESCRIPTION variant is supported, as more than one variant of REQUESTOR, CLIENT PROXY, and/or INVOKER are supported. For example, interface repositories might derive their information from interfaces defined using an interface description language.

In distributed object middleware that supports more than one programming language, INTERFACE DESCRIPTIONS must be given in a programming-language independent syntax. This requires tools that translate the INTERFACE DESCRIPTION into different languages. INTERFACE DESCRIPTIONS are an important means for building interoperable distributed systems. The distributed object middleware provides a language binding, in addition to the INTERFACE DESCRIPTIONS, to define generic conversion rules to/from a programming language.

INTERFACE DESCRIPTIONS separate interfaces from implementations. Thus the software engineering principle of *separation of concerns* is supported, as well as exchangeability of implementations. This means that clients can rely on stable interfaces, while remote object implementations can be changed. However, interface changes cannot be avoided in all cases, especially, in a distributed setting where server application developers have no control over client code and its deployment. The research community is still searching for ways to cope with such interface changes. The *Extension Interface* pattern [SSRB00] is one possible solution.

The CLIENT PROXY typically represents the same interface as described by the INTERFACE DESCRIPTION, although in some cases there might be differences. First, the operations may have additional parameters for technical reasons, such as explicit context passing. Alternatively, the CLIENT PROXY might provide additional operations, for example for life-cycle management. Finally, the client proxy may act as an *Adapter* [GHJV95]. For example, when the INTERFACE DESCRIPTION is updated, a CLIENT PROXY may represent the old interface, as it was before the interface change, and translate invocations if possible.

Note that in some cases using REQUESTORS directly, without an INTERFACE DESCRIPTION, might be an option. Suppose, for example, that you receive the invocation or location information (such as remote object type, OBJECT ID, method name, or host name and port) at runtime from a server and the client cannot be stopped in cases of interface violations. Performing the invocation and handling the REMOTING ERROR might be the much simpler solution than, for example, compiling a CLIENT PROXY from an INTERFACE DESCRIPTION on the fly.

Remoting Error

Remote communication between clients and remote objects is inherently unreliable.

❈ ❈ ❈

Although it is desirable that access to remote objects is transparent to clients, actual implementations of distributed object middleware can never achieve this goal completely, due to the inherent unreliability of communication networks. Apart from errors in the remote object itself, additional types of error can occur when communicating across machine boundaries. Examples are network failures, server crashes, or unavailable remote objects. Clients need to be able to cope with such errors.

In addition to errors occurring within the remote object as a consequence of faults in business logic, such as an attempt to transfer money from an empty account, other types of error are a consequence of the distribution of client and remote object across separate processes and possibly also separate machines. Clients and servers typically fail independently of each other, since they run in separate processes. In addition, the network connection between them can fail, or provide only intermittent service.

The client should be able to distinguish between errors that are due to the use of a distributed infrastructure and errors that are due to the application logic inside remote objects.

Therefore:

Detect and propagate errors inside the distributed object middleware. Distinguish between errors that arise from distribution and remote communication, and errors that arise from the application logic inside remote objects. Clients can then handle these types of REMOTING ERROR differently. INVOKER, REQUESTOR, and the REQUEST

HANDLERS detect REMOTING ERRORS that are due to communication and dispatching problems.

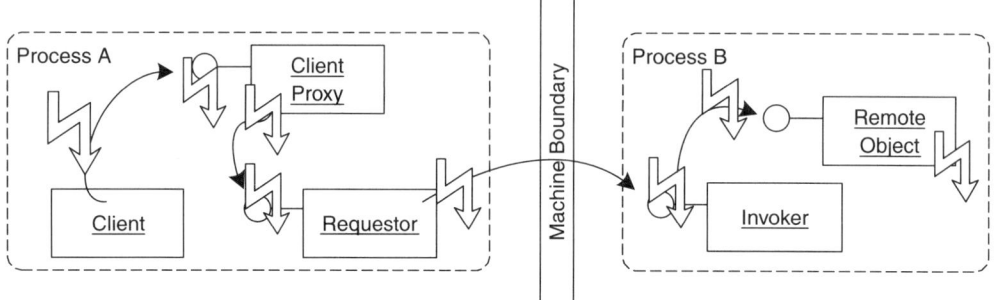

Problems that occur during a remote invocation are reported via the REQUESTOR to the CLIENT PROXY, or directly to the client, as a REMOTING ERROR.

The client has to be able to differentiate critical REMOTING ERRORS, such as server crashes or network outages, from less critical errors, such as 'object not found' errors. For example, as a reaction to a unavailable server, the client, including the involved REQUESTOR and CLIENT REQUEST HANDLER, might have to clean up resources related to the remote objects on the server application.

REMOTING ERRORS detected inside the server application need to be transported back to the client as the result of a remote method invocation. INVOKER, REQUESTOR, and/or CLIENT PROXY will forward the error to the client. Other errors, such as timeouts or an unreachable server application, can be detected directly by the client infrastructure itself. Again, REQUESTOR and/or CLIENT PROXY will forward the error to the client.

INVOKERS and SERVER REQUEST HANDLERS send back special reply messages in the case of a REMOTING ERROR. These messages should include a reason to the error, or at least a guess at what might have gone wrong. If REMOTING ERRORS are not to influence regular communication, separate communication channels dedicated to error reporting may be used.

Note that the mechanisms that are employed to report a REMOTING ERROR to the actual client within the client process depend on the programming language. In most modern programming languages, exceptions are used. To distinguish REMOTING ERRORS from application errors, exceptions reporting REMOTING ERRORS typically inherit from a system-provided exception base class such as `RemotingError`. Specific kinds of REMOTING ERRORS are implemented using subclasses. Alternatively, such as in the case of DCOM, special return values such as integers in a specific range are used to signal REMOTING ERRORS. The language also determines whether the client can be forced to handle the exception, such as in Java, or whether it is left to the client to provide a catch clause, such as in C++ and C#. In the latter case, when no catch-clause is provided, the client developer of course risks undefined application behavior.

The reported error must contain enough information for the client to take sensible action to handle the error and possibly to recover from it. If the REMOTING ERROR is caused by a problem in the local network stack, there is usually not much the client can do. But if there is a problem on the server side, the client may use LOOKUP to find another compatible remote object or server application, and try again.

Not all REMOTING ERRORS raised by the server side need to be reported to the client application – the client-side distributed object middleware may handle some of these automatically, depending on the configuration of the system. For example, a REQUESTOR can be configured to contact a different server application if the original one is not available, or the CLIENT REQUEST HANDLER can automatically re-send messages to handle short, temporary network outages transparently to the client.

Besides recovery from errors, another important goal of sending detailed REMOTING ERRORS is debugging distributed applications. The client and server application should log REMOTING ERRORS in the order they occurred, to help in the localization of bugs.

By making server and network errors visible to the client, the REMOTING ERROR pattern addresses the inherent unreliability of network communication in distributed environments. A liability of using the pattern is the necessity for programmers to deal with the new types of error when developing client applications. Ignoring these errors is not an option – the REMOTING ERROR pattern gives the client at least a chance to recover from the error and/or perform meaningful error logging.

Interactions among the patterns

The patterns illustrated in this chapter form the basic building blocks of distributed object middleware. Note that it is not necessary for each pattern actually to form a component, or module, in the software architecture. The patterns should rather be seen as *roles*. A software component can play multiple roles at the same time – that is, it can participate in a number of patterns. Or, a pattern implementation can be spread over several software components.

The basic remoting patterns form a logical *layer* architecture that is symmetrical between client and server. The following illustration shows this.

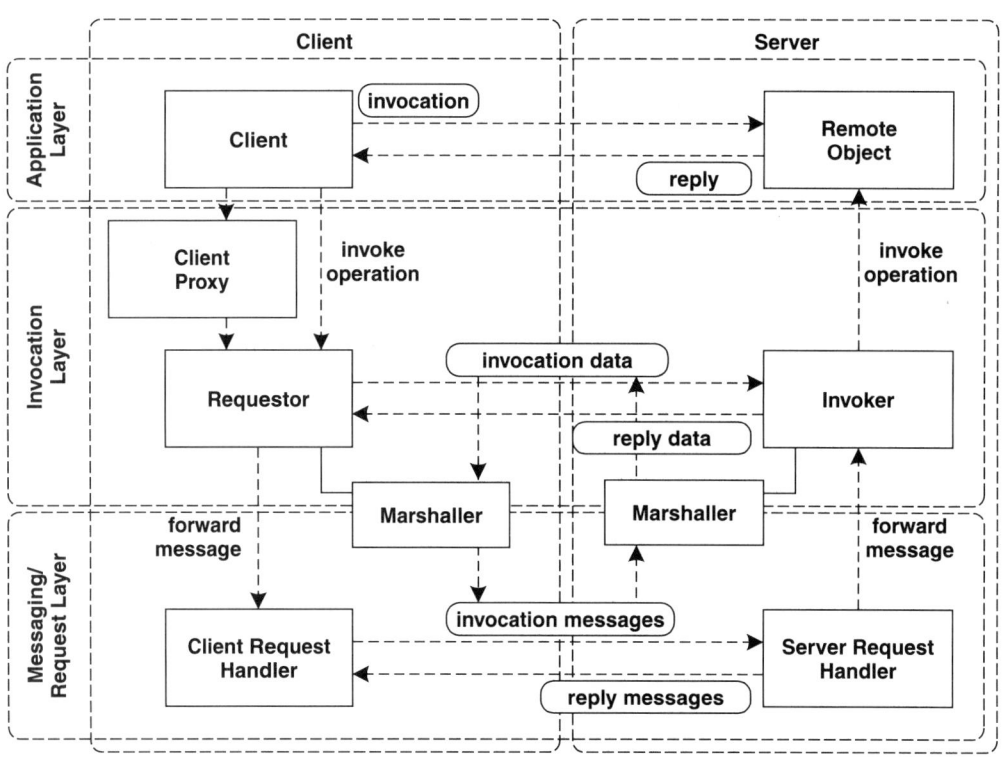

The sequence diagrams that follow illustrate the dynamics of some of the interactions among the patterns. Note that for reasons of brevity, we do not consider all technical implementation details in those diagrams.

Interactions among the patterns

That is, only the necessary operation parameters are shown, helper objects are omitted, and so on.

The following sequence diagram shows a basic invocation sequence on the client side. A CLIENT PROXY builds up the invocation using the REQUESTOR. All invocation data is stored in an invocation data object so that the invocation data can be passed among the participants of the invocation process. The REQUESTOR uses the MARSHALLER to build up a Message object, which is sent across the network by the CLIENT REQUEST HANDLER. A similar approach is used for the reply, although this is not shown in the diagram. The message is received by the CLIENT REQUEST HANDLER and returned to the REQUESTOR. It demarshals the message using the MARSHALLER and returns the de-marshaled reply to the CLIENT PROXY which, in turn, returns this result to the client.

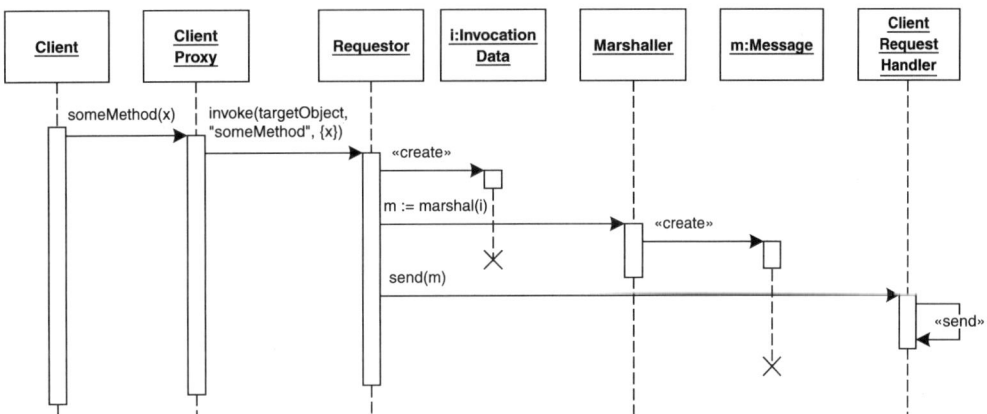

On the server side, the mechanics are similar, but happen in reverse order. This is exemplified in the next sequence diagram. Again, we do not show how return values are handled.

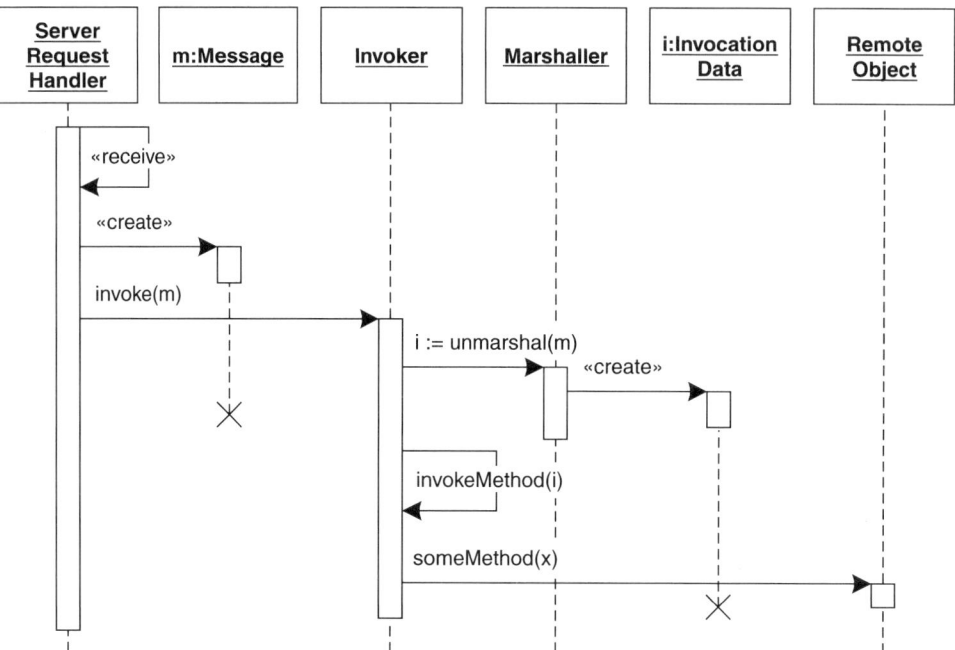

In this example we presume that there is only one INVOKER. The SERVER REQUEST HANDLER does not have to do any demarshaling to find out which INVOKER to use. The INVOKER uses the MARSHALLER to re-create the invocation data object that was marshaled on the client side. Using the information in that object, the INVOKER performs the invocation.

Now consider a slightly more complex situation. In the next diagram, we use a registry for INVOKERS, where INVOKERS can be registered to be responsible for particular remote object types. For example, different INVOKERS might implement different activation strategies. The SERVER REQUEST HANDLER must be able to decode the ID of the remote object type or the OBJECT ID that contains the remote object's type. Using this information, the INVOKER can be selected from the registry.

Further, each INVOKER contains an instance list of the objects it can invoke. Thus the INVOKER has to get the target remote object from the instance list – using its ID – before the object can be invoked.

Interactions among the patterns

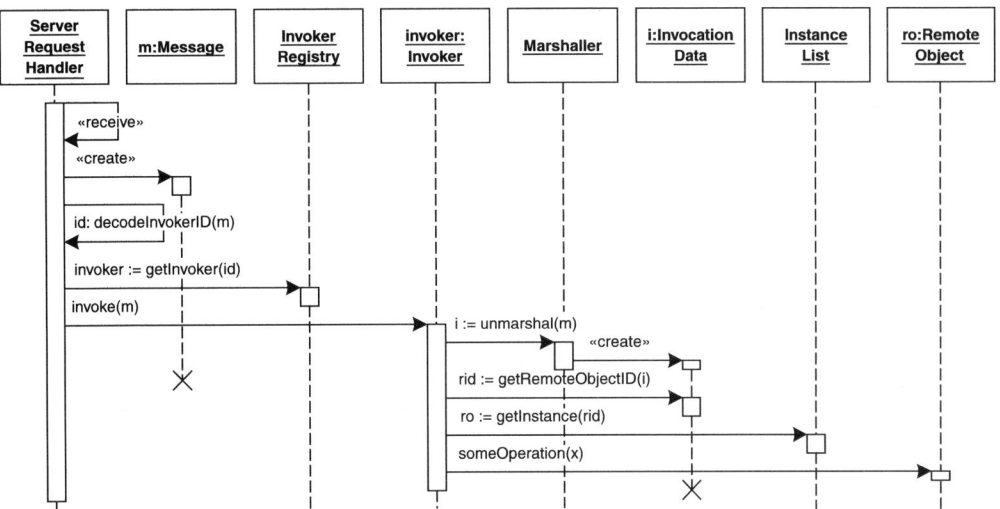

Assuming everything works fine in the above sequence diagram, the result of the invocation is returned to the client. If no object corresponding to the OBJECT ID is registered in the instance list, a REMOTING ERROR would have to be raised. In this case a REMOTING ERROR is sent back to the client.

If a REMOTING ERROR arrives at the client side, the REQUESTOR raises an exception instead of handing back the result. This sequence is illustrated in the following sequence diagram. In the diagram, the REMOTING ERROR is propagated to the client. Here, the CLIENT REQUEST

HANDLER creates an object describing the error and then raises an exception to be handled by the client.

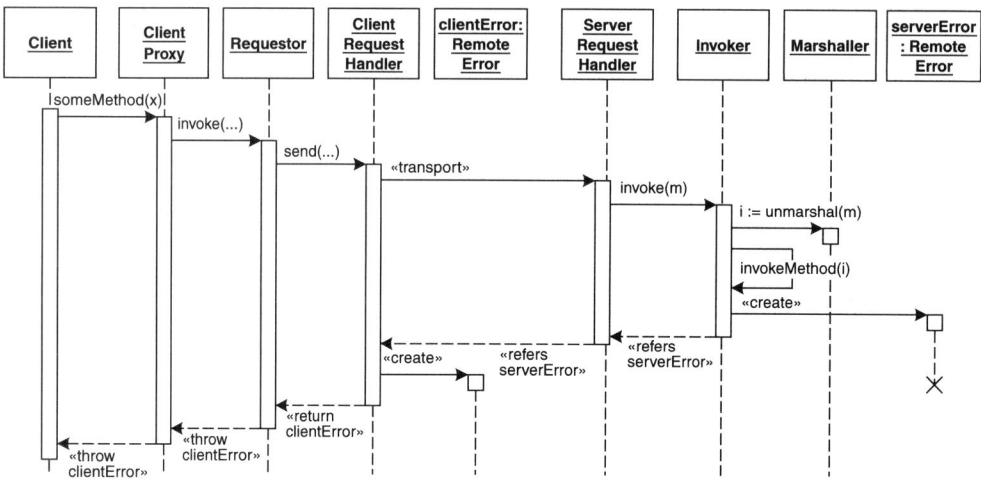

Note that technically two REMOTING ERROR objects are involved: server-Error is the object created in the server application, whereas clientError is the error object created on the client side to signal the REMOTING ERROR to the original caller. The two objects contain the same error information: this information must be marshaled on server side and be transmitted to the client side.

Instead of propagating the REMOTING ERROR to the client, the REQUESTOR or CLIENT PROXY might handle the error transparently. The next diagram shows an example in which the REQUESTOR tries to contact a different server application, because the original one could not be reached. This allows this special REQUESTOR to be able to handle

Interactions among the patterns

the REMOTING ERROR caused by the server being unreachable in a way that is transparent to the client.

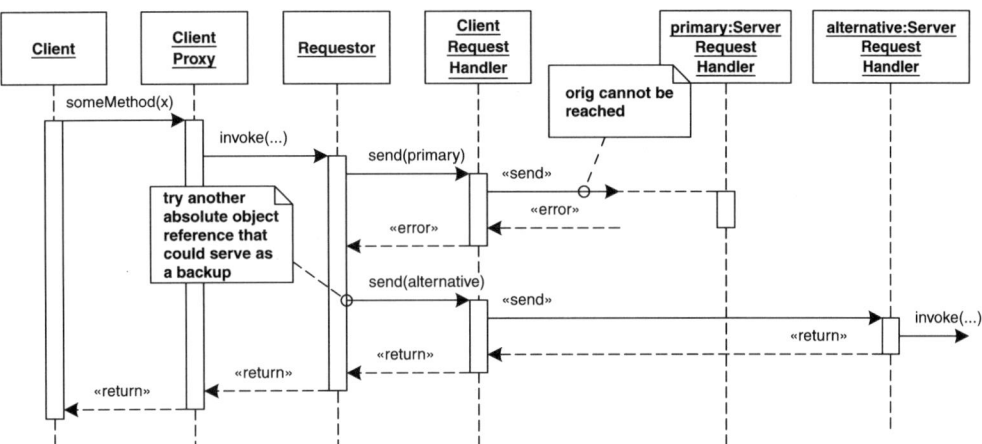

4 Identification Patterns

This chapter documents patterns for the identification, addressing, and look-up of remote objects. This includes the assignment of logical OBJECT IDS for each remote object instance, as well as the notion of ABSOLUTE OBJECT REFERENCES that allow remote objects to be identified and addressed uniquely by remote clients. The LOOKUP pattern describes how to associate remote objects with properties, and how to search for them later using those properties. Typical examples of properties used for LOOKUP are human readable names and name-value pairs.

The figure below illustrates the relationship of the Identification patterns to each other and to the basic Remoting Patterns from the previous section.

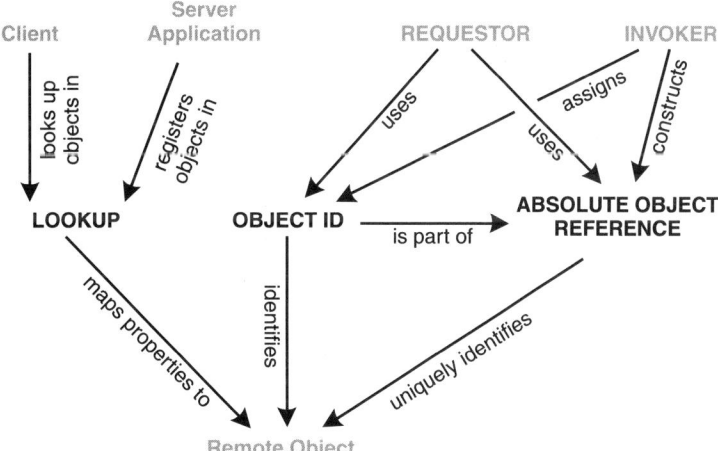

Object ID

The INVOKER has to select between registered remote objects to dispatch an invocation request.

❊ ❊ ❊

The INVOKER is responsible for dispatching invocations received from the SERVER REQUEST HANDLER. It invokes the operation of a remote object on behalf of a client. However, the INVOKER handles invocations for several remote objects, and has to determine the remote object corresponding to a particular invocation.

In a local environment, when a client invokes an operation on an object, the object is typically identified by its unique memory address. In distributed object middleware, using the memory address for identification does not work, because client and server run in different address spaces. A pointer to a memory address in a server refers to different data than in the client. Memory addresses are therefore not suitable for identification of remote objects in distributed object middleware.

When a request arrives from a client at the INVOKER, the INVOKER needs to know to which of potentially many remote objects the invocation must be dispatched. On the client side, the remote object must be identified, so that an invocation request can refer to the correct remote object when it arrives at the INVOKER.

Therefore:

Associate each remote object instance with an OBJECT ID that is unique in the context of the INVOKER with which the remote object is registered. The client, or the CLIENT PROXY respectively, has to provide the OBJECT ID, so that the REQUESTOR can include it in the

invocation and the INVOKER can dispatch the request to the correct remote object.

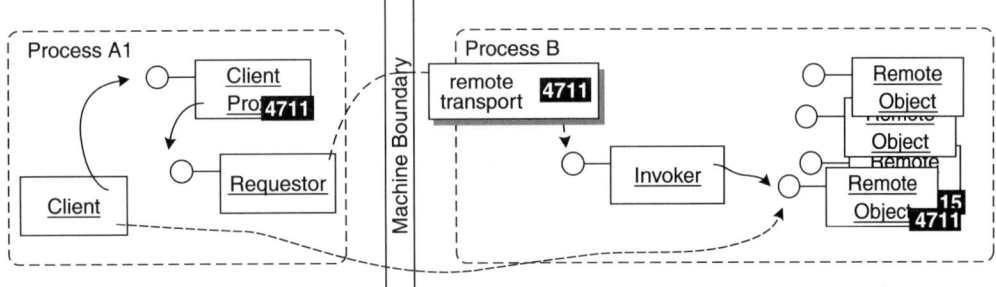

The CLIENT PROXY hands over an invocation to the REQUESTOR, providing the OBJECT ID of the target remote object. The OBJECT ID is sent with the invocation request to the INVOKER. Once the invocation arrives at the INVOKER, the INVOKER uses the OBJECT ID contained in the request to look up the correct instance. Then it invokes the operation on this instance.

A remote object's OBJECT ID can be any kind of identifier, but it is usually a numerical value (32 or 64 bits) or a string-based identifier. The range of possible values of the type used must be large enough to distinguish all remote objects registered at the same time in an INVOKER. The OBJECT ID has to be unique only inside an INVOKER, as we assume the correct server and correct INVOKER have already been identified by other means. Clients use ABSOLUTE OBJECT REFERENCES for absolute identification of the server, the INVOKER, and the remote object.

Another important aspect of OBJECT IDS is comparing for equality of remote objects. It is often necessary to find out whether or not two CLIENT PROXIES refer to the same remote object. It should be possible to perform this comparison without contacting the remote object and incurring communication overhead. The most efficient means to perform such a comparison is by comparing the OBJECT IDS of the targets in the client. But since the OBJECT IDS are often unique only inside one INVOKER, such comparisons need to be handled with care. Some distributed object middleware implementations therefore use globally-unique OBJECT IDS. Several algorithms are available to create identifiers that are unique over space and time and still have a practical and useful length (see for example [Ope97]). A globally-unique OBJECT ID is different from an ABSOLUTE OBJECT REFERENCE, as the ABSOLUTE OBJECT REFERENCE also contains location information on how to contact the server over the network.

Using OBJECT IDS with the INVOKER pattern enables advanced lifecycle control features, such as those provided by CLIENT-DEPENDENT INSTANCE, STATIC INSTANCE, PER-REQUEST INSTANCE, LAZY ACQUISITION, and POOLING. Those patterns require remote objects to be logically addressable. That is, clients are able to invoke operations on instances that are not physically present, but are instantiated or acquired from a pool on demand by the INVOKER. This behavior is typically delegated by the INVOKER to the LIFECYCLE MANAGER.

OBJECT IDS identify remote objects, rather than the servants realizing the remote object at runtime, because remote objects do not necessarily map one-to-one to physical instances within the server application. For example, the OBJECT ID of a PER-REQUEST INSTANCE identifies the remote object rather than the individual servant handling the request, because the servant is created only after the request arrives. Thus it is not possible to reference the servant with an ID before the request arrives at the server.

A particular remote object can be represented by a CLIENT PROXY in the client address space. All invocations that originate from this CLIENT PROXY should reach the same remote object. As the REQUESTOR and CLIENT REQUEST HANDLER are generic, the identity of the remote object is stored therefore inside the CLIENT PROXY.

Note that the use of the OBJECT ID pattern in distributed object middleware is not mandatory. It is also possible to identify an object by the network connection over which a request arrives. This only works if each remote object has its own dedicated network connection, however. It is done in some embedded systems, in which there is only a very limited and statically-known number of remote objects. Using connection-based object identification saves dispatching overhead and improves performance. For more details about server-side connection handling in distributed object middleware, refer to the SERVER REQUEST HANDLER pattern.

Absolute Object Reference

The INVOKER uses OBJECT IDS to dispatch the invocation to the target remote object.

❄ ❄ ❄

The OBJECT ID of a remote object allows the INVOKER to dispatch the remote invocation to the correct target object. However, the REQUESTOR, in combination with the CLIENT REQUEST HANDLER, has first to deliver the invocation containing the target remote object's OBJECT ID to the SERVER REQUEST HANDLER and INVOKER.

The client invokes operations via a REQUESTOR, or using a CLIENT PROXY, and the REQUESTOR forwards the invocation via REQUEST HANDLERS to the INVOKER. To allow a client to address the remote object, its OBJECT ID is included in the remote invocation, allowing the INVOKER to dispatch it correctly. Before the INVOKER can do this, however, the invocation request has to reach the correct INVOKER. The client therefore needs to associate the network endpoint of the INVOKER and the SERVER REQUEST HANDLER with the OBJECT ID, respectively. Note that this is independent of the uniqueness of the OBJECT ID. Even if the OBJECT ID is globally unique, the REQUESTOR and CLIENT REQUEST HANDLER respectively need to determine where to send the invocation request.

The simplest way to associate network endpoints with OBJECT IDS would be for the client to keep a map that relates OBJECT IDS and network endpoints. The manual and explicit maintenance of such a map is tedious, and it is cumbersome in cases where references to remote objects have to be exchanged between clients.

Therefore:

Provide ABSOLUTE OBJECT REFERENCES that uniquely identify the INVOKER and the remote object. Let the ABSOLUTE OBJECT REFERENCE include endpoint information, for example the host and port number of the network peer, the ID of the INVOKER, as well as the OBJECT ID of the target remote object. Clients exchange references to

remote objects by exchanging the respective ABSOLUTE OBJECT REFERENCES.

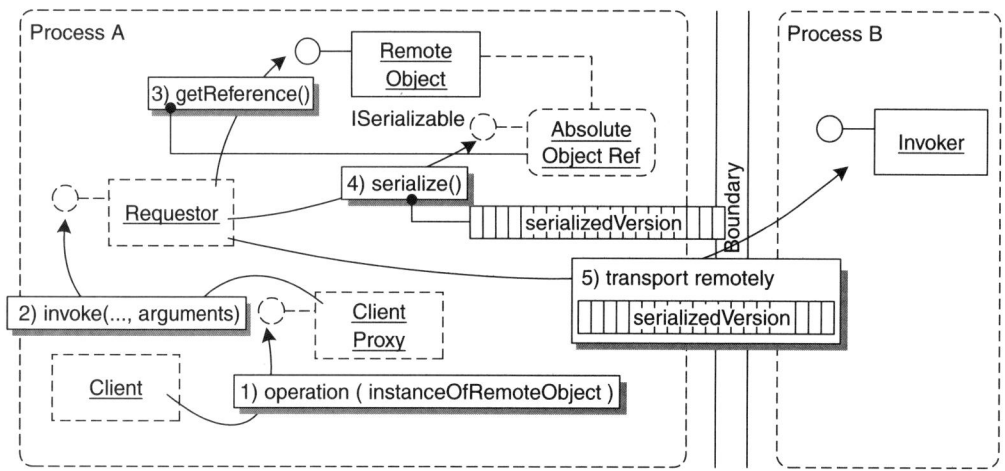

A client invokes an operation that accepts a reference to another remote object as parameter. Before marshaling the parameter, the REQUESTOR retrieves the ABSOLUTE OBJECT REFERENCE to the remote object. The serialized version of the instance is then sent to the INVOKER as part of the invocation request.

❆ ❆ ❆

An ABSOLUTE OBJECT REFERENCE must contain enough information for the client to contact the INVOKER with which the remote object is registered, as well as the OBJECT ID of the remote object. Depending on the environment and technology, endpoint information (such as host and port) is sufficient, but sometimes also protocol information needs to be added. Additionally, in the case of multiple INVOKERS, the INVOKER needs to be identified, too.

If the distributed object middleware uses a predefined default protocol, it is sufficient for the reference to contain the target endpoint. Since there is no choice, the client knows which protocol to use to contact the INVOKER.

Alternatively, if the distributed object middleware supports several protocols, the protocol to be used by the CLIENT REQUEST HANDLER has to be included in the reference. For example, CORBA object references always specify the protocol, as well as the host name, port,

INVOKER ID, and OBJECT ID, where INVOKER ID and OBJECT ID are encoded in binary format as a separate opaque part of the object reference.

When references to other remote objects are passed as parameters between clients and remote objects, the ABSOLUTE OBJECT REFERENCES are exchanged between them. Since the references are locally represented as CLIENT PROXIES of the corresponding remote objects, the MARSHALLER gets the ABSOLUTE OBJECT REFERENCE from the CLIENT PROXY. In the reverse direction – from server to client – a parameter containing an ABSOLUTE OBJECT REFERENCE leads to the instantiation of a CLIENT PROXY, requiring the availability of the necessary CLIENT PROXY classes on the receiver's side. In some systems/languages, especially if they are interpreted, the construction of CLIENT PROXIES can be done on the fly using reflection and runtime code generation. Alternatively, some distributed object middleware systems allow complete CLIENT PROXY implementations to be sent across the network.

The choice between making an object remotely accessible via pass-by-reference or pass-by-value, which involves the serialization and transmission of the object's state, and sometimes even code, depends on the use case and the heterogeneity of the environment. If client and server application use the same programming language, it might be possible to pass state and code. For example, to pass code, RMI transmits a URL reference to a location that provides the Java class code. But in most cases of pass-by-value only the state is transmitted, a suitable implementation being assumed to be available in the receiving process. For more detail, see Chapter 13, *Related Concepts, Technologies, and Patterns*, specifically the discussion on mobile code.

ABSOLUTE OBJECT REFERENCES may be opaque to client applications. That is, it is not possible for the client to construct a reference and access the remote object. The main reasons for opaqueness are to avoid the risk of creating unusable references based on wrong identity assumptions, and to allow the middleware to add special dispatching hints to the ABSOLUTE OBJECT REFERENCE, for example for optimization. Nevertheless, practice proved opaque references to be cumbersome, since they requires LOOKUP or explicit/manual distribution of the opaque references. Later versions of distributed object middleware systems therefore also allow for non-opaque references – see corbaloc [OMG04a] and Ice [Zer04]. Today, middleware technologies support either or both forms of ABSOLUTE OBJECT REFERENCES: opaque references that contain dispatching and optimization hints, as well as non-opaque references that can be constructed by the client application. Non-opaque references are typically only used for initial access to key remote objects of the distributed application. URIs are often used for that purpose.

ABSOLUTE OBJECT REFERENCES are either transient or persistent:

- Transient ABSOLUTE OBJECT REFERENCES become invalid after the remote object has been deactivated or the server application has restarted. A client that has obtained an ABSOLUTE OBJECT REFERENCE cannot be sure that the remote object it references still exists. Often, LEASING is used to manage the validity of references, and to allow the INVOKER to passivate or remove a remote object to which client reference no longer exist.
- Persistent ABSOLUTE OBJECT REFERENCES are valid even after the server application has been restarted, but the remote object needs to be registered with the same INVOKER and endpoint configuration. Persistent object references are supported by CORBA, for example.

To cope with changing transient references, distributed systems often use indirection through a lookup service. LOOKUP allows 'persistent' logical names to be mapped to (transient) ABSOLUTE OBJECT REFERENCES. The same principle is applied by LOCATION FORWARDERS in load-balancing scenarios: an additional level of indirection translates a persistent reference into a transient reference.

To keep existing ABSOLUTE OBJECT REFERENCES valid after remote objects have been moved to a different server application, either LOCATION FORWARDERS are used or the ABSOLUTE OBJECT REFERENCE is made to contain several endpoints, so that the REQUESTOR has alternatives when communication with the original endpoint fails. This is of interest in scenarios that require automatic failover. Note that this only works when the remote objects are stateless, or the state of the remote objects is replicated among the various server applications.

Lookup

Client applications want to use services provided by remote objects.

❋ ❋ ❋

To use a service provided by a remote object, a client has to obtain an ABSOLUTE OBJECT REFERENCE to the respective object. Further, the remote object providing the service might change over time, either because another instance takes over the role, or because the server application has been restarted, so that the transient reference changes. Despite such changes, clients need a valid initial reference to access the service.

ABSOLUTE OBJECT REFERENCES for the remote objects can typically be serialized into a string and exchanged between server application and client manually via configuration files, or even e-mail. But doing this on every client restart or change of configuration is tedious.

Reusing references obtained during previous runs of the client program has to be done with care, because the reference to the remote object might be transient, and therefore might have become invalid as a consequence of a server application restart, or the relocation of the service on another remote object hosted by a different server application. Even in the case of non-opaque ABSOLUTE OBJECT REFERENCES – references constructed by the client – the client would have to know the endpoint information, INVOKER ID and OBJECT ID. Clients typically do not know this information, because this would compromise the goal of location transparency, one of the fundamental concepts of distributed object middleware.

Another way to obtain a reference for a specific remote object is to invoke an operation of some other remote object that returns the desired reference. However, where does the client get the reference to the 'other' remote object from?

Therefore:

Implement a lookup service as part of the distributed object middleware. Let server applications register references to remote objects and associate them with properties. Clients then use the lookup service to query for the ABSOLUTE OBJECT REFERENCES of remote

objects based on these properties. The most common case is to use unique names for each reference of a remote object.

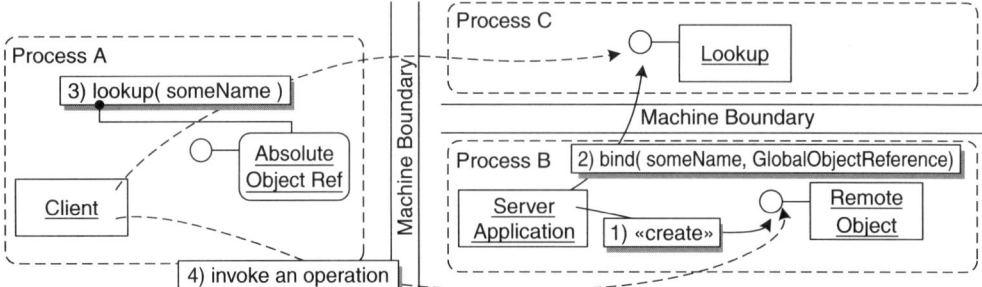

The server application binds the reference of a remote object to a symbolic name in the lookup service after instantiating the remote object. The client looks up the ABSOLUTE OBJECT REFERENCE using the same symbolic name, gets the reference returned, and finally invokes an operation on the remote object.

❄ ❄ ❄

The lookup service provides an interface to bind and look up ABSOLUTE OBJECT REFERENCES to properties, and is typically implemented as a remote object itself. Of course clients need to know the reference to the remote object implementing the lookup service before they can query it. This leads to a kind of chickesn-and-egg problem, as LOOKUP cannot be used to find the lookup service. To solve this, clients typically are manually configured using a persistent ABSOLUTE OBJECT REFERENCE to the lookup service, or use some kind of multicast to search in the local network for a lookup service instance. The lookup service is considered a *well-known* object.

If the lookup service uses names, the names typically are structured hierarchically, just like qualified names in a file system. For example, the following string could be a valid name:

/com/mycompany/accounting/accountfactory

The last element of such a structured name is usually called a *binding*, whereas all other parts are called *contexts*. Obviously contexts can be nested. Lookup services based on unique, structured names are often called *naming services*.

More complex lookup services use arbitrary properties, typically implemented as name-value pairs. The server application uses the lookup service to associate the properties and their associated values with the respective remote object. Clients can query for references by specifying expressions such as:

printertype="hplaser" and location="building10" and color="true"

The lookup service returns a set of references that conform to the query. Lookup services supporting such complex queries are often referred to as a *trading service*.

Even complex lookup services provide a generic interface for the type of remote object returned from a query. When using CLIENT PROXIES, clients have to cast the returned reference to the correct type. It is important to understand that the registration of a remote object in a lookup service does not necessarily mean that the instance is physically created, only that it is legal for clients to invoke operations on it. Of course, this only works if INVOKERS are able to create references to remote objects not yet activated and maintain the mapping between the reference and the remote object type. As a consequence, these not-yet-existing objects need to be created on demand once an invocation arrives at the respective INVOKER. More details on decoupling of reference creation and remote object activation are provided in Chapter 5, *Lifecycle Management Patterns*.

To avoid the lookup service being filled with dangling references – references to objects that are no longer available – a server application should unbind a reference when it stops serving it. To manage unbinding automatically, the lookup service should use LEASING for the bindings: when a server application registers a remote object, the lookup service establishes a lease that the server application must renew periodically. If the server does not remove the binding, for example due to a crash of the server application, the lease will eventually time out and the lookup service can remove the reference, along with the properties.

LOOKUP can also be used for load balancing, by registering more than one remote object for a property/name entry in the lookup service, and having the lookup service dispatch those reference on a random, round-robin, or load-based basis.

To avoid performance bottlenecks and single points of failure, clients should use LOOKUP sparsely. For example, you should only register factory objects, in the sense of *Factory Method* [GHJV95] and *Abstract Factory* [GHJV95], and obtain further references through them. To further reduce the chances for failure, lookup services are typically replicated and/or federated across several hosts. Keeping the replicas consistent does incur a performance overhead, which is another reason for storing only a few important initial objects in the LOOKUP service.

This pattern was originally documented in POSA3 [KJ04].

Interactions among the patterns

The three patterns introduced in this chapter are used for locating objects. The use of the OBJECT ID pattern has already been implicitly shown in the sequence diagram examples in Chapter 3, *Basic Remoting Patterns*, where the OBJECT ID was used by the INVOKER to find the target remote object in its list of instances.

The following sequence diagram shows how a server application registers the reference of a remote object in LOOKUP and how a client uses the lookup service to retrieve this reference. The ABSOLUTE OBJECT REFERENCE of the lookup service has been configured manually, both in the server application and in the client application. Both server application and client use a framework facade to retrieve the initial reference to the lookup service. Here the framework facade acts a utility class providing access to the middleware's core features. The lookup service is itself implemented as a remote object, offering the operations bind for registering remote objects and lookup for looking up ABSOLUTE OBJECT REFERENCES of remote objects.

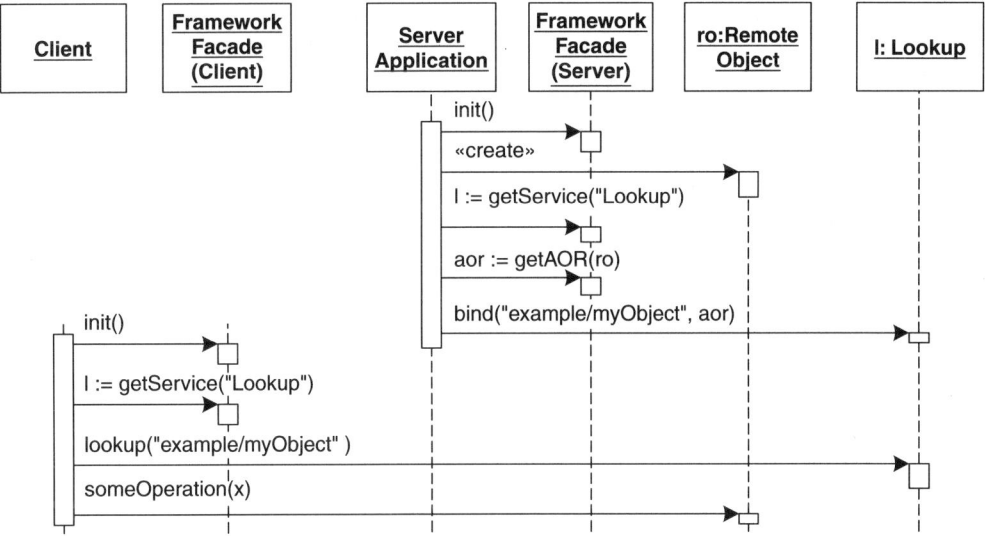

The next illustration shows how a client invokes an operation of a remote object, passing another remote object as parameter. The MARSHALLER gets the invocation parameters and recognizes that some of them are remote objects located on a server. In this example, the

MARSHALLER converts these parameters into ABSOLUTE OBJECT REFERENCES. The ABSOLUTE OBJECT REFERENCES are stored in the CLIENT PROXIES of the remote objects and are obtained using the operation getAOR. This information is then handed over to the CLIENT REQUEST HANDLER by the REQUESTOR.

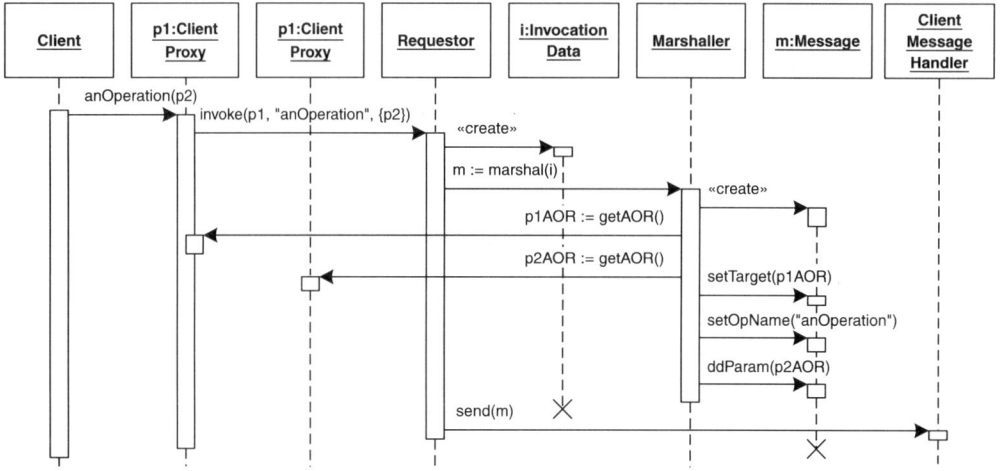

5 Lifecycle Management Patterns

This chapter presents patterns for managing the lifecycle of remote objects. The patterns describe behaviors and strategies, not building blocks, and are therefore different than the patterns in the previous chapters. The patterns are typically implemented with the help of the LIFECYCLE MANAGER pattern, which is presented in Chapter 7, *Extended Infrastructure Patterns*.

This chapter is structured as follows: first, we describe three basic patterns for remote object lifecycle management, STATIC INSTANCE, PER-REQUEST INSTANCE, and CLIENT-DEPENDENT INSTANCE. These patterns are illustrated by usage examples of how clients typically use remote objects. Then we present three resource-management patterns, LAZY ACQUISITION [KJ04], POOLING [KJ04], and LEASING [KJ04], as well as a pattern for state management in the context of remote objects, PASSIVATION [VSW02]. All four patterns have already been described in existing literature, although in different contexts. Finally, we describe typical use cases that show how the patterns can be combined to optimize resource use in distributed applications.

In the context of this chapter, we need to explicitly consider the *servant* of a remote object. The servant is the runtime object that represents a remote object in the server application. Since the relationship between a servant and a remote object is not strictly one-to-one for all the activation strategies described in this chapter, it is essential to distinguish these concepts. See the discussion of 'remote objects' in Chapter 2, *Pattern Language Overview* (page 19) for more details on the relationship of remote object and servant. The basic idea of distinguishing servant and remote object is also described as a *Virtual Instance* [HV99, VSW02].

To understand the issues of lifecycle management better, the concept of stateful and stateless objects is important. In object-oriented programming each object has state as soon as it has member variables. This is also true for remote objects, but additionally it is important to distinguish whether the remote object state is persistent or transient with respect to subsequent invocations. If the state is transient, the remote object is considered stateless: if the state is persistent, the remote object is considered stateful.

Transient state can, but need not, be persisted. For example, if the object only has read-only state, it does not require persistence of state. Persistent state must be written to a database in case the remote object is temporarily deactivated. Since persistent state must be persisted (see PASSIVATION), stateful remote objects are more costly to activate and deactivate, and in consequence are kept for longer in memory, occupying valuable resources. Remote objects with transient state can be managed using POOLING, which requires fewer memory resources.

A brief note on activation and deactivation is appropriate. By the term *activation*, we mean every action that is necessary for the distributed object middleware to make a remote object ready to receive an invocation. This typically includes instantiation of the servant, initialization, and registration with the INVOKER and LIFECYCLE MANGER. Additionally, it can also include registration with the lookup service and the restoration of the remote object's state. *Deactivation* means reversing the activation steps, such as persisting remote object state, unregistering the remote object, and possibly even destroying the servant. Note that deactivation is not the same as PASSIVATION. PASSIVATION keeps the remote object available to clients while temporarily removing its servant from the server applications's memory.

Basic lifecycle patterns

The chapter starts with the following three basic lifecycle patterns that describe strategies for the lifecycle management of remote objects:

- STATIC INSTANCES are remote objects whose servant's lifetime is independent of the lifetime and the access patterns of their clients. Notionally they live forever and are accessible to all clients in the distributed system.
- In the case of a PER-REQUEST INSTANCE, the distributed object middleware's LIFECYCLE MANAGER (logically) creates and destroys new servants for every individual method invocation.
- CLIENT-DEPENDENT INSTANCES rely on the client to instantiate a remote object and its servant explicitly. A CLIENT-DEPENDENT

Basic lifecycle patterns

INSTANCE is destroyed either on a client's explicit request, or by the LIFECYCLE MANAGER once its lease has expired.

The following illustration shows the relationships between the patterns. We have already shown their relationships to the patterns LAZY ACQUISITION, POOLING, LEASING, and PASSIVATION, which are introduced in the second part of this chapter.

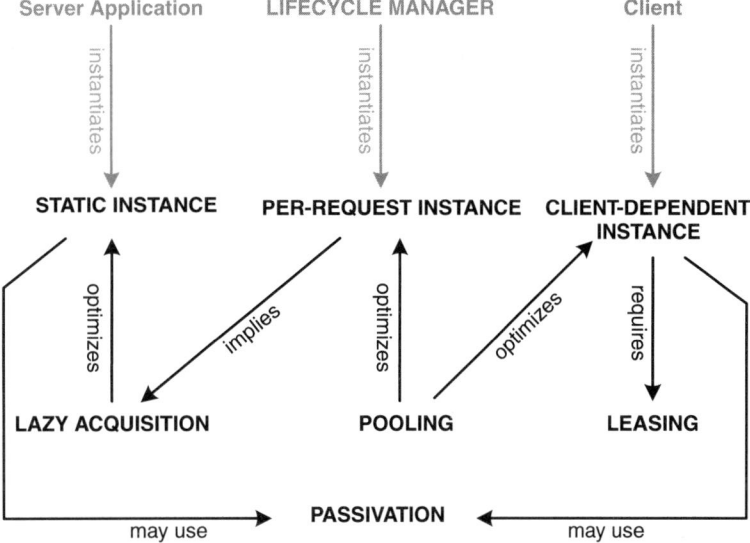

Static Instance

A remote object offers a service that is independent of any specific client.

❊ ❊ ❊

The server application has to provide a number of previously-known remote objects instances – the number may even be fixed over the lifetime of the server application. The remote objects must be available for a long period without any predetermined expiration timeout. The remote object's state must not be lost between individual invocations, and must be available to all clients.

As an example, consider a factory control system in which a central control system coordinates a set of machines. Each machine has its own control computer that runs a server application. Such a machine typically consists of a predefined number of subsystems such as sensors and actuators. To coordinate the manufacturing process, the central control software needs to communicate with these subsystems. Using distributed object middleware each subsystem (actuator, sensor) can be realized as a remote object that can be accessed by the central control software, and potentially other clients, such as a monitoring application.

When remote objects represent physical devices, as in this scenario, the number and types of remote objects is previously known and typically does not change, because it directly corresponds to the physically installed devices. The lifecycle and state of the remote objects is independent of the client's lifecycle: in the case of the scenario, the state and lifecycle is associated with the physical device.

Therefore:

Provide STATIC INSTANCES of remote objects that are independent of the client's state and lifecycle. These STATIC INSTANCES are activated before any client's use, typically as early as during application start-up, and deactivated when the application shuts

down. For easy accessibility by clients, the instances are registered in LOOKUP after their activation.

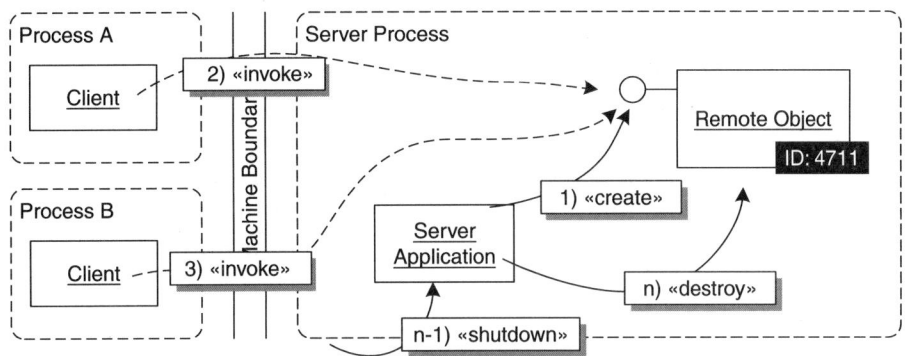

During initialization of the server application a number of STATIC INSTANCES are activated, becoming available for use by clients. Once the server application shuts down, all STATIC INSTANCES are deactivated.

❄ ❄ ❄

STATIC INSTANCES are typically activated eagerly, as described by the *Eager Acquisition* [KJ04] pattern. STATIC INSTANCE servants are acquired before their first use to optimize runtime behavior, allowing for fast and predictable access times. Such behavior is especially important for embedded and real-time scenarios.

Using eager activation of remote objects can be a problem, because the servant's resources remain acquired for the lifetime of the server application. The system might not have enough physical resources to host all the remote objects at the same time. Applications with a large numbers of STATIC INSTANCES have to consider alternatives to reduce the resource consumption. Examples of such alternatives are:

- Instead of *Eager Acquisition*, LAZY ACQUISITION can be used to instantiate a servant for the remote objects only when they are actually accessed. As a consequence, though, predictability is lost, and invocation times might increase, which is often a reason for using STATIC INSTANCES in the first place.
- To save and restore the state of the remote object, PASSIVATION can be used to temporarily remove servants from memory if the remote object is not accessed by clients for a specific interval. A

new servant, containing the state that has been saved previously, will be created when the next invocation request arrives.

Stateless STATIC INSTANCES are advantageous for supporting load balancing and failover techniques. The remote objects are simply replicated using LOOKUP-based techniques, or by applying LOCATION FORWARDER to redirect messages to one of the replicas. Matters become more complicated if state has to be replicated, however. One of the easiest solutions is to establish shared state between the STATIC INSTANCES, for example in a shared database. In *Chapter 13, Related Concepts, Technologies, and Patterns*, we discuss further patterns from [DL04] to improve availability and scalability.

Since a STATIC INSTANCE is accessed by many clients concurrently, either the servant needs to be thread-safe, or the INVOKER needs to serialize the access.

Per-Request Instance

A remote object offers a service that does not require maintaining state.

❊ ❊ ❊

A server application serves remote objects that are accessed by a large number of clients, and access to the remote objects needs to be highly scalable with respect to the number of clients. When many clients access the same remote object concurrently, the performance of the server application decreases dramatically due to synchronization overhead.

Consider a system that provides information on stock prices. A client invokes operations by passing in a stock symbol (such as 'DCX' for Daimler Chrysler) to query the current quote and some historical data to compute a trend graph. To retrieve the stock information, the remote object implementing the queries typically performs one or several queries on a database, processes the results, and returns them to the client.

In this and similar scenarios, individual invocations are independent of each other. Semantically, it does not matter whether the invocations of individual clients are handled sequentially or concurrently. They do not modify any shared state, they just return read-only information.

Implementing this service as a STATIC INSTANCE would cause a bottleneck, because all clients would use the same instance, requiring it to serialize access as a consequence. On the other hand, using multiple STATIC INSTANCES to distribute the load better would waste resources in situations of low system load.

Therefore:

Let the distributed object middleware activate a new servant for each invocation. This servant handles the request, returns the results, and is then deactivated. While the client expects to get a new instance from request to request, the activation and deactivation can be optimized internally, for example by using POOLING of servants.

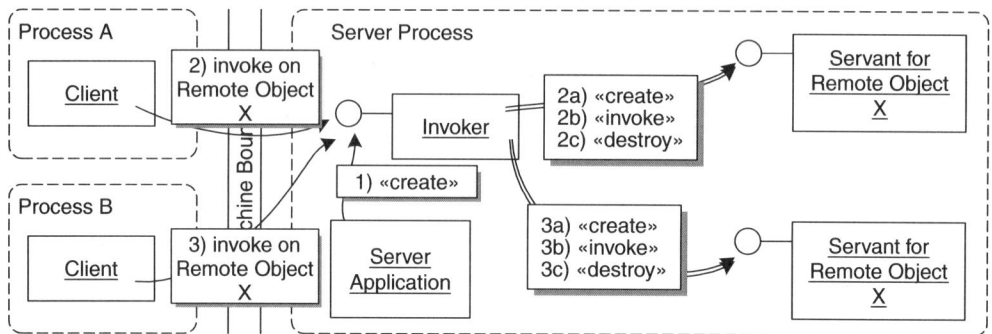

For each invocation on a specific remote object, the INVOKER creates a new servant, dispatches the invocation to the newly-created servant, waits for the result, then destroys the servant.

The PER-REQUEST INSTANCE pattern uses the *Lazy Acquisition* [KJ04] activation strategy. Activating a PER-REQUEST INSTANCE results in the preparation of the LIFECYCLE MANAGER to accept requests for the respective remote object. No servant is created to actually represent the remote object. Only when a request arrives for the previously-activated remote object does the LIFECYCLE MANAGER create a new servant to handle the request, and discards it after the invocation on the servant returns. The client's reference to the remote object will be valid all the time. The OBJECT ID of a PER-REQUEST INSTANCE logically identifies the REMOTE OBJECT, not the individual servant. This is necessary because the servant does not exist before the request arrives, and so cannot be referenced by the OBJECT ID.

Depending on the resources available to the server application, the strategy chosen by PER-REQUEST INSTANCES can scale very well, and concurrency is not an issue on the servant level, since each request has its own instance. However, there are also some drawbacks. For example, PER-REQUEST INSTANCES require that the remote objects are stateless with regards to the client. That is, all invocations must be self-contained. Clients must not expect persistence of changes made to the object's state between two invocations of the same (or different) client – they talk to a new servant for each invocation.

Of course, a PER-REQUEST INSTANCE can change shared state that is kept outside the servant itself, for example in an associated database. The invocation would have to refer to that shared state somehow, for example by specifying the primary key of the data to be altered.

As long as the servants of PER-REQUEST INSTANCES do not access and change shared state (in session objects or in a database), developers need not be concerned about multi-threading issues, and can leave it to the LIFECYCLE MANAGER to decide how many requests should be handled in parallel. This mainly depends on the number of threads that can run concurrently without an unacceptable performance penalty. However, if the LIFECYCLE MANAGER uses several threads, developers need to be careful when accessing shared resources (especially for write access). Access to such resources must be protected using synchronization primitives, for example by introducing critical regions in the servant, or by placing a monitor around shared data. Managing concurrent access to shared resources can be handled inside remote objects themselves, or by using *Proxies* [GHJV95] that protect the resources (see *Managed Resource* in [VSW02]).

Distributed object middleware implementations leave optimizations, such as the number of threads, to the LIFECYCLE MANAGER and INVOKER. Server developers have only to limit this number to make sure that the system is not overloaded by too many threads. If too many concurrent requests arrive, it is the task of the INVOKER to serialize these invocations, or alternatively to signal an overload condition to the client using a suitable REMOTING ERROR.

In some systems, creating and destroying large numbers of servants, as well as acquiring and releasing their resources, can be very expensive, limiting the scalability of the system. To remedy this problem, POOLING techniques can be used, as will be explained later.

Client-Dependent Instance

Clients use services provided by remote objects.

In situations in which the application logic of the remote object extends the logic of the client, it becomes important to think about where to put the common state of both. Keeping the common state solely in the client requires the client to transmit its state with every invocation. Keeping the common state solely in the server, for example in a STATIC INSTANCE, requires complex mechanisms to keep the states of individual clients separate inside the remote object.

As an example, consider a server farm that provides sophisticated image processing of radio-astronomical data. The server application provides a set of stateless algorithm objects, each performing a specific transformation of the image. A client processes an image using a sequence of such algorithms, each subsequent algorithm operates on the result of the previous one. The exact nature, sequence, and configuration of the algorithms used depends on the scientific goals of the client. That is, the client inspects intermediate results and decides how to proceed.

To implement this scenario, a large volume of state needs to be stored for each client: the original image, the current image after the execution of the last algorithm, diagnostic messages and problems that occurred during processing that could influence the accuracy of the result, as well as the sequence of algorithms applied to the image and their parameterization. All this state is client-specific – the images and results of one client typically have nothing to do with the images and results of another client. Transmitting the image data repeatedly between client and server is very inefficient because of the huge size of astronomical data sets.

Therefore:

Provide remote objects whose lifetime is controlled by clients. Clients create CLIENT-DEPENDENT INSTANCES on request and destroy them when no longer needed. As an instance is *owned* by a client, the client can consider the state of the instance to be private. Clients

Basic lifecycle patterns

typically use a *factory* remote object to request the creation of new instances.

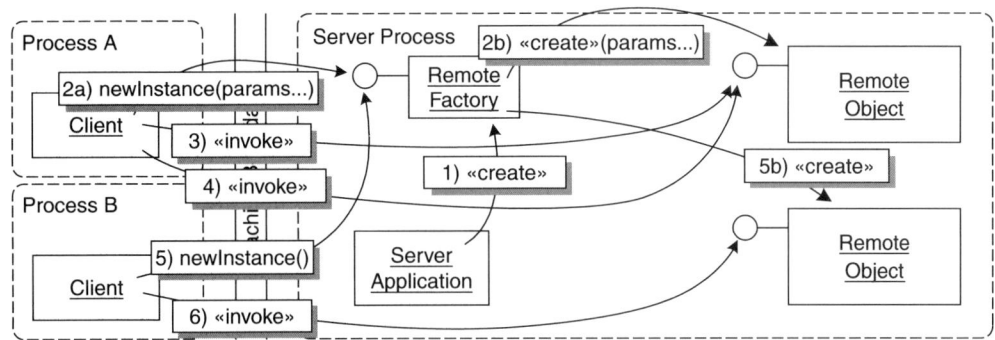

A *factory* remote object is created by the server application and made available to clients using LOOKUP. Clients use this factory to create and configure CLIENT-DEPENDENT INSTANCES. The client then invokes operations on its instance, and destroys the instance when it no longer needs it.

❄ ❄ ❄

The most obvious difference between CLIENT-DEPENDENT INSTANCES and using STATIC INSTANCES and PER-REQUEST INSTANCES is that an additional component is introduced, the factory. This is necessary to allow clients to request a CLIENT-DEPENDENT INSTANCE that is specific to the client. In the case of a STATIC INSTANCE or a PER-REQUEST INSTANCE, creation and activation of the remote object is handled by the SERVER APPLICATION and/or the distributed object middleware.

The factory itself is typically a STATIC INSTANCE. When invoked by a client, it creates the requested CLIENT-DEPENDENT INSTANCE and returns the ABSOLUTE OBJECT REFERENCE of the newly-created instance to the client.

As explained above, CLIENT-DEPENDENT INSTANCES typically are considered to be accessed by a single client only. As a consequence, no concurrency issues need be taken care of in the servant, with regard to client requests and its own state. If CLIENT-DEPENDENT INSTANCES can be accessed concurrently (for example, because a client can open multiple browser windows that are not coordinated), some kind of synchronization has to be implemented on the server side.

In addition, access to global shared resources from within CLIENT-DEPENDENT INSTANCES still needs to be serialized.

To ensure that only one client accesses a CLIENT-DEPENDENT INSTANCE, the factory will only provide operations to create *new* instances. It is not possible to ask the factory to return some previously-created instance. The client therefore has to store the reference to the instance, and it is the client's own responsibility whether to pass the reference to other clients.

Lifecycle management of CLIENT-DEPENDENT INSTANCES is easy if clients behave well. The clients are required to signal when to `destroy` the remote object, permitting the server application to remove the servant from memory. However, if a client forgets to invoke `destroy`, or if a client crashes, the server application may end up with orphan CLIENT-DEPENDENT INSTANCES. To avoid this, LEASING [KJ04] is used. This allows the removal of orphan CLIENT-DEPENDENT INSTANCES when the lease period expires.

There are potential problems with the lifecycle model of CLIENT-DEPENDENT INSTANCES, though. The more clients a server application has, the more CLIENT-DEPENDENT INSTANCES might be created. Thus the server application is no longer in control of its own resources. This can be a serious issue for large, publicly-available systems in which you cannot control the number and behavior of the clients. To overcome this problem, the LIFECYCLE MANAGER can use PASSIVATION. PASSIVATION temporarily evicts a servant from memory, persist its state and creates a new servant – with the previously-saved state – upon the next client request.

General resource management patterns

After introducing the three basic lifecycle management patterns for remote objects, we will now describe three resource management patterns originally described in [KJ04] – LAZY ACQUISITION, POOLING, and LEASING – as well as a state management pattern originally described in [VSW02], PASSIVATION. We provide specializations of these patterns in the context of distributed object middleware.

After presenting the patterns, we will combine them with the basic lifecycle management patterns to show typical implementation strategies for lifecycle management of remote objects.

- LAZY ACQUISITION defers the creation of a servant for a remote object to the latest possible time – the actual invocation of an operation on the remote object.
- POOLING describes how instantiation and destruction of servants of remote objects can be avoided by recycling servants that are no longer needed. Besides servants, there are many other resources that can be pooled in distributed object middleware, such as threads and connections – see the pattern descriptions of CLIENT REQUEST HANDLER and SERVER REQUEST HANDLER, for example. Note that we refer to the original *Pooling* pattern in [KJ04] in these cases.
- LEASING explains how the resources of remote objects' servants that are no longer needed can be reclaimed reliably. LEASING associates time-based leases with a servant, which clients have to extend to use the remote objects.
- Finally, PASSIVATION temporarily evicts servants from memory if the remote object is, for example, not accessed by clients for a specific period of time.

The implementation of the lifecycle management patterns in distributed object middleware relies on the LIFECYCLE MANAGER as the key participant. The LIFECYCLE MANAGER is responsible for actually acquiring, pooling, leasing, and passivating the remote objects.

Lazy Acquisition

STATIC INSTANCES must be managed efficiently.

❊ ❊ ❊

Creating servants for all the remote objects that might possibly be accessed by clients during server application start-up can result in waste of resources. The total resources needed for all servants might even exceed the physically-available resources in the server process. Additionally, instantiating all servants during server application start-up leads to long start-up times.

Acquiring resources and instantiating servants always has a cost in CPU cycles. If servants are instantiated long before their use, valuable resources such as server application memory are wasted to keep them alive. This influences the overall availability of resources as well as the stability of the system – if resources become scarce, client requests might stay unfulfilled, or the system might crash, since it cannot cope gracefully with resource starvation.

Additionally, if servants are instantiated too eagerly, the system start-up time will be unnecessarily long. However, systems are expected to start up quickly to be available for use by clients.

Therefore:

Instantiate servants only when their respective remote objects are actually invoked by clients. However, let clients assume that remote objects are always available. The INVOKER triggers the LIFECYCLE MANAGER to lazily instantiate the servant when it is accessed by a client.

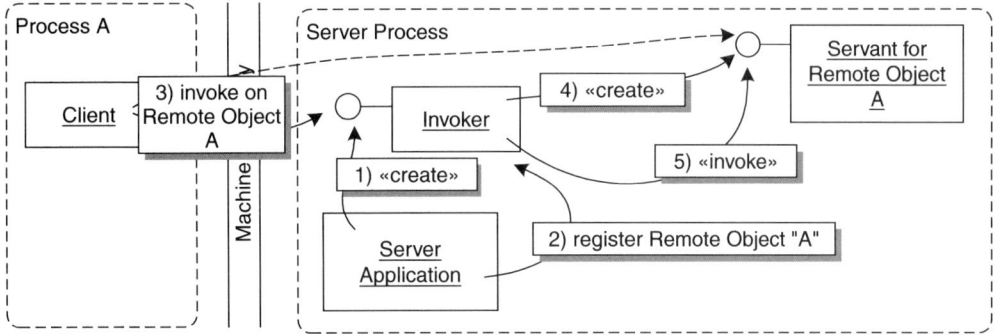

A remote object type has been registered with the INVOKER during server application start-up, but the servant has to be instantiated lazily. Upon the first request, therefore, the INVOKER creates a servant lazily. This servant is subsequently used by other client requests.

❅ ❅ ❅

As soon as clients hold an ABSOLUTE OBJECT REFERENCE for a remote object, they naturally assume the remote object is available. While this is true, a servant need not necessarily be created to serve the requests. For example, resource constraints might lead to decoupling of remote objects and their servants.

Upon a request to a lazily-acquired remote object, the INVOKER checks whether a servant is already available for the remote object. If this is not the case, it will trigger the LIFECYCLE MANAGER to instantiate a servant for the remote object. In this way only the remote objects that are actually accessed have a physical representation in the server application.

Initial resource consumption is significantly lower using LAZY ACQUISITION when compared to instantiating remote objects eagerly during start-up. A drawback is that this pattern also introduces some complexity in the LIFECYCLE MANAGER, which now has to check for the existence of servants. Further, this check, and the LAZY ACQUISITION of the servants, introduces some delay. Access times become more unpredictable, which might be a problem in time-sensitive, embedded systems. Large and complex objects save most resources when acquired lazily, but also take the longest to acquire. If this is a problem, *Partial Acquisition* [KJ04] is a possible solution, which acquires parts of a servant immediately and other parts lazily.

Before considering LAZY ACQUISITION as a solution to a resource shortage, you should be sure that a large number of remote object servants is actually needed. There is always the danger that LAZY ACQUISITION is used to minimize the consequences of a poor design in which too many remote objects are activated unnecessarily. That is, you should first think about ways to reduce the resource consumption of your server application, for example by evicting or reusing unused remote objects. Only if this fails should you think about more complex resource management techniques such as LAZY ACQUISITION.

Note also that LAZY ACQUISITION only solves half the problem. Eventually all remote objects will have been accessed. This means that a large number of remote objects will have a servant, consuming large amounts of server application resources. So, in addition to instantiating servants lazily, we also need a means to dispose of servants that are not currently needed. PASSIVATION, LEASING, and POOLING can help here. An *Evictor* [KJ04] that manages the destruction (eviction) of objects is also a possible solution.

A PER-REQUEST INSTANCE can be seen as an extreme form of LAZY ACQUISITION: a new servant for a PER-REQUEST INSTANCE is lazily instantiated when an invocation arrives, and is evicted directly after the invocation.

The LAZY ACQUISITION pattern is documented in more detail in [KJ04].

Pooling

Every remote object instance consumes server application resources.

❄ ❄ ❄

Instantiating and destroying servants regularly, as in the case of PER-REQUEST INSTANCES, causes a lot of overhead in terms of additional load for the server. Among other issues, memory needs to be allocated, initialization code for the servants needs to be executed, and the servants have to be registered with the distributed object middleware.

The overhead of creating and destroying servants heavily influences the scalability, performance, and stability of the server application. Scalability is impacted negatively because the CPU cycles needed for the acquisition and release of resources are not available to serve the requests of other clients. The performance for each invocation is slow, because the resource acquisitions during each invocation need time to execute. Where servants are not destroyed, for example to save the overhead of destruction, stability is at risk, since resource contention might occur and new invocations might not get served.

Besides these reasons, predictability of invocation times is degraded – especially in environments that rely on garbage collection, such as Java. Garbage collection will be necessary from time to time to clean up the large number of discarded servants, causing the server performance to degrade substantially.

Therefore:

Introduce a pool of servants for each remote object type hosted by the server application. When an invocation arrives for a remote object, take a servant from the pool, handle the request, and put it back into the pool. Subsequent invocations will follow the same procedure when reusing the instance. The remote object's state is removed from the servant before it is put into the pool, while servants taken from the pool are initialized with the state of the remote object they should represent.

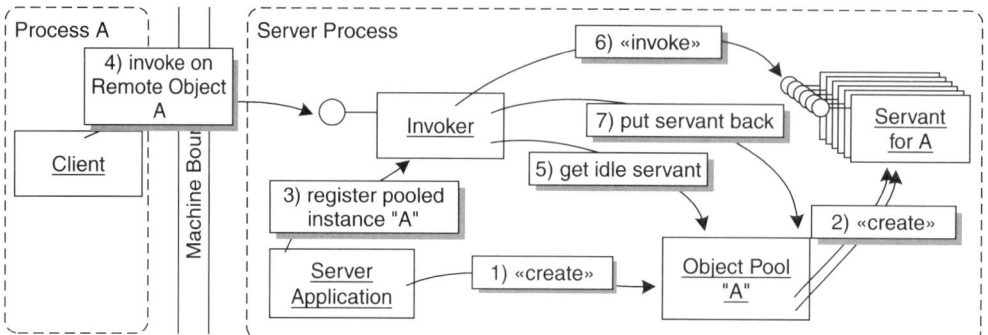

The server application creates an object pool, which in turn creates a number of servant instances. The remote object type is registered as a pooled instance. Upon invocation, the INVOKER takes an idle servant from the pool and performs the invocation using this servant. After the invocation has finished, the servant is put back into the pool.

❊ ❊ ❊

The pool uses *Eager Acquisition* [KJ04] to instantiate a limited number of servants during pool creation, to improve performance. If more servants are needed, the pool may grow dynamically up to a predefined limit. If that limit is reached, further invocations need to be queued. Of course, dynamic growth and queuing negatively impact performance and predictability. When fewer servants are needed than are available in the pool, the pool evicts servants.

POOLING avoids the overhead of repeated instantiation, initialization, and destruction of servants. A servant managed by a pool might handle invocations for different remote objects of the same type during its lifetime. That is, the identity and the state the servants represents changes over time. The LIFECYCLE MANAGER has to initialize the servant when taken from the pool, and deinitialize it when it puts it back. Initialization and deinitialization result in some overhead. As a consequence, POOLING is especially well-suited for remote objects that do not have identity and state: stateless remote objects. Here, all servants in a pool are considered equal. An invocation can be handled by any of the instances in the pool without any further set-up or initialization.

The management of stateful remote objects is more complicated. When servants for remote objects are fetched from the pool, the LIFECYCLE MANAGER has to trigger them via a *Lifecycle Callback* operation [VSW02].

Triggered by the lifecycle callback, the servant taken from the pool acquires the state of the entity it represents in the context of the invocation. Alternatively, the LIFECYCLE MANAGER can supply a stateful servant with the required state directly. To associate the state correctly, the LIFECYCLE MANAGER differentiates between remote objects using their OBJECT IDS. Advanced lifecycle management strategies such as these are implemented, for example, by server-side component infrastructures, as documented in [VSW02].

The POOLING pattern is presented in more detail in [KJ04].

Leasing

Clients consume server application resources, for example by using CLIENT-DEPENDENT INSTANCES.

❋ ❋ ❋

Remote objects and their servants that are no longer needed should be released in time to free unused system resources. However, the LIFECYCLE MANAGER cannot determine when a particular remote object is no longer used so that it can release it safely. In most scenarios, neither the LIFECYCLE MANAGER nor the remote object itself have knowledge of the clients, and so do not know whether they intend to access the remote objects in the future.

Consider a stateful remote object that is accessed by a single client, such as a CLIENT-DEPENDENT INSTANCE. The easiest way for a LIFECYCLE MANAGER to know that a remote object is no longer needed is when the client invokes a destroy operation on the remote object. When this operation is invoked by a client, the remote object destroys itself and its resources – specifically the servant – can be reclaimed. There is a problem, though: if a client does not call the destroy operation, the remote object might live forever, and the server application cannot reclaim the servant resources.

There might be several reasons why a client fails to call the destroy operation. Clients can simply be buggy, and thus not call the destroy operation, they can crash unexpectedly, or the network connection may become unavailable.

Therefore:

Associate each client's use of a remote object with a time-based lease. When the lease for a particular client expires, the server application may assume that the client no longer needs the remote object. As soon as all leases for a remote object have expired, the servant is destroyed by the LIFECYCLE MANAGER, and the remote object can be unregistered from the distributed object middleware. It is the responsibility of the client to renew the lease for as long as it requires the remote object to be available.

General resource management patterns

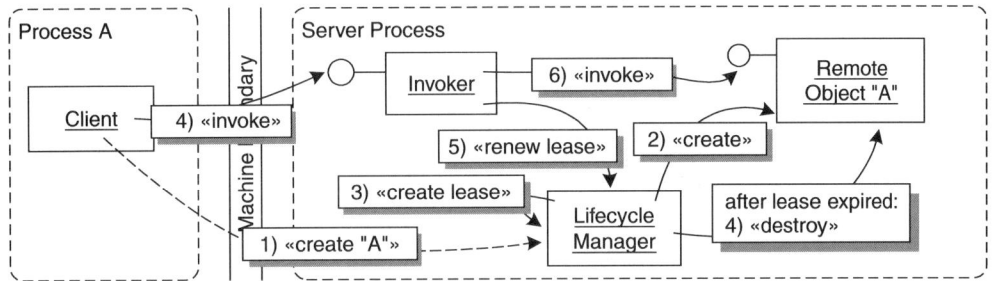

A CLIENT-DEPENDENT INSTANCE is created by the LIFECYCLE MANAGER together with a lease for the instance. During an invocation, the lease is automatically renewed. After a specified time without lease renewal, the lease expires, and so the LIFECYCLE MANAGER destroys the leased instance.

❊ ❊ ❊

LEASING frees clients from explicitly releasing unused remote objects. Since leases are only valid for a limited period, they must be renewed regularly. There are three basic ways in which lease renewal can be handled:

- A client's lease for a remote object is implicitly renewed with each invocation of the remote object. This requires the client to invoke the remote object at intervals that are shorter than the lease period, to keep remote objects alive.

- The client can be required to invoke the renewal operation explicitly on the lease before the lease period ends. Here, the client can influence the duration of the lease by specifying a lease extension period as part of the lease extension request. Explicit renewal might also be needed in the above case, in which the client's invocation interval is longer than the lease period. Network latency should also be considered when short lease periods are used.

- The distributed object middleware informs the client of a lease's upcoming expiration, allowing the client to specify an extension period. The client does not have to keep track of lease expiration itself, and thus the logic to manage the lifecycle of its remote objects becomes simpler. On the other hand, as network communication is unreliable, lease expiration messages might get lost and remote objects might be destroyed unintentionally. A further liability is that clients need to be able to handle such messages, which typically requires them to provide callback remote objects, so they have to be servers, too.

As far as the lease period is concerned, there is a trade-off between:

- Short periods, which cause less resources to be wasted, when clients no longer use remote objects
- Long periods, which minimize communication overhead due to regular lease renewals

Leases are not only beneficial within server applications, but also to clients. Clients typically only notice the unavailability of remote objects when an REMOTING ERROR is returned in reply to an invocation. Using LEASING, clients can potentially notice the unavailability of remote objects earlier, when the lease expires and lease renewal fails. This avoids the accumulation of dangling references, keeping the system more stable and up to date.

To avoid complicating client application logic, the lease management is often handled by the CLIENT PROXY, to make it transparent to the client application. Note that this still preserves the most important goal of using leases: if the client crashes, the CLIENT PROXY will also fail, and no further lease extensions will be requested.

If multiple clients use the same remote object, reference counting [Hen01] helps to keep track of the individual leases. When a lease is granted, the reference count is increased, when a lease expires, the reference count is decreased.

The LEASING pattern is documented in more detail in [KJ04].

Passivation

The server application provides stateful remote objects such as CLIENT-DEPENDENT INSTANCES or STATIC INSTANCES.

❋ ❋ ❋

Remote objects might not be accessed by a client for a long time. Even if remote objects are not used, their servants still consume server resources. As a consequence, the server application uses more resources than is actually necessary at any one time. In systems with large numbers of remote objects this can compromise performance and stability.

Neither the server application nor the distributed object middleware know when clients will access a remote object. From a client's perspective, the remote object must be available to handle invocations at all times.

However, keeping stateful remote objects such as CLIENT-DEPENDENT INSTANCES or STATIC INSTANCES active, even when clients do not invoke operations for longer periods, consumes server resources. Occupied resources lead to more contention, which degrades server application performance, scalability, and ultimately stability.

Therefore:

Temporarily remove an unused servant from memory when it has not been accessed by clients for a predefined period. This process is called PASSIVATION. If the INVOKER receives an invocation for a remote object that has been passivated, the LIFECYCLE MANAGER creates a new servant for the remote object before dispatching the invocation. In the case of a stateful remote object, the state of the remote object is stored in persistent storage during PASSIVATION. During recreation, the LIFECYCLE MANAGER initializes the newly-created servant with the persisted state.

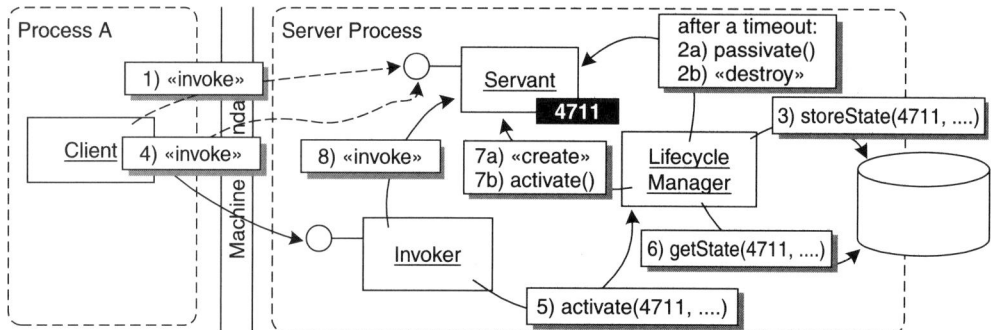

A remote object is passivated after an invocation, and its state is stored to a persistent storage. Later, a subsequent invocation arrives for the object, and the INVOKER informs the LIFECYCLE MANAGER. The LIFECYCLE MANAGER creates a new servant for the remote object, after which the INVOKER can perform the invocation on that new servant.

❄ ❄ ❄

PASSIVATION typically requires *Lifecycle Callback* operations [VSW02], such as `activate` and `passivate`, to be implemented by the remote object's servant. The operations are used by the LIFECYCLE MANAGER to notify the servant before it is passivated. In this way the servant can release used resources. A similar notification is necessary immediately after the servant has been reactivated, to re-acquire the previously-released resources.

The remote object has to persist its state while it is passivated. It can either do this on its own in the context of the *Lifecycle Callback* operations just mentioned, or the LIFECYCLE MANAGER can persist and read the state of its objects to and from a persistent storage automatically.

PASSIVATION usually involves a significant overhead, comparable to paging in operating systems. The need to passivate should therefore be avoided whenever possible. To achieve this, the server should have enough memory to keep all servants active, at least for relatively short-lived instances. A need for heavy PASSIVATION is usually a clear indication of insufficient server resources.

This pattern has been described in the context of server component infrastructures in [VSW02].

Interactions among the patterns

This section details the relationships among the patterns presented in this chapter. We first show which of the four patterns described in the second half of the chapter can be usefully combined with the three basic activation strategies. We then provide typical best practices for such combinations. The following table presents an overview.

	STATIC INSTANCE	PER-REQUEST INSTANCE	CLIENT-DEPENDENT INSTANCE
LAZY ACQUISITION	*useful*	*implicitly useful*	*implicitly useful*
POOLING	*not useful*	*very useful*	*useful*
LEASING	*sometimes useful*	*not useful*	*very useful*
PASSIVATION	*sometimes useful*	*not useful*	*very useful*

Let's discuss these combinations. Instead of eagerly instantiating a STATIC INSTANCE servant at program start-up, you can wait until a client attempts to invoke an operation on the object by using LAZY ACQUISITION. This does not change anything about the fact that the number of instances is predetermined, for example by the presence of physical devices. Acquisition of resources can be postponed until they are actually needed. The caveat is, though, that the first invocation of the instance takes longer than subsequent ones, which can be problematic in the context of embedded or real-time systems.

POOLING is not very useful for STATIC INSTANCES, because in most cases STATIC INSTANCES represent physical entities or similar concepts with their own identity and state. LEASING might be useful to remove a STATIC INSTANCE when clients are no longer interested in using the remote object. PASSIVATION can be used to evict servants temporarily until they are used again. Of course, this sacrifices some of the predictability of access times for STATIC INSTANCES, because an invocation will take longer if a new servant has to be created.

For pure PER-REQUEST INSTANCES, LAZY ACQUISITION is used implicitly. A new servant is lazily created just in time for each request that arrives at the server application. LEASING does not make sense at all for PER-REQUEST INSTANCES, because the servant is destroyed immediately after handling an invocation. PER-REQUEST INSTANCES are suited ideally for optimization through POOLING. As PER-REQUEST INSTANCES are always stateless, a servant pool can easily be created, taking an instance from the pool to serve each invocation. PASSIVATION is not useful here, since there is no state.

If many CLIENT-DEPENDENT INSTANCES are created *and* destroyed by clients, it makes sense to use POOLING and initialize the servants with the parameters supplied by the client, instead of creating new servants all the time.

CLIENT-DEPENDENT INSTANCES are the primary use case for LEASING. As outlined in the description of the LEASING pattern, CLIENT-DEPENDENT INSTANCES are typically implemented using LEASING to make sure the server application has a way of reclaiming remote objects and their servants if they are no longer accessed and have not been explicitly destroyed, for example as a consequence of a crashed client. Since CLIENT-DEPENDENT INSTANCES are typically stateful, PASSIVATION is useful. Support of PASSIVATION is important, if the state must remain available even when the client is off-line for an extended period. In such scenarios, PASSIVATION of CLIENT-DEPENDENT INSTANCES can reduce a server's resource usage significantly.

Lifecycle management best practices

Embedded and real-time applications typically rely on STATIC INSTANCES. This is because the remote objects often resemble physical devices (or functionality associated with them), and the configuration is fairly static. There is therefore no need to use techniques that mainly address dynamic resource management scenarios, such as LAZY ACQUISITION and PASSIVATION. The static configuration ensures that enough resources are available, and that they can be acquired at server application start-up.

While the number of clients in embedded and real-time applications is often known in advance, this is usually not the case in business applications. Business applications are often built using server-side component technologies such as Enterprise Java Beans (EJB) [Sun04d], CORBA Components (CCM) [Sev04], or Microsoft's COM+ [Mic04d]. We will now consider how component containers manage the lifecycles of their components.

Containers help the developer to focus on functional issues when implementing components, leaving the management of technical issues to the container [VSW02]. All major component containers available today support different kind of components, featuring different lifecycle models.

The selection of lifecycle models implemented by component containers can be seen as best practice, because they try to cover the typical requirements of most developers. All component containers provide so-called *Service Components* [VSW02]. These are stateless components whose lifecycle is typically implemented by PER-REQUEST INSTANCES, optimized using POOLING, or as STATIC INSTANCES.

Session Components [VSW02] are basically CLIENT-DEPENDENT INSTANCES that provide no support for concurrent access, because it is assumed that only one client accesses a specific instance at a time. They are created at the client's request, and often have leases associated with them. LEASING is a two-step process here:

- If an instance is not accessed for a specific period, the instance is passivated – its state is written to persistent storage and the servant itself is destroyed.
- When a new request arrives for such a passivated instance, a new servant is created lazily and its state restored from disk.

PASSIVATION helps to save the resources of instances that are not accessed for a while. Only after longer periods is the remote object (including its state) actually destroyed, and so cannot be reactivated.

Entity Components [VSW02] are typical examples of stateless remote objects that use POOLING to optimize resource consumption. From a client's perspective, however, *Entity Components* have state that represents business entities, such as customers, orders, or products. The state of these business entities is kept in persistent storage and transferred to and from pooled servants by the LIFECYCLE MANAGER of the container. As with all stateless pooled remote objects, LEASING is not necessary (the servants stay in the pool, and the state is persistent). In the case of entity components, however, destroying an instance means deleting the persistent state of an instance. This is therefore a business operation and not a means to manage resources technically.

Note that, as mentioned before, such more elaborate lifecycle management strategies are typically the domain of component containers. These provide a lifecycle management framework that also deals with advanced technical aspects such as transactions, security, and failover.

More details about component infrastructures can be found in [VSW02]. See also Chapter 13, *Related Concepts, Technologies, and Patterns*.

Lifecycle interaction sequences

This section gives some examples of typical lifecycles. In all the following diagrams we assume that the invocation data is demarshaled and that an object containing the invocation data is already instantiated. To illustrate these tasks, the following sequence diagram shows the steps that we assume to have already happened in all the subsequent diagrams. The INVOKER triggers demarshal ling and receives the newly-created invocation data object as a result. This object is used for further tasks, such as lifecycle management, as indicated in the diagram. After these tasks have been completed, the actual invocation of the remote object takes place.

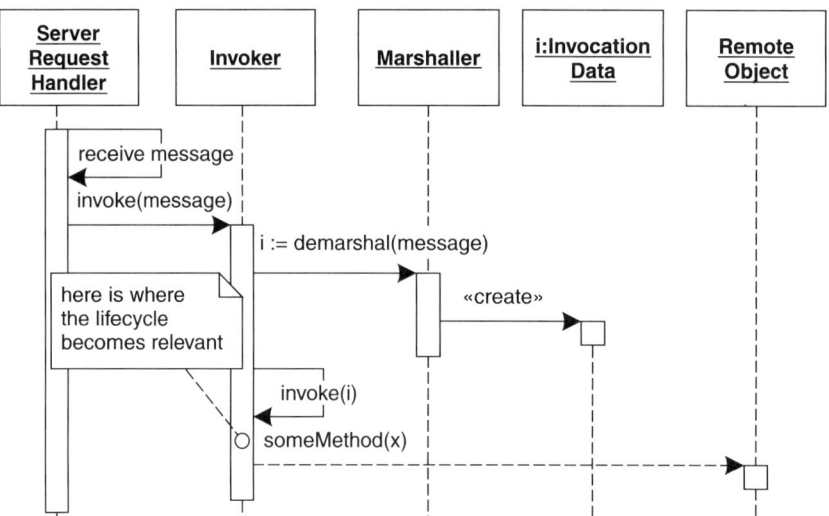

In the following examples, we also assume that there is only one INVOKER in the system. This manages a set of LIFECYCLE MANAGERS that implement different activation strategies.

The following sequence diagram shows a simple, non-pooled PER-REQUEST INSTANCE.

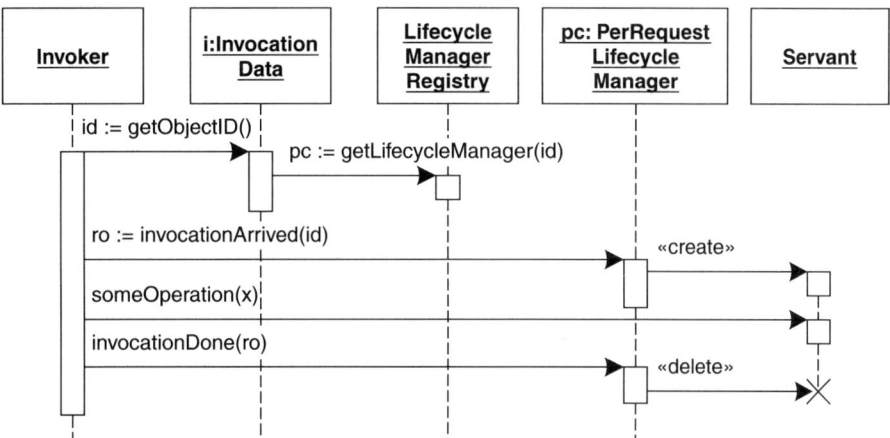

The LIFECYCLE MANAGER implements the *Strategy* pattern [GHJV95]. All concrete LIFECYCLE MANAGERS support the same interface, but have different implementations. The `LifecycleManagerRegistry` class keeps track of all LIFECYCLE MANAGERS in the system, as well as their relationship to remote objects and their servants.

To associate a remote object with a specific LIFECYCLE MANAGER, a well-defined registration procedure must be followed. In the example above, we would not register a specific remote object instance with the LIFECYCLE MANAGER, but rather a specific *type*. The LIFECYCLE MANAGER realizes PER-REQUEST INSTANCES. That is, it instantiates the remote object type for each request by creating a new servant.

The process of registering a remote object with its LIFECYCLE MANAGER depends on the strategy implemented by the LIFECYCLE MANAGER. In the other two lifecycle strategy patterns, STATIC INSTANCE and CLIENT-DEPENDENT INSTANCE, concrete remote object instances are registered with the LIFECYCLE MANAGER. It is therefore a good idea to let the LIFECYCLE MANAGER handle the registration process. Internally, the LIFECYCLE MANAGER updates the `LifecycleManagerRegistry`. In this example, the registry must of course support both registration of particular objects (for STATIC INSTANCES and CLIENT-DEPENDENT INSTANCES) and of object types (for PER-REQUEST INSTANCES). This can be realized by registering the OBJECT ID of the remote object rather than the individual servants. The different LIFECYCLE MANAGERS map the OBJECT IDS to servants when an invocation arrives.

The next diagram shows an example of how to simplify the management tasks of PER-REQUEST INSTANCES, such as registering them in the lookup service. Here, the registration operation of the LIFECYCLE MANAGER returns a proxy for the PER-REQUEST INSTANCE. This proxy is used inside the server application when other components refer to the PER-REQUEST INSTANCES. Thus it is possible to interact with PER-REQUEST INSTANCES as ordinary objects, even though no servant is yet instantiated, or multiple servants are instantiated at the same time. The following sequence diagram shows how this could look.

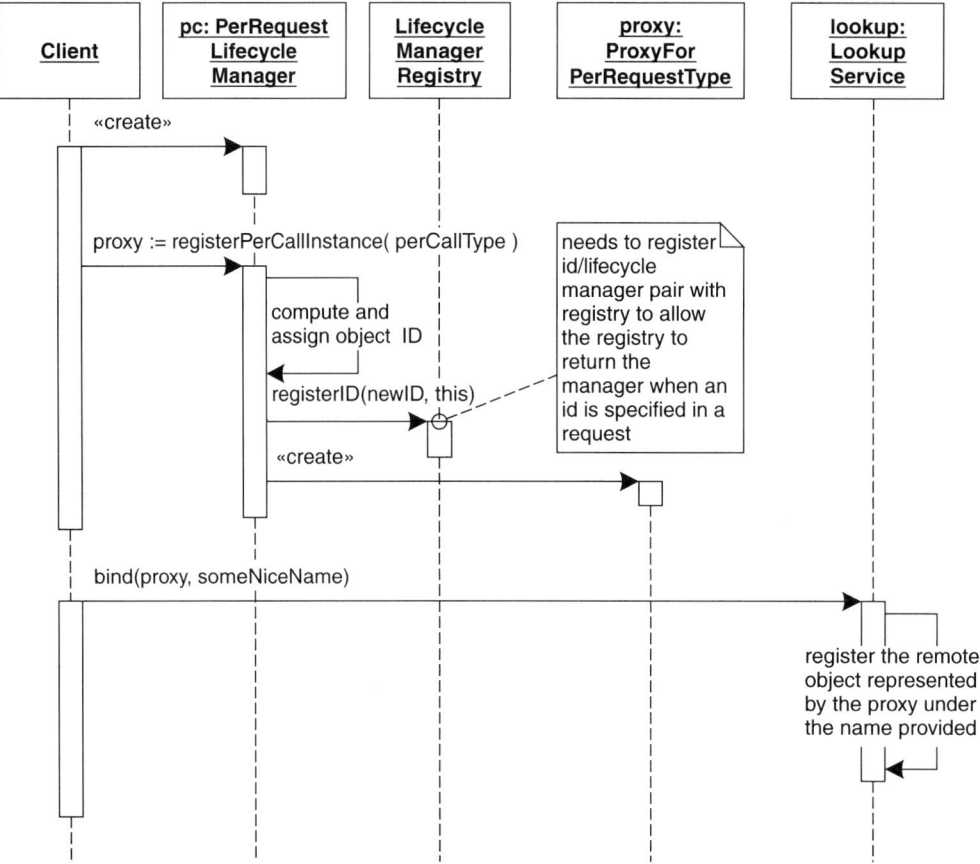

Interactions among the patterns

We will now return to the activation strategies. As explained above, PER-REQUEST INSTANCES are typically optimized using POOLING. The following sequence diagrams show how this could be implemented. The first one shows the pool creation process. A PER-REQUEST INSTANCE is first registered with the LIFECYCLE MANAGER. This triggers the creation of an instance pool. The pool in turn instantiates a number of servants as pooled instances.

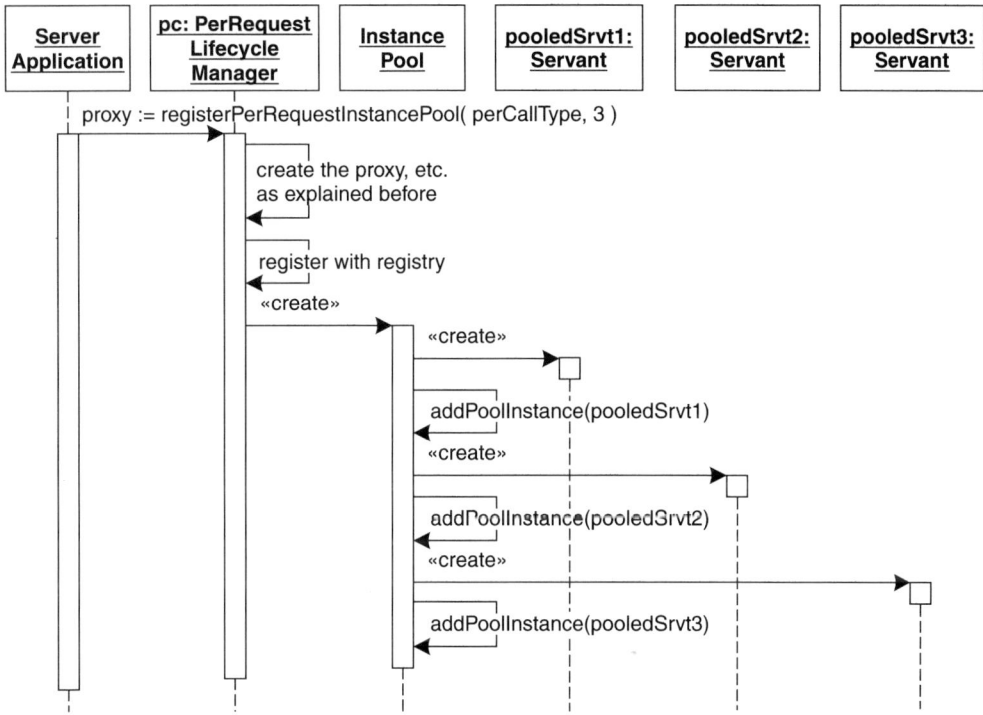

The following diagram shows how a PER-REQUEST INSTANCE is actually accessed when an invocation arrives for it. The LIFECYCLE MANAGER is informed that the invocation has arrived. Next, it looks up an idle servant in the instance pool and returns it. The instance is then used to execute the invocation. Finally, the instance is returned to the pool.

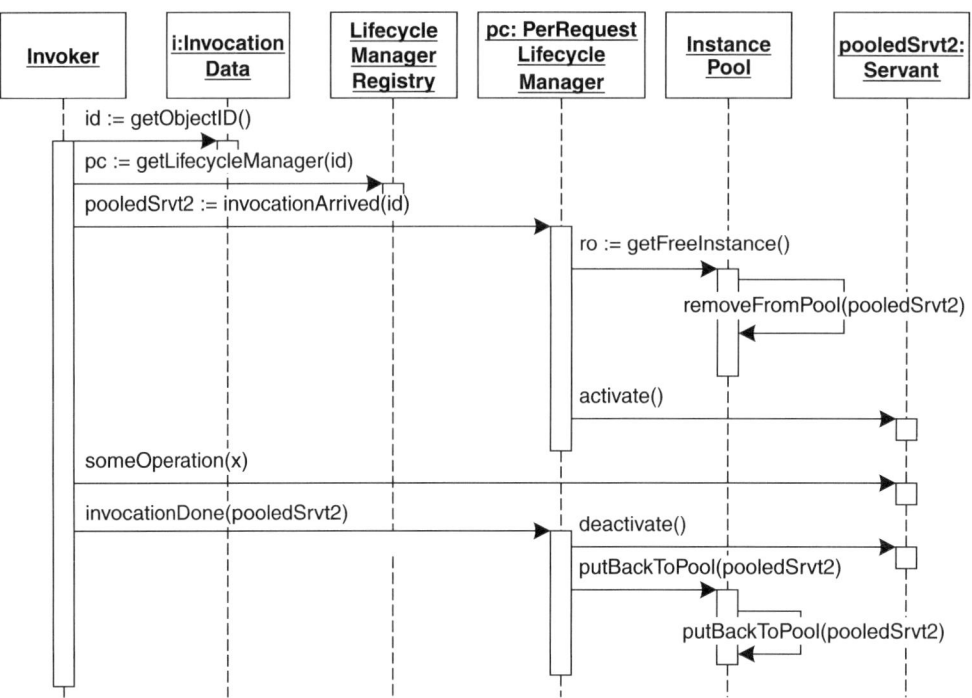

Note how the LIFECYCLE MANAGER uses the activate *Lifecycle Operation* [VSW02] to allow the servant to do some initialization when it is taken from the pool – for example to acquire resources. The reverse is done in deactivate, called after the invocation has been handled and just before the servant is put back into the pool.

We do not illustrate STATIC INSTANCES for two reasons. First, a STATIC INSTANCE that is not instantiated lazily is trivial, and is implicitly illustrated with many other examples given in the previous chapters: the server application simply instantiates the remote object's servant and registers it with a LIFECYCLE MANAGER for STATIC INSTANCES, which just remembers the servant and forwards invocations to it. Second, when LAZY ACQUISITION is used, the process is basically the same as in the PER-REQUEST INSTANCE example shown above, except that the single servant so created is not destroyed, and can serve subsequent invocations. Specifically this also requires a type-based registration and a proxy, as in the example illustrated above.

More examples of POOLING, especially POOLING of persistent, stateful remote objects, are shown at the end of Chapter 7, *Extended Infrastructure Patterns*, to illustrate the LIFECYCLE MANAGER and CONFIGURATION GROUP patterns.

The diagrams that follow illustrate CLIENT-DEPENDENT INSTANCES in more detail. The next diagram shows how a client accesses a CLIENT-DEPENDENT INSTANCE using a factory remote object. Here the factory is used to create the CLIENT-DEPENDENT INSTANCE, and the instance is explicitly destroyed by the client after a number of invocations.

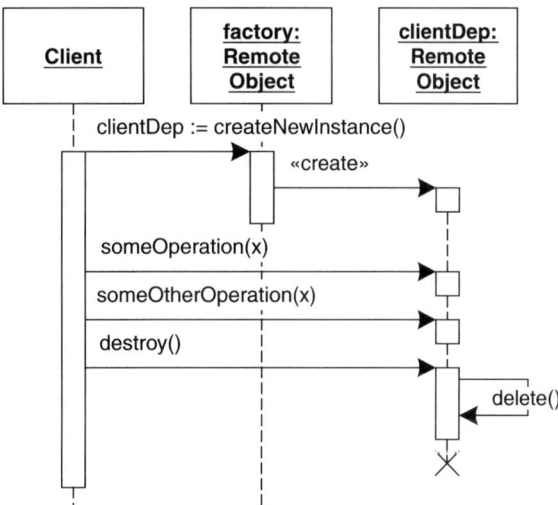

The more interesting tasks happen 'under the hood' of the distributed object middleware, of course. The next sequence diagrams tries to illustrate this. First, we have to initialize the respective LIFECYCLE MANAGER and create the factory. This job is done by the server application, as the next sequence diagram shows.

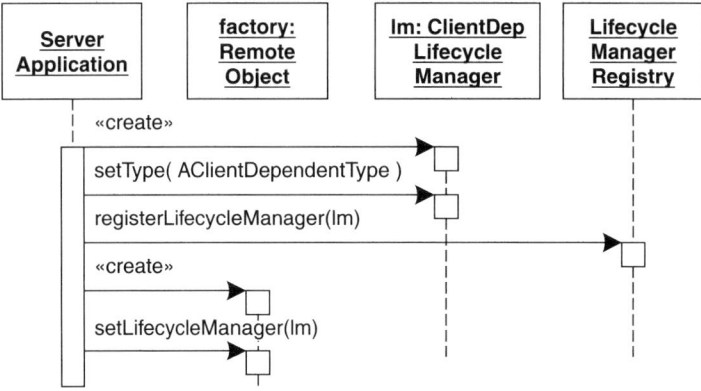

An important aspect for CLIENT-DEPENDENT INSTANCES is the management via LEASING, so that remote object instances that are no longer needed are removed automatically. The diagram below shows how a client requests the creation of a new CLIENT-DEPENDENT INSTANCE. The LIFECYCLE MANAGER keeps track of the instance and the lease. The lease is configured with the lease time and the leased object instance. The configured lease is registered with a lease manager that keeps track of the instantiated leases.

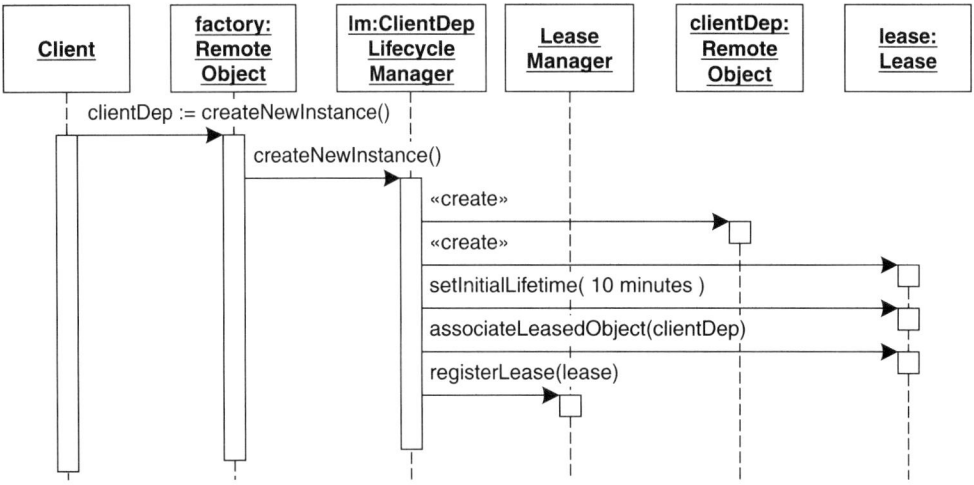

Interactions among the patterns

The next illustration addresses the issue of invoking an operation on a CLIENT-DEPENDENT INSTANCE with leases. In this case, the INVOKER and the associated LIFECYCLE MANAGER have to ensure that the lease is still valid before the object can be invoked. There are two scenarios:

- The OBJECT ID is unknown to the lifecycle manager, for example because its lease has expired and it has been removed. The invocation then results in a REMOTING ERROR.
- The lease is ok and the object can be found. The lease is then renewed and the invocation is performed on the leased instance.

We show these two cases in the following diagram.

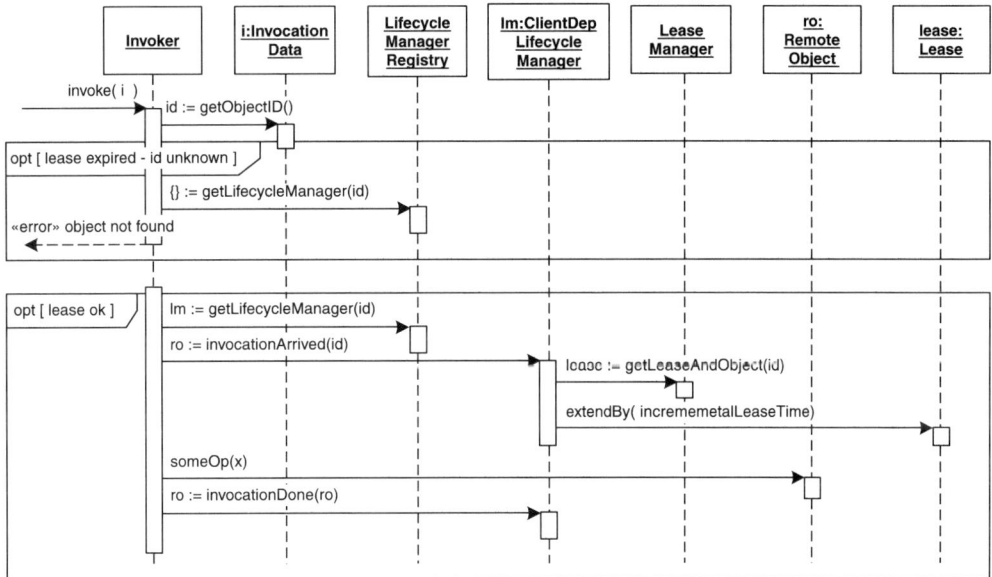

The next diagram shows how lease expiration is handled. Leases are handed out on a per-client and remote object basis. Several potential approaches exist:

- Check lease validity whenever a request arrives. If the lease has expired in the mean time, the remote object is deactivated and the lease is deleted. An error is reported to the client.
- Have a background thread check all leases in turn, continuously, and delete those remote objects and leases that are no longer valid.
- Register a callback function for the point in time at which a remote object's lease is expected to expire. The callback function can then check whether the remote object can be deactivated. This approach is often used in event-based systems.

The first approach seems simplest, but has a serious drawback: if a client does not invoke the remote object regularly, the system will not notice the lease expiration, and the remote object will not be deactivated. As a consequence, one or other of the second two approaches is necessary in all cases. However, it can still be useful to combine on-request-checks with a background thread solution, as this avoids situations in which the lease has expired but the background thread has not yet run.

Interactions among the patterns

The figure below shows the first alternative. An invocation arrives and the lease is obtained. However, this lease has expired. As a reaction to this, the remote object instance, the lease instance, and the registration of the remote object in the lifecycle manager registry are deleted. A REMOTING ERROR is reported to the client.

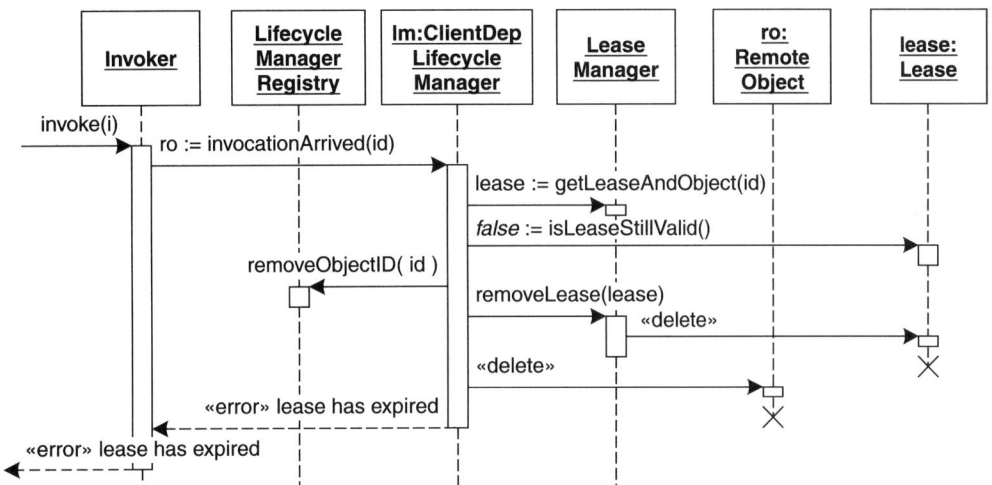

The background thread variant is rather simple and therefore is not shown – it just scans all the leases managed by the lease manager, and if one expires, executes the same deactivation steps as shown above. In this example, the background thread and the lease manager are integral parts of the CLIENT-DEPENDENT INSTANCE'S LIFECYCLE MANAGER.

The third variant, using an event-based callback, needs to register the callback during creation. All deactivation steps shown above need to be performed by the callback.

The remaining sequence diagrams show how PASSIVATION works. A background thread checks for instances whose PASSIVATION timeout has been reached and must be passivated. The instance is passivated by a `passivate` operation, then destroyed. Again, this variant can also be implemented using an event-system-based callback that is executed recurringly after a specific time.

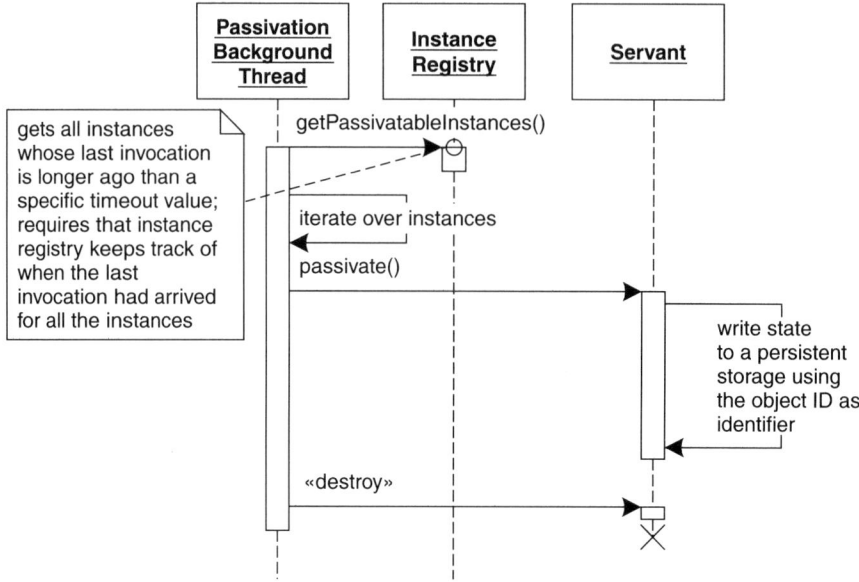

The final diagram shows how the LIFECYCLE MANAGER reactivates a previously-passivated remote object when a new invocation for the remote object arrives. First an empty instance is created, then it is filled

Interactions among the patterns

with the state from the database during the `activate` operation. The INVOKER performs the invocation on this new instance.

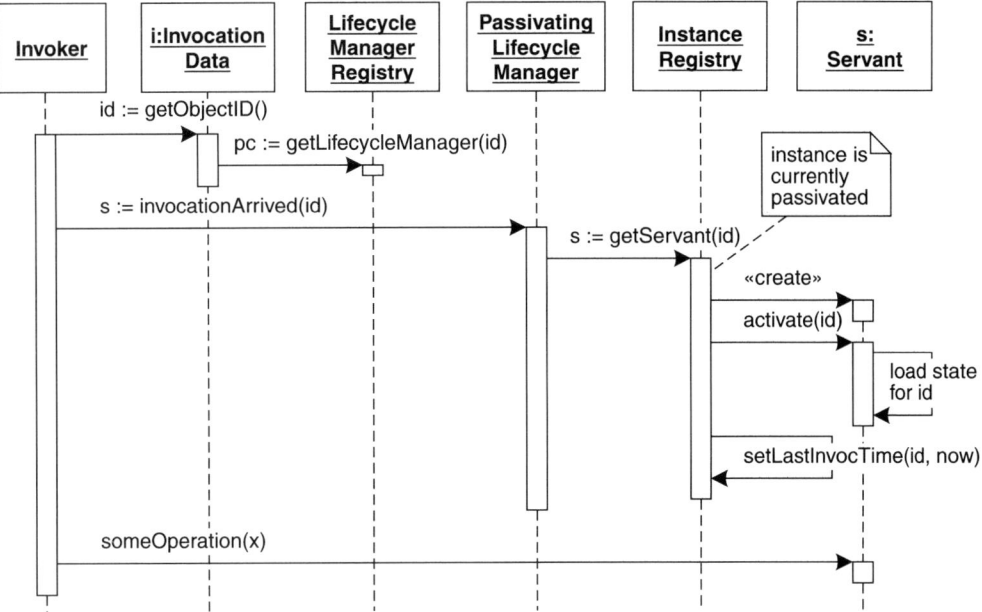

6 Extension Patterns

Message processing in distributed object middleware follows a *Layers* [BMR+96] architecture, as shown in the illustration below. The layers architecture partitions and encapsulates mutual responsibilities. Each layer interacts only with the next higher and lower layer.

Application	Remote Object Server Application Client
Invocation	CLIENT PROXY REQUESTOR INVOKER
Request Handling	CLIENT REQUEST HANDLER SERVER REQUEST HANDLER
Communication	*Reactor* *Acceptor Connector* *Leader/Followers*

The following layers can be identified:

- *Application.* The top-level layer of the message processing architecture of distributed object middleware consists of clients that perform invocations and remote objects that serve invocations.
- *Invocation.* Beneath the application layer, CLIENT PROXY, REQUESTOR, and INVOKER are responsible for marshaling/de-marshaling and multiplexing/demultiplexing of invocations/replies.
- *Request handling.* In the next layer, the REQUESTOR uses a CLIENT REQUEST HANDLER, and the INVOKER is served by a SERVER REQUEST HANDLER. This layer is responsible for the basic tasks of establishing connections and message passing between client and server.

- *Communication*. The communication layer is responsible for defining the basic message flow and managing the operating system resources, such as connections, handles, or threads. Depending on the concrete architecture, this layer uses the *Reactor* [SSRB00] pattern and/or *Acceptor/Connector* [SSRB00] pattern.

Each layer only depends on the layers adjacent to it. To introduce new services, layers might have to be extended. Depending on the purpose of an extension, the extension can be made in any layer, on both the client and the server side. Typical extensions are the introduction of security, transaction, or logging support of remote invocations. For example, security issues such as authorization are typically introduced by extending the invocation layer, so that the extended behavior is transparent to the application. Other security issues, such as using a secure transport protocol, require modifications to the request handling and communication layers.

In this chapter we present patterns for extending the *Layers* architecture of message processing in distributed object middleware. Note that there is a certain symmetry between client and server in the layered architecture. This is because the processing patterns at each layer depend on their remote counterpart. The same is true for many typical extension tasks: they also have to be performed both on the client side and the server side. Consider authorization, for example, as a possible security extension. The client would have to provide the user credentials, and the server side would have to verify those credentials. Thus both sides have to be extended in parallel to support authorization.

Extension Patterns

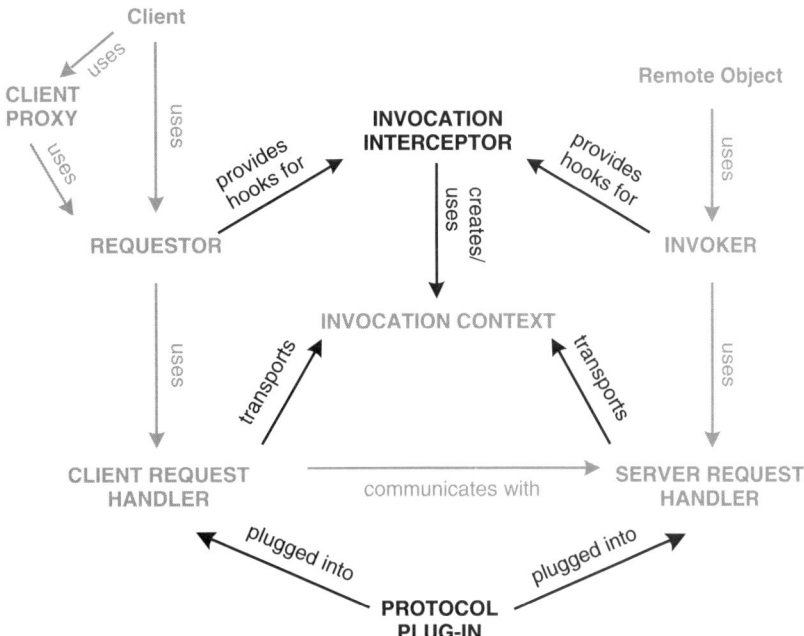

INVOCATION INTERCEPTORS extend message processing by intercepting a message before and/or after it passes a layer. These can be configured at almost every level, even though typically they are used in the REQUESTOR and INVOKER. The granularity can be per server application, per remote object, or per CONFIGURATION GROUP. Other combinations are also possible, but less common. See Chapter 7, *Extended Infrastructure Patterns*.

To handle issues such as transactions or security, invocations need to contain more information than just the operation name and its parameters, for example some kind of transaction ID or security credentials. For that purpose INVOCATION CONTEXTS are exchanged transparently between CLIENT REQUEST HANDLER and SERVER REQUEST HANDLER. INVOCATION INTERCEPTORS on the client side and the server side can create and consume INVOCATION CONTEXT data to communicate with their counterpart on the remote side. INVOCATION INTERCEPTORS apply the *Interceptor* [SSRB00] pattern to remote communication.

A PROTOCOL PLUG-IN can be used by developers to exchange or adapt the transport protocol. Such plug-ins are plugged into the CLIENT REQUEST HANDLER and SERVER REQUEST HANDLER. This approach can be used for optimizing the communication protocols, used for particular applications, or for supporting new protocols.

Invocation Interceptor

Distributed applications need to transparently integrate add-on services.

❊ ❊ ❊

In addition to hosting remote objects, the server application often has to provide a number of add-on services, such as transactions, logging, or security. The clients and remote objects themselves should be independent of those services.

Consider the typical concern of security in distributed object middleware: remote objects need to be protected from unauthorized access. The remote objects themselves should not have to worry about authorization – they should be accessible with or without authorization enabled. When the server application needs to enforce security, the client must add the relevant credentials, such as user name and password, to the request.

In addition to security, there are many other issues that might potentially have to be added to the invocation path, such as transactions, logging, persistence, and so on. Since these are add-on services, clients and remote object implementations should not be coupled with such features. It should be possible to selectively enable and disable them without changing their implementations.

Therefore:

Provide hooks in the invocation path, for example in the INVOKER and REQUESTOR, to plug in INVOCATION INTERCEPTORS. INVOCATION INTERCEPTORS are invoked before and after request and reply messages pass the hook. Provide the interceptor with all the necessary information to allow it to provide meaningful add-on services,

such as operation name, parameters, OBJECT ID, and, if used, the INVOCATION CONTEXT.

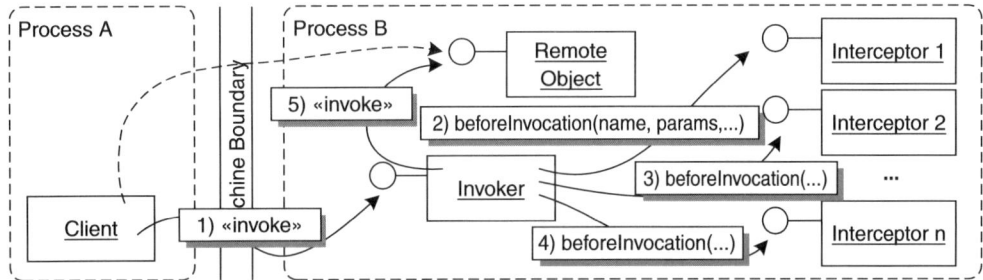

The INVOKER receives an invocation and checks whether INVOCATION INTERCEPTORS are registered for the remote object. If so, the interceptor is invoked before and after the actual invocation.

❅ ❅ ❅

INVOCATION INTERCEPTORS allow for the transparent integration of additional orthogonal services. These additional services are independent of the individual clients and remote objects.

If more than one INVOCATION INTERCEPTOR is applicable to an invocation, the interceptors are often interdependent. In most cases, therefore, they are arranged in a chain of interceptors. Each INVOCATION INTERCEPTOR forwards the invocation to the next interceptor in the chain. Alternatively, the components that provide the hooks, such as REQUESTOR and INVOKER, can manage the passing of information between elements of the chain.

An INVOCATION INTERCEPTOR can use the invocation data to do whatever it wants. The INVOCATION INTERCEPTOR might just read the passed parameters, modify them, or even interrupt further processing and report a REMOTING ERROR to the client. Note that there are distributed object middleware systems that do not permit the modification of all the invocation data.

INVOCATION INTERCEPTORS are configured typically via external configuration files or via programming interfaces. External configuration has the advantage that it allows the interceptors to be modified without recompilation. A programmatic interface has the advantage that INVOCATION INTERCEPTORS can be added and removed dynamically at runtime.

INVOCATION INTERCEPTORS can only access the information that is available at the abstraction layer where their hook is located. For example, in the CLIENT REQUEST HANDLER and SERVER REQUEST HANDLER, only marshaled information in byte stream format is available, whereas in hooks in the REQUESTOR/INVOKER layer, individual data items, such as operation name and parameters, are directly accessible. Based on this difference, the use cases are different also. For example, encryption is typically handled at the request handling layer, as this task operates on byte streams and not individual data items. On the other hand, logging will typically be implemented on the REQUESTOR/INVOKER level, since the data items that should be logged are available in their native format.

If the INVOCATION INTERCEPTOR requires more information than is usually available in the invocation message, an INVOCATION CONTEXT can be used to transport additional data between client to server. A typical design provides an INVOCATION INTERCEPTOR in the client, which adds specific information to the INVOCATION CONTEXT, and a corresponding INVOCATION INTERCEPTOR in the server that consumes this information, thus providing some service that uses this data.

INVOCATION INTERCEPTORS consume additional resources and add complexity to the overall architecture. Further, entities such as the INVOKER can no longer rely on what they receive or send, as parameters might have been modified by intermediate INVOCATION INTERCEPTORS. If safety is a primary concern, this can become problematic and therefore requires proper control, for example via programming guidelines.

The issues addressed by INVOCATION INTERCEPTORS can be also solved using aspect-oriented solutions [KLM+97]. Such solutions are interesting specifically if no hooks are available in the distributed object middleware. General purpose aspect languages, such as AspectJ [KHH+01], can be used transparently to integrate the same features that INVOCATION INTERCEPTORS are typically used for. For a discussion of aspect-oriented programming (AOP) in the context of remoting, see Chapter 13, *Related Concepts, Technologies, and Patterns* and Appendix A, *Extending AOP Frameworks for Remoting*.

The INVOCATION INTERCEPTOR is a specialization of *Interceptor* [SSRB00] for distributed object middleware.

Invocation Context

Add-on services are plugged into the distributed object middleware.

❊ ❊ ❊

Remote invocations typically only contain necessary information, such as operation name, OBJECT ID, and parameters. But INVOCATION INTERCEPTORS often need additional information to provide add-on services. A straightforward solution would be to add this information to the operation signature of remote objects. But this would prevent the transparent integration of add-on services, which is the goal in the first place, as signatures would change depending on the requirements of the add-on services. Changing operation signatures for reasons other than business logic is tedious and error-prone.

When the server application has to provide add-on services transparently, the client-side and the server-side distributed object middleware have to share contextual information, such as a transaction ID or security credentials. If this information changes on either the client or server side, it needs to be transported to the other side. In the case of transactions, the transaction ID has to be transported between client and server for every remote invocation, so that both can participate in the same transaction.

The operation signature of remote objects should not need to be changed to transport this additional information. This is not only because it is tedious to maintain, but also because the contextual information is not always necessary, since the add-on service may be optional and can be turned on and off. If contextual information were to be part of the operation signature, it would waste network bandwidth in the case in which the add-on service is turned off.

In general, contextual information required by add-on services cannot be anticipated by either the distributed object middleware itself, or by remote object developers – it needs to be extensible independently.

Therefore:

Bundle contextual information in an extensible INVOCATION CONTEXT data structure that is transferred between client and remote object with every remote invocation. For transparent integration, INVOCATION INTERCEPTORS can be used to add and consume this information.

The format and data types used for the contextual information in the INVOCATION CONTEXT depend on the use case.

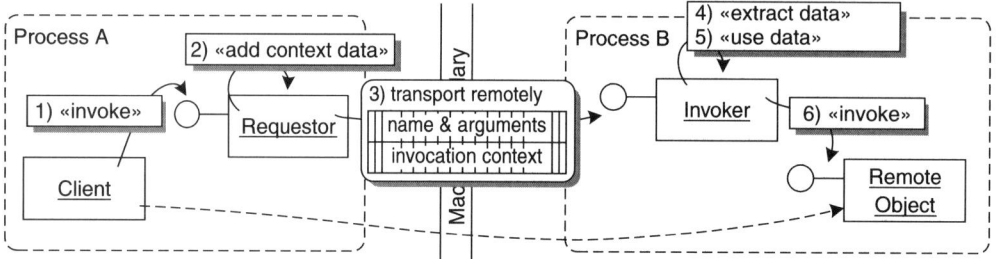

The client invokes an operation. The REQUESTOR adds the required contextual information in the INVOCATION CONTEXT. The INVOKER extracts the information, uses it, and invokes the operation of the remote object. Typically, the information is added and used by application-specific INVOCATION INTERCEPTORS.

Insertion, extraction, and use of INVOCATION CONTEXT information is hidden inside distributed object middleware components, specifically INVOCATION INTERCEPTORS, the REQUESTOR, or the INVOKER. The application logic of clients and remote objects remains independent of INVOCATION CONTEXT information. This works well because in most cases the information in the INVOCATION CONTEXT is only of interest to the add-on service. For situations in which the remote object needs access to INVOCATION CONTEXT data, the distributed object middleware provides a well-defined API.

The data in the INVOCATION CONTEXT has to be marshaled just like every other item of information contained in an invocation. As a consequence, the same limitations apply as for operations parameters: the MARSHALLER used must support the data types used.

The client- and server-side components that make use of the INVOCATION CONTEXT information must adhere to the same protocol, which means they must agree on a common data structure inside the INVOCATION CONTEXT.

Using INVOCATION CONTEXTS, add-on services such as transaction support or security can communicate transparently, that is, without the explicit support of clients and remote objects. The remote objects are kept independent of any contextual data transferred. While INVOCATION CONTEXTS provide a useful and flexible extension mechanism, using them increases the footprint of every remote invocation to which they are added.

Protocol Plug-In

A CLIENT REQUEST HANDLER and a SERVER REQUEST HANDLER adhere to the same communication protocol.

❄ ❄ ❄

Developers of client and server applications often need to control the communication protocol used by the CLIENT REQUEST HANDLER and SERVER REQUEST HANDLER. In some cases, differences in network technologies require the use of specialized protocols, in other cases, existing protocols need to be optimized to meet real-time constraints. Sometimes it might even be necessary to support multiple protocols at the same time. Communication protocols should be configurable by developers, who might have only a limited knowledge of low-level protocol details.

There are several situations in which the developer of a distributed application cannot abstract from the implementation details of distributed object middleware at the communication protocol layer, and needs to control the communication protocol used explicitly:

- Specialized network technologies require specialized communication protocols. If multiple network adapters have to be used by the same client or server, each adapter might need to be accessed using a different communication protocol.
- Specialized custom MARSHALLERS that provide optimized serialization mechanisms might require specialized communication protocols to be used to actually transport the serialized data.
- The distributed application needs to fulfil varying QoS requirements. To effectively fulfil these QoS requirements, the facilities provided by the communication protocol have to be used differently, and perhaps need to be optimized at a low level.
- The implementation strategies of the communication protocol, such as the handling of priorities, need to be optimized for the most common use case of the distributed application to achieve the desired predictability.
- Firewalls might prohibit the use of default communication protocols. Specialized communication protocols are required that are

able to cross firewalls. Adaptations to the new protocol may be necessary to cope with differences in the network environment.

Therefore:

Provide PROTOCOL PLUG-INS to extend CLIENT REQUEST HANDLERS and SERVER REQUEST HANDLERS. Let the PROTOCOL PLUG-INS provide a common interface to allow them to be configured from higher layers of the distributed object middleware.

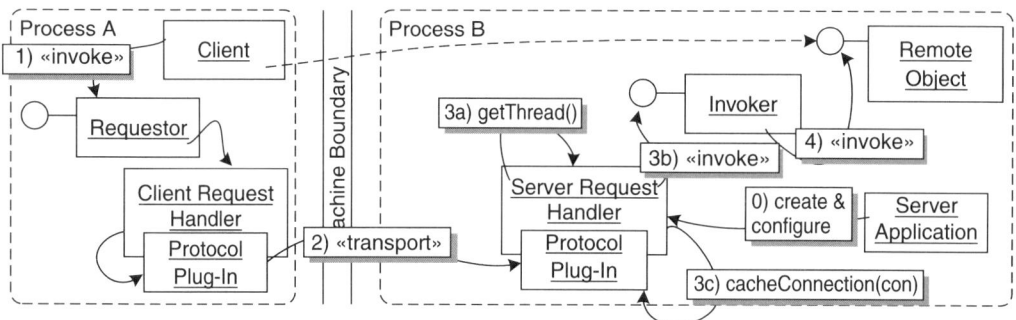

The PROTOCOL PLUG-INS are created, configured, and used inside the CLIENT REQUEST HANDLER and SERVER REQUEST HANDLER, respectively. In heterogeneous environments the CLIENT REQUEST HANDLER selects the plug-in based on the properties and supported communication protocol of SERVER REQUEST HANDLER. For optimization, connections may be cached using PROTOCOL PLUG-INS.

❊ ❊ ❊

To ensure interoperability, the CLIENT REQUEST HANDLER and SERVER REQUEST HANDLER need to support the same communication protocol, or at least compatible PROTOCOL PLUG-INS, simultaneously.

PROTOCOL PLUG-INS can be integrated using INVOCATION INTERCEPTORS in a chain of interceptors. Architectures that follow this design, such as ART [Vin02b] or Apache Axis (see Chapter 11, *Web Services Technology Projection*), distinguish several kinds of INVOCATION INTERCEPTORS, for example transport interceptors, protocol interceptors, and general interceptors.

Some communication protocols, such as CAN [Cia04], require very special handling. For example, packet sizes are severely limited, and requests and replies usually have to be mapped to pre-defined messages types on the CAN network. This requires close cooperation between a custom MARSHALLERS and the PROTOCOL PLUG-IN.

For the configuration of PROTOCOL PLUG-IN parameters, the PROTOCOL PLUG-INs offer either an API or a configuration file. Typical parameters are QoS properties including packet sizes and timeouts to be used by the communication protocol. In most cases those details are only customized by CLIENT REQUEST HANDLERS and SERVER REQUEST HANDLERS. Which plug-in is used is transparent to the distributed application. In certain cases, for example when *Reflection* [BMR+96] is supported, it can be beneficial to configure such parameters from inside the application, as this allows the application to adapt to changing environments. However, most of this is the topic of current research.

If more than one PROTOCOL PLUG-IN is involved in parallel, that is, if a remote object can be reached using more than one network, the SERVER REQUEST HANDLER must ensure that the reply message is sent using the correct protocol, or else the reply will never reach the original client.

To summarize, PROTOCOL PLUG-INS provide several advantages: they abstract from communication protocol details, they allow for flexible support of several communication protocols, and they allow for configuration and optimization of the communication protocols used.

Interactions among the patterns

The following sequence diagram shows how a client uses an INVOCATION INTERCEPTOR to add a security token to each invocation. The security token will be used within the server application to authenticate the client.

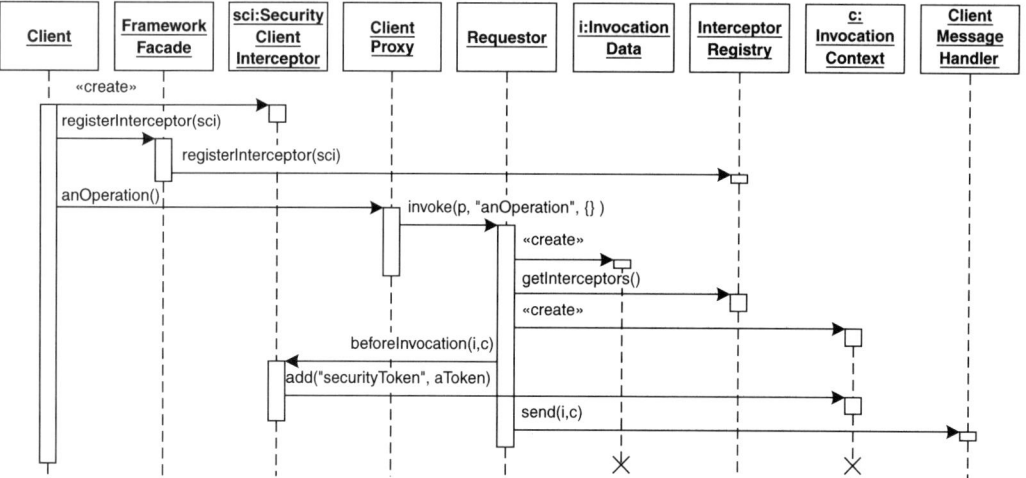

As the diagram shows, the client registers a security interceptor with the framework facade, a *Facade* [GHJV95] object that provides access to the distributed object middleware infrastructure on start-up. When the client invokes an operation, the REQUESTOR uses the registered INVOCATION INTERCEPTORS to add the security token to the INVOCATION CONTEXT transparently.

The invocation itself is passed to the interceptors as an invocation data object. Potentially, the interceptors can change the information in this object and thereby manipulate the invocation. The same happens on the server side.

The respective parts in the server application are shown next. An INVOCATION INTERCEPTOR is used to access the security token in the INVOCATION CONTEXT. The token is used to authenticate the client, and the operation is invoked only if access can be granted. If the token is invalid, a security exception is raised and a REMOTING ERROR is sent back to the client. In the following sequence diagram, we assume that the interceptor has been registered by the server application upon start-up, using the server-side framework facade. Here, the interceptor decides

Interactions among the patterns **139**

whether the invocation can be performed or, if the security token is not valid, the invocation is rejected using a security exception.

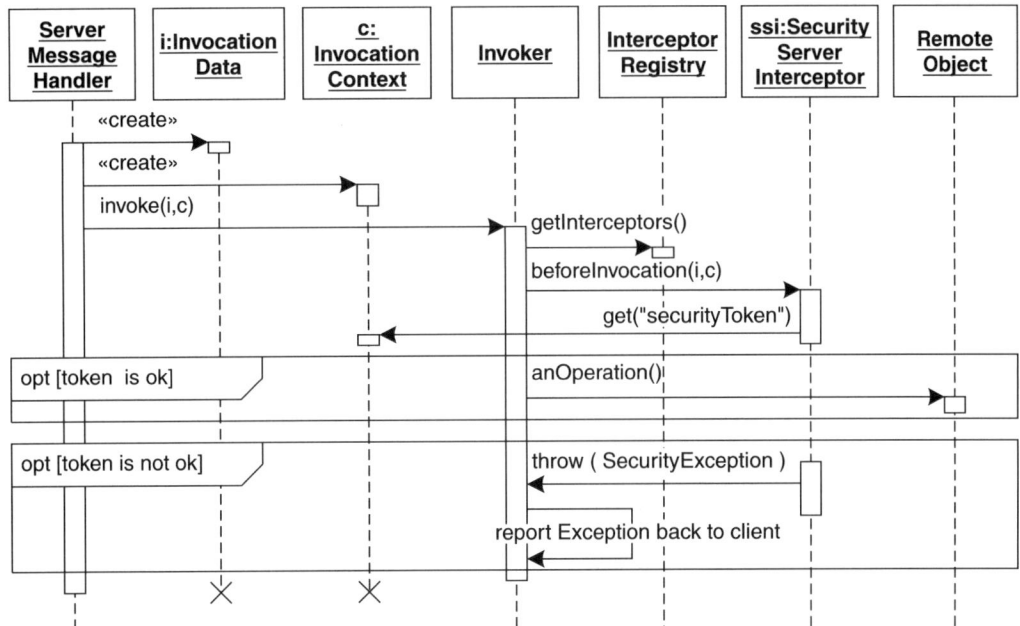

Session handling is another interesting feature that can be implemented easily using the patterns introduced in this chapter. As explained more deeply in Chapter 13, *Related Concepts, Technologies, and Patterns*, sessions can be used to provide state to otherwise stateless remote objects. Using a client-specific session object, instead of making all the remote objects stateful, CLIENT-DEPENDENT INSTANCES makes scalability, failover, and load-balancing easier to achieve in most cases.

The example in the next diagram uses non-persistent sessions. These are only stored in memory by the SessionRegistry. If persistent sessions must be supported, the respective INVOCATION INTERCEPTOR would have to make sure the session data is loaded in beforeInvocation and also save potential changes in afterInvocation. In the example below, beforeInvocation handles the session using the session registry and afterInvocation does nothing. The sequence diagram shows two session-handling scenarios:

- The session does not yet exist. A session object is created, added to the session registry, then used for the invocation.

- A session object is found. It can therefore be obtained and used for the invocation.

In the sequence diagram, we see that the remote object instance can optionally interact with the session object. Here, we store and retrieve values from the session object. This requires the remote object to know the current session object. The INVOCATION INTERCEPTOR can be used to add this information to the invocation.

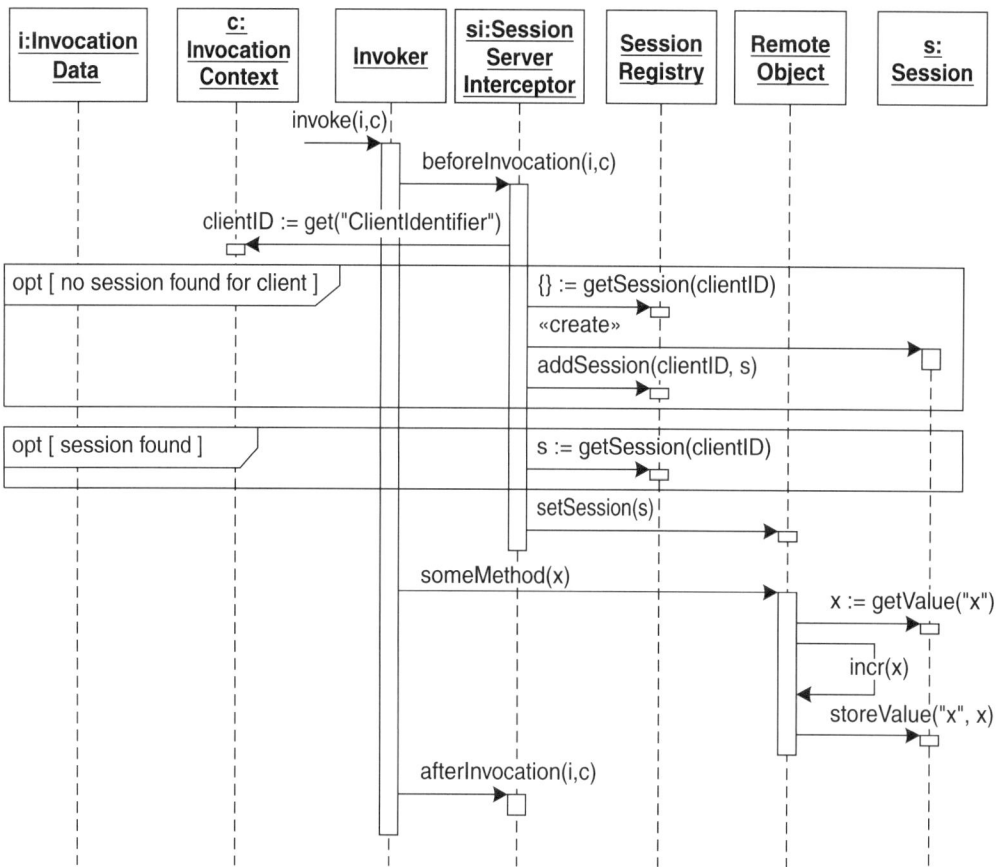

7 Extended Infrastructure Patterns

This chapter presents patterns that are used to implement advanced features of distributed object middleware. While they are part of the infrastructure, they are still visible and relevant to the developer who is using distributed object middleware.

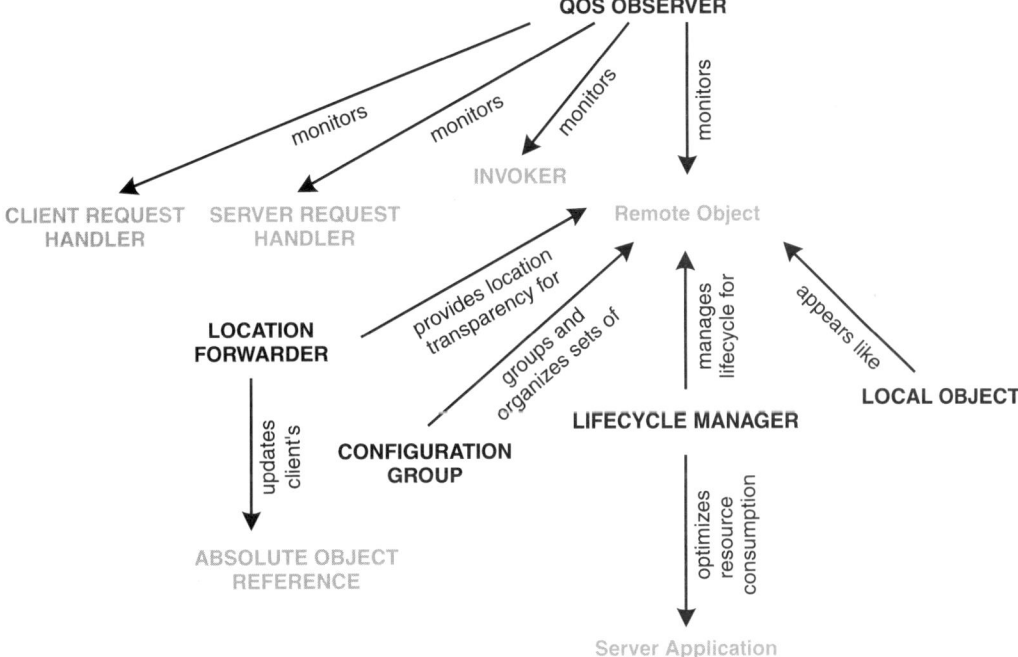

The LIFECYCLE MANAGER is responsible for managing the activation, deactivation, and other more advanced lifecycle issues of remote objects. It is based on the concept of separating remote objects from their servants, as introduced Chapter 5, *Lifecycle Management Patterns*.

CONFIGURATION GROUPS are used to configure the lifecycle, synchronization, and other properties of groups of remote objects.

QOS OBSERVERS are used to monitor service properties such as performance of various constituents of the system, such as the INVOKER, the SERVER REQUEST HANDLER, or even the remote objects themselves. QOS OBSERVERS help to ensure overall quality of service (QoS) constraints by properly tuning the distributed object middleware.

The LOCATION FORWARDER takes care of automatic forwarding of invocation messages to other server applications, for example if the target remote object has moved to another server application. A LOCATION FORWARDER can also update clients by returning a new ABSOLUTE OBJECT REFERENCE of the remote object, to be used instead of the original reference.

Distributed object middleware constituents that need to be accessed by application code appear as LOCAL OBJECTS. LOCAL OBJECTS are provided to simplify programming models by supporting the same parameter passing and other rules that are used for remote objects. However, LOCAL OBJECTS are not accessible remotely.

Lifecycle Manager

The server application has to manage different types of lifecycles for remote objects.

❊ ❊ ❊

The lifecycle of remote objects needs to be managed by server applications. Based on configuration, usage scenarios, and available resources, servants have to be instantiated, initialized, or destroyed. Most importantly, all this has to be coordinated.

The server application has to manage its resources efficiently. For example, it should ensure that only those servants of remote objects that are actually needed at a specific time are loaded into memory.

It is not only the creation and loading of servants that is expensive, but also their destruction and clean-up. Clean-up and destruction might involve invoking a destructor, releasing an ABSOLUTE OBJECT REFERENCE, invoking custom clean-up routines, and recycling servants using POOLING.

The lifecycle strategies should not be mixed with other parts of the distributed object middleware, as the strategies can become quite complex, but need to be highly configurable. Specifically, it should be possible for application developers to customize lifecycle strategies, or even implement their own lifecycle strategies.

Therefore:

Use a LIFECYCLE MANAGER to manage the lifecycle of remote objects and their servants. Let the LIFECYCLE MANAGER trigger lifecycle operations for servants of remote objects according to their configured lifecycle strategy. For servants that have to be aware of lifecycle events, provide *Lifecycle Callback* **operations [VSW02]. The LIFECYCLE MANAGER will use these operations to notify the servant of**

upcoming lifecycle events. This allows servants to prepare for the events accordingly.

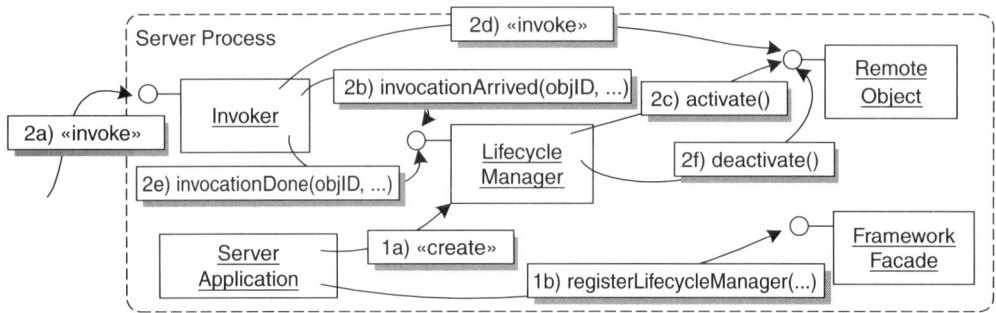

A LIFECYCLE MANAGER is typically created by the server application during start-up, and is registered with the distributed object middleware's INVOKER. Before an invocation is dispatched, the INVOKER informs the lifecycle manager. If the servant is not active, the LIFECYCLE MANAGER activates it. The INVOKER dispatches the invocation. After the invocation returns, the LIFECYCLE MANAGER is informed again and can deactivate the servant if required.

❊ ❊ ❊

The LIFECYCLE MANAGER enables modularization of the lifecycle strategies, including activation, PASSIVATION, POOLING, LEASING and eviction, as explained in Chapter 5, *Lifecycle Management Patterns*. Such strategies are important for optimization of performance, stability, and scalability.

The LIFECYCLE MANAGER, with its strategies, is either implemented as part of the INVOKER, or closely collaborates with it. If multiple different lifecycle strategies have to be provided, different LIFECYCLE MANAGERS can be available in the same server application.

The INVOKER triggers the LIFECYCLE MANAGER before and after each invocation. This allows the LIFECYCLE MANAGER to manage the creation, initialization, and destruction of servants.

For complex remote objects, for example those that have non-trivial state, it can become necessary to involve the servants in lifecycle management by informing them about upcoming lifecycle events. For this, the LIFECYCLE MANAGER invokes *Lifecycle Callback* operations implemented by the servant. For example, when using PASSIVATION, a remote object's state has to be saved to persistent storage before the servant is destroyed. After the servant has been resurrected, the servant has to reload its previously saved state. Both events are triggered by the LIFECYCLE MANAGER via *Lifecycle Callback* operations, just before the servant is passivated and just after resurrection.

Triggering the LIFECYCLE MANAGER can be hard-coded inside the INVOKER, but it can also be 'plugged in' using an INVOCATION INTERCEPTOR. Besides the synchronous involvement of the LIFECYCLE MANAGER when triggered by an INVOKER, a LIFECYCLE MANAGER implementation can also become active asynchronously, for example to scan for remote objects that should be destroyed because some lease has expired.

To decouple remote objects from servants, the LIFECYCLE MANAGER must maintain the association between OBJECT ID and servant. This mapping is either kept separately in the LIFECYCLE MANAGER or is reused from the INVOKER. Additionally, the LIFECYCLE MANAGER also has to store information about which lifecycle state each servant is in.

Besides all the advantages of decoupling lifecycle strategies from the INVOKER, the LIFECYCLE MANAGER also incurs a slight performance overhead, as it has to be invoked on every request of a remote object.

The LIFECYCLE MANAGER pattern applies the *Resource Lifecycle Manager* pattern [KJ04] to the management of remote objects. It integrates several existing patterns, such as *Activator* [Sta00] and *Evictor* [HV99].

Configuration Group

A server application manages remote objects that require similar configurations.

❊ ❊ ❊

In many applications remote objects need to be configured with various properties, such as quality of service (QoS), lifecycle management, or protocol support. Configuring such properties per server application is often not flexible enough, and configuring them separately for each individual remote object might lead to an implementation overhead.

The implementations of LIFECYCLE MANAGER, PROTOCOL PLUG-INS, MARSHALLER, and INVOCATION INTERCEPTORS need to be to be configured to support the way in which invocations are actually handled. Specifically, some remote objects might require different configurations of distributed object middleware constituents than other remote objects.

Configuring the framework constituents for each remote object separately is tedious, and incurs implementation and resource-usage overhead. For example, to configure the priorities of all remote objects in an embedded system, and to align those priorities, requires a lot of implementation effort. It is also hard to track the priorities that have been assigned.

A global configuration for the complete server application is usually not sufficient either. In a vehicle, for example, a brake control remote object will have to run at a higher priority than an air conditioning remote object, although both might be hosted by the same server application.

Therefore:

Provide CONFIGURATION GROUPS that group remote objects with common properties, for example the same QoS properties or the same lifecycle. A server application can have multiple CONFIGURATION GROUPS at the same time. Configuration properties for the

constituents, such as LIFECYCLE MANAGER, PROTOCOL PLUG-INS, and so on, are specified at the CONFIGURATION GROUP level.

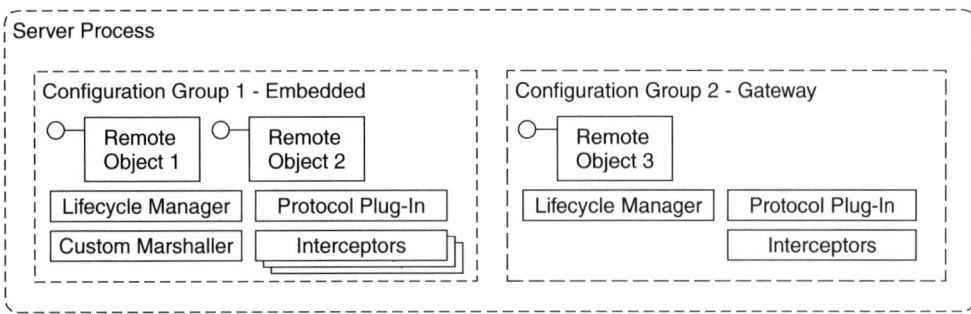

The figure depicts two CONFIGURATION GROUPS in a server application: one group for embedded objects and one group for gateway objects. The LIFECYCLE MANAGER, PROTOCOL PLUG-IN, MARSHALLER, and INVOCATION INTERCEPTORS are configured accordingly.

❊ ❊ ❊

Remote objects requiring the same configuration of the distributed object middleware, such as transaction support, pooling, or security checks, are registered with the same CONFIGURATION GROUP. The CONFIGURATION GROUP is set up in advance, before remote objects register with it and before invocations are dispatched to them.

The implementation of CONFIGURATION GROUPS is often tightly integrated with the SERVER REQUEST HANDLER and INVOKERS in distributed object middleware. This is necessary, because many properties, such as execution priority, invocation of INVOCATION INTERCEPTORS, or lifecycle management of remote objects, have to be configured at the proper dispatching level. Due to the configuration differences, distributed object middleware that supports CONFIGURATION GROUPS might have several differently-configured SERVER REQUEST HANDLERS and INVOKERS.

The configuration of the distributed object middleware constituents, such as INVOKER or LIFECYCLE MANAGER, can be simplified by associating the CONFIGURATION GROUP with each of them. The constituents are either statically configured with a configuration, or retrieve their configuration from the CONFIGURATION GROUP when the invocation is passed through them. The later approach avoids the need for multiple instances of the constituents, one for each configuration. Dynamic adaptation to configuration properties is especially effective if the constituents are implemented as chained INVOCATION INTERCEPTORS, because interceptors can easily be dynamically composed in different chains for different remote objects or groups of objects.

CONFIGURATION GROUPS are typically represented as LOCAL OBJECTS so that developers can configure them programmatically and eventually change configuration at runtime, disallowing remote access. A good way to maintain an overview of possible configurations is to organize CONFIGURATION GROUPS into hierarchies of CONFIGURATION GROUPS. To model commonalities, configurations may be inherited by child configurations from parent configurations, unless the child overwrites a configuration parameter with its own, more specific, values.

The collective configuration of remote objects via CONFIGURATION GROUPS eases administration and reduces the risk of incompatible configurations of remote objects.

However, if remote objects substantially differ in their required properties, so that many different CONFIGURATION GROUPS become necessary, CONFIGURATION GROUPS may cause additional complexity.

Local Object

The distributed object middleware needs to provide interfaces for constituents that need to be configured.

❋ ❋ ❋

To configure policies and parameters in distributed object framework constituents, such as PROTOCOL PLUG-INS, CONFIGURATION GROUPS, or LIFECYCLE MANAGERS, the application programmer must have access to their interfaces. The interfaces must not be accessible remotely, as they should only be configured by the server application developer. However, for consistency reasons, the interfaces should behave similarly to those of remote objects for parameter passing rules, memory management, and invocation syntax.

Many constituents of distributed object middleware need to be accessed and/or configured:

- The LIFECYCLE MANAGER must be configured with activation and eviction strategies.
- PROTOCOL PLUG-INS must be set and configured.
- CONFIGURATION GROUPS must be set up and remote objects registered.
- INVOCATION INTERCEPTORS must be created and set up.
- INVOCATION CONTEXT objects, such as the current transaction or a security context, must be accessible.

The interfaces of those constituents must not be accessible remotely, in order to avoid inconsistencies and privacy violations. The interfaces should behave like the interfaces of remote objects, so that the server application developer does not have to deal with two different programming models. For example, they should have the same parameter-passing semantics, they should be constructed the same way, and possibly even be registered/found using LOOKUP.

Therefore:

Provide LOCAL OBJECTS to allow application developers on both the client and server side to access configuration and status parameters of the distributed object middleware's constituents. Ensure that the

LOCAL OBJECTS adhere to the same parameter passing rules, memory management, and invocation syntax as remote objects. However, do not make them accessible remotely.

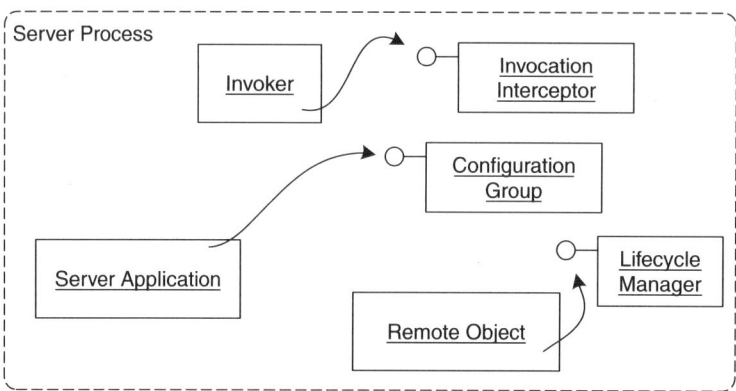

The server application and the implementations of remote objects access LOCAL OBJECTS as if they were remote objects.

❅ ❅ ❅

LOCAL OBJECTS make specific constituents of distributed object middleware, such as LIFECYCLE MANAGERS and PROTOCOL PLUG-INS, accessible for server application developers. Other constituents of the distributed object middleware are implemented as regular objects to which the application programmer has no access.

To avoid remote access, it is necessary to ensure that it is impossible to create ABSOLUTE OBJECT REFERENCES for LOCAL OBJECTS. Without the existence of ABSOLUTE OBJECT REFERENCES for LOCAL OBJECTS, remote clients are prevented from access to a LOCAL OBJECT.

LOCAL OBJECTS allow for a consistent programming model between remote objects and the distributed object middleware's internal constituents. For distributed object middleware systems that have to support several platforms and/or programming languages, LOCAL OBJECTS help to standardize APIs among the different implementations. APIs of LIFECYCLE MANAGERS, PROTOCOL PLUG-INS, and so on can be defined using the INTERFACE DESCRIPTION provided by the distributed object middleware. For example, an interface description language can be used for defining these constituents, and the standard language mapping can be used to define the programming language-dependent API.

QoS Observer

You want to control application-specific quality of service properties, such as bandwidth, response times, or priorities, when clients access remote objects.

❋ ❋ ❋

Distributed object middleware constituents, such as REQUEST HANDLERS, MARSHALLERS, PROTOCOL PLUG-INS, CONFIGURATION GROUPS, provide hooks to implement a wide variety of quality of service characteristics. Applications might want to react to changes in the quality of service currently provided. The application-specific code to react to such changes should be decoupled from the middleware itself.

Consider a situation in which response times need to be guaranteed to clients. The response time is determined, for example, by the available network bandwidth, the network traffic, and the load on the server application. To ensure that the required response times are met, a reasonable strategy is to stop accepting requests from new clients when the response time reaches a certain threshold. To do this, you need to be able to monitor the (average) response time and decline further clients if the quality of service deteriorates.

To be able to react to QoS changes, monitoring of quality of service characteristics is usually necessary. Because the QoS thresholds and the object's reactions are typically application-specific, QoS monitoring functionality should be accessible and configurable by application developers.

Therefore:

Provide hooks in the distributed object middleware constituents where application developers can register QOS OBSERVERS. The observers are informed about relevant quality of service parameters, such as message sizes, invocation counts, or execution times. Since the QOS OBSERVERS are application specific, they can contain code to react appropriately if service quality gets worse.

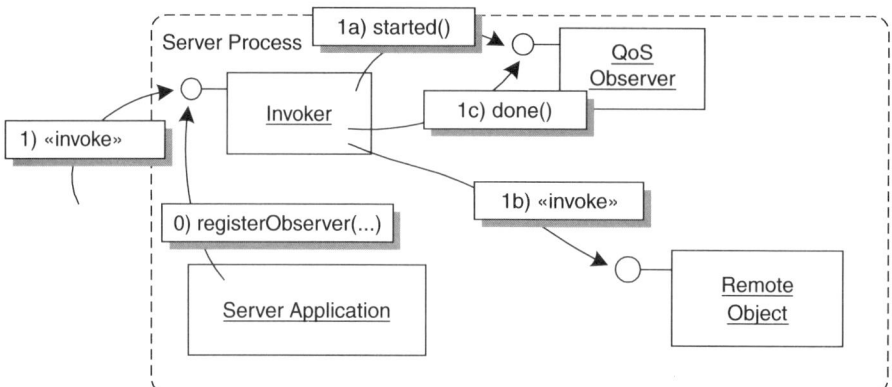

On start-up, QOS OBSERVER implementations are registered with the INVOKER, or any other relevant framework constituent. The INVOKER notifies the QOS OBSERVERS of the start and end of each invocation. The QOS OBSERVERS can obtain relevant invocation data, such as duration and size, from the constituent with which it is registered.

❄ ❄ ❄

On start-up application-specific QOS OBSERVERS are registered with the constituents whose quality of service they should observe. Typical candidates are CLIENT and SERVER REQUEST HANDLER, MARSHALLER, PROTOCOL PLUG-IN, INVOKER, REQUESTOR, and LIFECYCLE MANAGER. The framework constituents report events, such as invocation start/invocation end, connection establishment, incoming invocations, return of invocation, marshaling started/ended. Configuration of the constituents should be done per CONFIGURATION GROUP. Triggered by the events, the QOS OBSERVERS check execution time, size, or other QoS characteristics.

The respective middleware constituents need to provide an API so that QOS OBSERVERS can query for additional relevant information. For example, the QOS OBSERVER might need to know which operation has been requested in the current request, or how large the message for the invocation actually was.

To minimize the performance overhead, it is important to ensure that the QOS OBSERVERS are only notified about changes for which they have registered.

The QOS OBSERVER allows relevant QoS properties to be monitored and reaction to events triggered by them. Applications benefit from observing QoS properties, as they can better adapt and react to critical situations.

QOS OBSERVERS are typically LOCAL OBJECTS. INVOCATION INTERCEPTORS can be used to implement specific quality of service observations, such as operation invocation times. Be aware that the monitoring and handling of QoS properties might influence the actual observations.

Location Forwarder

Invocations of remote objects arrive at the INVOKER and the INVOKER should dispatch them.

❋ ❋ ❋

Remote objects might be located in a different server application than the one at which the invocation arrives. Reasons for this could be that remote objects are put onto multiple servers to achieve load balancing or fault tolerance, or that the remote objects were moved to other server applications. The invocations should reach the correct remote object transparently, even if it exists in another server application.

The lifetime of server applications can be very long – some are expected never to shut down, even though the world around them changes. The deployment of remote objects can change, for example because of resource shortage in the original server application, but existing ABSOLUTE OBJECT REFERENCES should stay valid and the invocation should still reach the target remote object.

Further, scalable and highly available distributed applications rely on load balancing and fault tolerance mechanisms:

- To achieve load balancing, typically remote objects are replicated so that the same requests can be served by multiple instances. It is necessary to coordinate the invocations of these instances. How can you delegate requests to multiple instances, while making the client believe it communicates with only one instance?

- One way to achieve fault tolerance, especially in the case of hardware faults, is to replicate remote objects and distribute them over several nodes. The replicated objects form a group of remote objects that all implement the same functionality. How can you make the invocation of such a group look as if only one remote object exists?

The general problem is that server applications have to collaborate when remote objects do not reside at the location to which the ABSOLUTE OBJECT REFERENCE points, either because they have been moved or aggregated.

Therefore:

For remote objects that the INVOKER cannot resolve locally, make a LOCATION FORWARDER forward invocations to the remote object in another server applications. The LOCATION FORWARDER looks up the actual location of the remote object based on its OBJECT ID. The result of this lookup is an ABSOLUTE OBJECT REFERENCE of another remote object. The LOCATION FORWARDER has two options: either it sends the client-side distributed object middleware an update notification about the new location, so that the client can retry the invocation on the new location, or it transparently forwards the invocation to the new location.

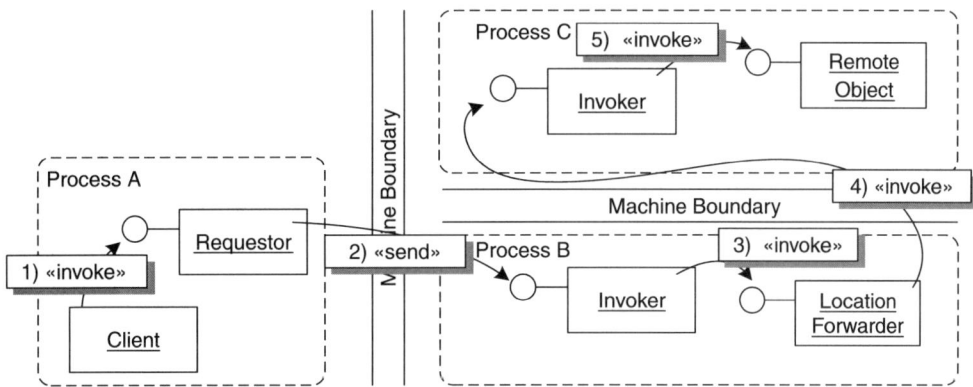

A client invokes an operation on a remote object. Because the instance has moved from one server application to another, the LOCATION FORWARDER forwards the invocation to the server application where the remote object currently resides.

❄ ❄ ❄

When a client performs an invocation using a particular ABSOLUTE OBJECT REFERENCE to a server application, the invocation will reach the INVOKER. If the INVOKER cannot resolve the target remote object locally, the INVOKER can delegate the invocation to a LOCATION FORWARDER. The LOCATION FORWARDER looks up the new location, represented as an ABSOLUTE OBJECT REFERENCE based on the OBJECT ID. The behavior that occurs after the new location has been resolved depends on the use case.

The following list explains variants of location forwarding, based on the scenarios mentioned above:

- If remote objects are moved to another server application, let the LOCATION FORWARDER inform the client of the move. Forwarding the invocation transparently to the new location would increase the load of the local server application, as it would have to perform this forwarding permanently. It is better therefore to let the client know of the move, so that it can send subsequent invocations directly to the new location.

- For the purpose of load balancing, the LOCATION FORWARDER acts as a load dispatcher. The LOCATION FORWARDER looks up the ABSOLUTE OBJECT REFERENCES to a set of remote objects and redirects the invocation to one of those remote objects. Inside the LOCATION FORWARDER, different load balancing algorithms can be applied, such as round robin or smallest number of clients. Again, the LOCATION FORWARDER can become a bottleneck if all invocations are routed through it. To avoid this, let the LOCATION FORWARDER update the client to distribute the load equally over the available instances.

- In the case of fault-tolerant systems, the LOCATION FORWARDER can act as part of the coordinator of an *Object Group* [Maf96], and thus forward invocations to all remote objects in the *Object Group*. The LOCATION FORWARDER does not update the client location unless a new coordinator for an *Object Group* is determined, in which case the client is updated with a reference to the new coordinator. In the same way, the LOCATION FORWARDER can be used as a distributor unit in the patterns *Fail-Stop Processor* [Sar02] and *Active Replication* [Sar02].

- A special case is the internal failure of a remote object, in which case the LOCATION FORWARDER should either update the client with the location of a working remote object of the same type, or forward the invocations until the failed remote object is repaired.

Using a LOCATION FORWARDER has the advantage that the deployment of a distributed application can be hidden from clients. This reduces the complexity from a client perspective and eases overall maintainability. ABSOLUTE OBJECT REFERENCES that clients have once obtained stay valid, even if the deployment of the remote object changes.

As with every additional level of indirection, the LOCATION FORWARDER incurs a performance overhead and increases the risk of failure. In the case of load balancing, a failed load dispatcher causes the complete distributed application to fail. A typical solution to this is the replication of the load dispatcher at a lower level, for example at the level of IP routing.

It can become confusing for developers of client applications if the location of a remote object is constantly updated. Optimizations that make assumptions about the location of the remote object become useless, as the remote object might have moved anywhere.

This pattern enables fault-tolerant systems to be built. A pattern language on this topic can be found in [Sar02, Sar03] – see Chapter 13, *Related Concepts, Technologies, and Patterns*.

Interactions among the patterns

First, let us look at the LIFECYCLE MANAGER. For illustrative purposes, we will show how persistent state can be realized for remote objects in combination with POOLING. In the following example we assume that the developers of the server application have configured the distributed object middleware to use a custom developed LIFECYCLE MANAGER. Note that these interactions are just examples of how the patterns can be implemented – many other alternatives exist.

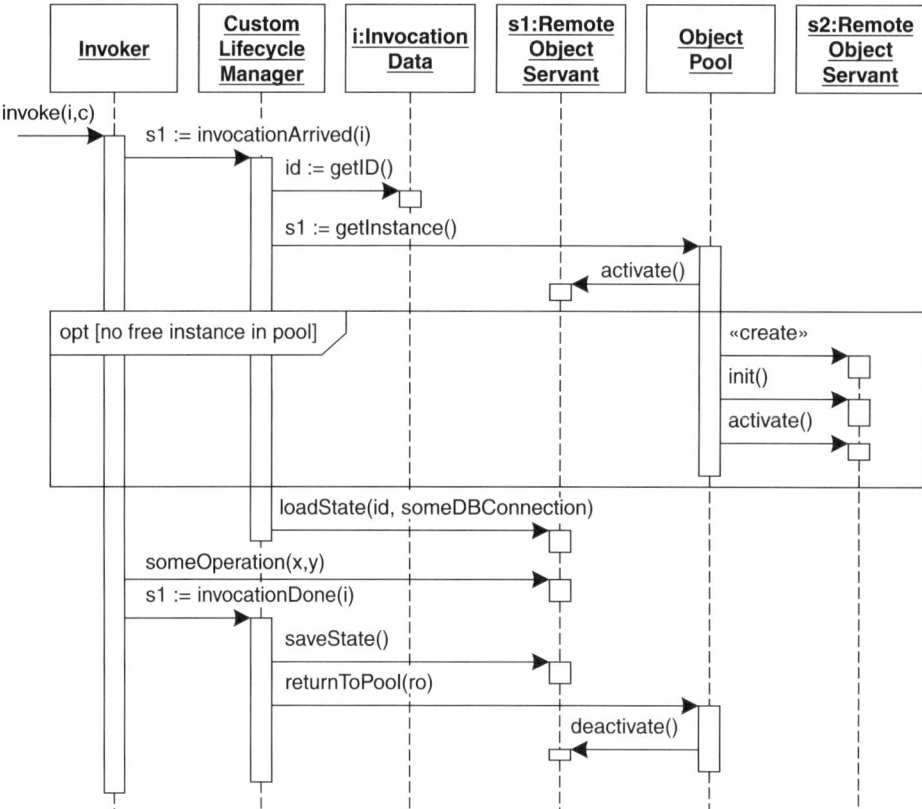

In the figure above the LIFECYCLE MANAGER obtains a servant from a pool of servants. After the servant is activated (or optionally created lazily), the state associated with the given OBJECT ID is loaded from persistent storage. The operation is executed, and finally the state of the remote object is passivated and the servant is put back into the pool.

Remote object servants that are to be used with this LIFECYCLE MANAGER need to implement up to five lifecycle operations [VSW02]: init, activate, and deactivate to be compatible with POOLING, and loadState and saveState to be compatible with the persistent state handling used by PASSIVATION.

Next we look at a possible scenario for CONFIGURATION GROUPS. Let us first look at how a server application sets up two CONFIGURATION GROUPS. One contains a LIFECYCLE MANAGER that uses pooling, whereas the other contains a persistency LIFECYCLE MANAGER, as well as a transaction INVOCATION INTERCEPTOR to make the persistency accesses transactional. For each of the CONFIGURATION GROUPS the group object has first to be instantiated. Next, INVOCATION INTERCEPTORS and LIFECYCLE MANAGERS for the group have to be created and registered. Finally, the group has itself to be registered with a group registry of the distributed object middleware.

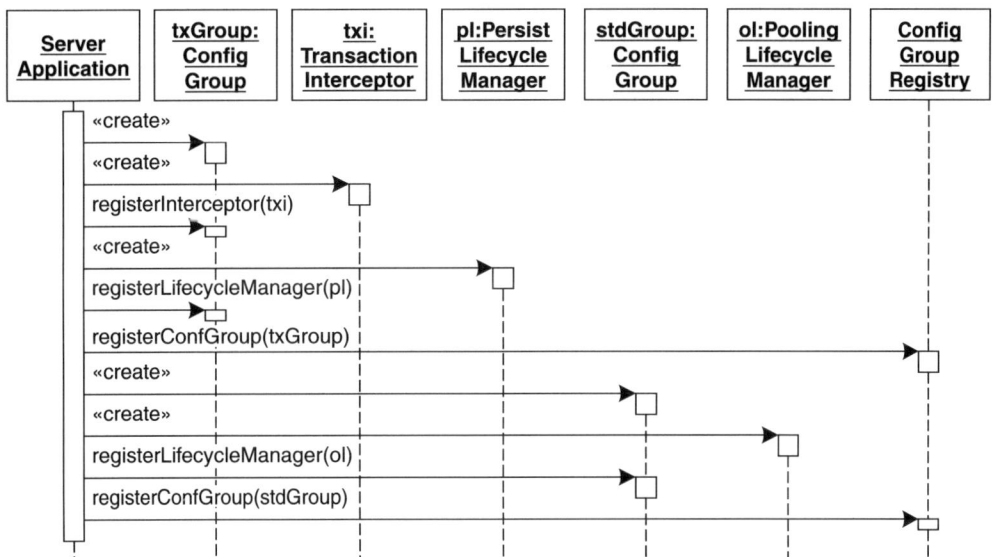

In the next step we have to create a set of remote objects and register them with the CONFIGURATION GROUPS.

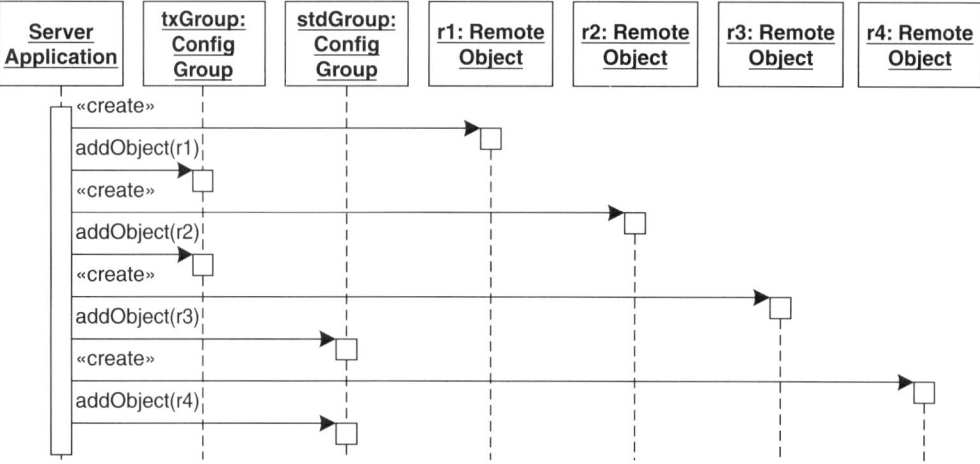

Now invocations can be handled by objects in the CONFIGURATION GROUP. In the next diagram we show how the invocation proceeds when using different CONFIGURATION GROUPS. We can see that the INVOKER first looks up the CONFIGURATION GROUP. Based on this group, the LIFECYCLE MANAGER is chosen, as well as the INVOCATION INTERCEPTORS. In the example the persistency group is chosen (txGroup). This causes the persistency interceptor and LIFECYCLE MANAGER to manage persistency of the remote object instance.

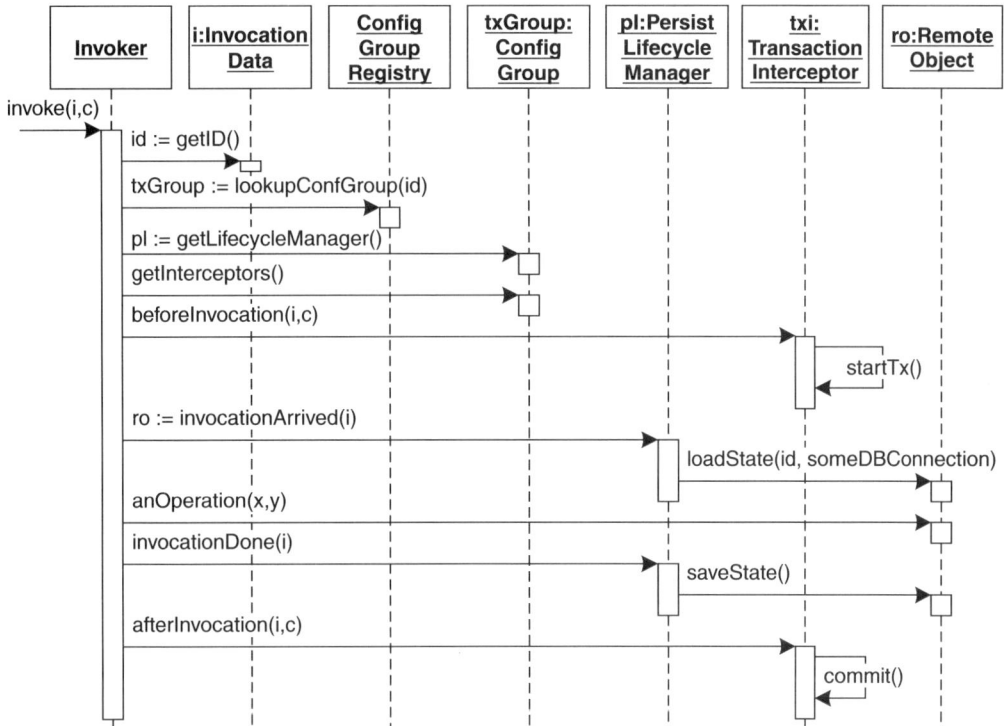

8 Invocation Asynchrony Patterns

This chapter deals with asynchronous invocations. Asynchronous invocations, in contrast to synchronous invocations, decouple the client from the server application. The client does not have to wait for the reply to arrive, and resumes its work imfmediately after a remote invocation is sent.

Asynchrony is often dictated by performance and throughput optimizations. By making use of the inherent asynchrony of most communication channels, developers can optimize their applications. Clients can continue with other work while waiting for replies to earlier invocations.

In particular we present the following four patterns in this chapter:

- FIRE AND FORGET describes best-effort delivery semantics for asynchronous operations that have void return types.
- SYNC WITH SERVER is similar to FIRE AND FORGET, as it also works only for void return types, but the client is notified about the successful delivery of the invocation to the server application.
- POLL OBJECTS provide clients with the means to query the distributed object middleware about whether an asynchronous reply to the request has arrived, and if so, to obtain the return value.
- RESULT CALLBACK actively notifies the requesting client of the returning result.

The figure below gives an overview of the interactions of the four invocation asynchrony patterns.

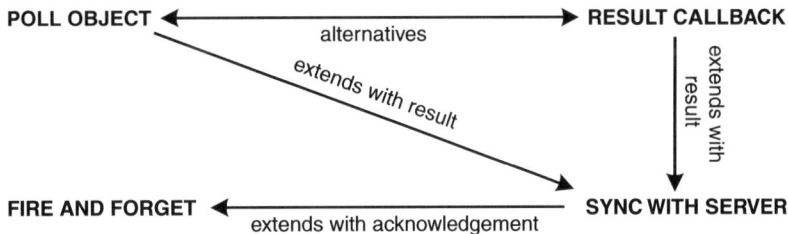

The following table illustrates the alternatives for applying the patterns. It distinguishes whether or not a result is sent to the client, whether or not the client receives an acknowledgement, and, if a result is sent to the client, whether it is the client's responsiblity to obtain the result, or whether it is informed using a callback.

	Acknowledgement to client	Result to client	Responsibility for result
FIRE AND FORGET	no	no	-
SYNC WITH SERVER	yes	no	-
POLL OBJECT	yes	yes	Client is responsible for obtaining the result.
RESULT CALLBACK	yes	yes	Client is informed via callback.

SYNC WITH SERVER should be applied when message delivery needs to be more reliable than it is with FIRE AND FORGET, although the invocation will still be unreliable compared, for example, to messaging protocols (see Chapter 13, *Related Concepts, Technologies, and Patterns*). The increased reliability is achieved by sending an acknowledgement back to the client on receipt of the request from the server. POLL OBJECT and RESULT CALLBACK not only provide an acknowledgement of receipt of the request, but also send back a reply. These two patterns therefore acknowledge implicitly that the request has been processed.

- POLL OBJECT should be used when the result must be processed by the same thread that sent out the request, but not immediately after arrival.
- In contrast, RESULT CALLBACK should be used when it is required to react on the result immediately after the arrival of the reply.

Fire and Forget

The server application provides remote objects with operations that neither have a return value nor report exceptions.

❋ ❋ ❋

In many situations a client application needs to invoke an operation on a remote object merely to notify the remote object of an event. The client does not expect a return value. Reliability of the invocation is not critical, as the invocation is used merely as a notification.

Consider a simple logging service implemented as a remote object. Clients use it to record log messages. Recording of log messages must not influence the execution of the client. For example, an invocation of the logging service must not block. Loss of individual log messages is acceptable.

Such a scenario is quite typical for distributed implementations of patterns such as *Model-View-Controller* [BMR+96] or *Observer* [GHJV95], especially if the view or observer is notified constantly and old data is stale data.

Therefore:

Provide FIRE AND FORGET operations. When invoked, the REQUESTOR sends the invocation across the network, returning control to the calling client immediately. The client does not receive any acknowledgement from the invocation of the operation either for success or failure.

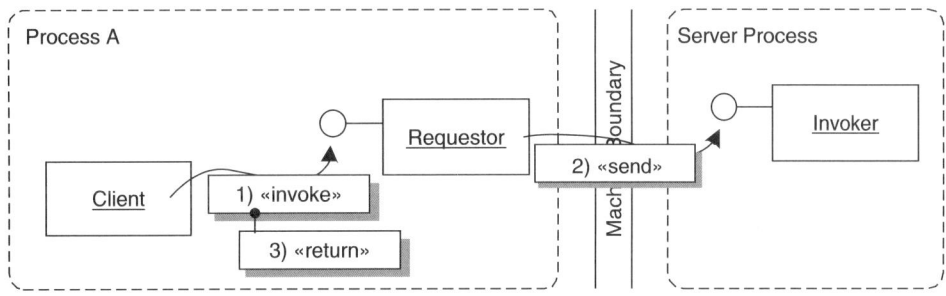

When the client invokes a FIRE AND FORGET operation, the REQUESTOR marshals the parameters and sends them to the server.

❋ ❋ ❋

The implementation of a FIRE AND FORGET operation can be done in several ways. For example:

- The REQUESTOR can put the bytes on the wire in the caller's thread, assuming the send operation does not block. Asynchronous I/O operations, supported by some operating systems, are of great help here to avoid blocking.

- Alternatively, the REQUESTOR can spawn a new thread that puts the bytes on the wire independently of the thread that invoked the remote operation. This variant also works when the send operation temporarily blocks. However, this variant has some drawbacks: it works only as long as the application does not get bogged down – from the operating system perspective – due to huge numbers of such threads, and as long as the existence of such threads does not overwhelm the underlying marshaling, protocol, and transport implementations due to things like lock contention. Another drawback of concurrent invocations is that an older invocation may bypass a more recent one.

As FIRE AND FORGET operations do not have to be reliably transported, an option is to use unreliable protocols such as UDP for their implementation. UDP is much cheaper than reliable protocols such as TCP.

The server-side distributed object middleware, primarily the INVOKER, differentiates between operations that do not require a reply, such as FIRE AND FORGET operations, and synchronous operations that do require a reply. For synchronous operations a reply is sent even if it has no return value.

When the remote invocation is performed in a separate thread, a thread pool can be used instead of spawning a new thread for each invocation, to avoid thread creation overhead.

If the distributed object middleware does not provide FIRE AND FORGET operations, the client application can emulate such behavior by spawning a thread itself and performing the invocation in that newly-created thread. Be aware, however, that such an emulation heavily influences scalability. In particular, many concurrent requests lead to many concurrent threads, decreasing overall system performance.

The benefit of the FIRE AND FORGET pattern is the asynchrony it provides compared to synchronous invocations. Client and remote object are decoupled, in the sense that the remote object executes independently of the client and the client does not block during the invocation. This means the pattern is very helpful in event-driven applications that do not rely on a continuous control flow or on return values. Further, it is important that the applications do not rely on successful transmission.

REMOTING ERRORS during the sending of the invocation to the remote object, or errors that were raised during the execution of the remote invocation, cannot be reported back to the client. The client is unaware of whether the invocation is executed successfully by the remote object. FIRE AND FORGET therefore usually has only 'best effort' semantics. The correctness of the application must not depend on the reliability of a FIRE AND FORGET operation invocation. To cope with this uncertainty, especially in situations in which the client expects some kind of action, clients typically use timeouts to trigger compensating actions.

Sync with Server

The server application provides remote objects with operations that neither have a return value nor report exceptions.

❋ ❋ ❋

FIRE AND FORGET is a useful but extreme solution, in the sense that it can only be used if the client can really afford to take the risk of not noticing that a remote invocation has not reached the targeted remote object. The other extreme is a synchronous invocation, in which a client is blocked until the remote method has executed successfully and the result returned. Sometimes a balance between these extremes is needed.

Consider a system that stores images in a database. The images are filtered before the images are stored in the database, for example using a Fourier transformation, which may take a long time. The client is not interested in the result of the transformation, only in a notification that it has been delivered as a message to the server. The client therefore does not need to block and wait for the result – it can continue executing as soon as the invocation has reached the remote object.

In this scenario the client only has to ensure that the invocation containing the image is transmitted successfully. From that point onwards it is the responsibility of the server application to ensure that the image is processed correctly and stored safely in the database.

Therefore:

Provide SYNC WITH SERVER semantics for remote invocations. The client sends the invocation, as in FIRE AND FORGET, but waits for a reply from the server application informing it about the successful reception (but *not* the execution) of the invocation. After the reply is received by the REQUESTOR, it returns control to the client and execution continues. The server application executes the invocation independently.

Sync with Server

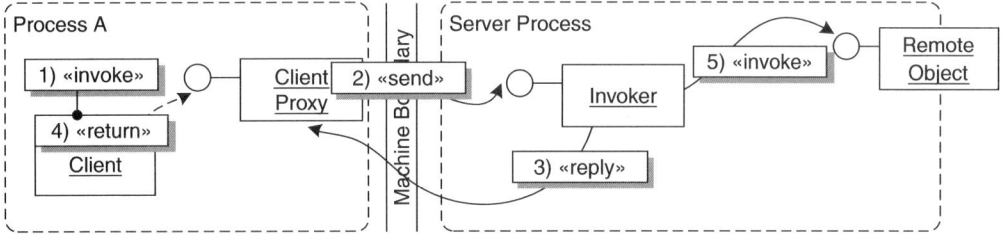

A client invokes a remote operation. The REQUESTOR puts the bytes of the invocation on the wire, as in FIRE AND FORGET, but then waits for a reply from the server application as an acknowledgment that the invocation has been received by the server.

In the SYNC WITH SERVER pattern, as in FIRE AND FORGET, no return value or out parameters of the remote operation are sent back to the client. The reply sent by the server application is only to inform the REQUESTOR about successful reception of the request.

If the distributed object middleware supports SYNC WITH SERVER operations, the SERVER REQUEST HANDLER can send an acknowledgment message immediately after reception of the invocation. Alternatively, if only synchronous invocations are supported, SYNC WITH SERVER can be emulated at the application level inside the operations of the remote object. The operation of the remote object spawns a new thread that performs the actual invocation, while the INVOKER thread that initially invoked the operation returns immediately and returns an acknowledgement back to the client.

Compared with FIRE AND FORGET, SYNC WITH SERVER operations ensure successful transmission, and thus make remote invocations more reliable. However, SYNC WITH SERVER incurs additional latency – the client has to wait until the reply from the server application arrives.

Note that the REQUESTOR can inform the client of system errors, such as failed transmission of the invocation. However, it cannot inform clients about application errors during the remote invocation in the remote object, because this happens asynchronously after the acknowledgement has already been sent to the server.

Poll Object

Invocations of remote objects must execute asynchronously, and the client depends on the results for further computations.

❄ ❄ ❄

There are situations in which an application needs to invoke an operation asynchronously, but still needs to know the results of the invocation. The client does not necessarily need the results immediately to continue its execution, and can decide for itself when to use the returned results.

Consider a client that needs to prepare a complex XML document to be stored in a relational database accessed through a remote object. The document should have an unique ID: this is generated by the database system. Typically a client would request an ID from the database, wait for the result, create the rest of the XML document, then forward the complete document to the remote object for storage in the database. A more efficient implementation would be to request the ID from the database first. Without waiting for the ID, the client can prepare the XML document, receive the result of the ID query, put it into the document, then forward the whole document to the remote object for storage.

In general, a client application should be able to make use of even short periods of latency, instead of blocking until a result arrives.

Therefore:

Provide POLL OBJECTS that receive the results of remote invocations on behalf of the client. The client subsequently uses the POLL OBJECT to query the result. It can either just query ('poll') whether the result is available, or it can block on the POLL OBJECT until the result becomes available. As long as the result remains unavailable from the POLL OBJECT, the client can continue with other tasks asynchronously.

Poll Object

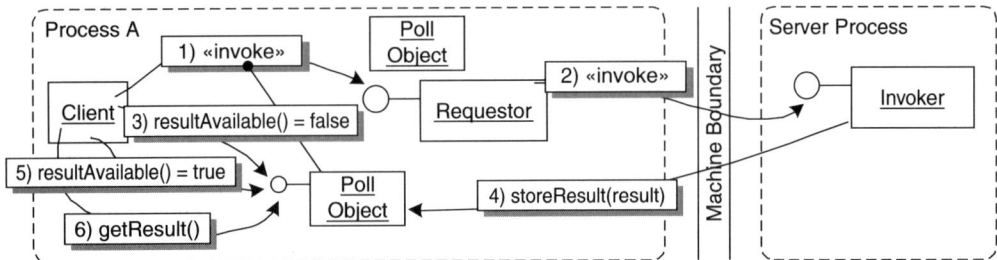

A client invokes a remote operation on the REQUESTOR, which in turn creates a POLL OBJECT to be returned to the client immediately. As long as the remote invocation has not returned, the 'result available' operation of the POLL OBJECT returns false. When the result becomes available, it is memorized in the POLL OBJECT. When it is next polled it returns true, and the client can fetch the result by calling the 'get result' operation.

❊ ❊ ❊

The POLL OBJECT has to provide at least two operations: one to check whether the result is available, the other to actually return the result to the calling client. Besides this client interface, an operation for storing the result received from the server is needed.

Most POLL OBJECT implementations also provide a blocking operation that allows clients to wait for the availability of the result if they choose to do so. The core idea of this pattern follows the *Futures* concept described in [Lea99], but POLL OBJECT extends it to distributed settings and allows the availability of the result to be queried in a non-blocking fashion – whereas with *Futures* this query would block.

POLL OBJECTS typically depend on the interface of the remote object. That is, the client requires a POLL OBJECT that offers the out parameters and return values of the remote object's operations. There are three options in the design of POLL OBJECTS:

- A separate POLL OBJECT type is provided for each remote operation. That is, the number of POLL OBJECT types for one remote object equals the number of remote operations of the remote object.

- One POLL OBJECT type is provided per remote object, and the operation to get the result must be provided for each of the remote object's operations, offering the out parameters and return values of that remote operation.
- A generic POLL OBJECT type is provided offering a 'get result' operation with a generic type, such as C's void* or Java's Object. It is the client's burden to provide the correct type conversions. In this variant static type checks are not possible.

Use POLL OBJECTS when the time until the result is received is expected to be relatively short, but long enough to allow the client to use the time for other computations. For longer wait periods, especially if the period cannot be estimated, use a RESULT CALLBACK. This is because it is hard to manage a potentially large number of POLL OBJECTS over a long period. A number of 'small' programming tasks would be required between the polls, and polling would have to be triggered constantly. This constant triggering can be avoid by using RESULT CALLBACKS.

POLL OBJECTS offer the benefit that the client application does not have to use an event-driven, completely asynchronous programming model, as is the case with RESULT CALLBACK, but can still make use of asynchrony.

From an implementation perspective, the CLIENT REQUEST HANDLER typically marks the invocation with an *Asynchronous Completion Token* [SSRB00], sends the invocation, and associates the POLL OBJECT with the *Asynchronous Completion Token*. When the reply returns, the client-side distributed object middleware dispatches the result to the corresponding POLL OBJECT, on which the client polls. Using *Asynchronous Completion Tokens* requires the server application to return the *Asynchronous Completion Token*, contained in the request, in the reply.

When using POLL OBJECTS, the client has to be changed slightly to do the polling. POLL OBJECTS either need to be generic, which typically requires programming language support, or they have to be specific to the remote object and its interface operations. In the latter case they are typically code-generated. More dynamic environments can use runtime means to create the types for POLL OBJECTS.

Result Callback

The server application provides remote objects with operations that have return values and/or may return errors. The result of the invocation is handled asynchronously.

❋ ❋ ❋

The client needs to be informed actively about results of asynchronously-invoked operations on a remote object. That is, if the result becomes available to the REQUESTOR, the client wants to be informed immediately, so that it can react on the availability of the result. In the meantime the client executes concurrently.

Consider an image-processing example. A client posts images to a remote object, specifying how the images should be processed. When the remote object has finished processing the image, it is available for download and is displayed subsequently on the client. The result of the processing operation is the URL from which the image can be downloaded. A typical client may have several images to process at the same time, and processing will take different times for each image, depending on image size and the calculations to be performed.

In such situations a client does not want to wait until an image has been processed before it submits the next. However, the client is interested in the result of the operation so that it can download the result promptly.

Therefore:

Provide a callback-based interface for remote invocations on the client. Upon an invocation, the client passes a RESULT CALLBACK object to the REQUESTOR. The invocation returns immediately after sending the invocation to the server. When the result is available, the distributed object middleware invokes a predefined operation on the RESULT CALLBACK object, passing it the result of the invocation.

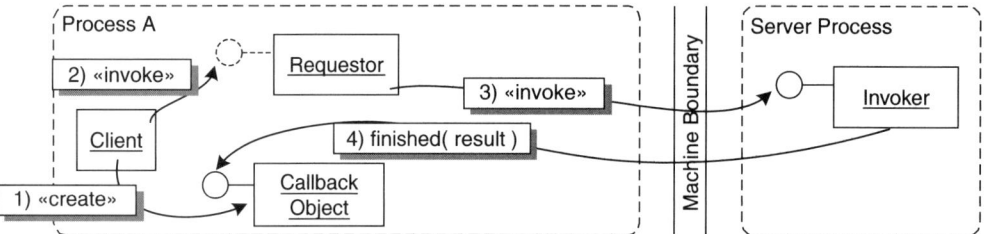

The client instantiates a callback object and invokes the operation on the REQUESTOR. When the result of the remote invocation returns, it is dispatched by the distributed object middleware to the callback object, calling a pre-defined callback method.

You can use the same or separate callback objects for each invocation of the same type. The correct callback object has to be identified somehow, however. There are different ways to implement this, although which works best depends on the application:

- When you want to use the same callback objects, you need an *Asynchronous Completion Token* [SSRB00] to associate the callback with the original invocation. An *Asynchronous Completion Token* contains information that identifies the callback object and the method responsible for handling the reply uniquely.
- In cases in which a separate callback object is used for each invocation, replies to requests do not need to be demultiplexed further among callback objects, so no *Asynchronous Completion Token* is necessary.

RESULT CALLBACKS allow the client to react immediately to the results of asynchronous invocations. As in the case of POLL OBJECT, the server application has nothing to do with the specifics of result handling in the client. The use of RESULT CALLBACKS requires an event-driven application design, whereas POLL OBJECTS allow a synchronous programming model to be used.

The RESULT CALLBACK pattern also incurs the liability that client code, namely the code doing the original asynchronous invocation and the code associated with the RESULT CALLBACK, is often executed concurrently in multiple thread contexts. The client code therefore needs to be prepared for that, for example when accessing shared resources. To dispatch replies to callback objects, the client side distributed object middleware needs an separate thread besides the client's thread invoking the original invocation.

Typical implementations require the client to provide a callback object as a remote object, which is registered with the client-side distributed object middleware on invocation of an asynchronous operation. There are two implementation options:

- The *client-side* distributed object middleware invokes the callback object when the result of the operation arrived.
- The *server-side* distributed object middleware invokes the callback object, typically using a new connection that sends an independent reply message.

In the second case, the client has to become a server as well, as it has to accept invocations on the callback object. The remote callback can become a problem in configurations in which a firewall exists between client and server: callback invocations using a new connection for the callback might get blocked by the firewall. The use of bidirectional connections is therefore advisable to allow requests to flow in both directions without requiring new connections.

The major difference between POLL OBJECT and RESULT CALLBACK is that RESULT CALLBACKS require an event-driven design, whereas POLL OBJECTS allow large parts of the client be written using a synchronous execution model, thus hiding the subtleties of asynchrony from the developer.

Interactions among the patterns

The patterns described in this chapter – FIRE AND FORGET, SYNC WITH SERVER, POLL OBJECT, and RESULT CALLBACK – are alternatives for synchronous (or blocking) invocations. In many distributed object middleware systems, more than one of them is supported, and it is the task of the developer to select the proper asynchrony pattern for the application.

Note that changing the invocation variant used in a client application usually requires changing the client code as well. The patterns cannot therefore simply be exchanged as *Strategies* [GHJV95]. This is mainly due to the fact that the different invocation alternatives require different code for result handling (blocking for the result, ignoring the result, polling the result, or event-based reaction to callback events). Such differences sometimes require major changes in the client code. For example, to convert a complex blocking client to an invocation model based on RESULT CALLBACKS is not a trivial task. It requires implementing an event model and an event loop, and breaking down complex operations into sequences of subsequent callbacks. If the callbacks can execute in parallel, some mechanism for synchronizing incoming results might also be required. Such differences between an event-based programming model and conventional, blocking invocations are one of the motivations behind the use of POLL OBJECTS – they provide a form of asynchrony, while keeping the program sequential in nature.

The following sequence diagrams show the different asynchronous invocation patterns in more detail. Let's start with FIRE AND FORGET. The first sequence diagram shows how FIRE AND FORGET can be implemented using asynchronous network facilities. We can see an ordinary client-side invocation, but instead of waiting for the result, the CLIENT REQUEST HANDLER returns directly to the client.

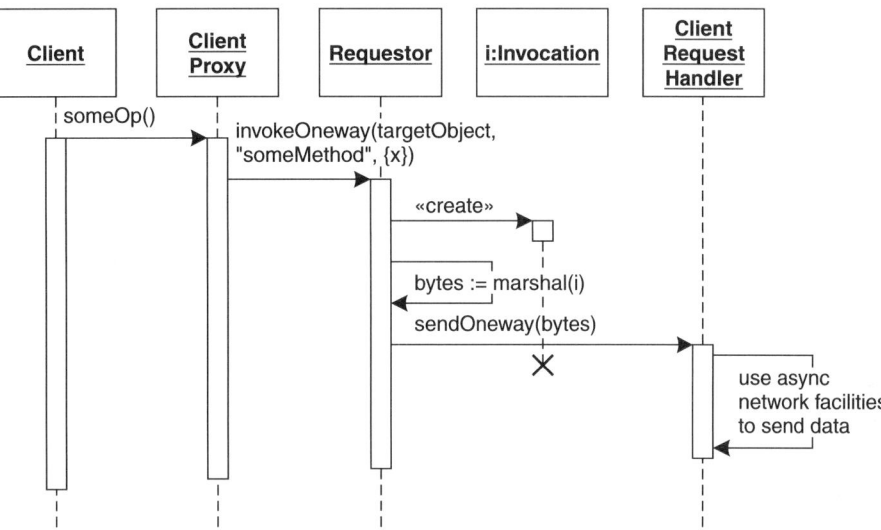

Alternatively, the client can use multithreading to implement FIRE AND FORGET operations. The invocation of the REQUESTOR returns immediately, while a separate thread performs the invocation. Decoupling between the client thread and the invocation thread must not be done at the level of the REQUESTOR, but can be implemented at the level of the CLIENT REQUEST HANDLER. Note that the additional thread incurs some overhead, which might become problematic if a large number of FIRE

AND FORGET operations are sent at the same time. The following diagram shows this variant.

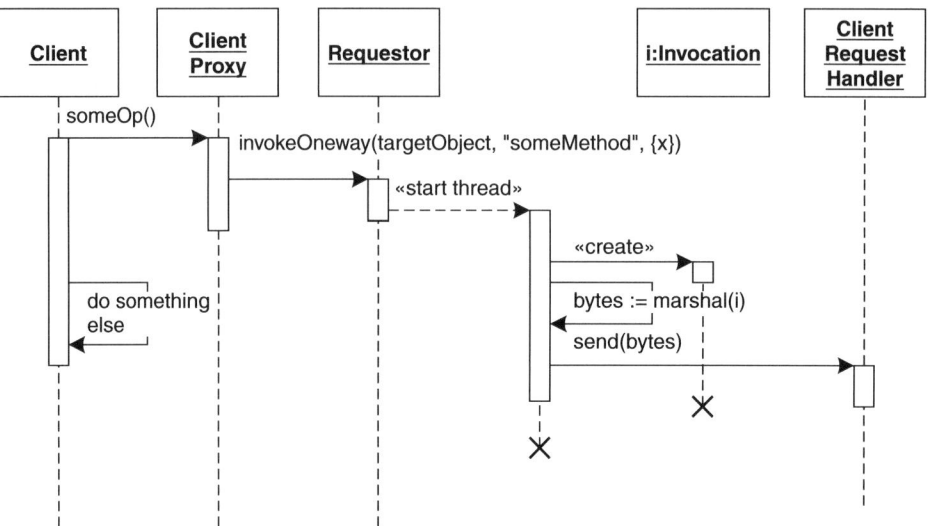

The next sequence diagram shows an example of SYNC WITH SERVER. Again there are two variants, one using network facilities and the other using multithreading, although now on the server side.

We show both alternatives in turn, starting with the variant that uses network facilities. In this case we carry out a normal synchronous method invocation. However, the CLIENT REQUEST HANDLER only waits until an acknowledgement from the SERVER REQUEST HANDLER is sent – the invocation has not yet been dispatched to the remote object.

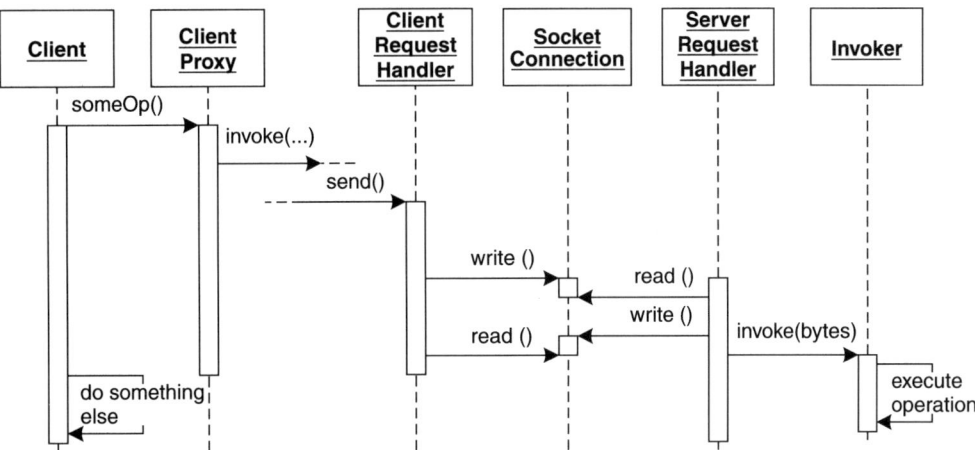

The second alternative uses a separate thread within the server application, here illustrated inside the INVOKER. In this case, the invocation data sent over the network has to have a flag that instructs the INVOKER to execute the operation asynchronously. This flag is not shown in the diagrams. This allows a synchronous acknowledgement to be received, but the invocation is performed asynchronously without making the client wait for a result.

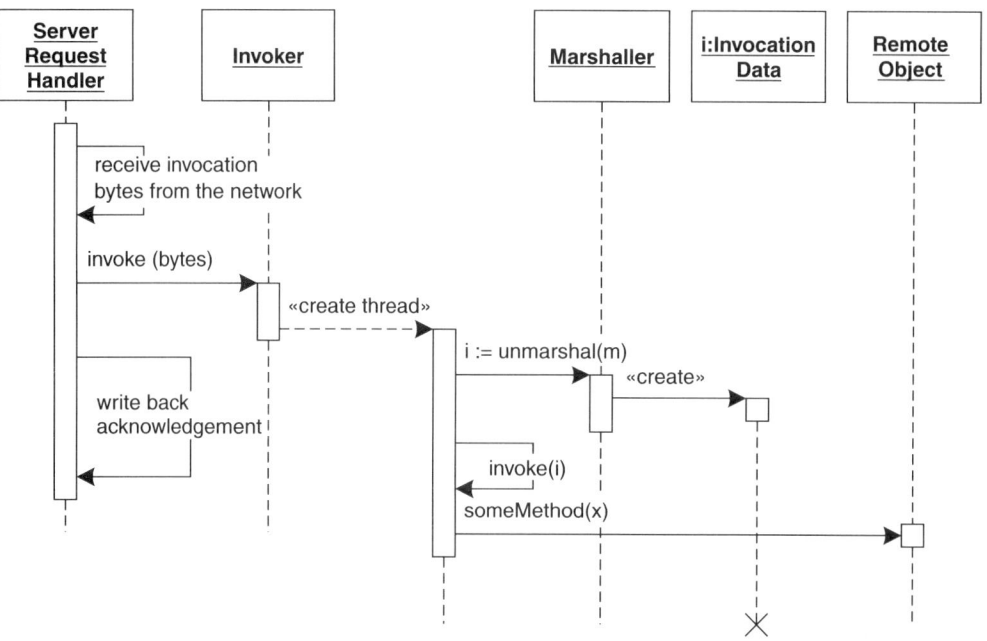

The next diagrams show examples of how POLL OBJECT and RESULT CALLBACK can be realized. We will show sequence diagrams for selected implementation alternatives.

For POLL OBJECT, a POLL OBJECT is returned to the client on asynchronous invocation. For RESULT CALLBACK, the client has to pass a callback object to the asynchronous invocation. In both cases the request is then delivered to the server, as in SYNC WITH SERVER. The difference is the way in which the POLL OBJECT and callback object are notified about the availability of the result. Two options exist:

- The POLL OBJECT/callback object is registered in the client-side distributed object middleware using the *Asynchronous Completion Token* sent as part of the request. The out parameters and return value are delivered to that POLL OBJECT/callback object by the client-side distributed object middleware. A separate thread inside the client-side distributed object middleware waits for the reply, and dispatches the reply to the proper POLL OBJECT/callback object. This can be a LOCAL OBJECT or a remote object.

- An ABSOLUTE OBJECT REFERENCE for the POLL OBJECT/callback object is sent to the server, together with a flag to indicate that the server-side distributed object middleware should send the reply back as a request to the POLL OBJECT/callback object in the client. The client becomes a server, as the POLL OBJECT/callback object has to be a remote object that can accept remote invocations.

What are the consequences of these approaches? In the first case, no changes are required in the server-side distributed object middleware – only the client needs to be adapted. The invocations are handled like synchronous invocations on the server side.

In the second case, the server-side distributed object middleware is involved in the implementation of the asynchrony, as it has to send back the reply as a request to the POLL OBJECT/callback object on the client side. This makes the client-side distributed object middleware easier to implement, but on the other hand the client has to become a server too.

A third but very inefficient alternative for POLL OBJECT is to poll remotely for the result on the original remote object. This is only worth considering if the client is a 'pure' client that has no means or resources to allow it to behave as a server.

Note that in all the implementation alternatives, the remote object implementation or interface does not change at all – all the asynchrony is handled by some part of the infrastructure.

The point of the above discussion is to demonstrate that the programming model for the two alternatives (POLL OBJECT and RESULT CALLBACK) is independent of its implementation. Both patterns can be implemented in either way, with the respective advantages and disadvantages explained above. The major difference between POLL OBJECT and RESULT CALLBACK is not how the distributed object middleware handles the asynchrony, but how the client accesses the result.

To illustrate this discussion, we first show an example using POLL OBJECT and the first implementation option, then an example using RESULT CALLBACK and the second implementation option. We assume that the CLIENT PROXY provides an additional operation for each operation on the remote object, prefixed with the `async_`, tag that invokes the remote operation using a POLL OBJECT. These operations have been generated into the proxy by the developer specifying a flag in the proxy generator that indicates that he wants to invoke the operations asynchronously. In this example the REQUESTOR creates a new thread and returns immediately to the client. This thread handles the invocation as usual and writes the result to the POLL OBJECT. The POLL OBJECT is polled by the client, and after the result arrives the client can obtain it using the operation getResult.

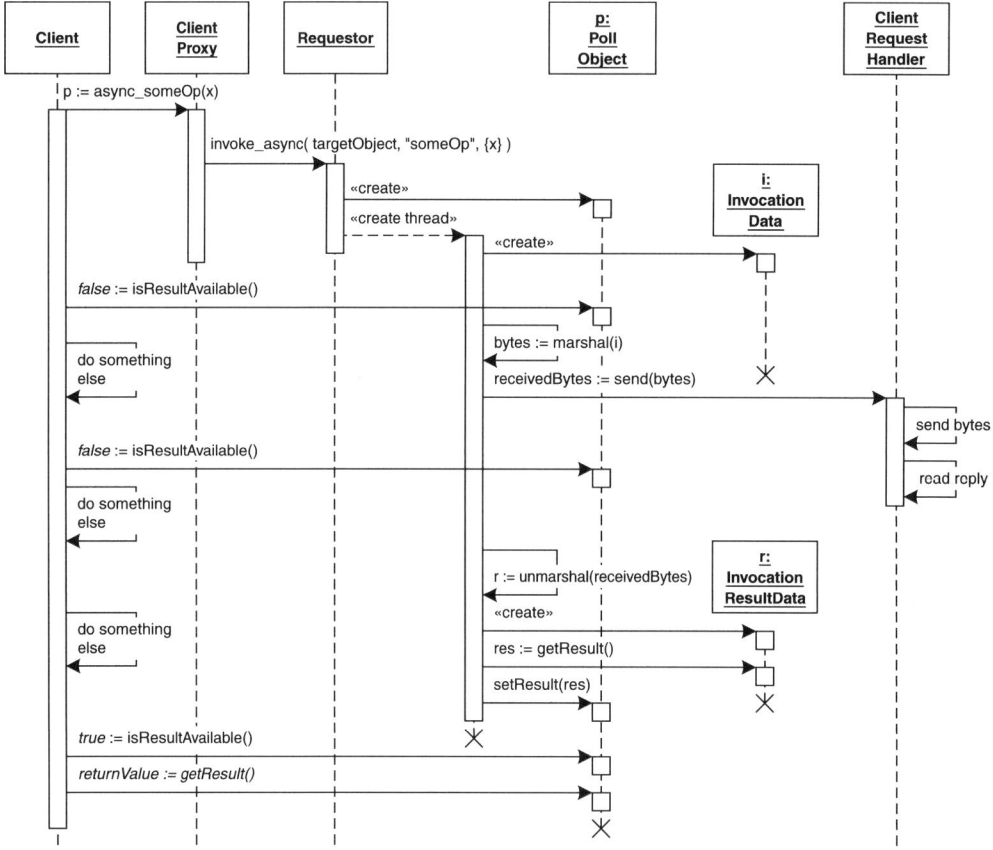

The sequence diagram above shows the POLL OBJECT dynamics when it is implemented using client-side asynchrony. If we were to implement RESULT CALLBACK in this way, the only difference would be that the client supplies the callback object to the async_ operation. The client-side distributed object middleware would then invoke the corresponding operation on the callback object from the separate thread.

The next section shows the implementation of RESULT CALLBACK using a 'real' callback from the server infrastructure. The client instantiates a separate callback object, although the client itself could also implement the required callback interface and its operations, respectively. We assume that there is a second variant of the async_... operation that takes the callback object as a parameter. The following diagram shows only the client-side part of the complete RESULT CALLBACK interaction.

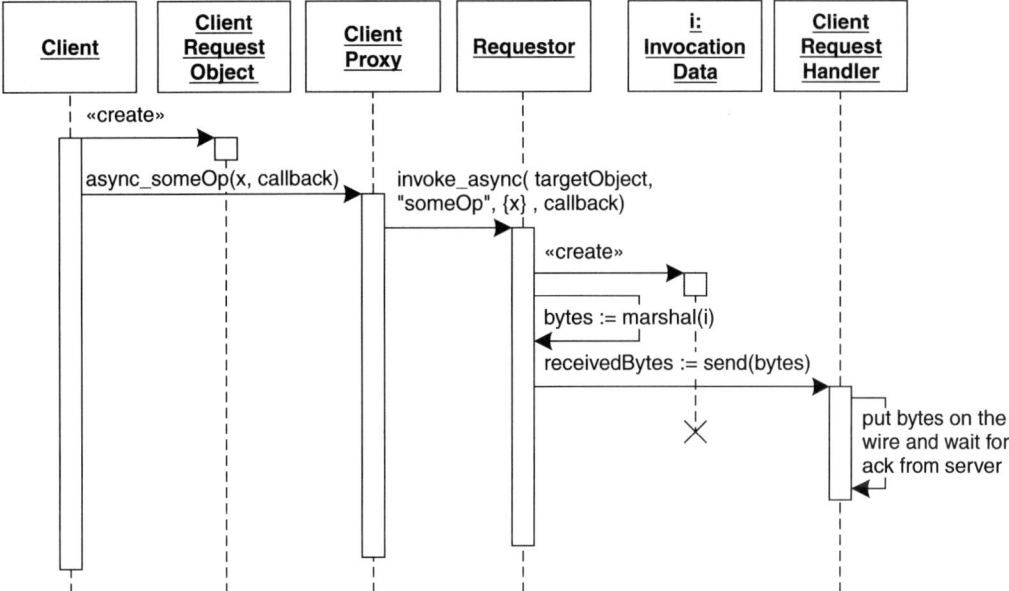

We assume at least SYNC WITH SERVER semantics for the request – the invocation only returns after the server application has acknowledged the receipt. The callback remote object is now accessible by the server infrastructure. A proxy is constructed in the usual way (using the ABSOLUTE OBJECT REFERENCE passed in the request), and the callback operation is called on it. Finally, we also assume that the SERVER

REQUEST HANDLER handles multithreading, so that no separate thread needs to be created in the INVOKER to handle the callback.

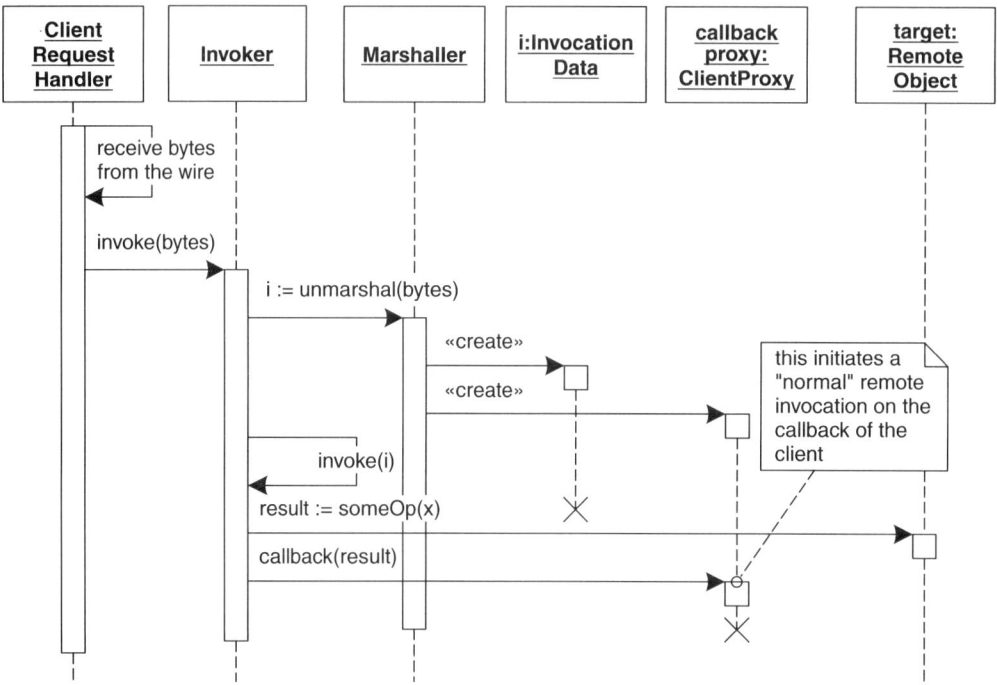

Note that when accessed asynchronously, a remote object is very similar to an *Active Object* in [SSRB00]. An *Active Object* decouples method invocation from method execution. The same holds true for remote objects that use any of patterns presented here for asynchronous communication. However, when remote objects are invoked synchronously, the invocation and execution of a method is not decoupled, even though they run in separate threads of control.

Active Objects typically create *Future* [Lea99] objects that clients use to retrieve the result from the method execution. The implementation of such *Future* objects follows the same concepts that are presented in RESULT CALLBACK and POLL OBJECT.

9 Technology Projections

In the pattern language presented in earlier chapters we did not provide known uses for each of the patterns, just generic examples. We provide more substantial examples for the whole pattern language in the following chapters, in which we look at a specific technology, show how the patterns are applied, and how they relate to each other. In these chapters we emphasize the focus on the pattern language as a whole – instead of focusing on single patterns within the language. Instead of calling these chapters 'Examples of the pattern language' we call them *technology projections*[1].

Each subsequent technology projection is intended to emphasize specific features of the pattern language:

- *.NET Remoting*. .NET Remoting provides a generally usable, flexible and well-defined distributed object middleware. It has a nice and consistent API and can easily be understood, even by novices. It is already widely used and is thus an important remoting technology. We use C# as the example programming language.
- *Web Services*. Web Services are currently one of the hottest topics in the IT industry. Basically, they provide an HTTP/XML-based remoting infrastructure. Our technology projection here focuses especially on interoperability. Java, as a programming language, and Apache Axis, as a framework, are used for most of the examples, but we also discuss other Web Services frameworks, such as .NET Web Services, IONA's Artix, and GLUE.
- *CORBA and Real-time CORBA*. CORBA is certainly the most complex, but also the most powerful and sophisticated distributed object middleware technology available today. In addition to being language-independent and platform-interoperable, there are also implementations for embedded and real-time applications. Our

---

1. 'Technology projection' is a term we first heard from Ulrich Eisenecker.

technology projection for CORBA will focus especially on quality of service aspects. C++ is used in the examples.

Please note that these chapters cannot serve as complete and full tutorials for the respective technologies. They are really just meant to help you understand the patterns, as well as the commonalities and trade-offs of the technologies.

Reading the technology projections will of course give you a basic understanding of the respective technology, but to use one of the described technologies in practice, you should probably also read a dedicated tutorial.

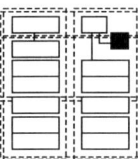

At the beginning of each of the three technology projections, we present a *pattern map* that illustrates the relationships between the Remoting Patterns and the architecture of the respective technology. To provide a guide to where we are in this overall architecture, in the left-hand margin we display thumbprints of the full pattern map shown on pages 190, 242 and 293. The thumbprint on the left shows an example that denotes that we are in the server application. This example is taken from the .NET technology projection.

10 .NET Remoting Technology Projection

.NET provides an easy to use but yet powerful distributed object middleware that follows the patterns described in the first part of this book very closely. .NET Remoting is a powerful and flexible distributed object middleware. We use the C# programming language exclusively for our examples, although we could have also used other .NET languages such as VB.NET or C++.NET.

Note that we cannot go into every detail of .NET Remoting in this chapter. You can find more information for example in [Bar02], [Ram02], and [Sta03].

A brief history of .NET Remoting

.NET Remoting was introduced as part of Microsoft's .NET platform. From the developer's perspective, .NET replaces the older Windows programming APIs such as the Windows 32-bit API (Win32 API), the Microsoft Foundation Classes (MFC) and, with regard to remoting, DCOM – although DCOM will live on as part of COM+ [Mic04d]. We don't want to compare DCOM and .NET Remoting here, except to say that they have almost nothing in common, and that developing with .NET Remoting is much simpler and more straightforward than DCOM [Gri97].

Note that, technically, .NET does not *replace* the older APIs, but it is built on top of them. This is, however, invisible to developers.

.NET Remoting is an infrastructure for distributed *objects*. It is not ideally suited to building service-oriented systems. Microsoft is planning to release a new product in 2006 (currently named Indigo) that provides a new programming model for Web Services-based, service-oriented systems on top of .NET. It will be possible to migrate .NET Remoting applications, as well as applications using .NET Enterprise services, to Indigo. At the time of writing, further information on

Indigo can be found at [Mic04b] – we also summarize some key concepts in *Outlook for the next generation* on page 235.

.NET concepts – a brief introduction

This section explains some basics that should be understood in outline before reading on.

Just as Java, .NET is based on a virtual machine architecture. The virtual machine is called *Common Language Runtime* (CLR), also named *runtime* in this section. The runtime runs programs written in '.NET assembler', the *Microsoft Intermediate Language* (MSIL). Many source languages can be compiled into MSIL, including C#, C++, VB.NET, Eiffel. Since everything is ultimately represented as MSIL, a great deal of language interoperability is possible. For example, you can let a C++ class inherit from a C# class.

.NET supports *namespaces* to avoid name clashes. Just as in C++, a namespace is logically a prefix to a name. Multiple classes can exist in the same namespace. In contrast to Java, there is no relationship between namespaces and the file system location of a class.

Assemblies are completely independent of namespaces: assemblies are the packaging format, a kind of archive, for a number of .NET artifacts, such as types, resources, and metadata (see below). The elements of a namespace can be scattered across several assemblies, and an assembly can contain elements from any number of namespaces. So, namespaces are a means to structure names logically, whereas assemblies are used to combine things that should be deployed together. It is of course good practice to establish some kind of relationship between namespaces and assemblies to avoid confusion, for example to put all the elements of one namespace into the same assembly.

.NET provides many features that are known from scripting or interpreted languages. For example, it provides reflection: it is possible to query an assembly for its contained artifacts, or to introspect a type to find out its attributes, operations, supertypes, and so on. It is also possible to create .NET types and assemblies on the fly. `CodeDOM` and the `Reflection.Emit` namespace provides facilities to define types, as well as their complete implementation.

Attributes are another very interesting feature. Many .NET elements, such as types, member definitions, operations, and so on, can be annotated with attributes in the source code. For example the [Serializable] attribute specifies that the annotated type should be marshaled by value in the case of a remote invocation. Developers can define their own attributes, which are .NET types themselves. The compiler then instantiates them and serializes them into the assembly, together with the compiled MSIL code. At runtime it is possible to use reflection to find out about the attributes of a .NET element and react accordingly.

In addition to processes and threads, there are additional execution concepts in .NET, such as *application domains*. While threads only define a separate, concurrent execution path, processes in addition define a protection domain. If one process crashes, other processes remain unaffected. As a consequence, communication between processes involves a significant overhead due to process context switching. .NET application domains provide the context of a protection domain independently of the separate, concurrent execution path, and without the context switching overhead.

.NET Remoting pattern map

The following illustration shows the basic structure of the .NET Remoting framework. It also contains annotations of pattern names showing which component is responsible for realizing which pattern.

The following overview does not show the behavioral patterns (*Lifecycle* Patterns and *Client Asynchrony* Patterns).

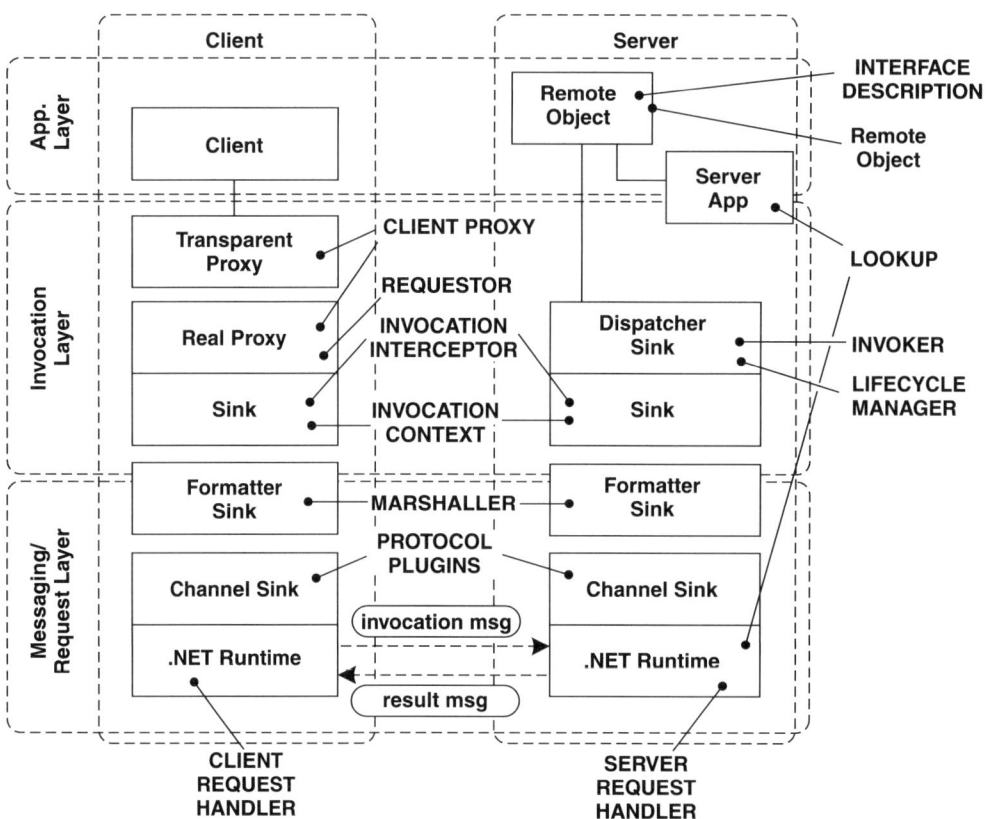

Thumbnails of this diagram in the margin serve as an orientation map during the course of this chapter, by highlighting the area of the above diagram to which a particular paragraph or section relates.

A simple .NET Remoting example

To introduce .NET Remoting we will start with a simple example. Instead of using the stereotypical 'Hello World!', we use a different but equally simple example in which we build a distributed system for the medical domain. Our introductory example comprises a remotely-accessible `PatientManager` object that provides access to the patients' data in a hospital's IT system.

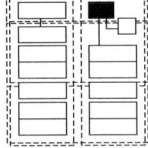
Let us consider the remote object first. In .NET, a remotely-accessible object must extend the `MarshalByRefObject` class, as shown in the following example. `MarshalByRefObject` is thus the base class for all remotely-accessible objects in .NET. The name is an allusion to the fact that the object will not be marshaled (that is, serialized) to a remote machine. Instead only the remote object's reference will be marshaled to the caller if an instance is passed as an operation parameter or as a return value.

```
using System;
namespace PatientManagementServer
{
  public class PatientManager: MarshalByRefObject
  {
    public PatientManager()
    {}
    public Patient getPatientInfo( String id )
    {
      return new Patient( id );
    }
  }
}
```

Here we define the `PatientManager` class, which provides a single operation to retrieve a `Patient` object. The class resides in the `PatientManagementServer` namespace.

.NET does not require a separate interface for remote objects – by default, the public operations of the implementation class are available remotely. To make sure we do not need the remote object class definition (`PatientManager`) in the client process, we provide an interface that defines publicly-available operations. In accordance with .NET naming conventions, this interface is called `IPatientManager`. It is located in a namespace `PatientManagementShared`, which we will use for the code that is required by client and server. The namespaces `PatientManagementServer` and `PatientManagementClient` will be used for server-only and client-only code, respectively.

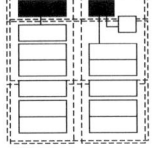

```
namespace PatientManagementShared
{
  public interface IPatientManager
  {
    Patient getPatientInfo( String patientID );
  }
}
```

The implementation must now of course implement this interface to ensure that the PatientManager is subtype-compatible with IPatientManager. This is necessary because the client will use the IPatientManager interface to declare references to remote PatientManager objects.

```
namespace PatientManagementServer
{
  public class PatientManager: MarshalByRefObject,
    IPatientManager
  {
    public PatientManager()
    {}
    public Patient getPatientInfo( String id )
    {
      return new Patient( id );
    }
  }
}
```

The operation getPatientInfo returns an instance of Patient. This class is a typical example of a *Data Transfer Object* [Fow03, Mic04c, Sun04a], which is serialized by value when transported between server and client (and vice versa). In .NET such objects need to contain the [Serializable] attribute in their class definition, as shown below. Note that, just as for the interface, the Patient class is also defined in the PatientManagementShared assembly, because it is used by both client and server.

```
namespace PatientManagementShared
{
  [Serializable]
  public class Patient
  {
    private String id = null;
    public Patient( String _id )
    {
      id = _id;
    }
    public String getID()
    {
      return id;
    }
  }
}
```

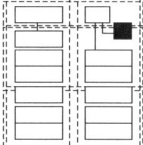

To continue, we need to get a suitable server application running for our initial example. This needs to set up the Remoting framework and publish the remote object(s). We postpone the details of setting up the

A simple .NET Remoting example

Remoting framework, and thus just use a 'black box' helper class[1] to do this for us, RemotingSupport. With this, the server application becomes extremely simple:

```
using System;
using RemotingHelper;
using System.Runtime.Remoting;
using PatientManagementShared;

namespace PatientManagementServer
{
  class Server
  {
    static void Main(string[] args)
    {
      RemotingSupport.setupServer();
      RemotingConfiguration.RegisterWellKnownServiceType(
        typeof(PatientManager), "PatientManager",
        WellKnownObjectMode.Singleton );
      RemotingSupport.waitForKeyPress();
    }
  }
}
```

The second line of the main method is the interesting part: here we publish the PatientManager remote object for access by clients. The registration also includes a definition of a name by which the remote object will be available to clients. The following URL will serve the purpose of an ABSOLUTE OBJECT REFERENCE:

```
http://<the serverHost>:<the port>/PatientManager
```

Note that there is no central LOOKUP system in .NET: clients have to know the host on which an object can be looked up by its name. They therefore must use the URL above. The URL contains information about the transport protocol used to access the object. Since .NET supports different communication *channels* (see below), it is possible, after appropriate configuration, to reach the same object using a different URL. An example using the TCP channel is:

```
tcp://<the serverHost>:<another port>/PatientManager
```

---

1. This class is not part of the .NET Remoting framework, we have implemented it for the sake of this example. The class itself consists just of a couple of lines, so it does not hide huge amounts of complex code. We show its implementation later.

Note also that we use LAZY ACQUISITION here. `WellKnownObject-Mode.Singleton` specifies that only one shared instance is accessible remotely at any time. This instance is created only when the first request for the `PatientManager` remote object arrives. For details of the activation mode, see *Activation and bootstrapping* on page 208.

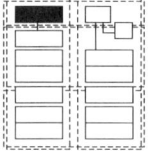

Last but not least, we need a client. This is also relatively straightforward:

```
namespace PatientManagementClient
{
  class Client
  {
    static void Main(string[] args)
    {
      RemotingSupport.setupClient();
      IPatientManager patientManager =
        (IPatientManager)Activator.
          GetObject(typeof(IPatientManager),
                   "http://localhost:6642/PatientManager" );
      Patient patient = patientManager.getPatientInfo("42");
      Console.WriteLine("ID of the "+
        "retrieved Patient:"+patient.getID());
    }
  }
}
```

First we invoke the `setupClient` operation on the `RemotingSupport` class. Then we look up the remote object using the URL scheme mentioned above. We use the `Activator` class provided by the .NET framework as a generic factory for all kinds of remote objects. The port 6642 is defined as part of the `RemotingSupport.setupServer` operation called by the `Server.Main` operation. Note that we use the interface to declare and downcast the returned object, not the implementation class. We then finally retrieve a `Patient` from the remote `PatientManager` and, for the sake of the example, ask it for its ID.

Setting up the framework

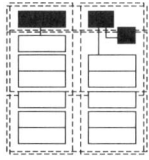

We use the `RemotingSupport` helper class to set up the Remoting framework. Internally, this class uses a .NET API to do the actual work. Alternatively, it is also possible to set up Remoting using certain elements in the application configuration XML file. Each .NET application can have an associated configuration file that controls various aspects of the application's use of the .NET framework. The file must be loaded by the program manually. The file contains, for example, the versions of assemblies that should be used, security information, as well as setup information for Remoting. Although we show a snippet of the XML file later in this chapter, we will not consider it in detail in this book.

Assemblies for the simple example

Assemblies in .NET are binary files that are used for deployment. An assembly is represented by a DLL (dynamically loaded library) or an executable. As recommended above, all elements of a particular namespace are put into the same assembly, so we use the following assemblies in this example:

- `PMShared` contains artifacts that are needed by client and server.
- `RemotingHelper` contains everything needed to set up the .NET Remoting framework.
- `PMServer` contains all the code for the server.
- `PMClient` contains all the code for the client.

The following illustration shows the assemblies, the classes they contain, and the dependencies among the assemblies.

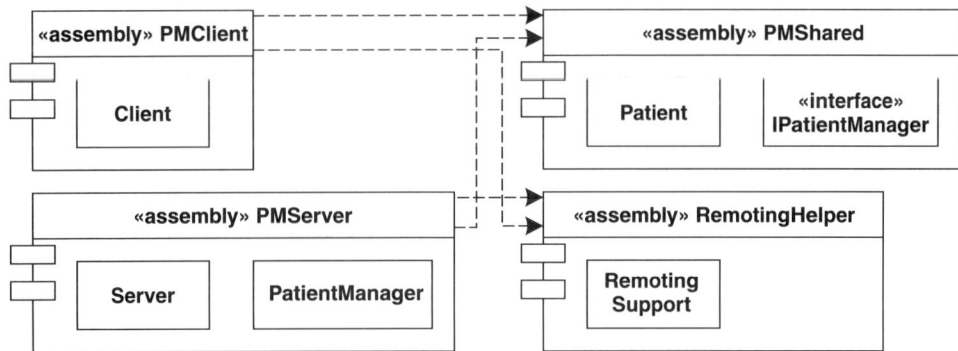

Remoting boundaries

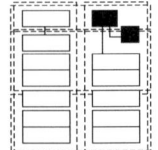 While distributed object middleware is typically used to communicate between two processes that are usually located on different machines, this is technically not completely correct for .NET Remoting.

.NET provides two important additional concepts: *application domains* and *contexts*. The following illustration shows the relationship of the concepts, while the next two sections explain some details.

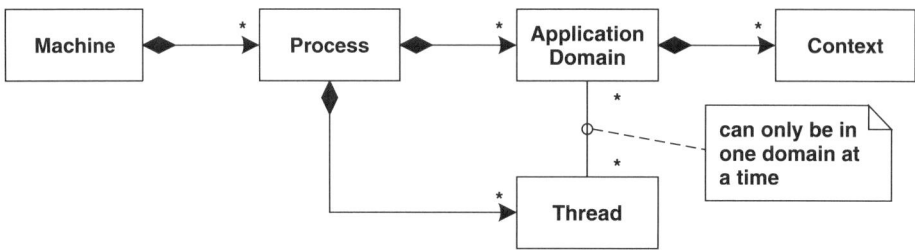

Application domains

In a .NET managed environment a process can contain several *application domains*. An application domain is a logically-separate 'space' inside a process. Applications running in different application domains are isolated from each other – faults in one application domain cannot affect the code running in other application domains inside the same process. This is mainly achieved by verifying the loaded MSIL code with respect to boundary violations. The code is only executed if no such violations are detected. As a consequence, application domains provide the same isolation features as processes, but with the additional benefit that communication between application domains need not cross process boundaries. Using application domains improves communication performance and scalability, since crossing process boundaries is avoided. However, to communicate between two application domains, .NET Remoting has to be used.

Note that application domains are not related to threads. An application domain can contain several threads, and a thread can cross application domains over time. There is a distinct relationship between assemblies and application domains, though. A specific assembly is always executed in one application domain. For example, you can run the same assembly in several application domains, in which case the code is shared, but the data is not.

Application domains can be set up manually using the `AppDomain.CreateDomain` operation. This takes a set of parameters such as the domain's working directory, the configuration file for the domain, as well as the search path the runtime uses to find assemblies. Once an application domain is set up, you can use the `Load` operation to load a specific assembly into the domain. `Unload` allows you unload the assembly without needing to stop the process. Finally, you can create instances of a `Type` in a specific application domain using the `CreateInstanceFrom` operation.

In the remainder of this chapter, we will however consider Remoting from the perspective of crossing process boundaries.

Contexts

Contexts provide a way to add INVOCATION INTERCEPTORS to objects running in the same application domain. Again, .NET Remoting is used to insert proxies that handle interception, thus contexts can be used as CONFIGURATION GROUPS. Details are explained later in the section on INVOCATION INTERCEPTORS, or in [Low03].

Basic internals of .NET Remoting

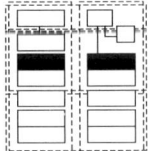

In contrast to other platforms, such as natively-compiled C++, the .NET platform is a relatively dynamic environment. This means that reflective information is available, instances can be asked for their types, and types can be modified, or even created, at runtime. As a consequence, many classes for which you would have to generate and compile source code manually on a native platform can be generated on the fly by the .NET runtime – no separate source code generation or compilation step is required.

An example of such an automatically-generated class is the CLIENT PROXY. You never see any source code for these classes, and there is no code-generated server-side skeleton as part of the INVOKER. The INVOKER – called a *dispatcher* in .NET – is a .NET framework component that uses reflection, as well as the information passed in remote method invocation requests, to invoke the target operation on the remote object dynamically.

As usual, the communication framework is an implementation of the BROKER pattern [BMR+96]. This, as well as the CLIENT REQUEST HANDLER and SERVER REQUEST HANDLER, form an integral part of the .NET framework, and are also supported by the .NET runtime itself.

Each remote object instance has a unique OBJECT ID. Using Visual Studio.NET's debugger, we can look into the state of a remote object instance and see the unique OBJECT ID, called _ObjURI. In case of our PatientManager, it looks like the following:

```
/e478bad4_a6c0_43a1_ae5e_4f7f9bd2c644/PatientManager
```

Another attribute of the PatientManager remote object instance is the ABSOLUTE OBJECT REFERENCE. This reference contains several attributes: among others, it contains the OBJECT ID shown above and the communication information in the form of one or more ChannelData objects. The URL is the same as the one we introduced before, which allows clients to access remote objects: tcp://172.20.2.13:6642

As we shall see later, a remote object can be accessed remotely through several different *channels*. Channels are communication paths that consist besides other things of a protocol and a serialization format. A channel is connected to a network endpoint with a specific configuration. In the case of TCP, this would be the IP address and the port, here 6642. Channels have to be configured when the server application is started.

Error handling in .NET

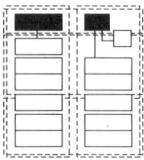

REMOTING ERRORS are reported using subclasses of System.SystemException. For example, if the CLIENT REQUEST HANDLER is unable to contact the server application because of network problems, it throws a WebException or a SocketException (both extending SystemException) to the client, depending on whether a TCP or an HTTP channel is used to access the remote object. To distinguish application-specific exceptions from REMOTING ERRORS clearly, a convention says that application exceptions must not subclass SystemException: instead it is recommended that you use `System.ApplicationException` as a base class. An example of a user-defined exception follows:

```
using System;
using System.Runtime.Serialization;

namespace PatientManagementShared
{
  [Serializable]
  public class InvalidPatientID: ApplicationException
  {
    public InvalidPatientID( String _message ) : base(_message)
    {
    }
    public InvalidPatientID(SerializationInfo info,
                     StreamingContext context):
                     base(info, context)
    {}
  }
}
```

Note that the class has to provide a so-called 'deserialization constructor' (the constructor with the `SerializationInfo` and `StreamingContext` parameters) and it has to be marked `[Serializable]`, otherwise the marshaling will not work. The exception's body is empty, because we have no additional parameters compared to `Exception`.

Server-activated Instances

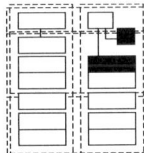

.NET provides two fundamentally different options for activating remote objects:

- Remote objects can be activated by the server. In this case, a client can just contact a remote object and does not have to worry about its creation and destruction.
- Remote objects can be created and destroyed explicitly by a client. The lifecycle of these CLIENT-DEPENDENT INSTANCES is thus controlled by a specific client, and not by the server.

This section considers alternatives for server-side activation, while the following section examines CLIENT-DEPENDENT INSTANCES more extensively.

.NET Remoting provides the following activation options for server activated objects. We will look at each of those in detail in the following sections:

- PER-REQUEST INSTANCES are created for each and every method invocation.
- STATIC INSTANCES can also be used, which have singleton semantics, meaning that there is always at most one instance in each .NET runtime.
- LAZY ACQUISITION results in a behavior similar to STATIC INSTANCES, but the instances are initialized on demand, whereas STATIC INSTANCES are instantiated manually, typically when the server application starts up.

Per-request instances

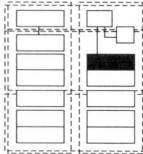

As we described in the pattern chapters, using PER-REQUEST INSTANCES requires remote objects to be stateless, because a new instance is created at each invocation. Developers have to be aware of this restriction, and ensure that remote objects are actually stateless – there is nothing in .NET that prevents developers from making PER-REQUEST INSTANCES stateful, possibly resulting in unexpected program behavior.

To implement a PER-REQUEST INSTANCE, all you have to do is to specify the SingleCall activation mode when you register the remote object with the Remoting framework. The code to do so in the server application is shown in the following fragment:

```
namespace PatientManagementServer
{
  class Server
  {
    static void Main(string[] args)
    {
      RemotingSupport.setupServer();
      RemotingConfiguration.RegisterWellKnownServiceType(
        typeof(PatientManager), "PatientManager",
        WellKnownObjectMode.SingleCall );
      RemotingSupport.waitForKeyPress();
    }
  }
}
```

Server-activated instances

To illustrate the effect of using PER-REQUEST INSTANCES, we have added some text output messages to the `PatientManager` remote object and the client. The next diagram shows the output from client and server, using a sequence diagram-like graphical syntax. The numbers in brackets denote OBJECT IDS.

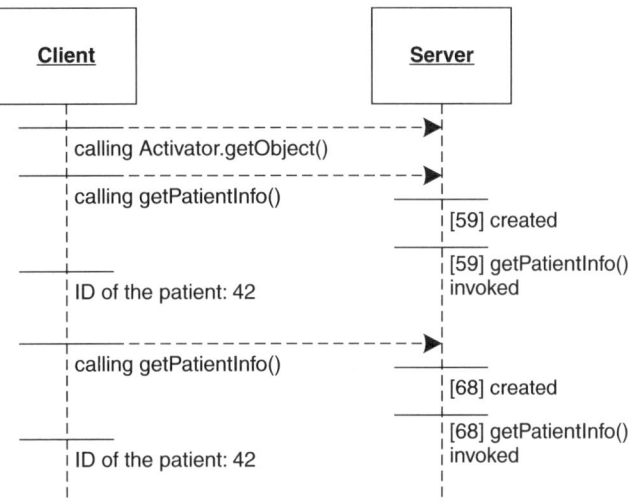

Two things can be observed: first of all, an instance is really only created when an operation is invoked, not when the object is acquired by the client calling `Activator.getObject`, or when the object is registered with the Remoting framework. Second, a new instance is actually created for each invocation (the OBJECT IDS are different): no POOLING is used here.

As each request has its own instance, you don't need to care about thread-safety – as long as you don't access shared resources.

Static instances

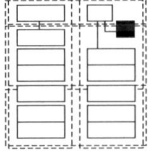

.NET Remoting also provides the possibility of using a STATIC INSTANCE. Instead of just registering a remote object type with the framework and letting the framework do the instantiation on demand, you instantiate the remote object manually and then publish the instance explicitly.

```
namespace PatientManagementServer
{
  class Server
  {
    static void Main(string[] args)
    {
      RemotingSupport.setupServer();
      PatientManager pm = new PatientManager();
      RemotingServices.Marshal(pm, "PatientManager");
      RemotingSupport.waitForKeyPress();
    }
  }
}
```

Here, the object is instantiated manually. After the instantiation in the second line of the Main operation, the remote object is published using the RemotingServices.Marshal operation. Note that this approach is a use of the *Eager Acquisition* pattern [KJ04].

Using STATIC INSTANCES has a number of additional advantages. You can call arbitrary constructors, whereas the alternative is always to use the Remoting framework's invocation of the remote object's default constructor. You can also control whether and when instances are created, and clients' access to instances will happen without a potential creation overhead. The following diagram shows the output obtained by running the program.

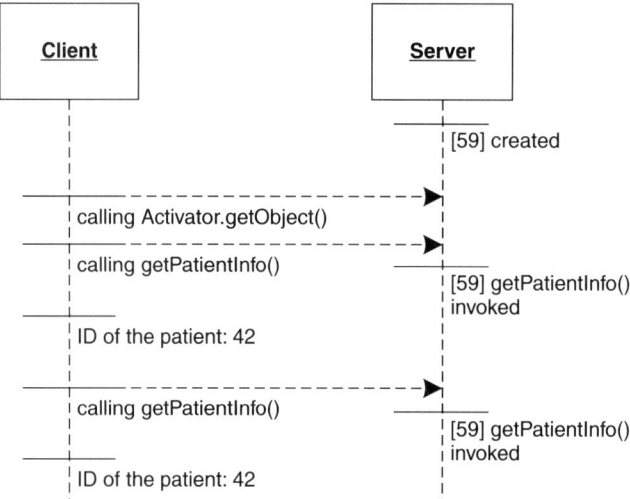

Server-activated instances

Note that just as with LAZY ACQUISITION, you have to add your own synchronization constructs when accessing shared resources.

You can publish several distinct instances of a particular remote object type with different names:

```
PatientManager pm = new PatientManager();
RemotingServices.Marshal(pm, "PatientManager");
PatientManager pm2 = new PatientManager();
RemotingServices.Marshal(pm2, "PatientManager2");
```

pm and pm2 are distinct instances, accessible through different names, and both can have their own separate state. Of course you can also publish several different instances when using other server-based activation techniques – you just have to register the same remote object type with different names. These then become different remote objects from the framework's perspective, both of which happen to use the same implementation class and interface. The following code shows this for PER-REQUEST INSTANCES:

```
namespace PatientManagementServer
{
  class Server
  {
    static void Main(string[] args)
    {
      RemotingSupport.setupServer();
      RemotingConfiguration.RegisterWellKnownServiceType(
        typeof(PatientManager), "PatientManager",
        WellKnownObjectMode.SingleCall );
      RemotingConfiguration.RegisterWellKnownServiceType(
        typeof(PatientManager), "PatientManager2",
        WellKnownObjectMode.SingleCall );
      RemotingSupport.waitForKeyPress();
    }
  }
}
```

As usual, a client can access any of the remote objects by using the Activator.GetObject operation, passing the URL that contains the respective object's name.

Lazy Acquisition

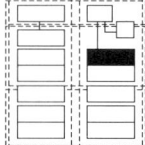

LAZY ACQUISITION activates an instance when a request arrives, and keeps it alive until its lease time expires. We discuss more about LEASING in *Client-dependent instances and Leasing* on page 208. When several requests arrive for the same remote object, all are handled by the same instance, one per common language runtime (CLR). This is why these instances are called *Singletons* in .NET. The .NET Remoting framework will potentially handle concurrent requests in several threads concurrently, so the remote object implementation has to be thread-safe. Configuring the framework to behave accordingly is again easy, you just pass WellKnownObjectMode.Singleton as the parameter to the RegisterWellKnownServiceType operation.

```
RemotingConfiguration.RegisterWellKnownServiceType(
   typeof(PatientManager), "PatientManager",
   WellKnownObjectMode.Singleton );
```

Again, we have added Console.Writeln statements at the relevant places in the code. The following diagrams illustrate the temporary sequence of these outputs.

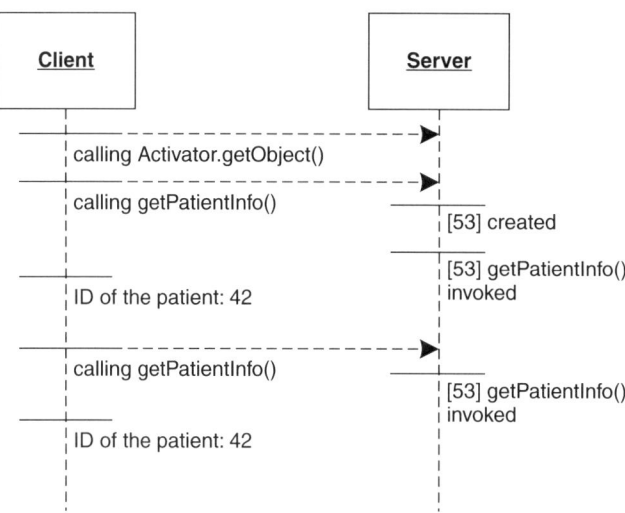

As you can see, only one instance is created on the server, even for multiple subsequent requests. If the lease time expires, the instance is

Server-activated instances

discarded. When a new invocation arrives, a new instance is created that will handle all requests until its own lease expires. If you want to avoid this behavior, you must ensure that the instance lives forever. To do this, you have to return `null` in `InitializeLifetimeService` of the particular remote object type. This is typically done in case of STATIC INSTANCES:

```
public class PatientManager: MarshalByRefObject, IPatientManager
{
  // all other operations as before
  public override object InitializeLifetimeService()
  {
    return null;
  }
}
```

Client-dependent instances and Leasing on page 208 provides more details about `InitializeLifetimeService` and leasing.

A more interesting situation occurs, however, when two clients concurrently call the `PatientManager` on the same server application. This situation is shown in the following diagram. Note that, since the two events happen at almost the same time, the two arrows almost overlap.

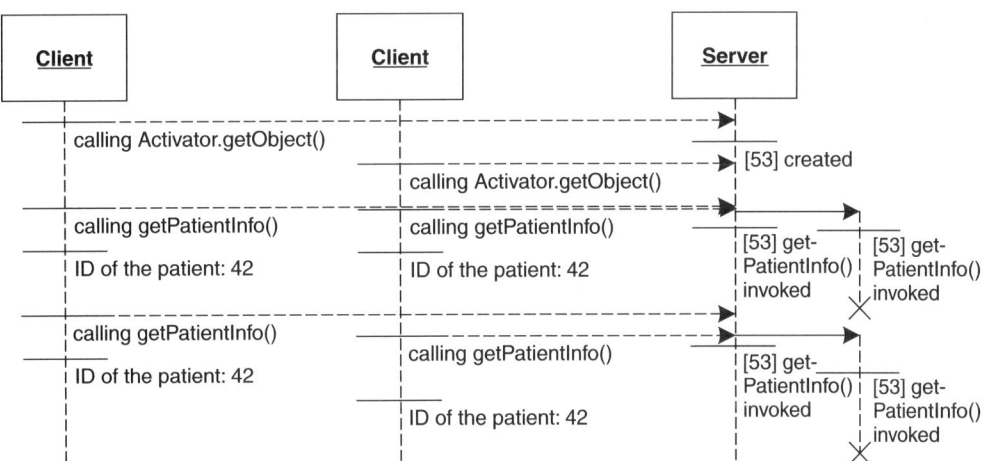

In this situation, the operation is invoked from within several threads (as illustrated by the two object lifelines of the server), but on the same instance. The constructor is called only once. Here, thread-safe programming is required as soon as shared resources require coordinated access from within the remote object.

The lifetime of the instances

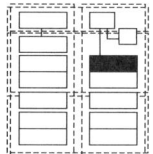

We first have to define what we mean by 'lifetime of instances'. There are two different 'lifetimes' for remote objects:

- One is the time the class's instance exists, that is, the time during which the object is managed by the .NET runtime, independent of the Remoting framework.
- The other lifetime is the duration during which the instance is managed by the Remoting framework and is remotely accessible.

Depending on the activation mode, the object either physically exists first and is then managed by the Remoting framework (as in case of STATIC INSTANCES), or the remote object type is managed by the framework first (with no instances yet in existence), and instances are created on demand, as in case of LAZY ACQUISITION, PER-REQUEST INSTANCES and CLIENT-DEPENDENT INSTANCES.

In the context of this section, we are mainly interested in the time during which an object is managed by the Remoting framework. Let's look at the different activation modes:

- In the case of a PER-REQUEST INSTANCE, the situation is fairly simple: the instance is created on request and immediately released after the invocation. Eventually the object is garbage-collected by the .NET runtime.
- In the other cases the object lives on until its lease expires. It is then discarded by the Remoting framework and eventually garbage collected. Usually you should ensure that the instance lives forever by returning null in InitializeLifetimeService. We will look into LEASING in more detail later when we discuss CLIENT-DEPENDENT INSTANCES.

The following diagram illustrates this discussion. It shows the lifetime of the remote object (above the dotted line) and the lifetime of actual

Server-activated instances

implementation objects (below the dotted line) for each of the activation modes.

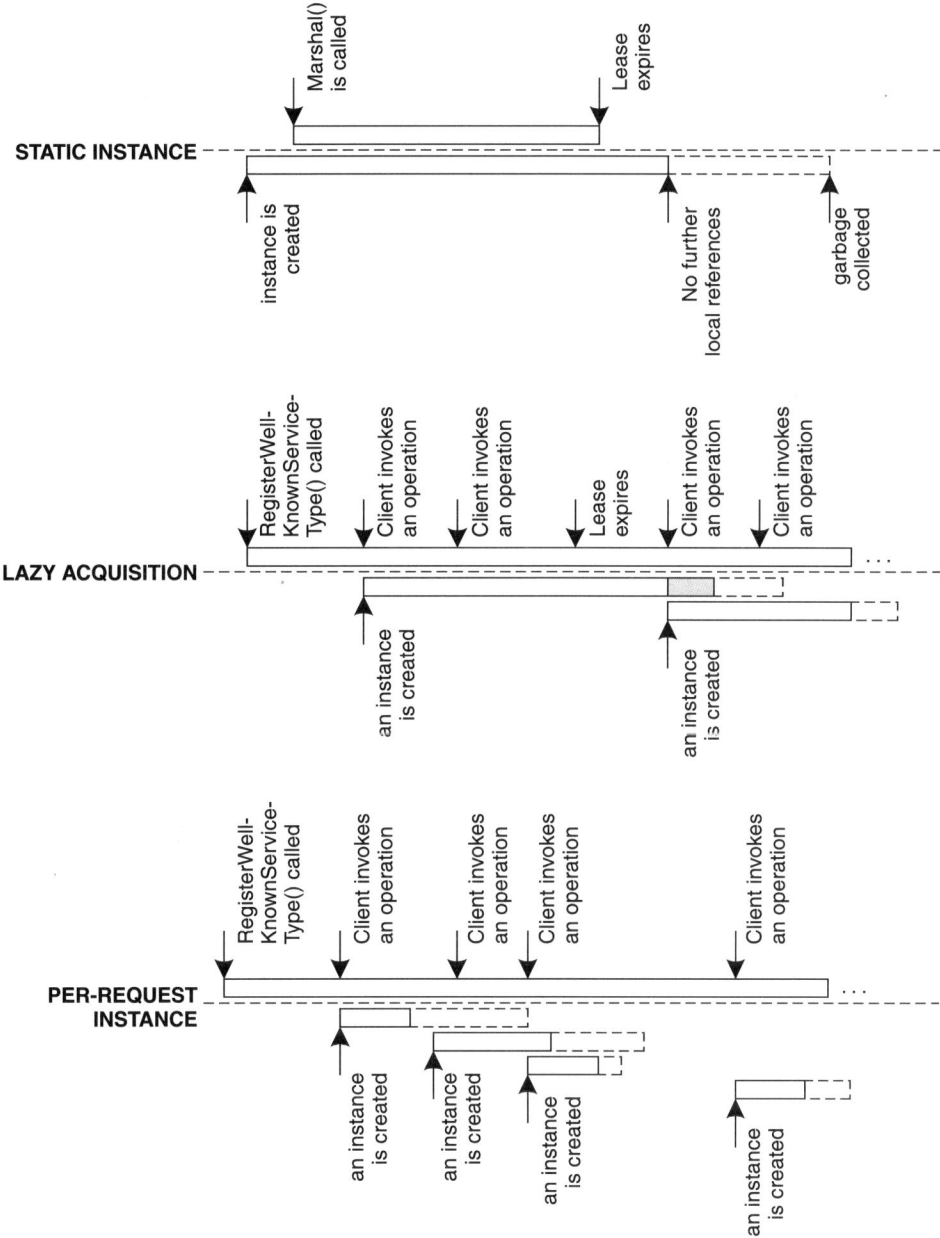

Client-dependent instances and Leasing

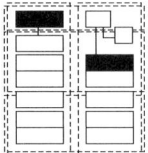

CLIENT-DEPENDENT INSTANCES are necessary if you need remote objects that are specific to a certain client and can keep (conversational) state on the client's behalf. Two aspects of CLIENT-DEPENDENT INSTANCES are specifically interesting:

- How they are created and accessed by a client
- How long they live

These two aspects are trivial for the other activation modes, because in all cases a generic factory can be used for activation (.NET's Activator class) and the lifetime of the instances is also non-critical:

- PER-REQUEST INSTANCES die just after serving a request
- Singletons are typically made to live forever

The next sections focus on these aspects in the context of CLIENT-DEPENDENT INSTANCES, and especially at the determination of when an instance is allowed to die, which is non-trivial.

Activation and bootstrapping

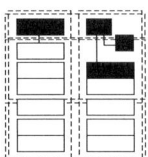

In .NET Remoting there are several ways in which a client can obtain a reference to a CLIENT-DEPENDENT INSTANCE:

- One is to call Activator.getObject. The Activator class is a generic factory provided as part of the .NET framework. It can be used to access any kind of remote object. This also works for CLIENT-DEPENDENT INSTANCES, but allows remote objects only to be instantiated using their default constructor. This is impractical, since a client typically wants to initialize its 'personal' instance by passing parameters to a constructor.

- Another alternative is to use the new operator that seamlessly instantiates a remote object instance on the *server* after correct configuration of the framework, although called in a client application. However, for this to work, you need the remote object's implementation class on the client, as opposed to just an interface, as the compiler will not allow you to call the new operator on an interface type. This is a bad approach, since clients should never depend on remote object implementation classes.

- A third option is to use a custom-built factory to instantiate the remote objects on the server application. In this approach, the factory is a STATIC INSTANCE or PER-REQUEST INSTANCE, and thus needs no additional bootstrapping. The factory can call whatever constructor is useful, and the parameters can be passed as parameters to the factory operation. The factory operation's return type is the interface type that is implemented by the remote object implementation class, and defines its remotely-available operations.

Since we consider the third option the most versatile and powerful, let us examine it more closely. Suppose that the CLIENT-DEPENDENT INSTANCE we want to create is an object that allows us to calculate the total amount of money that will be billed to a health insurance company for a patient's stay in hospital. Because such calculations can become rather complex (at least in Germany, as a result of the intricacies of the German health system), it is not possible to do this within one stateless remote operation call. We need CLIENT-DEPENDENT INSTANCES, one for each pending calculation. We therefore introduce a new example, the `Pricing` remote object, that will be stateful and client-activated.

As we mentioned before, we want to use a factory to allow the client to create new `Pricing` instances. This factory is called `PricingFactory`. We also introduce the interface `IPricing` that will be used by the client to access the Pricing remote object. The following class diagram shows the setup.

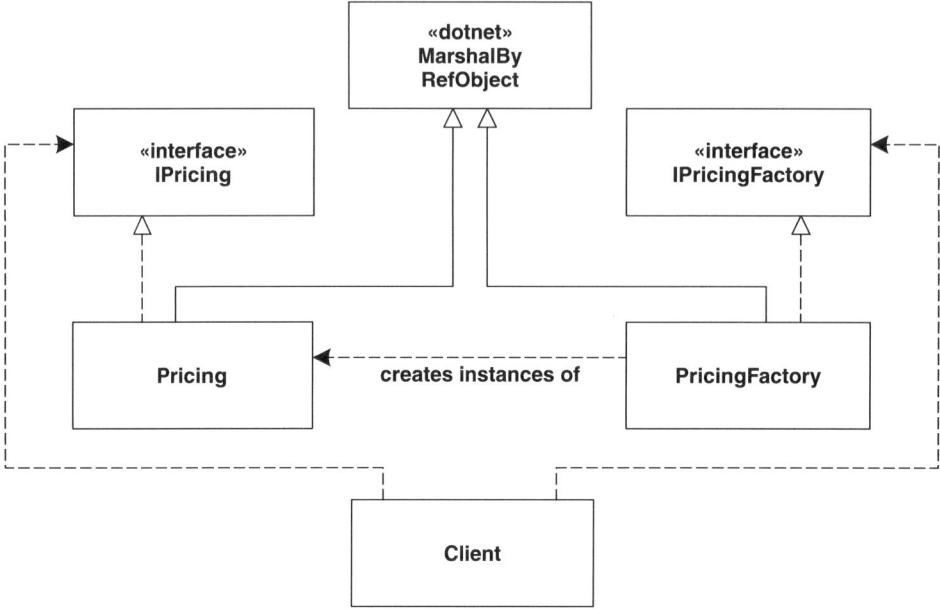

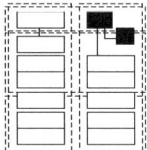

We'll start with the interface of the factory:

```
namespace PatientManagementShared
{
  public interface IPricingFactory
  {
    IPricing getPricingInstance( Patient patient );
  }
}
```

The factory operation returns a new instance of a class that implements the IPricing interface, such as a Pricing. The instance is initialized with the `Patient` that has been passed to the factory. The implementation for the factory interface is shown next. It is fairly simple:

```
namespace PatientManagementServer
{
  public class PricingFactory : MarshalByRefObject,
    IPricingFactory
  {
    public IPricing getPricingInstance( Patient patient )
    {
      return new Pricing( patient );
    }
  }
}
```

The implementation simply returns a new instance of the `Pricing` remote object. The `PricingFactory` will be registered as a lazily instantiated object, just as described above. This approach permits the client to only work with the interface (`IPricing`) and we can call a non-default constructor (the one with the `Patient` parameter). The only drawback is the additional complexity for client and server that is required to handle the factory object, and the development of the factory class by the developer.

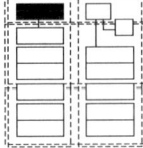

The only additional code required on the client is the factory's interface. So how does the code look from the client's perspective? The following code extract shows an example.

```
// retrieve a Patient object from a PatientManager
RemotingSupport.setupClient();
IPatientManager patientManager =
  (IPatientManager)Activator.GetObject(
    typeof( IPatientManager ),
    "tcp://localhost:6642/PatientManager" );
Patient patient = patientManager.getPatientInfo("42");

// retrieve the PricingFactory
IPricingFactory pf = (IPricingFactory)Activator.GetObject(
  typeof( IPricingFactory ),
  "tcp://localhost:6642/PricingFactory" );

// get an instance of a pricing object and work with it
IPricing p = pf.getPricingInstance(patient);
p.addDiagnosticKey( new Key("09098") );
p.addDiagnosticKey( new Key("23473") );
double total = p.getTotalPrice();
```

In the code you can see how the client retrieves a `PatientManager` object in the first section using the `Activator`. The second section retrieves the factory using the same approach (because it is also stateless) and the third section uses the factory to obtain an instance of `IPricing`.

Up to this point there is no difference between CLIENT-DEPENDENT INSTANCES and the other activation modes. It gets interesting, however, when we consider how long an instance actually lives before it is considered 'invalid' by the framework. The following discussion is also important for LAZY ACQUISITION and STATIC INSTANCES, because they might also need to be removed once their lease expires. This is typically not what is intended, so they have to be made to live forever.

Implementing lease management

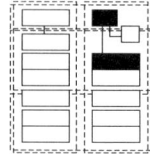

.NET Remoting uses the LEASING pattern. A lease is basically a temporarily limited permission for a remote object instance to exist and to be accessed by clients. Each instance has a counter (called *Time To Live*, or *TTL*) that determines how long the instance is allowed to live. .NET uses the following policies to determine the lifetime of an instance:

- An instance has an `InitialLeaseTime` that determines how long the instance lives initially after creation.
- On each method invocation, the remaining TTL is set to the specified `RenewalOnCallTime`.
- When the instance's TTL reaches zero (that is, when no method has been invoked for the remaining TTL) then a *sponsor* will be contacted by the LEASING manager, if one is registered for the respective instance. The sponsor can increase the TTL to make sure the instance does not die, even though the lease had expired.
- If the sponsor does not increase the TTL, or if no sponsor is registered for the instance, the instance is discarded by the Remoting framework and eventually garbage-collected.

The default values for the initial lease time is five minutes, and the renewal on call time defaults to two minutes. For many application scenarios this is not suitable, and shorter or longer periods might be appropriate. It is easily possible to change these settings – either on an application-wide level, on a remote object type level, or per remote object instance. Let's look at changing the LEASING settings for a particular remote object type.

Client-dependent instances and Leasing

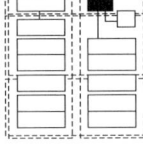

The `Pricing` implementation could look something like the following:

```
namespace PatientManagementServer
{
  public class Pricing : MarshalByRefObject, IPricing
  {
    private Patient patient = null;
    private ArrayList keys = new ArrayList();

    public Pricing( Patient _patient ) {
      patient = _patient;
    }

    public void addKey( DiagonsticKey key ) {
      keys.Add( key );
    }

    public double getTotalPrice() {
      return keys.Count;
    }

    public Patient getPatient() {
      return patient;
    }
  }
}
```

This implementation uses the system-wide defaults. To change these for this particular remote object type, we have to override the `InitializeLifetimeService` operation in the following way:

```
namespace PatientManagementServer
{
  public class Pricing : MarshalByRefObject, IPricing
  {
    // the other operations as before

    public override object InitializeLifetimeService()
    {
      ILease lease = (ILease)base.InitializeLifetimeService();
      if ( lease.CurrentState == LeaseState.Initial )
      {
        lease.InitialLeaseTime = TimeSpan.FromSeconds(10*60);
        lease.RenewOnCallTime = TimeSpan.FromSeconds(5*60);
      }
      return lease;
    }
  }
}
```

As you can see, we set the initial lease time to 10 minutes and the renewal interval at each method call to 5 minutes.

If you want to make sure your instance lives forever (that is, until program termination), you just return `null` in `InitializeLifetimeService`. This is typically done in case of STATIC INSTANCES:

```
public class PreconfiguredEx : MarshalByRefObject, IPricing
{
  public override object InitializeLifetimeService()
  {
    return null;
  }
}
```

When a client accesses an instance that is no longer accessible because its lease has timed out, the client receives a `RemotingException`:

```
Unhandled Exception: System.Runtime.Remoting.RemotingException:
Object </6ddffc7/1.rem> has been disconnected or does not exist
at the server.
```

The last hope – sponsors

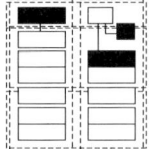

We mentioned the concept of a *sponsor* before. Sponsors are the 'last hope' for a remote object if its lease expires. The lease manager contacts the sponsor and asks it whether it should renew the lease for the instance that is ready to die. Sponsors must implement the `ISponsor` interface, which is very simple:

```
public interface ISponsor {
  TimeSpan Renewal( Ilease lease );
}
```

The following is a simple example of a sponsor that allows its associated instance an extended lifetime of 20 minutes:

```
namespace RemotingTestApp
{
  public class Sponsor : ISponsor
  {
    public TimeSpan Renewal( ILease lease )
    {
      return TimeSpan.FromMinutes(20);
    }
  }
}
```

The respective instance would have to die immediately if the sponsor returns `TimeSpan.Zero`.

Sponsors can be remote objects themselves. This means that the client of a CLIENT-DEPENDENT INSTANCE can host a sponsor object that determines the lifetime of the associated CLIENT-DEPENDENT INSTANCE.

In addition, the lease manager on the server application will only try to contact the sponsors – of which there can be several per remote object – for a specific period, which can be defined in the `InitializeLifetimeService` operation. After not reaching the sponsor(s) in the specified time, the lease manager gives up and the instance is finally discarded.

Remote sponsors and the timeout together provide a flexible and practical scheme for distributed garbage collection. Here are two examples:

- If all remote sponsors for CLIENT-DEPENDENT INSTANCES are located in the respective client processes, then, should this client go away (for example terminate without logging off, or just crash) the client-side sponsor will disappear with it and no new lease renewals will be sponsored. The CLIENT-DEPENDENT INSTANCE on the server application will be discarded and eventually garbage-collected.
- Alternatively, you can deploy a sponsor on the server application, make it remotely accessible, and use keep-alive pings from the client to determine its own lifetime – thus determining the time during which it is available for the lease manager.

Depending on the strategy implemented, there might be a performance penalty due to messages being sent between the lease manager and the sponsor.

More advanced lifecycle management

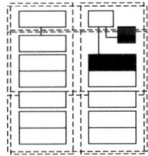

More advanced lifecycle management options are not directly available in Versions 1.x of the .NET framework. Specifically, POOLING of remote objects is not available. In the case of the `SingleCall` activation strategy a new instance is created for each invocation. After the invocation, it is discarded and eventually garbage-collected. This strategy assumes that garbage collection does not impose an unacceptable performance penalty. Of course it is possible to deploy your remote objects as COM+ [Mic04d] components where POOLING is supported. Visual Studio provides tool support for this and other forms of deployment.

In the case of the *Singleton* activation strategy, the instance lives until its lease expires (and no sponsor votes to keep the instance alive). There is no PASSIVATION of state if an instance is not accessed for a while.

Cases in which optimizations such as POOLING are necessary requires developers to built it manually. How can this be achieved? Let us take a closer look at POOLING. This strategy is obviously only necessary if the objects that are pooled are either expensive to create or to destroy, or if the resources they represent are limited. The following diagram shows the basic constituents of a self-made pooling infrastructure.

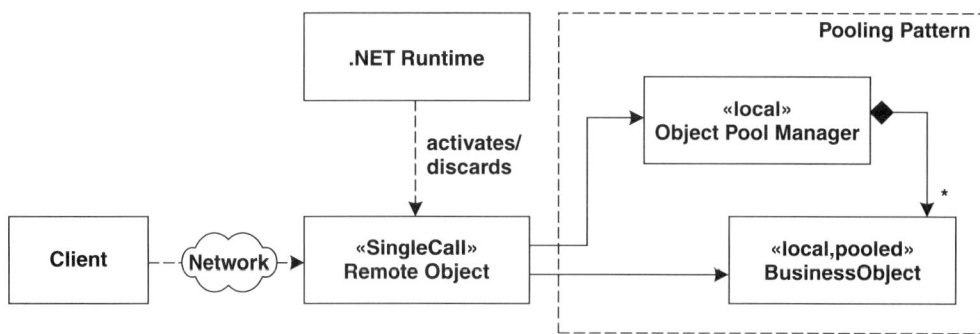

In this example we use a `SingleCall` remote object that is remotely accessible and acts as the interface to the client. Its lifecycle is managed by the .NET runtime – nothing special so far. This remote object, however, does not do very much, and merely delegates to another object (which we call *business object* here) which does the actual work. The remote object acquires an instance of the business object through an object pool manager. So the resources that should be pooled are kept by the business object, which itself is pooled. The remote object, with its framework-managed `SingleCall` lifecycle, merely acts as a kind of proxy delegating to the pooled business object. Of course you have to develop your own synchronization and lifecycle code. This is non-trivial, so it would be nice if the .NET framework did this for us.

For PASSIVATION the same discussion applies. .NET Remoting does not support it directly, but COM+ provides support for this feature. Again, a PASSIVATION infrastructure can be implemented along the same lines. It can even be seen as an extension of the POOLING infrastructure we looked at previously. In this case, the pool manager would also be responsible for passivating and activating objects as they go into and out of the pool by persisting the objects' state.

Note that in effect we are building our own LIFECYCLE MANAGER here.

Internals of .NET Remoting

Many aspects of the framework we describe with our patterns in the first part of the book are completely invisible to the .NET Remoting developer. This is because these features are supported by the .NET runtime, and thus are provided to the developer transparently. We discuss these internals in this section.

Request handlers

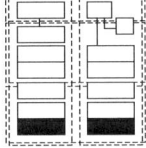

CLIENT REQUEST HANDLER and SERVER REQUEST HANDLER are provided by the .NET runtime. Every CLR instance is capable of receiving remote invocations from other runtimes. However, this does not imply that runtimes that currently do not host any remote objects consume resources for the provisioning of the remoting infrastructure. The necessary infrastructure is only started once remote objects are actually hosted by a CLR instance. Network resources (such as sockets) are only acquired when they are really needed.

The integration of remoting as an integral part of the .NET framework and runtime has advantages as well as liabilities. On the plus side, the developer does not have to worry about the details of how remoting is technically handled, as it is part of the platform. In addition, the API for accessing remote objects is the same in every .NET environment – there is no great variability of distributed object libraries.

On the downside, the problem of this approach is that the developer does not have very much control over how .NET manages threads, network resources (such as sockets), memory, activation and deactivation of objects, and so on. Compare this to CORBA, where the developer can take full control of these aspects if necessary. .NET Remoting is a typical example where this kind of flexibility is sacrificed for ease of use. The learning curve should be as gentle as possible, so that Remoting technology can be made available to as many developers as possible. Performance-critical applications that do not fit the access patterns assumed by the .NET framework developers at Microsoft are hard to realize in such an environment. In the typical office or enterprise world this should only seldom be a real problem. In distributed embedded real-time systems, however, such an approach usually does not work – but that is not the typical usage scenario for the .NET framework.

Note that this does not mean that .NET Remoting is not flexible. On the contrary, it is *very* flexible with regard to application-level/infrastructure-level adaptations: leases, sponsors, message sinks, and custom channels provide an excellent way of adapting .NET Remoting to specific application requirements. Details are provided in *Extensibility of .NET Remoting* on page 221.

Client Proxies and Interface Description

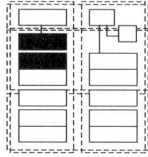

As usual in any distributed object middleware, a CLIENT PROXY is used by the client to invoke operations. The CLIENT PROXY is subsequently responsible for forwarding the request over the network to the remote object. The CLIENT PROXY is a local object in the client's address space and thus can receive ordinary, local method invocations.

In .NET Remoting, the CLIENT PROXY is separated into two parts:

- The so-called *transparent proxy* is the CLIENT PROXY in the sense of this pattern language. It has the same interface as the remote object and forwards invocations across the network.
- The *real proxy* is actually a part of the client-side facilities of the .NET Remoting infrastructure. It receives the invocation data from the transparent proxy and forwards it over the network. It therefore plays the role of the REQUESTOR. However, it is not accessible by the client program directly.

As explained in the CLIENT PROXY and REQUESTOR patterns, this separation into transparent and real proxy does make sense, because only the transparent proxy is specific to the interface of the remote object, while the real proxy is independent of this interface. The same real proxy class is common to all kinds of remote objects, which is the reason why it is actually a part of the .NET framework. The following illustration shows this:

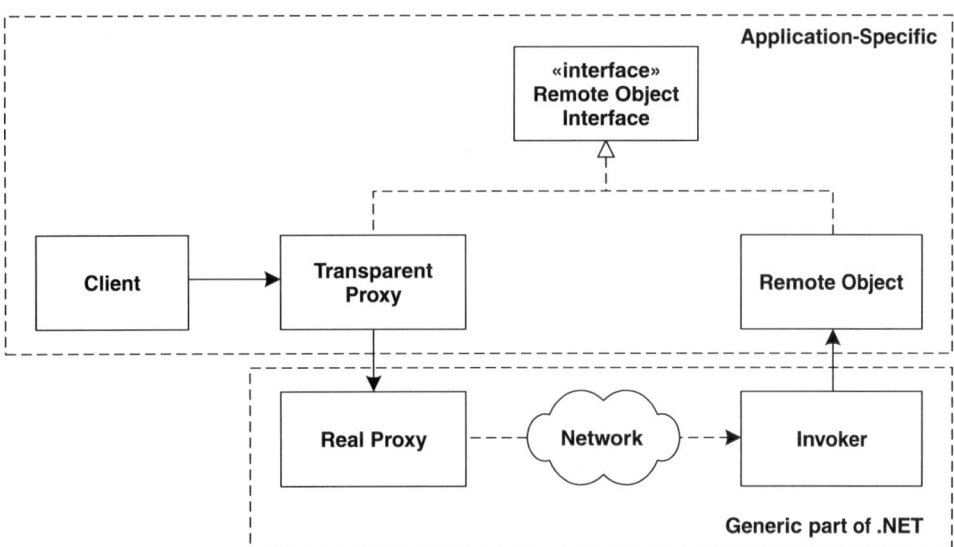

The interesting thing about the transparent proxy is that you never really see its implementation code. There is no explicit code generation step involved here. While in CORBA, for example, you have to manually code-generate the CLIENT PROXY, this is not necessary in .NET. .NET Remoting takes advantage of the features provided by the .NET runtime which transparently generates the proxy on the fly.

Let's look at this a little bit more closely. If a client wants to communicate with a remote object, typically it uses the Activator.GetObject operation to obtain a reference. This operation returns a CLIENT PROXY for the requested remote object, optionally contacting the server application to physically create the instance (depending on the activation mode). The client specifies two parameters: the type of the remote object (as an instance of the Type type) as well as a URL that points to the required object. Since the client passes the type object to the operation, this approach requires the remote object type to be available on the client already. There is thus no need to transfer the interface to the client as part of the Activator.GetObject call.

The returned transparent proxy implements the interface of the remote object by forwarding each method invocation to the real proxy that is connected to the server. The on-the-fly code generation is made possible by the Reflection.Emit namespace's classes, which can be used to generate MSIL code at runtime, packaging it into an in-memory assembly for direct execution in the running CLR instance.

To find out about the interface of the remote object (the interface that must also be used for the generated transparent proxy), the client runtime uses reflection on the type parameter given in the Activator.getObject call.

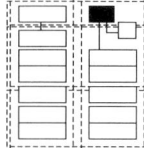

So what exactly is the interface of a remote object? .NET does not require developers to define an explicit interface for remote objects. By default, the public methods of the remote object class constitute the interface of the remote object. To allow the client to use reflection to build the transparent proxy, this implies that the implementation of the remote object is actually available to the client. However, it is not good design practice to transfer the implementation class's code to the client merely to invoke remote operation invocations.

It is therefore good practice to define an explicit interface for remote objects, as illustrated in the following code fragments.

```
namespace PatientManagementShared
{
  public interface IPatientManager
  {
    Patient getPatientInfo( String id );
  }
}
```

The remote object hosted by the server then has to implement this interface:

```
namespace PatientManagementServer
{
  public class PatientManager : MarshalByRefObject,
    IPatientManager
  {
    public Patient getPatientInfo( String id )
    {
      return new Patient( id );
    }
  }
}
```

Using this idiom, only the code of the interface IPatientManager needs to be available on the client, the implementation class is used only on the server. Note that the implementation code is not necessary at the client anyway, since the implementation on the client side must only package the invocation and forward it to the real proxy.

As a consequence of this process, we can write code that uses only the interface type on the client, as opposed to the remote object implementation class:

```
IPricingFactory pf = (IPricingFactory)Activator.GetObject(
    typeof( IPricingFactory ),
    "tcp://localhost:6642/PricingFactory" );
```

Extensibility of .NET Remoting

In this section we look at some advanced features of .NET Remoting, which are mostly concerned with extensibility. These include:

- INVOCATION INTERCEPTORS, which provide hooks into .NET Remoting's message-handling architecture
- INVOCATION CONTEXTS, which allow additional data to be sent with remote method invocations
- PROTOCOL PLUG-INS, which allow for adaptation of the communication protocol
- Custom MARSHALLERS, which allow adaptation of the marshaling format for specific needs

Intercepting the invocation stream

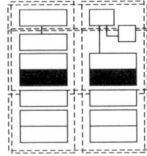

This section provides some details about how .NET Remoting works internally and how developers can extend its functionality. Note that for reasons of brevity we cannot delve into too much detail here. Please refer to [Ram02] for more information.

.NET can use several communication *channels* for access to remote objects. A channel provides a specific configuration for accessing remote objects. This includes protocols, the endpoint configuration, a message serializer and, as we shall see, INVOCATION INTERCEPTORS, if required. The Remoting framework in .NET is built as a layered system. Let's look at the following illustration first.

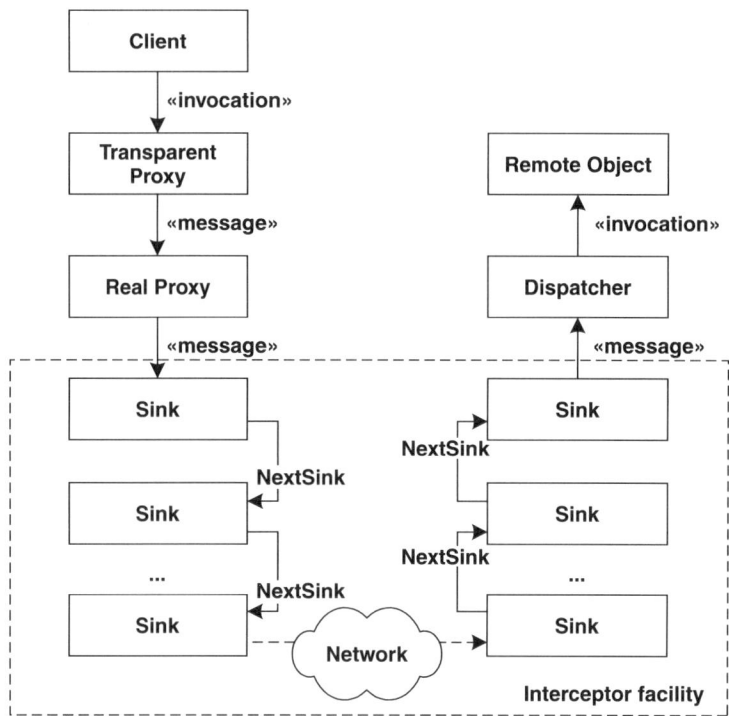

To implement INVOCATION INTERCEPTORS, .NET uses a set of *sinks*. As the above illustration shows, the sinks are organized as a chain in which each sink knows and invokes its successor (NextSink) after it has provided a specific aspect of the functionality required for the message transfer. The 'entry point' into this stack is provided by the transparent proxy, which transforms the invocation into a message. The message object contains information about the target object, the invoked operation, and the parameters. Its interface is defined as follows:

```
public interface IMessage
{
   IDictionary Properties{ get; }
}
```

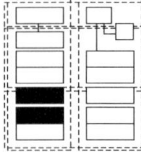

The message is then forwarded to the real proxy, which forwards the message to the top-most sink in the stack.

The message sink chain on the server and the client side are conceptually similar but not identical. Let's look at the client side. There are two very important sinks that play a vital role in the framework:

Extensibility of .NET Remoting

- The *formatter sink* serializes the message objects into a format suitable for transfer over the network.
- The *channel sink* handles the actual transfer of the serialized message over the network.

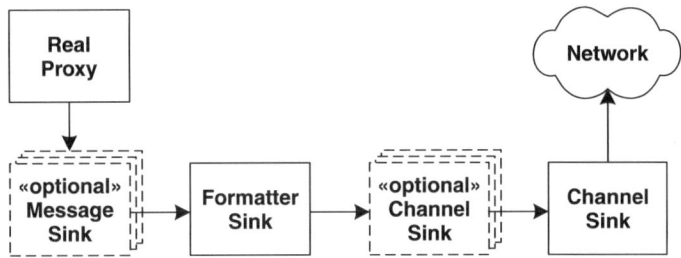

The extensibility of the .NET framework is largely due to the fact that it is possible to register application-specific sinks, and thereby provide invocation interception. There are sinks that have to be configured statically (that is, when a channel is created, using either the API or the XML configuration file) and others, the dynamic sinks, that can be configured into the chain at runtime. The static sinks can be further grouped into two types:

- *Message Sinks* intercept the stream when the message object is still in object form and not yet serialized
- *Channel Sinks* operate on the already-serialized messages

As the two kinds of sinks work with different data (message object vs. serialized data stream), their interfaces are different. The following interface is the one used for those sinks working on the message level (that is, before the message has been marshaled):

```
public interface IMessageSink
{
  IMessageSink NextSink{ get; }
  IMessageCtrl AsyncProcessMessage( IMessage msg,
                                    IMessageSink replySink );
  IMessage SyncProcessMessage(IMessage msg);
}
```

The two kinds of sinks are marked «optional» in the above illustration because you need not necessarily have them in a system: the minimum

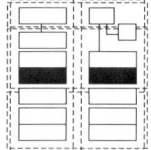

system configuration consists of a formatter sink, a channel sink, and some additional sinks that are beyond the scope of this book.

Sinks can either just inspect messages or modify them. For example, a channel sink can encrypt the message stream. The fragment of code below shows the interface of a dynamic sink:

```
public interface IDynamicMessageSink {
  void processMessageStart( IMessage request,
                            bool clientSide, bool isAsync );
  void processMessageFinish( IMessage reply,
                             bool clientSide, bool isAsync );
}
```

The `processMessageStart` operation is called by the framework when a request message is sent to the server. The message is passed as an argument. `processMessageFinish` is called for the reply.

On the server side, there is also a formatter sink, which deserializes a request and serializes the reply, as well as a channel sink, which handles network communication. For many tasks, the client- and server-side sinks must be compatible, for example using the same formatters on both sides. The same is true for custom sinks. If you plug in an encryption sink on the client, you need a compatible decryption sink on the server. Note that there are also sinks that do not need collaboration from 'the other side' – for example a logging sink.

It is also worth noting that the .NET framework itself uses sinks extensively. For example, there is an `SDLChannelSink` that creates WSDL [CCM+01] INTERFACE DESCRIPTIONS for a .NET Remoting interface.

Invocation interception using contexts

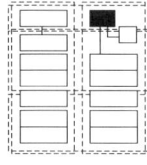

It is possible to associate objects running in the same (or different) application domains with different contexts. A context basically defines the services the runtime should apply to the objects within the context. Developers can associate objects with a context explicitly, making this feature an implementation of CONFIGURATION GROUPS. By associating a remote object with a specific context, you can define how the framework handles the object.

The services provided by a context:

- Are implemented using INVOCATION INTERCEPTORS, basically in the same way as explained in the section above
- Are requested for a specific type by adding specific ContextAttributes to the type

While the purpose of this facility is to allow framework developers to add their own interception-based services, some services are provided by the .NET framework directly. For example, you can ensure that concurrent access to instances of the SomeClass class is synchronized by applying the [Synchronization] attribute to a ContextBoundObject:

```
using System.Runtime.Remoting.Contexts;
[Synchronization]
public class SomeClass: ContextBoundObject
{...}
```

The implementation follows the same approach as in the case of remoting. A transparent proxy is generated; the real proxy forwards the invocation message (an instance of IMessage) to the first sink in the chain which, after doing its work, forwards the message to the next sink, until it reaches the StackBuilderSink, and finally, the destination object.

To implement a sink that can be used in such a scenario, developers have to implement the IMessageSink interface, which has been shown before.

Since communication inside contexts does not have to cross application domain, or even process, boundaries, no expensive marshaling is required when invocations between client and remote object are performed. An efficient CrossContextChannel is provided by the .NET framework. More details are beyond the scope of this book and can be found at [Low03].

Note that the context feature provides only a limited implementation of CONFIGURATION GROUPS, since many key characteristics cannot be defined using contexts, such as activation modes, associations between channels and contexts, as well as (thread) priorities.

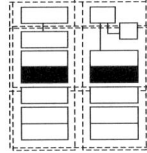

Invocation Contexts

INVOCATION CONTEXTS, which are known as CallContexts in .NET, can be used to transport information from a client to a remote object (and back) that is not part of the invocation data (target object, operation name, and parameters). Examples include security credentials, transaction information, or session IDs. The main motivations for using INVOCATION CONTEXTS are that the signature of the remote object operations should not need to feature these additional parameters, and that the client does not need to provide them explicitly when invoking an operation. This allows the addition of context data without changing clients or remote objects, and development of frameworks that handle this kind of data (and the associated services) transparently to the developer. So how do these additional information items get inserted into the INVOCATION CONTEXT? They are inserted typically by INVOCATION INTERCEPTORS (aka sinks) on the client and the server.

Let's first look at the API that allows passing of context data from client to server. In principle, the data is an associative array that contains name-value pairs:

```
SomeObject someObject = new SomeObject();
CallContext.setData( "itemName", someObject );
```

On the server, you can obtain the data item again:

```
SomeObject someObject =
   (SomeObject)CallContext.getData( "itemName");
```

The only precondition that must hold is that all objects that should be transferred as part of a `CallContext` must implement the `ILogicalThread-Affinitive` interface – a simple marker interface. The following is a legal class for `CallContext` transfers:

```
public class SomeObject : ILogicalThreadAffinitive {
}
```

Typically, the call context is populated and used from within custom sinks.

Protocol Plug-ins and custom Marshallers

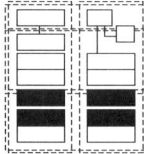

.NET provides pluggable message formats as well as exchangeable network stacks. As you have seen above, this variability is realized using sinks, which are implementations of the INVOCATION INTERCEPTOR pattern. .NET provides two ways of configuring the channels for sinks, and specifically for message formats and network stack adapters: using an API from within the application, or using an XML configuration file. We will look at both alternatives in turn.

In previous examples, you have typically seen the statements `RemotingSupport.setupClient` and `RemotingSupport.setupServer`. These are utility functions that hide the setup of formatters and network stacks. The following is the code from the `RemotingSupport` class:

```
namespace RemotingHelper
{
  public class RemotingSupport
  {
    public static void setupServer()
    {
      TcpChannel channel = new TcpChannel(6642);
      ChannelServices.RegisterChannel(channel);
    }
    public static void setupClient()
    {
      TcpChannel channel = new TcpChannel();
      ChannelServices.RegisterChannel(channel);
    }
  }
}
```

`setupServer` instantiates `TcpChannel` and listens on port 6642. The client also defines a `TcpChannel`, although we do not specify the port, because the client sockets will connect to whatever server port specified in the parameters of the `Activator.GetObject` operation.

The same configuration data can be specified in a configuration file:

```
<!-- file myapp.exe.config -->
<configuration>
  <system.runtime.remoting>
    <application>
      <channels>
        <channel ref="tcp" port="6642"/>
      </channels>
    </application>
  </system.runtime.remoting>
</configuration>
```

To configure an application, the configuration file must be loaded from within the application:

```
RemotingConfiguration.Configure( "myapp.exe.config" );
```

If you want to specify a specific formatter to be used in the server, you can add the following elements to your configuration file:

```
<channels>
  <channel ref="tcp" port="6642">
    <formatter ref="binary"/>
  </channel>
</channels>
```

To provide application-specific PROTOCOL PLUG-INS or custom MARSHALLERS, developers can implement their own classes for these two tasks and register them with the .NET Remoting framework. Details of this are beyond the scope of this book, however.

Note that there is no association between a channel and a particular remote object. All remote objects hosted by a server can be reached by all channels that are configured for the server.

For an example of a custom PROTOCOL PLUG-IN for .NET, see the IIOP implementation for .NET described in [OG03], or Borland's Janeva [Bor04].

QoS Observers and Location Forwarders

QOS OBSERVERS are not provided by .NET Remoting out of the box. However, it is fairly simple to build your own facilities here using sinks. You can define a message sink on the server side, where developers can register QOS OBSERVERS that are then notified if messages arrive for a specific remote object.

LOCATION FORWARDERS are not provided by .NET Remoting either.

Asynchronous communication

.NET provides a comfortable API for asynchronous remote communication. In fact, the facilities are not only usable for remote invocations, but also for local invocations. As you will see, the runtime, with its dynamic features provides the basis for the functionality.

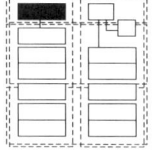

Asynchronous invocations are handled exclusively by the client of an invocation. This means that the remote object, as well as the server runtime, is not affected by asynchrony. While this is an advantage, there is also a serious problem with this approach: all the asynchrony is handled by executing code in a separate thread on the client side. This approach is not always the most efficient one, because threads are potentially expensive. In some cases you could use network characteristics (such as the UDP protocol), or a different server implementation, to implement asynchrony. As all this happens internally within the Remoting framework however, you cannot easily adapt the behavior to your own requirements.

When reading the following explanations of .NET Remoting's asynchronous communication features, you should bear in mind that you can of course also implement your own approach. For example, you can implement server-side asynchrony using an asynchronous handler as a server-side message sink. However, this requires more intricate programming, as well as changes to the server application configuration: you would have to add a specific message sink to realize this form of server-side asynchrony support.

The asynchronous features in .NET are implemented using *delegates*. Since they play a central role in understanding asynchrony, we will start with an introduction to delegates. Consider the class `SimpleCalculator`:

```
public class SimpleCalculator {
  public int add( int a, int b ) {
    return a+b;
  }
}
```

A delegate can be seen as a kind of 'object-oriented function pointer.' In our example, we want to be able to define a 'function pointer' to the `add` method. As with function pointers, say, in C, a delegate is typed by the method signature and the return type. So let's define a delegate that can point to methods that have two `int`s as arguments, and also return an `int`.

```
public class ThisIsAnotherClass {
  delegate int ExampleDelegate( int, int );
}
```

A delegate is a type declaration (in fact it's a reference type) and instances can be created. The instance takes the actual method to which the instance should point as an argument. This target operation's signature needs to be compatible.

```
public class ThisIsAnotherClass {
  delegate int ExampleDelegate( int, int );
  public void ExampleOperation() {
    SimpleCalculator sc = new SimpleCalculator();
    ExampleDelegate d = new ExampleDelegate( sc.add );
    int sum = d( 3, 7 ); // d calls sc.add(), sum is now 7
  }
}
```

The constructor of a delegate receives the target operation that should be invoked when an invocation is performed on the delegate (that is, during the invocation d(3,7)). In the example, the invocation d(3,7) calls the add operation of the sc object indirectly.

Delegates in .NET can also point to multiple methods at the same time. In that case, .NET builds a linked list of method pointers internally and calls each method in turn when the delegate is invoked. This feature is heavily used in .NET's event mechanism, but is not relevant to the following discussion.

Poll Objects

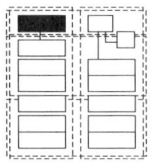

What is the relationship between delegates and asynchronous remote method invocations? Let's start by looking at the POLL OBJECT pattern and its implementation in .NET. Consider again our example of the remote version of the SimpleCalculator. We first look up an instance of the class:

```
ISimpleCalculator sc = (ISimpleCalculator)Activator.GetObject(
    typeof( ISimpleCalculator ),
    "tcp://localhost:6642/SimpleCalculator" );
```

We can then declare a delegate to the add operation of this object. In fact the delegate is actually defined for the transparent proxy instance that is returned from the Activator.GetObject operation:

```
delegate int RemoteAddCallDelegate( int, int );
```

Asynchronous communication

We now instantiate the delegate, pointing to the add operation of sc:

```
RemoteAddCallDelegate racd = new RemoteAddCallDelegate( sc.add );
```

You can now call an operation BeginInvoke on this delegate instance that will invoke the delegate's target operation asynchronously:

```
racd.BeginInvoke( 3, 4, null, null );
```

BeginInvoke is code-generated automatically by the compiler when it comes across the delegate declaration. It has (in this case) four parameters. The first two are the two ints of the add operation. Other operations have other parameters, depending on the signature of the target operation. The other two parameters will have null values in the example above – these are used for callbacks, which we explain below.

Invoking the operation executes the operation asynchronously. Of course, there is no POLL OBJECT yet. However, the BeginInvoke operation returns an instance of IAsyncResult which serves as the POLL OBJECT:

```
IAsyncResult ares = racd.BeginInvoke( 3, 4, null, null );
```

We can now do several things with this IAsyncResult. First of all, we can ask the object whether the result of the operation is available yet. This is a non-blocking operation and returns a bool:

```
bool isResultAvailable = ares.isCompleted;
```

We can also do a blocking wait until the result arrives:

```
ares.AsyncWaitHandle.WaitOne();
```

The main point of the POLL OBJECT, however, is to provide access to the return value of the asynchronously-invoked operation. The EndInvoke operation of the delegate allows access to it:

```
int sum = racd.EndInvoke( ares );
```

We have now invoked the operation asynchronously and received the result back to the calling thread. Note that no explicit downcast of the result was necessary. The compiler knows that the delegate returns an int.

It is also possible to catch exceptions thrown by the asynchronously-invoked operation. To do this, simply surround the EndInvoke operation in a try/catch clause:

```
try {
  int sum = racd.EndInvoke( ares );
  Console.WriteLine( "result:" + sum );
} catch ( Exception e ) {
  Console.WriteLine( "oops, exception:" + e );
}
```

Result Callbacks

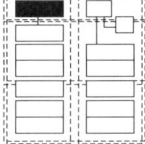

RESULT CALLBACKS are implemented on top of what we have seen above, namely delegates and the IAsyncResult interface. To provide a RESULT CALLBACK, we need a callback operation that is called by the .NET framework once the result of an asynchronous operation becomes available. Such a callback must be a void operation that takes exactly one argument of type IAsyncResult:

```
public class ThisIsAnotherClass {
  public void TheResultIsHere( IAsyncResult res ) {
    // ...
  }
  // ...
}
```

The invocation of the asynchronous operation works as before, except that the first null argument is replaced by an AsyncCallback delegate instance pointing to the callback operation:

```
public class ThisIsAnotherClass {
  // ...
  public void ExampleOperation() {
    // obtain a RemoteAddCallDelegate instance as above
    racd.BeginInvoke( 3, 4,
                new AsyncCallback(this.TheResultIsHere),
                null );
  }
}
```

When the result is available, the .NET framework invokes the delegate instance, that is, the TheResultIsHere operation of the current instance of the class ThisIsAnotherClass. In this operation we can now access the result in the same way as before:

```
public class ThisIsAnotherClass {
  public void TheResultIsHere( IAsyncResult res ) {
    RemoteAddCallDelegate racd = (RemoteAddCallDelegate)
      ((AsyncResult)res).AsyncDelegate;
    Console.WriteLine( "result: " + racd.EndInvoke(res) );
  }
}
```

The compiler creates the EndInvoke operation in a way that returns the result of the target operation – without a manual downcast.

.NET also supports the *Asynchronous Completion Token* (ACT) pattern [SSRB00]. The last parameter to BeginInvoke, null in the example here, can be used to supply an arbitrary value (the ACT) that can be accessed from the callback method to identify the asynchronous request.

Oneway operations

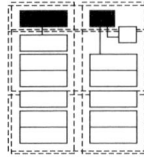

Oneway operations are the .NET implementation of FIRE AND FORGET; that is, the .NET framework provides best-effort semantics. In other words, nobody knows whether the operation is actually executed. Oneway operations – when used in the simplest way – provide no feedback about the result of an invocation execution, be it a return value or an exception. This is the reason why oneway operations must have a void return type.

To make an operation a oneway, the operation declaration needs to specify this. Oneway operations have to have the [OneWay] attribute. The following example shows this:

```
public interface ILogger {
  [OneWay()]
  void logMessage( string message );
  void store();
}
```

The logMessage operation is declared to be oneway. Invocations of this operation therefore have FIRE AND FORGET semantics, while the store operation is not oneway – it is invoked synchronously. The client can now invoke the operation without the `BeginInvoke/EndInvoke` construct, as the following example shows:

```
ILogger logger = (ILogger)Activator.GetObject(
        typeof( ILogger ), "tcp://localhost:6642/logger" );
logger.logMessage( "hello!" );
```

This invocation is handled asynchronously, although it looks like a normal synchronous method call. There is an important point to make here, though: although we have modified the interface definition of the remote object by adding the [OneWay] attribute, the asynchrony is still handled on the client! When the transparent proxy is generated by the runtime, its implementation contains the necessary code to invoke the operation in a separate thread. Note the difference to the other asynchronous invocation techniques explained in this chapter: in the case of POLL OBJECTS and RESULT CALLBACKS, it is the caller of the operation that decides whether the operation should be called synchronously or asynchronously. In case of oneway operations, it is defined as part of the operation's interface, so the server (the provider of the interface) decides that the operation should always be invoked asynchronously.

Let's finally look at exceptions. Exceptions thrown by the remote object's oneway operation are ignored, and are not reported back to the client. The same is true for exceptions thrown by the CLIENT PROXY or framework. For example, if the server application is down or unreachable, the operation *still succeeds* from a client's point of view. No exception is thrown, although the invocation never reaches the server. Note that this is true even if you invoke the oneway operation using delegates plus `BeginInvoke/EndInvoke` and enclose the `EndInvoke` call into a try/catch clause.

Other asynchronous invocation modes

In .NET, SYNC WITH SERVER semantics are not supported out of the box: all the asynchrony we have described is implemented with the help of threads on the client side. If we need SYNC WITH SERVER, we have to implement it ourselves. This means however that the server needs to be changed. The simplest way to achieve this is to execute the business logic on the server in a separate thread. This could be implemented in the operation itself, or with the help of a suitable message sink.

Outlook for the next generation

Indigo is Microsoft's upcoming technology for distributed ('connected') systems. Indigo subsumes several current APIs and technologies, such as .NET Remoting, ASMX and COM+. It is a service-oriented framework that makes communication boundaries explicit, as opposed to trying to hide them, as most other current remoting frameworks do. Indigo is based on a messaging abstraction, but in contrast to current messaging infrastructures it provides convenient support for request/reply style programming and other higher-level programming models, as well as additional services such as transaction and security. Indigo also provides transport over several protocols, among them the well-known Web Services infrastructure based on SOAP. Several hosting environments are supported. Indigo components can be run inside normal applications, as a Windows service, or in the context of the IIS.

Core Components

At its core, Indigo consists of the following components:

- *Ports* constitute network endpoints that can be addressed remotely, and also define the supported protocol.
- *Message Handlers* contain the actual application logic to handle the messages.
- *Channels* connect ports with message handlers. Channels are used to configure additional services, such as transactions and security, and to configure the programming model, such as reliable or unreliable messaging.

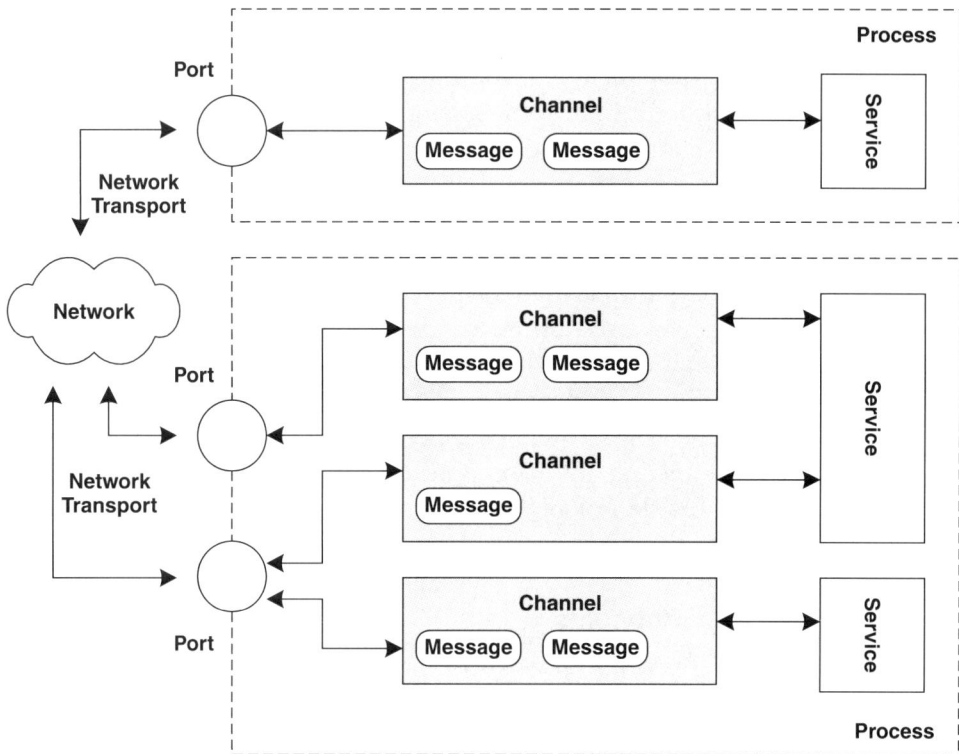

Application developers first have to define ports, then configure the channels that provide access to the ports (including a channel's services), and finally register message handlers with the ports. Note that there is no notion of a server or a client, since any process can receive and send messages.

Pattern mapping in Indigo

Ports implement the CLIENT REQUEST HANDLER and SERVER REQUEST HANDLER patterns. Channels fulfill multiple roles:

- They implement the role of a REQUESTOR, accepting Message objects
- They are part of the INVOKER, dispatching incoming Message objects to registered Message Handlers
- They are INVOCATION INTERCEPTORS, in the sense that additional services can be 'plugged in' to the channel

OBJECT IDS are strings, such as 'simple'. ABSOLUTE OBJECT REFERENCES further define the protocol, the host, and the port at which the service is provided, so that a complete ABSOLUTE OBJECT REFERENCE looks like this: soap://localhost:50000/simple.

As messaging is by its very nature asynchronous, a specific set-up is needed to use it for synchronous invocations. For a client-side synchronous request/reply messaging style, a separate RequestReplyManager, provided by the framework, must be used to send requests and receive results synchronously. For server-side synchronous request/reply style, a SyncMessageHandler must be used.

.NET Remoting technology projection has shown how easy using distributed object middleware can be. As soon as more advanced usage scenarios have to be addressed, however, a basic understanding of the inner workings is still necessary, for example of interception points using sinks, application domains, and lifecycle management via leases and sponsors.

11 Web Services Technology Projection

Web Services provide a standardized means of service-based interoperation between distributed software applications. These applications can run on a variety of platforms, and use different programming languages, and/or frameworks. The use of Web Services on the World Wide Web is expanding rapidly as the need for application-to-application communication and interoperability grows [BHM+03].

The goals of Web Services go beyond those of classical middleware frameworks such as CORBA, DCOM, or RMI: they aim at standardized support for higher-level interactions such as service and process flow orchestration, enterprise application integration (EAI), and provision of a 'middleware for middleware' [Vin03].

Web Services are defined by a number of protocols and standards. The implementations of these protocols and standards in different Web Services frameworks vary, but share many characteristics. For example, the APIs used in Web Services frameworks are not standardized, although they are typically quite simple. We use Apache Axis [Apa04b] as a representative and well-known Web Services framework in the main part of this technology projection. This chapter shows how Axis is designed using the patterns presented in this book. We also discuss other Web Services frameworks towards the end of this chapter, namely GLUE [Min04], Microsoft's .NET Web Services, IONA's Artix, and Leela [Zdu04c]. These frameworks are only discussed briefly to illustrate interesting characteristics of how the patterns are used by these frameworks.

A brief history of Web Services

Before we take an in-depth look 'under the hood' of current Web Services frameworks, let's take a brief look at the bigger picture and understand the motivation for Web Services.

Consider a situation in which multiple business processes are co-existing and cutting across multiple departments, or even companies. Each of these parties has its own IT infrastructure, which probably includes many different pre-existing applications, programming languages, component and middleware platforms (for example J2EE, .NET, CORBA, or MQSeries), backends, and third-party systems such as ERP or CRM systems. Somehow this heterogeneous IT landscape has to be integrated.

The goal of Web Services is to integrate such heterogeneous environments by enabling a standardized, *Service-Oriented Architecture* (SOA). The basic concept of an SOA is quite trivial: a service is offered using a message-oriented remote interface that employs some kind of well-defined INTERFACE DESCRIPTION. The service can be implemented, for example, as a remote object, or as any other kind of service implementation, such as a set of procedures. The service advertises itself at a central service, the lookup service. This lookup service realizes the pattern LOOKUP, and is implemented as a STATIC INSTANCE. Applications can therefore look up the advertised services by name or properties to find details of how to interact with the service.

There are many things that are called 'Web Services'. For the purpose of this chapter, and without prejudice towards other definitions, we will use the following definition, which is similar to that of [BHM+03]:

> *A Web Service is a software system designed to support interoperable machine-to-machine interaction over a network. It has an interface described in a machine-processable format (specifically WSDL). Other systems interact with the Web Service in a manner prescribed by its description using messages (specifically SOAP messages). Messages are conveyed typically using HTTP with an XML serialization, in conjunction with other Web-related standards, but any other communication protocol can be used for message delivery as well.*

Web Services emerged from the World Wide Web (WWW). The WWW was designed initially for unstructured information exchange. The information in HTML text is primarily designed to be used by humans. Over time the Web was used for machine-to-machine communication as well, such as e-commerce applications and business-to-business (B2B) communication. XML [BPS98] and many XML-based standards have emerged to facilitate structured information exchange on the Web.

Early e-services, however, have exposed their interfaces in an ad-hoc manner, meaning that no standardized interoperability existed between services.

The XML-RPC specification was released in 1999 [Win99] as a simple remote procedure call definition. To further facilitate automated access to complex services, a group of companies, including IBM and Microsoft, and more recently the W3C, have released a number of Web Services standards. These include SOAP [BEK+00], WSDL [CCM+01], and UDDI [Oas02]. SOAP is the successor to XML-RPC.

Today's Web Services are distributed services with WSDL interfaces. They are more often message-oriented than RPC-oriented. WSDL allows for a variety of transports, protocols, and message formats. SOAP over HTTP is just one possible Web Services protocol.

A number of successful middleware frameworks, such as CORBA, DCOM, .NET Remoting, or RMI, have been around for a while and can also be used to build complex services. The question therefore arises: aren't Web Services just reinventing the wheel? In the middleware integration world, however, interoperability problems occurred that are similar to the early inter-operation problems of e-services. As Steve Vinoski puts it [Vin03]: "Unfortunately, middleware's success and proliferation has recreated – at a higher level – the very problem it was designed to address. Rather than having to deal with multiple different operating systems, today's distributed-application developers face multiple middleware approaches." Among other things, a goal of Web Services is to provide a 'middleware for middleware.'

In this section we explain some central differences of the Web Services approach compared to other middleware approaches. Internally, Web Services are implemented using the same remoting patterns as other distributed object middleware systems – which is what we try to convey in the remainder of this technology projection.

Web Services are designed around the stateless exchange of messages. This design is originally due to the stateless nature of the HTTP protocol. In HTTP, stateful interactions are implemented as extensions on top of HTTP, such as cookies or sessions. Web Services use a similar stateless request/reply scheme for a message-oriented interaction, leading to a loose coupling of clients and servers.

SOAP is an XML-based message exchange format that is used in almost all Web Services frameworks available to date. It can be extended in various ways, including secure, reliable, multi-part, multi-party, and/or multi-network transport of messages. This also allows the messaging infrastructure to provide authentication, encryption, access control, transaction processing, routing, delivery confirmation, and so on. SOAP has quickly become a de-facto standard in the Web Services domain. It is often equated to 'Web Services' in general, although this is not quite correct, as there are other Web Services protocols around, and most applications of Web Services use more technical infrastructure than just a message-exchange protocol. As shown below, there is a 'stack' of different components (which often differ in different implementations) that together provide a Web Services infrastructure.

WSDL is used for XML-based service descriptions commonly understood by Web Services producers and consumers – among other information, it contains INTERFACE DESCRIPTIONS. It facilitates interoperability across heterogeneous systems by providing the precise structure and data types of the messages.

Web Services do not require any particular communication protocol. For example, HTTP, other Internet protocols such as SMTP and FTP, generic interface APIs such as JMS, other distributed object protocols such as IIOP, or almost any other communication protocol can be used. Most Web Services implementations today, however, use HTTP as their communication protocol.

Above the level of individual message exchanges, Web Services standardize process descriptions. This includes UDDI as a lookup service, a kind of service that can be found in many other distributed object middleware as well. But it also includes XML-based standards for higher-level business transactions, multi-part and stateful sequences of messages, and the aggregation of elementary processes into composite processes. For example, the Business Process Execution Language for Web Services (BPEL4WS) [ACD+03] is an XML-based workflow definition language that allows businesses to describe business processes that can both consume and provide Web Services. BPEL emerged from IBM's WSFL and Microsoft's XLANG. The WS-Coordination [CCC+03] and WS-Transaction [CCC+02] specifications complement BPEL4WS, in that they provide a Web Services-based approach to improving the dependability of automated, long-running business transactions in an

A brief history of Web Services

extensible and interoperable way. The Business Process Management Initiative specifies the Business Process Modelling Language (BPML) [Bpm02]. BPML provides an abstracted execution model for collaborative and transactional business processes based on the concept of transactional finite-state machines.

In addition to specific messaging and description technologies, the Web Services architecture also provides for security and management. These are complex areas that are applied on multiple levels of the Web Services architecture.

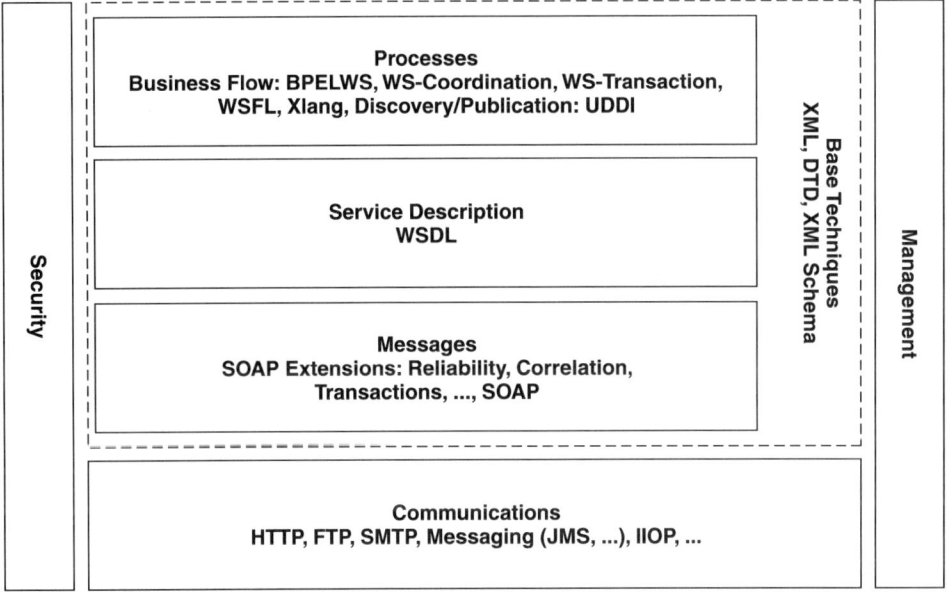

The figure above shows a high level architecture for Web Services [BHM+03]. Note that XML is the basis of the Web Services architecture. One can provide a Web Services framework that works without SOAP or WSDL, but XML is seen as more fundamental for two reasons [BHM+03]. First, XML provides the extensibility and vendor, platform, and language neutrality that is the key to loosely-coupled, standards-based interoperability. Second, XML helps to blur the distinction between payload data and protocol data, allowing easier mapping and bridging between different communications protocols, because the same tools and frameworks can be used.

Web Services pattern map

The following diagram summarizes the use of the Remoting Patterns within the Web Services architectures we describe here. We use the terms from Apache Axis in the figure, but this general static architecture is very similar in the other Web Services frameworks that are discussed towards the end of the chapter. Note that purely dynamic patterns, such as those in Chapter 5, *Lifecycle Management Patterns* or Chapter 8, *Invocation Asynchrony Patterns*, are not illustrated in the figure.

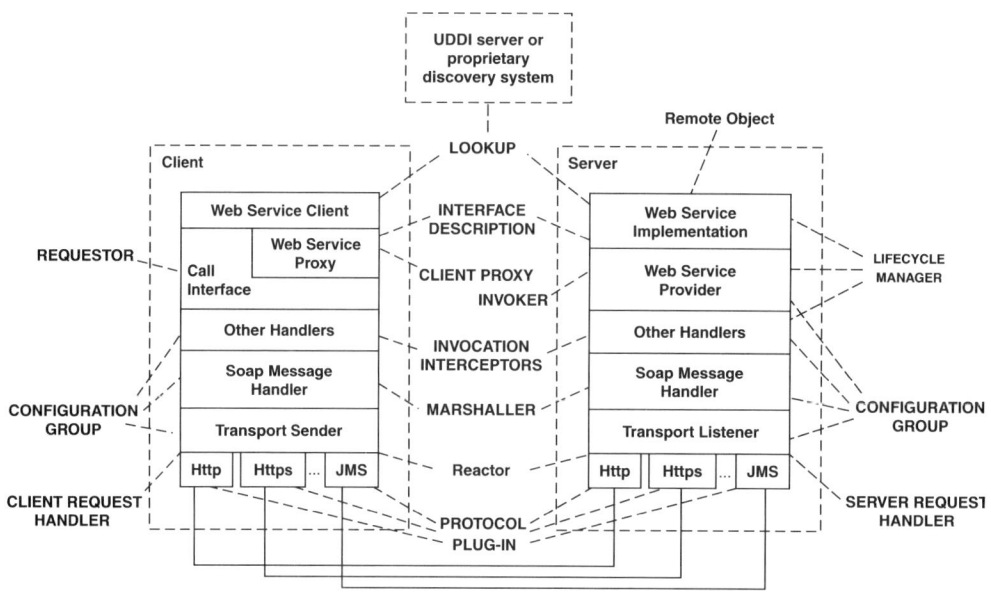

SOAP messages

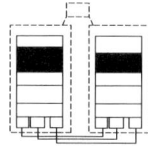

SOAP [BEK+00] is a standard, XML-based protocol used for invoking Web Services via messages. It supports RPC-style invocations (request/reply) and other distribution paradigms, such as asynchronous messaging or oneway messages. From a developer's perspective a SOAP implementation provides the *Layer* [BMR+96] of REQUESTOR, CLIENT PROXY, and INVOKER.

In this section, we discuss two ways to use SOAP from the perspective of developers of Web Services clients or server applications. First, we show how to construct an invocation of remote objects dynamically using a REQUESTOR and INVOKER. Second, we discuss how to use the INTERFACE DESCRIPTION language WSDL to generate CLIENT PROXY and INVOKER. Axis supports the client invocation models defined by the Sun's JAX-RPC API standard [Sun04b].

Dynamic invocation of remote objects on the server side

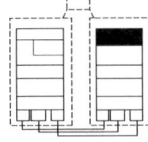

Let's look at an Apache Axis example to explain how the *Basic Remoting Patterns* are realized for Web Services. We will discover that the Axis framework offers quite simple APIs. Most other Web Services frameworks offer simple interfaces to provide or access a Web Service as well.

As an introductory example, let us consider using a SOAP-based Web Service that provides a simple date service in Java with Apache Axis. First we have to implement the service provider as an ordinary Java class:

```
package simpleDateService;
import java.util.*;
import java.text.SimpleDateFormat;

public class DateService {
  public String getDate (String format) {
    Date today = new Date();
    SimpleDateFormat formatter =
      new SimpleDateFormat(format);
    String result = formatter.format(today);
    return result;
  }
  public String getDate () {
    return getDate("EEE d MMM yyyy");
  }
}
```

This simple date service class provides two methods for querying the current date (and time), one using a default format (without a parameter) and one using the given format parameter. The remote objects offered by our Web Services application are instances of the DateService class.

Note that a Web Services remote object does not have to be implemented as an object internally. For example, it can instead by implemented by a set of procedures. In this way Web Services can be used to provide an object-oriented view of a procedural application.

In the Axis framework, the simplest way to provide a Web Service in a server is to use a SOAP INVOKER. The INVOKER is set up when the object is deployed to the Web Server and runs on the Web Server. We have to tell the INVOKER which services it provides and which operations are exported by each service. This is done in an XML file, called the *deployment descriptor*:

```
<deployment xmlns="http://xml.apache.org/axis/wsdd/"
    xmlns:java="http://xml.apache.org/axis/wsdd/providers/java">
  <service name="DateService" provider="java:RPC">
    <parameter name="className"
      value="simpleDateService.DateService"/>
    <parameter name="allowedMethods" value="getDate"/>
  </service>
</deployment>
```

When this deployment descriptor is sent to the Axis engine running in the Web application server, the INVOKER is informed that it supports a new Web Service with the symbolic ID DateService. This ID is used as an OBJECT ID for the Web Service. Whenever the corresponding URL, such as:

```
http://localhost:8080/axis/services/DateService
```

is accessed by a SOAP client, the INVOKER knows that an instance of the class simpleDateService.DateService is responsible for handling the invocation. Thus, when an invocation reaches the server, the INVOKER looks up the class, creates a PER-REQUEST INSTANCE of the class, and lets the instance handle the request.

In the SOAP request the operation name and parameters of the invocation are encoded. Before the invocation is performed, it is checked that the invocation is an 'allowed method' (here only the operation getDate is valid). It is additionally checked that the parameter number and types are also valid. If one of these invocation preliminaries is not valid, a SOAP REMOTING ERROR is returned to the client, otherwise the result of the operation invocation.

During the deployment we have announced to the server that the OBJECT ID DateService has to be mapped to an instance (here a PER-REQUEST INSTANCE) of the class simpleDateService.DateService.

Almost all Web Services frameworks provide some dynamic form of deployment. That is, remote objects can be registered and de-registered with the INVOKER dynamically. However, not all frameworks use an XML-based deployment descriptor. This XML-based deployment scheme is flexible and common for Java application servers. It decouples deployment code from application code. Compared with deployment code that is hard-coded within the application code, as in the case of GLUE (discussed below), the downsides are an additional level of complexity for developers and an overhead for XML processing. XML can only define the deployment in a declarative manner, whereas programmatic deployment specifications can also define a deployment behavior, such as a conditional deployment.

Note that URLs are used as ABSOLUTE OBJECT REFERENCES by a client to access a Web Service. Using URLs as ABSOLUTE OBJECT REFERENCES is simple and eases integration of Web Services with existing Web protocols such as HTTP, FTP, or DNS. However, URLs do not necessarily stay stable over the time: for example, when the server is started on another machine or when the machine's host name changes, the ABSOLUTE OBJECT REFERENCES have to be updated in all clients.

The Internet's Domain Name System (DNS) [Moc87] realizes a variant of LOOKUP that is used for finding the host that belongs to an URL. By changing the DNS entry, we can update the information provided to clients – thus the DNS can be used as a LOCATION FORWARDER when URLs are used as ABSOLUTE OBJECT REFERENCES. Note that DNS is not primarily designed for this task. For example, it takes a relatively long time to update DNS entries. A better solution to this problem might be to use HTTP Redirect [FGM+97] or other forwarding approaches. These approaches realize a LOCATION FORWARDER for Web Services directly on the original server, and thus have an immediate effect.

Constructing an invocation with a requestor on the client side

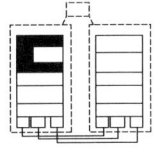
On the client side we have to write a Web Services client that accesses the SOAP INVOKER via the network. The Axis framework provides a REQUESTOR that enables users to construct requests dynamically. The

details of transporting the invocation across the network using SOAP are then handled by the Axis framework:

```
public class DateClient {
  public static void main(String [] args) {
    try {
      Options options = new Options(args);
      String endpointURL = options.getURL();
      String formatString;
      Object[] arguments = null;

      args = options.getRemainingArgs();
      if ((args == null) || (args.length < 1)) {
        formatString = null;
      } else {
        formatString = args[0];
      }

      Service service = new Service();
      Call call = (Call) service.createCall();

      call.setTargetEndpointAddress(
        new java.net.URL(endpointURL));
      call.setOperationName("getDate");
      if (formatString != null) {
        call.addParameter("format",
                    XMLType.XSD_STRING, ParameterMode.IN);
        arguments = new Object[] { formatString };
      }
      call.setReturnType(
        org.apache.axis.encoding.XMLType.XSD_STRING);
      String result = (String) call.invoke(arguments);
      System.out.println("Date: " + result);
    } catch (Exception e) {
      System.err.println(e.toString());
    }
  }
}
```

In this example the client takes the command-line arguments provided by the user, and accesses one of the two operations provided by the remote object. The Call class provided by the framework implements the REQUESTOR pattern, which lets us construct an invocation from a given URL, an operation name, parameters, and a return type. The Service class is used as a the starting point for access to SOAP Web Services on client side. In the example it provides a *Factory Method*

[GHJV95] `createCall` to create an instance of the `Call` class. Example invocations of the above client program are:

```
% java simpleDateService.DateClient
  -lhttp://localhost:8080/axis/services/DateService
% java simpleDateService.DateClient
  -lhttp://localhost:8080/axis/services/DateService "dd.MM.yy"
```

Generating the Invoker and Client Proxy code using WSDL

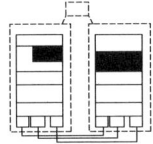

The dynamic invocation variants of REQUESTOR and INVOKER used above avoid static stubs for clients and so-called 'skeletons' for the server side. The goal is to configure service information, which is very flexible and generic. Another benefit is that the client has full control over the invocation. As the INVOKER handles all the details of the invocation, it requires only a proper deployment descriptor to deploy or un-deploy any Java class as a Web Service in the Web Services engine running on a Web Server. However, the disadvantage of this approach is that the client has to deal with remoting details directly, such as constructing the `Call` object and handling argument types. Sometimes this level of detail is required, for example when we want to control the way in which `Call` objects are constructed. In other cases we can use an INTERFACE DESCRIPTION to hide the details of the remote invocation: we can generate CLIENT PROXY and INVOKER code from the INTERFACE DESCRIPTION, so that the client developer does not have to deal with the details of the SOAP invocation.

Web Services Description Language (WSDL) [CCM+01] is a standard, XML-based language for INTERFACE DESCRIPTIONS of Web Services. It is based on the following abstract definitions and bindings:

- *Types* contain data type definitions that are required for later use in the messages.
- *Messages* are abstract definitions of the data being exchanged. They are organized in one or more logical parts. Each part has a type, and the types are extensible.
- A *port type*[1] is a named set of abstract operations and the abstract messages involved.
- *Operations* describe the abstract behavior supported by the service.
- A *binding* defines message format and protocol details for operations and messages defined by a particular port type.

---

1. Note that port type is renamed to *interface* in the recent WSDL 2.0 specification.

- A *port*[2] defines an individual endpoint for a binding. That is, it maps the abstract communication scheme of the binding to a concrete communication protocol.
- *Service*s are defined as a collection of ports.

Each port has one binding, and each binding has a single port type. Each service, in contrast, can have multiple ports. Each of these ports is an alternative way to access the service. Note that WSDL describes the concept of PROTOCOL PLUG-INS in this way – we will see in later sections how the Web Services framework architecture mirrors this extensibility with communication protocols. The following figure shows how the elements of WSDL inter-relate. We can see that WSDL distinguishes elements for the abstract interface specification of services (port types, operations, and messages), the access binding specifications, and the concrete collection of endpoints (ports) in a service.

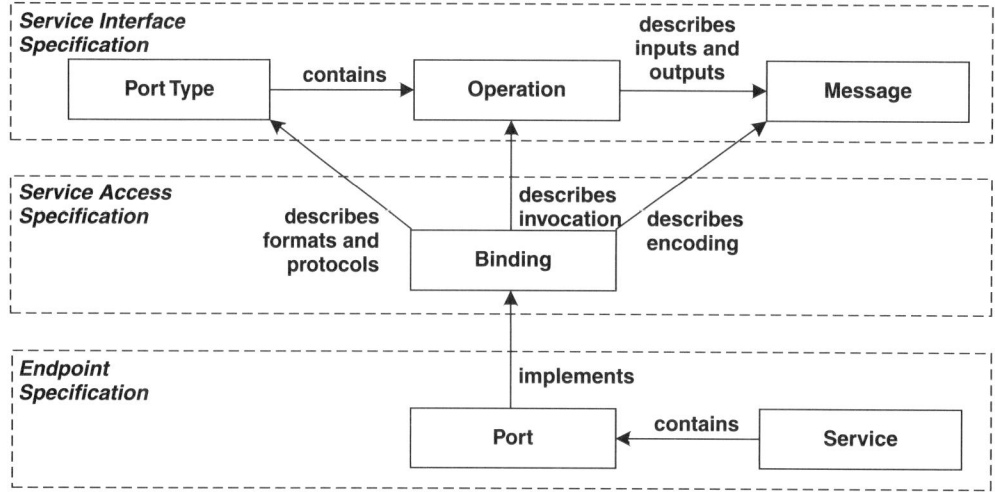

In contrast to other INTERFACE DESCRIPTIONS in other distributed object middleware, this scheme is relatively complex. The reason for this complexity is that the INTERFACE DESCRIPTION of a Web Service not only describes the remote object's interfaces, but also the protocol binding, how it can be reached, and its location. Because the protocols used might be quite diverse, we require a very generic binding scheme. Therefore almost all Web Services frameworks provide some means of

---

2. Note that port is renamed to *endpoint* in the recent WSDL 2.0 specification

generating the WSDL code for deployed Web Services or Web Services classes automatically. In many cases, this generated WSDL code can be accessed or downloaded remotely. Thus clients can download the INTERFACE DESCRIPTION describing how to access a Web Service, and can then generate a CLIENT PROXY on the fly.

Example of Invoker and Client Proxy generation and invocation using WSDL

Now that we have explained WSDL in general, let's see an example in Axis. In Axis two generation tools are provided: one to generate a WSDL description from an existing Java class (Java2WSDL), and one to generate CLIENT PROXY and INVOKER code from WSDL (WSDL2Java). Axis follows the JAX-RPC specification [Sun04b] when generating Java client bindings from WSDL. The main advantage of using WSDL is to avoid having to write the stub and binding (or skeleton) classes, as well as the deployment descriptors, by hand. The WSDL generation tool is also integrated in the Axis engine: for a deployed service, Axis allows developers to invoke a method to generate WSDL for a service on the fly (the WSDL output can for example be viewed via a Web browser).

As an example, we simply define the remote object's services in the programming language used (here, Java):

```
package wsdlDate;
public interface SimpleDate {
  public String getDate (String arg);
  public String getDate ();
}
```

We also implement these methods in a remote object class SimpleDateImpl:

```
public class SimpleDateImpl implements SimpleDate {
  ...
}
```

Now we can use the Axis tool Java2WSDL to create a WSDL file from the INTERFACE DESCRIPTION:

```
java org.apache.axis.wsdl.Java2WSDL -o wsdlDate/Date.wsdl
  -l "http://localhost:8080/axis/services/wsdlDate"
  -n urn:wsdlDate -p "wsdlDate" urn:wsdlDate wsdlDate.SimpleDate
```

The tool generates the INTERFACE DESCRIPTION using reflective information obtained from the remote object interface. All missing information (such as service name, namespace, package, and address) is provided as command line parameters to the tool. The generated WSDL file defines the request and reply messages, the service interface, the SOAP binding of the service, and the URL address of the service. The part of this WSDL file, describing the service, looks as follows:

```
...
<wsdl:message name="getDateResponse">
  <wsdl:part name="getDateReturn" type="xsd:string"/>
</wsdl:message>
...
<wsdl:portType name="SimpleDate">
  <wsdl:operation name="getDate" parameterOrder="in0">
    <wsdl:input name="getDateRequest"
      message="intf:getDateRequest"/>
    <wsdl:output name="getDateResponse"
      message="intf:getDateResponse"/>
  </wsdl:operation>
  <wsdl:operation name="getDate">
    ...
  </wsdl:operation>
</wsdl:portType>

<wsdl:binding name="wsdlDateSoapBinding" type="intf:SimpleDate">
  <wsdlsoap:binding style="rpc"
    transport="http://schemas.xmlsoap.org/soap/http"/>
  <wsdl:operation name="getDate">
    <wsdl:message name="getDateResponse">
      <wsdl:part name="getDateReturn" type="xsd:string"/>
    </wsdl:message>
    ...
  </wsdl:operation>
  <wsdl:operation name="getDate">
    ...
  </wsdl:operation>
</wsdl:binding>

<wsdl:service name="SimpleDateService">
  <wsdl:port name="wsdlDate"
    binding="intf:wsdlDateSoapBinding">
    <wsdlsoap:address
      location="http://localhost:8080/axis/services/wsdlDate"/>
  </wsdl:port>
</wsdl:service>
```

The above WSDL code introduces a number of messages that are later used to define operations in port types. The port type SimpleDate is provided with two operations, both named getDate. The first of these operations accepts a parameter, the other none. The possible inputs and outputs of operations, defined in the portType section, are the messages declared in the messages section before it. The following WSDL binding maps the port type to a SOAP RPC invocation. The service is then used to map the port to the binding and configure the Web Services location.

An alternative to using generative tools on the server side that create WSDL is to generate WSDL code directly from the deployed service at runtime. This has the advantage that the deployment information (such as service name, namespace, package, and address) is available and does not have to be specified using command-line parameters. GLUE uses this variant, while Axis provides both variants.

The following figure shows the classes that are generated on the client and server side for the example.

The package wsdlDate contains the user-defined classes, as described above. The package wsdlDate.ws contains the classes generated from the classes in the package wsdlDate. These generated classes are, in particular:

- WsdlDateSoapBindingImpl is a generated part of the INVOKER (in other middleware systems this part is called skeleton or server side stub) that invokes the remote object on server side.
- WsdlDateSoapBindingStub is a CLIENT PROXY corresponding to the generated INVOKER part to be used on client side.
- The common interface SimpleDate is used both on client and server side, as it is required for both CLIENT PROXY and INVOKER.
- SimpleDateService is a factory interface to create instances of SimpleDate.
- SimpleDateServiceLocator is a concrete factory class for the CLIENT PROXY. It is to be used on client side.

If WSDL is generated from the deployed service, only the client-side classes need to be generated using the tool WSDL2Java (this can be specified using a command-line option). In other frameworks, such as

GLUE, the CLIENT PROXY can also be generated on the fly (see the discussion of GLUE on page 281).

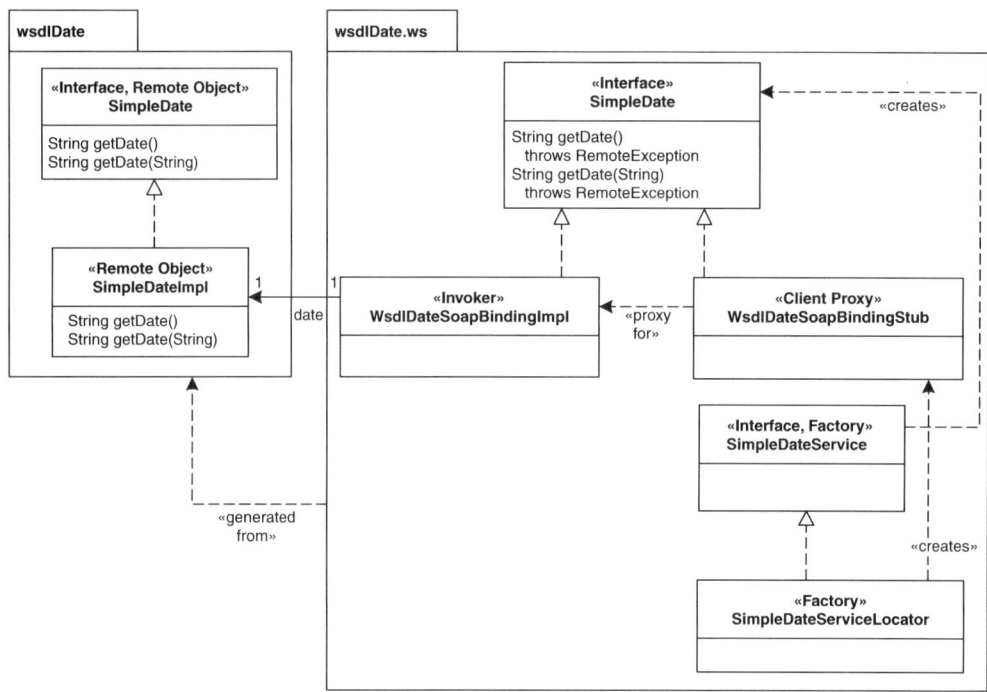

The interface `SimpleDate` is the interface provided remotely. It is implemented by the server side binding and the generated CLIENT PROXY. The interface's operations throw a REMOTING ERROR (here a `java.rmi.RemoteException`).

The generated package on the server side provides classes to be used by the INVOKER. `WsdlDateSoapBindingImpl` implements the interface described in the WSDL file. It does not contain the Web Services implementation, but uses wrapper methods that simply forward invocations to the Web Services implementation. This class is hooked into the INVOKER using the RPC provider – see the following sections. Besides this class, two XML files are generated: `deploy.wsdd` to deploy the Web Service, and `undeploy.wsdd` to undeploy the Web Service from the Axis engine.

On the client side, WsdlDateSoapBindingStub contains a SOAP-based implementation of the CLIENT PROXY interface. SimpleDateService contains an interface to access the service from the client. That means in particular that it provides a factory for the SimpleDate CLIENT PROXY interface. SimpleDateServiceLocator contains an implementation of the CLIENT PROXY factory that creates objects of the type WsdlDateSoapBindingStub.

The resulting runtime architecture and the interfaces and implementations used in this architectures are depicted in the figure below.

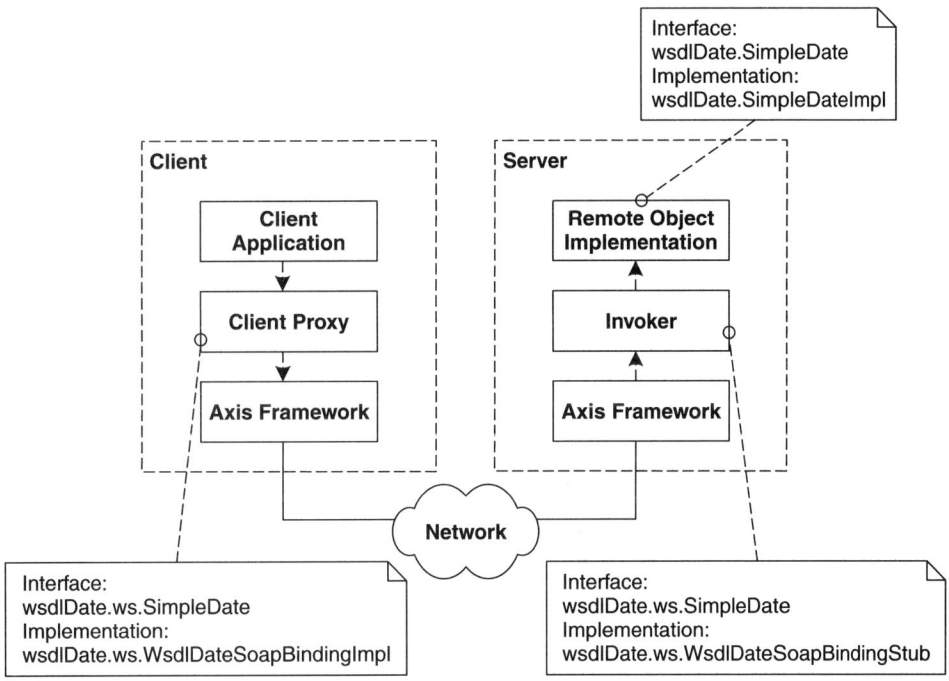

To create these files automatically, we have to invoke the WSDL2Java tool:

```
java org.apache.axis.wsdl.WSDL2Java -o . -d Session -s
   -p wsdlDate.ws wsdlDate/Date.wsdl
```

On the client side, a simpler client than the dynamic invocation client from the previous section can be implemented that abstracts from most of the distribution details. The following client code instantiates the factory, creates a CLIENT PROXY, and performs two remote invocations:

```
package wsdlDate;
public class DateClient {
  public static void main(String [] args) throws Exception {
    wsdlDate.ws.SimpleDateService service =
      new wsdlDate.ws.SimpleDateServiceLocator();
    wsdlDate.ws.SimpleDate dateProxy = service.getwsdlDate();
    System.out.println(dateProxy.getDate());
    System.out.println(dateProxy.getDate("dd-MM-yyyy"));
  }
}
```

The use of INTERFACE DESCRIPTION in Axis and other Web Services frameworks combines the benefits of using reflective code as a local interface repository with INTERFACE DESCRIPTIONS that can be sent to the client. WSDL is mainly used for providing interoperability and platform independence of Web Services implementations. With a WSDL description of a Web Service – say obtained with a lookup service such as UDDI, or downloaded from the server – the developer can generate a CLIENT PROXY that also works with Web Services frameworks or programming languages other than Axis/Java. In this way, for example, a .NET Web Services client can access the Web Services implementation written in Axis/Java. Hence most Web Services frameworks generate WSDL code dynamically from a deployed Web Service and offer this WSDL code to be downloaded by remote clients.

Message processing in Axis

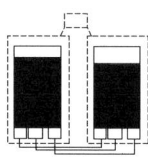

Now that we have looked at the implementer's view of REQUESTOR, CLIENT PROXY, and INVOKER, let's explore the internal message processing architecture of Axis.

There are many tasks to be performed within a Web Services REQUESTOR and INVOKER, both for the request and reply of an invoked service:

- Within the REQUESTOR, the invocation has to be constructed, marshaled as an XML message, and handed to the CLIENT REQUEST HANDLER. When the reply has arrived, it has to be obtained from the CLIENT REQUEST HANDLER, de-marshaled, and handed back to the client.

- Within the server-side INVOKER, the invocation has to be received from the SERVER REQUEST HANDLER, a MARSHALLER has to de-marshal the SOAP XML text, the service has to be looked up and invoked, the reply has to be marshaled again as SOAP XML text, and it has to be handed back to the SERVER REQUEST HANDLER. Invocations can either use a REQUESTOR-based invocation scheme (as in the first example above) or a CLIENT PROXY-based invocation scheme (as in the second example above using WSDL).
- Within both REQUESTOR and INVOKER there are many add-on tasks, for example integration with the access control mechanisms of the Web Server, logging, session handling, and many more.

There are several things we can observe:

- There are many different, orthogonal tasks to be performed for a message.
- There is a symmetry of the tasks to be performed for request and reply.
- The three tasks, mentioned above, occur on client side and server side.
- The invocation scheme and add-ons have to be extensible flexibly.

These forces are addressed in the Axis architecture by a combination of REQUESTOR, INVOKER, INVOCATION CONTEXT, INVOCATION INTERCEPTOR, and CLIENT/SERVER REQUEST HANDLER. This message processing architecture is used both on client side and server side – in its client and server variant, respectively. The basic idea is to construct the message-processing scheme and any add-on service as chained handlers. Handlers are ordered in a chain, and each invocation has to pass each handler in the chain, before it reaches the actual remote object. Each handler supports an operation `invoke` that is executed when an invocation passes it (which means that the handler implements the pattern *Command* [GHJV95]). The handler chain is used to implement an INVOCATION INTERCEPTOR architecture, similar to the architecture described in [Vin02b].

Each handler provides an operation `invoke` that implements the handler's task. This operation is invoked whenever a message passes the handler in the chain. A message can pass a handler either as a request or a reply, both on the client side and the server side. That is, the REQUESTOR passes each request message through the client-side handlers until the last handler in the chain is reached. This last handler (called a 'sender' in Axis) hands the message to the CLIENT REQUEST HANDLER, which sends the request across the network. On the server side the SERVER REQUEST HANDLER receives the request message and passes it through the server handler chain until the INVOKER (called a 'provider' in Axis) is reached. The provider actually invokes the Web Services remote object. After the remote object has returned, the provider turns the request into either a reply or a REMOTING ERROR. The reply is passed in reverse order through the respective handler chains – first on the server side and then on the client side.

Many different providers are implemented in Axis, including a Java provider, a CORBA provider, an EJB provider, a JMS Messaging provider, an RMI provider, and others. These providers are responsible for looking up the target object and invoking the target operation, after they have checked that it is allowed to invoke it, according to the deployment descriptor. Thus the provider abstraction supports heterogeneity for the implementation of Web Services remote objects.

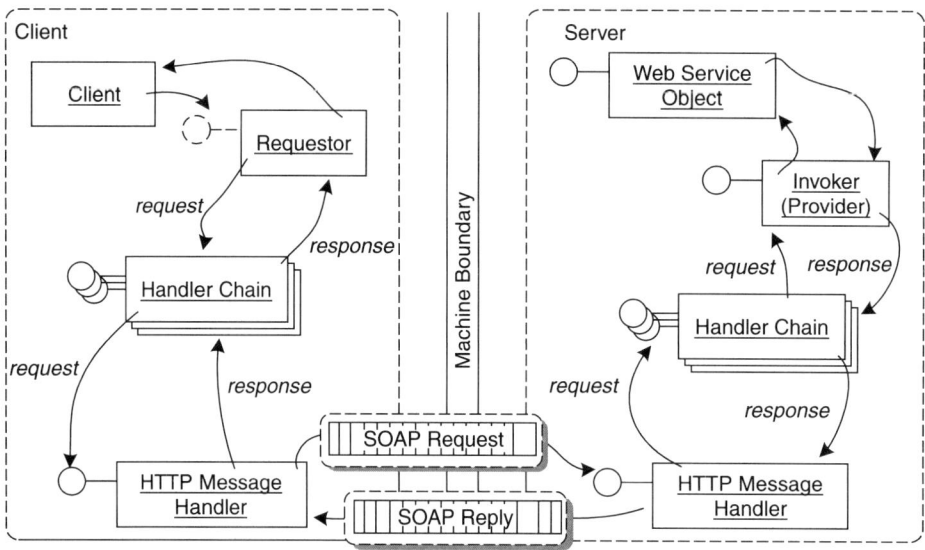

In the above figure, we can see an example of how the CLIENT PROXY invokes the chain of handlers with a request. After the client-side

Message processing in Axis

handler chain is traversed, the CLIENT REQUEST HANDLER passes the message across the network. The SERVER REQUEST HANDLER passes the received requests through the server-side handler chain. The last handler is the provider, which invokes the service and turns the request into a reply. The reply then traverses the server-side and client-side handler chains in reverse order.

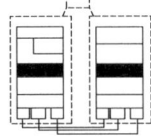

Note that all handlers between REQUESTOR and CLIENT REQUEST HANDLER on the client side and all handlers between INVOKER and SERVER REQUEST HANDLER on the server side are INVOCATION INTERCEPTORS. These can perform tasks *before* an invocation, when a request passes the handler, and *after* an invocation, when a reply passes the handler.

Basic tasks of REQUESTOR, CLIENT/SERVER REQUEST HANDLERS, and INVOKER are implemented as INVOCATION INTERCEPTORS. Examples are:

- Interacting with the transport listener provided by the SERVER REQUEST HANDLER.
- Invoking the MARSHALLER.
- Calling the URLMapper (a handler for mapping URLs to service names).

Orthogonal extensions of message processing are also handled by the same INVOCATION INTERCEPTOR architecture. Examples of such extensions are:

- LogHandler, for simple logging.
- SoapMonitorHandler, for connecting to a SOAP Monitor tool.
- DebugHandler, for setting the debug level dynamically based on the value of a SOAP header element.
- HTTPAuth, for HTTP-specific basic authentication.

To make INVOKERS and INVOCATION INTERCEPTORS work in handler chains as described above, one more pattern is used that is of particular importance in the architecture. An INVOCATION CONTEXT (called the MessageContext in Axis) has to be created first, before the message is sent through the handler chain. In this way different handlers can retrieve the data of the message and can potentially manipulate it. In Axis, the INVOCATION CONTEXT class MessageContext associates with the message object, which itself aggregates the message parts (such as SOAP parts and attachments). The corresponding class structure is illustrated in the following figure.

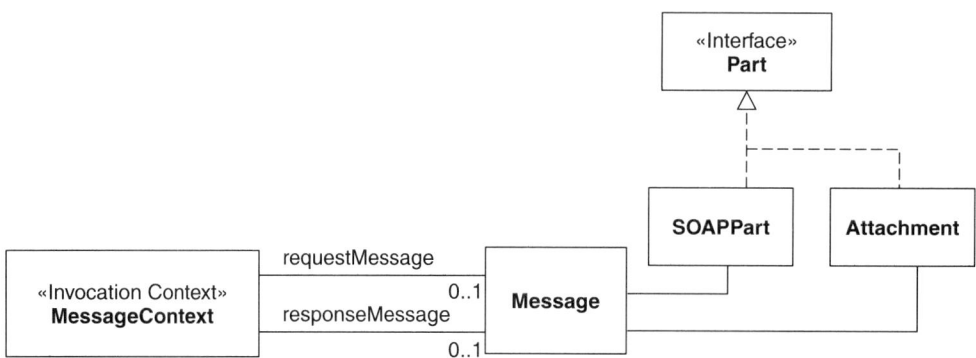

Here an INVOCATION CONTEXT is used on both the client and the server side. Each message context object is associated with two message objects, one for the request message and one for the response message. The MessageContext class stores the invocation data of the message, such the target service identifier and the operation name, as well as the context information, such as a session object (if required by the service), the transport protocol name, and authentication information (user name, password, and so on).

The last handler in the client side handler chain (the sender) and the provider in the server side handler chain are also called 'pivot points', because they turn the message from a request into a reply. A flag havePassedPivot on the MessageContext indicates whether this pivot point has been reached. That is, each handler can discover, using a method getPastPivot, whether it is currently processing a request or a reply.

Let us consider the predefined class LogHandler as an example of a handler class. It is implemented as follows:

```java
public class LogHandler extends BasicHandler {
  ...
  public void invoke(MessageContext msgContext) throws AxisFault
{
    ...
    if (msgContext.getPastPivot() == false) {
      start = System.currentTimeMillis();
    } else {
      logMessages(msgContext);
    }
    ...
  }
  private void logMessages(MessageContext msgContext)
    throws AxisFault {
    ...
    Message inMsg = msgContext.getRequestMessage();
    Message outMsg = msgContext.getResponseMessage();
    if (start != -1) {
      writer.println( "= " + Messages.getMessage("elapsed00",
                      "" + (System.currentTimeMillis()
                         - start)));
    }
    writer.println( "= " + Messages.getMessage("inMsg00",
        (inMsg == null ? "null" : inMsg.getSOAPPartAsString())));
    writer.println( "= " + Messages.getMessage("outMsg00",
        (outMsg == null ? "null" : outMsg.getSOAPPartAsString())));
    ...
  }
  public void onFault(MessageContext msgContext) {
    try {
      logMessages(msgContext);
    } catch (AxisFault axisFault) {
      ...
    }
  }
  ...
}
```

The class is used as an INVOCATION INTERCEPTOR in the request flow and response flow. Its `invoke` operation is invoked automatically whenever a message passes its position in a handler chain. In the request flow the class remembers the start time. In the response flow the class logs the message. It uses the INVOCATION CONTEXT to obtain the request message and the reply message. The previously-stored start time is used to calculate the processing time of the service, if available.

Handler classes are used by specification in the deployment descriptor. For example, we can configure the logging handler:

```
<handler name="logger"
  type="java:org.apache.axis.handlers.LogHandler"/>
```

Now we can further compose handlers into chains:

```
<chain name="myChain"/>
  <handler type="logger"/>
  <handler type="authentication"/>
</chain>
```

Either chains or individual handlers can be used in service descriptions. We can put the handler into the request flow, the response flow, or both, for example:

```
<service name="DateService" provider="java:RPC">
  ...
  <requestFlow>
    <handler type="myChain"/>
  </requestFlow>
</service>
```

Note that the order of handlers is important. The order is handled conceptually in Axis by ordering the chains in three parts: transport chain, global chain, and service chain. Chain and flow definitions are a way to define CONFIGURATION GROUPS for Axis Web Services, implemented by handlers. These configurations can be reused for different services.

The INVOCATION INTERCEPTOR-based message processing architecture of Axis has a similar structure as the Adaptive Runtime Architecture (ART) [Vin02b]. An INVOCATION INTERCEPTOR-based message processing architecture has the advantage of being highly generic, flexible, and adaptive. Almost the identical architecture can be (re)used on both the client side and the server side, as explained above. The Web Service domain requires high flexibility in the invocation schemes used, providers, protocols, marshaling, and diverse add-on services.

The flexibility of the Axis message processing architecture is not for free. The disadvantages of this highly flexible and reusable architecture are its complexity and its potential performance overhead. INVOCATION INTERCEPTOR-based architectures need not necessarily be slower than other BROKER architectures [Vin02b]. But an INVOCATION INTERCEPTOR mechanism that is not properly designed and implemented can easily lead to substantial performance degradation. Reasons for this are that interceptors require some additional indirections, dynamic lookups, and instantiations and destruction of interceptors. Some Web Services frameworks use a much simpler and less flexible message processing architecture – for an example, see the discussion of GLUE on page 281.

JAX-RPC handlers

Sun's JAX-RPC API [Sun04b] supports a slightly different handler model than Axis, but can also be used with Axis. Axis, on the other hand, has a more flexible INVOCATION INTERCEPTOR architecture than JAX-RPC. However, over time it might be deprecated in favor of the JAX-RPC standard, as that provides portability across application servers. From the perspective of the pattern language both are similar. We therefore do not discuss the differences in detail, but only mention that JAX-RPC handlers have a slightly different interface:

```
public interface Handler {
  boolean handleRequest(MessageContext ctx);
  boolean handleResponse(MessageContext ctx);
  boolean handleFault(MessageContext ctx);
}
```

This JAX-RPC handler interface is not compatible with the Axis handler interface, explained above. Axis enables you to use JAX-RPC handlers by using an *Adapter* [GHJV95] class JAXRPCHandler. This *Adapter* class has the responsibility of translating the Axis handler interface, which is expected by the Axis handler chain, into the interface provided by an JAX-RPC compliant handler. The concrete JAX-RPC handler to be used (in the example below, this it is called MyHandler) is given to the *Adapter* as a parameter in the XML deployment descriptor. The JAXRPCHandler instance in the handler chain then forwards invocations to the MyHandler instance:

```
<requestFlow>
  <handler type="java:org.apache.axis.handlers.JAXRPCHandler">
    <parameter name="scope" value="session"/>
    <parameter name="className"
      value="test.MyHandler"/>
  </handler>
</requestFlow>
<responseFlow>
  <handler type="java:org.apache.axis.handlers.JAXRPCHandler">
    <parameter name="scope" value="session"/>
    <parameter name="className" value="test.MyHandler"/>
  </handler>
</responseFlow>
```

Protocol integration in Web Services

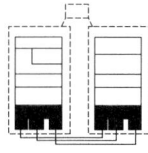

Next, let's take a closer look at the lowest layer of message processing in a Web Services framework: the communication layer. At this layer the heterogeneity of communication protocols in Web Services frameworks is provided. Most Web Services frameworks provide for some extensibility at this layer, even though slightly different REQUEST HANDLER/PROTOCOL PLUG-IN architectures are used.

In the default case that HTTP is used as a communication protocol, on the server side a Web Services framework has to behave like a Web server. That means that the HTTP server has to be informed that specific HTTP requests (for example, all requests on a specific port or URL extension) are handled by the Web Services framework. If such a port is accessed, the HTTP server does not handle the message itself, but forwards it to the SERVER REQUEST HANDLER of the Web Services framework. A Web Services framework can either be plugged into a server or be embedded in a server.

The typical communication protocol used by Web Services request handlers is HTTP. SOAP also allows for other communication protocols, however. Such a variability of communication protocols can be implemented with PROTOCOL PLUG-INS for the protocols supported. On top of the PROTOCOL PLUG-INS, all protocols are handled in the same way as HTTP. For example, the same INVOKER can be used for all protocols. Axis supports PROTOCOL PLUG-INS for HTTP, Java Messaging Service (JMS), SMTP, and local Java invocations.

PROTOCOL PLUG-INS need to be defined for both client side and server side. In Axis there are two main elements of the client-side PROTOCOL PLUG-INS:

- *Transport*. Axis contains a transport abstraction from which specific transport classes, such as HTTP transport, SMTP transport, JMS transport, and so on, inherit. The main task of the transport is to create an INVOCATION CONTEXT that is specific for the chosen communication protocol. For example, the HTTP message context may contain HTTP cookie options. The JMS message context contains JMS options like message priority and 'time to live.' The transport is set up (by the CLIENT PROXY) before the handler chain is traversed. This is important, because some handlers may depend on a knowledge of which transport is used. For example, session handling can only set cookie options if HTTP is used, otherwise the session information has to be transported in the SOAP header.

- *Sender.* There is a sender for each supported protocol, such as HTTP sender, JMS sender, SMTP sender, and so on. A sender is a special handler that is used as the last handler in the client side handler chain. It actually sends a request message across the network using the sender's communication protocol (and may wait for the result in the case of a blocking invocation). Obviously therefore the sender must be specific for the transport protocol. The relevant sender class is chosen based on the transport name given in the INVOCATION CONTEXT of a request.

On the server side, classes for receiving messages from a communication protocol are defined. These implement the SERVER REQUEST HANDLERS of the Web Services framework. The respective servers of the different communication protocols contain a *Reactor* [SSRB00] that reacts to network events and informs the SERVER REQUEST HANDLERS. On the server side there are also PROTOCOL PLUG-INS for the different protocols supported, in particular:

- For HTTP, a servlet is provided that can be used with any Java HTTP server that supports servlets (that is, a servlet container such as Tomcat) [Apa04c].
- Axis also implements a simple stand-alone HTTP server, although it is intended for testing purposes only.
- For JMS, a `MessageListener` is implemented that handles JMS messages using a JMS worker class. This class uses Java's JMS implementation as the actual JMS server.
- For SMTP, a simple `MailServer` is defined that connects to a mail server.

In all cases the SERVER REQUEST HANDLER is connected to the relevant server implementation of the PROTOCOL PLUG-IN, and *observes* the network events generated by the server. The server lets the SERVER REQUEST HANDLER handle specific incoming requests. For example, a specific port or range of URLs can be redirected to the SERVER REQUEST HANDLER. For each request that arrives, the SERVER REQUEST HANDLER sets up the server-side INVOCATION CONTEXT and invokes the server-side handler chain (as described in the previous section).

Note that many typical SERVER REQUEST HANDLER tasks are handled by the respective server implementation of the PROTOCOL PLUG-IN, such as listening to the port, (de-)marshaling on the level of the communication protocol (that is, HTTP, SMTP, and so on), performance optimizations, and so on. The Web Services framework's SERVER REQUEST HANDLER only performs high-level tasks at the level of SOAP and above. Similarly, lower-level CLIENT REQUEST HANDLER tasks are performed by existing client APIs. Building on existing middleware and protocol implementations is quite typical for the Web Services domain. This is because existing client and server implementations usually can be reused, as the protocols used are originally designed for tasks other than Web Services, and Web Services frameworks are implemented as an integration layer on top of these implementations.

Because of these reasons, the CLIENT and SERVER REQUEST HANDLERS and PROTOCOL PLUG-INS of the Web Services framework are relatively generic and allow for simple exchange of the communication protocol in use. A disadvantage of this architecture is that no one protocol implements the functionality of all other protocols supported. For example, simple session handling is possible via HTTP cookies, but cookies are specific to HTTP and not supported by protocols such as JMS and SMTP.

Marshaling using SOAP XML encoding

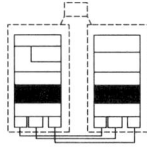

The MARSHALLER is a handler (an INVOCATION INTERCEPTOR) in the request and response flow that uses the SOAP implementation to encode messages in SOAP XML format and decode messages from SOAP XML format. During encoding it produces the SOAP message structure, and during decoding it extracts the information from it.

Each SOAP message has a so-called 'envelope'. The SOAP envelope is a simple wrapper for the content. The envelope can have an optional header that contains control information, for example for routing or authorization. Each SOAP message has a SOAP body that contains the message payload. Attachments can hold other types of data, such as binary data, un-encoded text, and so on.

Marshaling using SOAP XML encoding

Consider the following simple SOAP invocation, taken from the SOAP interoperability suite. It specifies the XML schemas used in the envelope, and in the body it invokes an operation `echoInteger` with one integer argument that has the value 42:

```xml
<?xml version="1.0" encoding="UTF-8"?>
  <soapenv:Envelope
      xmlns:soapenv="http://schemas.xmlsoap.org/soap/envelope/"
      xmlns:xsd="http://www.w3.org/2001/XMLSchema"
      xmlns:xsi="http://www.w3.org/2001/XMLSchema-instance">
    <soapenv:Body>
      <ns1:echoInteger soapenv:encodingStyle=
          "http://schemas.xmlsoap.org/soap/encoding/"
          xmlns:ns1="http://soapinterop.org/">
        <inputInteger xsi:type="xsd:int">42</inputInteger>
      </ns1:echoInteger>
    </soapenv:Body>
  </soapenv:Envelope>
```

The SOAP server can respond to this invocation with a similar message, also referencing relevant XML schemas and namespaces in the envelope. A reply to the operation invocation is embedded in the body with a return type and value, again an integer with the value 42:

```xml
<?xml version="1.0" encoding="utf-8"?>
  <soap:Envelope xmlns:soap=
      "http://schemas.xmlsoap.org/soap/envelope/"
      xmlns:soapenc="http://schemas.xmlsoap.org/soap/encoding/"
      xmlns:tns="http://soapinterop.org/"
      xmlns:types="http://soapinterop.org/"
      xmlns:xsi="http://www.w3.org/2001/XMLSchema-instance"
      xmlns:xsd="http://www.w3.org/2001/XMLSchema">
    <soap:Body soap:encodingStyle=
        "http://schemas.xmlsoap.org/soap/encoding">
      <types:echoIntegerResponse>
        <return xsi:type="xsd:int">42</return>
      </types:echoIntegerResponse>
    </soap:Body>
  </soap:Envelope>
```

The encoding for the message can be specified in the SOAP body. There are two commonly-used formats:

- *RPC encoding*. The SOAP specification defines RPC encoding (`http://schemas.xmlsoap.org/soap/encoding`). This encoding style aims to provide RPC invocations in the fashion of CORBA or Java RMI. Invocation parameters and the result are encoded in the body. RPC encoding defines primitive types, arrays, and structures of these types. Operations can have in/out and out parameters in addition to the return value.

- *Document literal.* An XML document with a format defined by a schema is transported with the SOAP messages. Compared to RPC encoding, document literal is more flexible, portable, and interoperable. Document literal requires code on the client and server sides to convert the data. .NET uses a variation of document literal with invocation parameters as children of root elements.

A SOAP message optionally contains a SOAP header, as well as add-on information such as authentication information, session-management information, or transaction-management information. This information represents the INVOCATION CONTEXT of a message at the SOAP level.

At runtime this information is represented by the class structure shown in the figure below. That is, the objects created by the MARSHALLER from the XML data, as well as the message representation before marshaling, conform to this class structure.

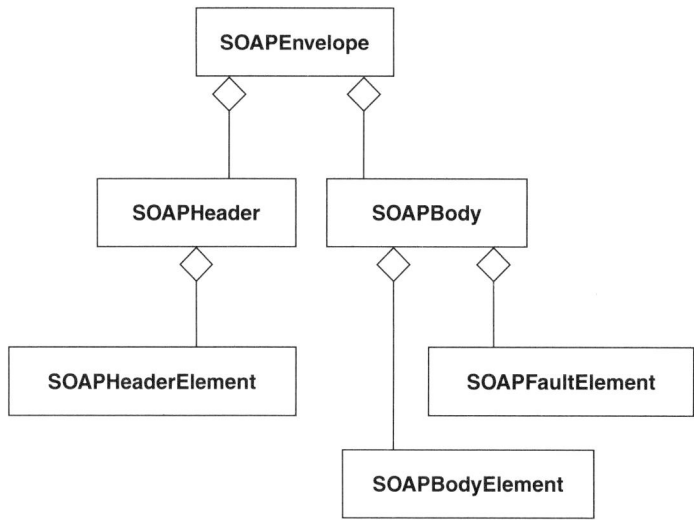

Not all kinds of INVOCATION CONTEXT data should be sent as part of the XML-encoded SOAP message. SOAP attachments are an extensible part of the INVOCATION CONTEXT. You should use attachments when you are planning to send large amounts of data. The advantage of this approach is that the SOAP processor does not have to perform any processing to obtain the attachment, because, when using attachments in SOAP, the SOAP message contains only a reference to the actual attachment data.

Lifecycle management in Web Services

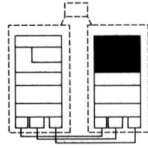

Axis supports the following lifecycle management patterns, using a *scope* option chosen in the deployment descriptor:

- PER-REQUEST INSTANCE. The HTTP protocol uses a simple request/response scheme for communication by default. This means that HTTP itself is stateless. Due to the service characteristics, the default lifecycle model of a Web Service is the PER-REQUEST INSTANCE. The PER-REQUEST INSTANCE is also stateless, as it only exists for the duration of one request, and does not maintain any state between subsequent requests. In Axis, such a PER-REQUEST INSTANCE is called a service with 'request' scope.

- STATIC INSTANCE. Axis also supports STATIC INSTANCES, where the so-called 'application' scope is chosen. This scope creates a remote object as a shared object that handles all requests for a particular Web Service.

- CLIENT-DEPENDENT INSTANCE. Sessions are supported either by HTTP cookies or by communication protocol-independent SOAP headers. If a service has 'session' scope, it creates a new object for each session-enabled client that accesses a service. With the session abstraction, CLIENT-DEPENDENT INSTANCES can be implemented for a service. Note that, as a second pattern, LEASING is required here to implement sessions. Each session object has a timeout, which can be set to a certain number of milliseconds. After the timeout expires, the session is invalidated. A `touch` operation can be invoked on the session object to renew the lease.

The standard Axis provider that exposes Java classes as services does not support POOLING for PER-REQUEST INSTANCES or CLIENT-DEPENDENT INSTANCES, although it would be no problem to add such a functionality here. Other providers are implemented as subclasses of this class. These subclasses have to override the *Factory Method* [GHJV95] `makeNewServiceObject` that creates the Java PER-REQUEST INSTANCES. The

POOLING functionalities of component frameworks such as EJB, for example, can therefore be used. (See the discussion in *Message processing in Axis* on page 256).

Note that Web servers and other communication protocol implementations usually pool the connections and/or worker threads that handle the HTTP requests.

The basic LIFECYCLE MANAGER of Axis is very simple. For services invoked with the standard Java provider, a `ServiceLifecycle` interface is implemented that has only `init` and `destroy` operations. This interface is invoked by the Java provider when the service objects are created and destroyed. The session implementation extends lifecycle management to handle the current session state of an object. The session implementation also manages LEASING for the session objects.

Other providers might hide frameworks that contain their own implementations of LIFECYCLE MANAGER, POOLING, and so on. For example, the `EJBProvider` hides the EJB component container that contains a LIFECYCLE MANAGER and a solution for POOLING. In other words, not all aspects of lifecycle management necessarily have to be handled within the Web Services framework – these can instead be provided by the service implementations.

Client-Side asynchrony

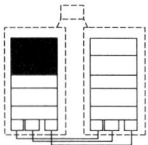

We have already provided two examples for client-side invocations, one building up the invocation at runtime with a REQUESTOR, the second using a CLIENT PROXY generated with WSDL. Both examples implement synchronous invocations.

Asynchrony supported by Axis and WSIF

The `Call` interface in Axis Version 1.0 only supports synchronous request-reply invocations and oneway invocations. The same options are also supported by other Web Services invocation frameworks for Java, such the Web Services Invocation Framework (WSIF) [Apa04a], a framework-independent invocation interface.

Oneways can be specified using WSDL, so they are supported by many Web Services frameworks. The oneway invocations follow the FIRE AND

FORGET pattern. Neither Axis nor WSIF support asynchronous invocations on the client side over synchronous protocols such as HTTP yet. That is, the other asynchrony patterns, SYNC WITH SERVER, RESULT CALLBACK, and POLL OBJECT, are not natively supported by Axis or WSIF.

However, both Axis and WSIF have PROTOCOL PLUG-INS for asynchronous messaging protocols such as Java Messaging Service (JMS). Support for asynchrony therefore is provided by a PROTOCOL PLUG-IN (for JMS), rather than implementing the asynchrony patterns on top of HTTP. This capability can be used to implement RESULT CALLBACKS with JMS messaging as the underlying protocol.

The general client programming model for asynchrony via a messaging protocol such as JMS is that the client sends an asynchronous remote invocation, and stores a correlation identifier (the term used for an *Asynchronous Completion Token* [SSRB00] in the messaging domain), together with the ID of a callback operation locally. It then proceeds with its work. The Web Service receives this invocation, sending a reply message back after processing the message. The client also acts as a messaging server able to receive replies. In JMS a `JMSListener` within the client waits for messages. When a message arrives, the `JMSListener` uses the correlation identifier sent back with the reply message to look up the associated callback operation, and invokes it.

Even though this scheme follows the RESULT CALLBACK pattern, problems might occur. Messaging protocols deal with a lot of additional aspects to support the QoS property 'reliability of message transfer.' In cases in which reliable message transport is not required, a messaging protocol is an overhead. Also, if HTTP is used, the messaging protocol might be problematic. In such cases we can implement the asynchrony patterns on top of synchronous invocations: this is explained in the next section.

Building asynchrony patterns on top of Axis

In this section we explain how to implement the client-side asynchrony patterns on top of Axis in a generic and efficient way. To achieve this we implement an asynchrony *Layer* on top of the synchronous invocation *Layer* provided by Axis. Please note that there is a certain overhead associated with this implementation, so that native support of a framework for asynchrony should generally be preferred.

We describe the Simple Asynchronous Invocation Framework for Web Services (SAIWS)[3] [ZVK03] here, an add-on for Apache Axis. An interesting aspect of this is that support for client-side asynchrony was designed – using the pattern language presented in this book – on top of a given distributed object middleware, and not at the lower-level layers of the distributed object middleware, as for example in the CORBA technology projection. SAIWS is intended to describe the concept of adding an asynchrony layer on top of a synchronous distributed object middleware – it is not intended to replace the integrated asynchrony provided at lower levels by some distributed object middleware systems.

In this framework we provide two kinds of REQUESTORS, one for synchronous invocations and one for asynchronous invocations. Both use the same invocation scheme. The synchronous REQUESTOR blocks the client until the reply returns. A client can invoke a synchronous REQUESTOR as follows:

```
SyncRequestor sr = new SyncRequestor();
String result =
   (String) sr.invoke(endpointURL, operationName, null, rt);
```

This REQUESTOR handles the invocation using the Axis `Call` interface presented previously, and after it has returned, returns to the client.

The asynchronous REQUESTOR is used in a similar way. It offers invocation methods that implement the client asynchrony patterns. The general structure of asynchronous invocation is quite similar to synchronous invocations - the only difference is that we pass an `AsyncHandler` and `clientACT` as arguments to the `invoke` operation, and do not wait for a result:

```
AsyncHandler ah = ...;
Object clientACT = ...;
AsyncRequestor ar = new asyncRequestor();
ar.invoke(ah, clientACT, endpointURL, operationName, null, rt);
// ... resume work
```

Note that the `clientACT` field is used here as a pure client-side implementation of an *Asynchronous Completion Token* (ACT) [SSRB00]. The

---

3. This framework can be downloaded from http://saiws.sourceforge.net.

Client-Side asynchrony

ACT pattern is used to let clients identify different results of asynchronous invocations when the reply has arrived.

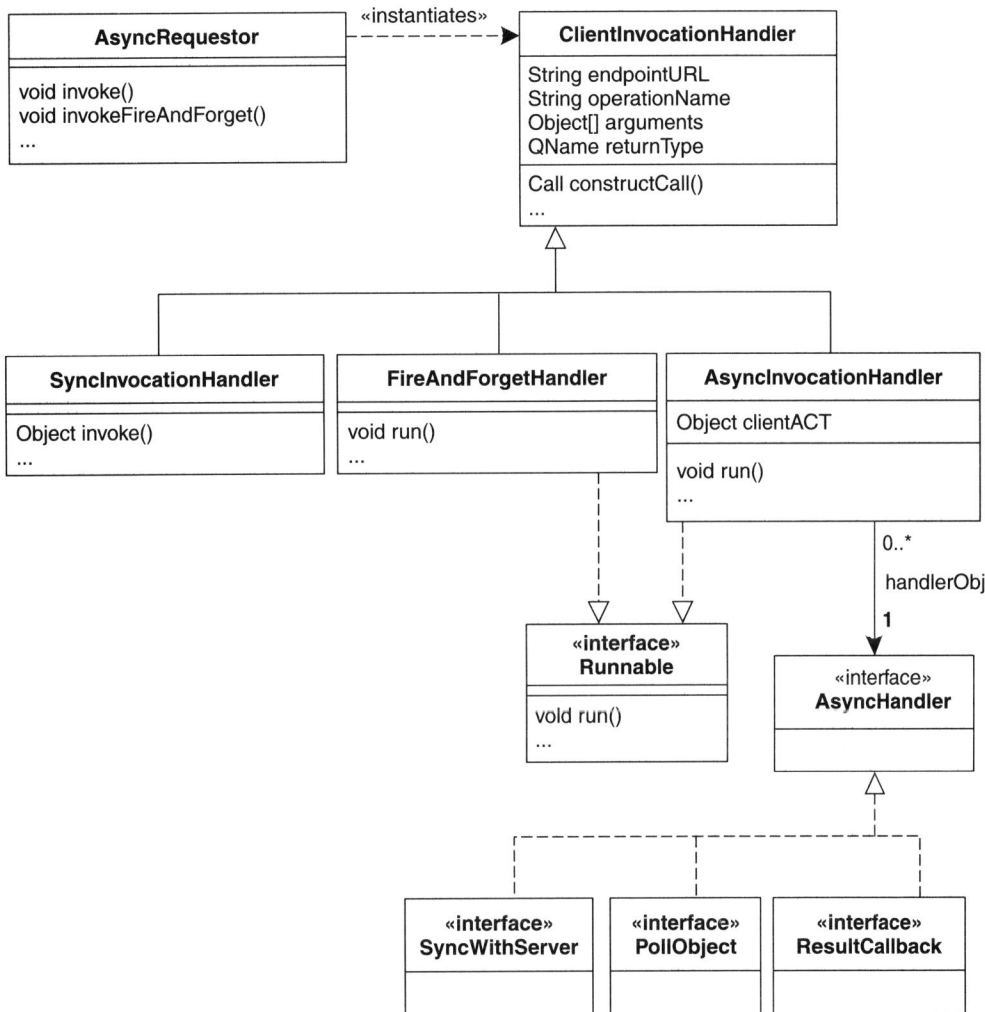

The synchronous invocation handler provides an `invoke` method that invokes a service synchronously and blocks. The asynchronous invocation handlers implement the `Runnable` interface. This interface indicates that the handler implements a variant of the *Command* pattern [GHJV95] that can be invoked in the handler's thread of control. Three `AsyncHandler` interfaces are provided for the different kinds of asynchronous invocations that follow SYNC WITH SERVER, POLL OBJECT, and RESULT CALLBACK.

The `AsyncInvocationHandler` decides which asynchrony pattern should be used on the basis of the kind of handler object: RESULT CALLBACK, POLL OBJECT, or SYNC WITH SERVER.

The FIRE AND FORGET pattern is not implemented in the `AsyncInvocationHandler` class, or as a subclass of it, because the WSDL standard that is used for INTERFACE DESCRIPTION of Web Services supports oneway operations. These are thus implemented by most Web Services frameworks that support WSDL. The `AsyncInvocationHandler` class does not therefore implement FIRE AND FORGET, but instead uses oneway invocations to support such operations. All other invocations dispatched by the `AsyncInvocationHandler` class are request-reply invocations.

A FIRE AND FORGET invocation executes in its own thread of control. It simply constructs the invocation, sends it, and the thread then terminates. A FIRE AND FORGET invocation is invoked by a special `invokeFireAndForget` method of the `AsyncClientProxy` class:

```
AsyncRequestor requestor = new AsyncRequestor();
requestor.invokeFireAndForget(endpointURL, operationName,
                              null, rt);
```

To deal with the asynchrony patterns RESULT CALLBACK, POLL OBJECT, or SYNC WITH SERVER, the client asynchrony handler types `ResultCallback`, `PollObject`, and `SyncWithServer` are provided. These are instantiated by the client and handed over to the REQUESTOR.

The asynchronous REQUESTOR handles the invocation with an `AsyncInvocationHandler`. Each invocation handler runs in its own thread of control and deals with one invocation. A thread pool is used to improve performance and reduce resource consumption. The client asynchrony handlers are sinks that are responsible for holding or handling the result for clients.

To make an asynchronous invocation, the client only has to instantiate the required client asynchrony handler (that is, a class implementing a subtype of `AsyncHandler`) and provide it to the REQUESTOR'S operation `invoke`. This operation is defined as follows:

```
public void invoke(AsyncHandler handler, Object clientACT,
    String endpointURL, String operationName,
    Object[] arguments, QName returnType)
  throws InterruptedException {...}
```

The parameter `handler` determines the handler object responsible and its type. It can be of any subtype of `AsyncHandler`. `clientACT` is a user-defined identifier for the invocation. The client can use the `clientACT` to correlate a specific result to an invocation. The four last arguments specify the service ID, operation name, and invocation data.

Consider a POLL OBJECT as an example of the use of an asynchronous invocation. The client might invoke a POLL OBJECT by first instantiating a corresponding handler, then providing the handler to the `invoke` operation. Subsequently, the client polls the POLL OBJECT for the result, working on other tasks until the result arrives:

```
AsyncRequestor requestor = new AsyncRequestor();
PollObject p = (PollObject) new SimplePollObject();
requestor.invoke(p, null, endpointURL, operationName, null, rt);
while (!p.resultArrived()) {
    // do some other task ...
}
System.out.println("Poll Object Result Arrived = " +
    p.getResult());
```

The class `SimplePollObject` implements the `PollObject` interface. Here the `clientACT` parameter is set to `null` because we can use the object reference in `p` to obtain the correct POLL OBJECT. More complex `AsyncHandlers` that handle multiple replies use the `clientACT` to identify the request belonging to a reply.

RESULT CALLBACK and SYNC WITH SERVER are used in the same way, but the respective `AsyncHandler` has to be used. For example, the following code instantiates a RESULT CALLBACK and then sends ten invocations, each handled by the same RESULT CALLBACK object. Each invocation gets an identifier as clientACT, so that the RESULT CALLBACK is able to identify the results when they arrive:

```
AsyncRequestor requestor = new AsyncRequestor();
ResultCallback r = (ResultCallback) new ResultCallbackQueue();
for (int i = 0; i < 10; i++) {
  String id = "invocation" + i;
  requestor.invoke(r, id, endpointURL, operationName,
                   null, rt);
}
```

Web Services and QoS

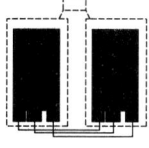

Even though there are quite a few emerging standards for Quality of Service (QoS) of Web Services, currently they should be seen only as a set of best practices. We want to summarize these here for the QoS properties of performance, accessibility, availability, reliability, and integrity.

Performance defines the number of requests for remote objects that are served in a given period of time. Performance is influenced by client and server processing times and network latency. Web Services frameworks contain a few typical performance bottlenecks compared to other distributed object middlewares, because XML processing requires various levels of XML parsing and validation. Unfortunately, not all Web Services frameworks apply best practices to maximize performance. These include the use of efficient XML parsers, avoiding XML validation in production mode (in situations where you are sure the XML data is valid), sending compressed XML over the network (for example by eliminating unnecessary spaces, or using binary representations), and caching of Web Services results. The Web Services developer can improve performance by using simple data types for SOAP interactions. Several tools are available to monitor the performance of Web Servers, mostly to debug Web sites or interactive Web applications. Many of these tools can be used to implement a QOS OBSERVER for Web Services running in a server as well (see for example [Jen02]).

Accessibility defines the capability of a remote object to serve clients' requests. This QoS property can be enhanced by the use of more powerful hardware, highly concurrent systems, or highly scalable systems. Best practices to enhance accessibility are:

- POOLING of services. This can be implemented by the service provider. In Axis POOLING is not supported by the Web Services framework. Pooled objects can use *Thread-Specific Storage* [SSRB00] to reduce the risk of lock contention and race conditions.

- Thread *Pooling* [KJ04] for the server's worker threads. This is provided by most servers of communication protocols used for Web Services. Specifically, modern Web Servers provide highly efficient *Pooling* architectures.

- Load balancing measures. These can improve scalability. Specifically, load balancing across multiple machines can be exploited for Web servers. A root server only checks the URL for the relevant server. It then redirects the requests to the server that is actually responsible for handling the request transparently, for example by using DNS aliasing, 'magic' routing, or HTTP Redirect. Redirection can be implemented as a LOCATION FORWARDER.

Availability defines whether a remote object is ready to service requests at a specific time. This QoS property is not tackled by Web Services frameworks directly. Web servers usually allow one to manage and log the server, which allows for a weak control of availability (by checking times of unavailability and long response in the log). Availability can be improved by fault-tolerant systems, or clustering.

Reliability defines the numbers of failed requests over time, as well as the ordered delivery of messages. HTTP, the standard communication protocol of Web Services, provides only best-effort delivery. Many Web Services frameworks support the use of messaging protocols to guarantee message delivery and message order.

Integrity can refer to both integrity of data and transaction integrity. Data integrity defines whether the transferred data is modified during transmission. Transactional integrity refers to the orchestration of a transaction that is longer than a single request. Both kinds of integrity are not handled in current Web Services frameworks. A number of Web Services standards exist to support transaction integrity and long-running business transactions, such as BPEL4WS [ACD+03], WS-Coordination [CCC+03], and WS-Transaction [CCC+02].

Web Services security

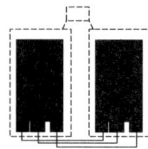

Security of remote invocations includes the authentication of clients, encryption of messages, and access control. Some support for authorization usually is provided in Web Services frameworks via the Basic or Digest Access Control mechanism of the HTTP protocol: in Axis, these are supported as a special handler. SSL encryption of the network traffic can be supported using HTTPS as a PROTOCOL PLUG-IN. Different XML standards are emerging currently to deal with security on a broader level. These are however not yet widely adopted by most Web Services frameworks. Examples are the XML encryption specification [ERI+02], the XML key management specification [FHF+01], and XML Signature [BBF+02]. It is quite typical for security to be supported either by a PROTOCOL PLUG-IN at the communication protocol level, or by an INVOCATION INTERCEPTOR as an extension of the message processing architecture. More complex security requirements can be coded in the Web Services themselves.

The simple security measures summarized above work for simple interactions. However, larger service-oriented architectures usually have additional security requirements. For example, problems arise if messages have to be routed across (untrusted) intermediaries, if more than one party needs control over security aspects, or if the messages need to be stored securely for later consumption. A number of security standards for Web Services are proposed to deal with these issues. WS-Security [ADH+02] is the premier standard for more complex authentication, confidentiality, and integrity of SOAP messages. It provides a framework for the exchange of X.509 certificates or SAML tokens. SAML [Oas03a] is an XML-based security protocol that provides the secure exchange of authentication and authorization assertions. WS-Trust [ABB+02] is another proposed standard for exchanging authentication and authorization assertions, but it is not yet as mature as SAML.

Security in a service-oriented architecture with a potentially large number of participants requires a means to discover the security policies supported by a partner without human intervention. XACML [Oas03b] allows developers to define access control policies. Web Services endpoints can be described with the mandatory features of service invocation, optional features that they support, and a preference order among those features. WS-Policy [BCH+03] provides a framework for defining the properties of Web Services as policy statements. Its security addendum WS-SecurityPolicy [DHH+02] can be used to describe the security properties of a Web Service.

Lookup of Web Services: UDDI

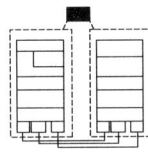

There are many possible ways to realize LOOKUP with Web Services, and there are a number of proprietary implementations. UDDI [Oas02] is a standard for an automated directory service that allows the developer to register and look up services. In contrast to many simple naming and property services, UDDI started with the vision of providing a world-wide, replicated registry for business services, similar to the Domain Name Service (DNS) for Internet domain names. A central registry server, called the Universal Business Registry (UBR), is provided by a number of vendors, including Microsoft and IBM.

All UDDI specifications use XML to define data structures. An UDDI registry includes four types of document that make up the simple basic data model of UDDI:

- A *business entity* is a UDDI record for a service provider
- A *business service* represents one or more deployed Web Services
- A *technical model* (tModel) can be associated with business entities or services
- A *binding template* binds the access point of a Web Service and its tModel

UDDI allows a service provider to register information about itself and the services it provides, such as the service provider's name, contact information, and description. Arbitrary contact information can be registered, including URLs that refer to Web Services. Technical details of a Web Service are also registered, such as the protocol supported. The most common Web Services protocols, such as HTTP and SMTP, are pre-registered in UDDI registries as so-called tModels. tModels are templates for technical protocol specifications in UDDI. A client can search for services that have an associated tModel that complies with one of the client's protocols.

This basic model of UDDI is too simple to describe all the information that is relevant to a business or a service. Instead of defining one highly-complex model for all systems, UDDI supports predefined and user-defined taxonomies for the identification and categorization of the information. The taxonomies are themselves tModels – that is, they can themselves be categorized.

An important aspect is the integration with the INTERFACE DESCRIPTION format WSDL. The WSDL port type and binding are mapped to tModel elements using categories predefined in UDDI. The role of the port element in WSDL is provided by the binding template: this associates an abstract communication scheme with a concrete communication protocol. The WSDL service element obviously matches the business service in UDDI.

UDDI was designed originally based on the business vision of the early days of Web Services. The idea was to provide services publicly and allow business partners to come together through it, for example by finding a required Web Service via UDDI. This vision has not yet gained much momentum, mainly because most businesses do not work this way: the first business transaction is normally preceded by a number of human-mediated selection steps, instead of letting your business partner be found automatically such as by UDDI.

UDDI Version 3 supports a number of improvements to make UDDI more usable in practice. Technical improvements include an improved API for accessing a UDDI registry, better performance, and mechanisms to support inheritance from taxonomies. Conceptual improvements include the support for multiple, federated UDDI registries, instead of the central UBR, as well as support for the exchange and synchronization of data between different UDDI instances.

Other Web Services frameworks

This section presents webMethods' (formerly: The Mind Electric) GLUE, Microsoft's .NET Web Services, and IONA's Artix as popular commercial Web Services implementations. We also discuss Leela, a framework that extends Web Services with concepts from P2P architectures, coordination technologies, and spontaneous networking.

GLUE

GLUE [Min04] is a commercial Web Services implementation in Java that is optimized for performance and ease of use. It can be run as a stand-alone application server, or in other application servers.

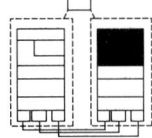

Similarly to Axis, any Java class can be published as a Web Service in GLUE. In contrast to Axis, however, a programmatic deployment is used primarily, instead of the XML deployment descriptor used by Axis. For example, to publish a Web Service of the class HelloWorld:

```
public class HelloWorld implements IHelloWorld {
  ...
}
```

you have to publish this class in a registry:

```
Registry.publish("helloworld", new HelloWorld());
```

The registry automatically generates a remotely-accessible WSDL INTERFACE DESCRIPTION for the Web Service. By default all public methods and interfaces of a remote object are accessible. Instead of publishing all methods, you can specify only that specific interfaces should be published. Even single methods can be published programmatically.

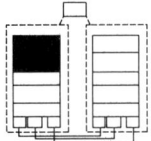

The registry is also provided on the client side, where it is used to bind to a Web Services remote object. This is done by retrieving the WSDL INTERFACE DESCRIPTION of the Web Service. A CLIENT PROXY is then generated from this INTERFACE DESCRIPTION. Finally, the CLIENT PROXY is cast to one of the Web Services' interfaces to allow for invocation of its methods. This can also be done programmatically:

```
String url = "http://localhost:8015/glue/helloworld.wsdl";
IHelloWorld hw = (IHelloWorld)
   Registry.bind(url, IHelloWorld.class);
```

Instead of generating the CLIENT PROXY dynamically, a helper class can be generated by the tool WSDL2Java. This helper class is then stored on disk and compiled. This is not as flexible as the dynamic retrieval of the WSDL file above, but avoids the overhead incurred by retrieving and processing the WSDL file at runtime. One can then bind to the helper instead of using the registry:

```
IHelloWorld hw = HelloWorldHelper.bind();
```

To facilitate ease of use, generating the CLIENT PROXY is the default in GLUE: the REQUESTOR is hidden from the developer. However, sometimes it is necessary to construct invocations dynamically, for example because the interface of a remote object is unknown before runtime. GLUE allows developers to access the REQUESTOR using the interface IProxy. Again, WSDL is used to bind to the Web Service – so GLUE generally uses the automatically-generated INTERFACE DESCRIPTION to ease the use of Web Services. When using the Axis REQUESTOR, in contrast, we have to deal with low-level details such as service endpoints. Here is an example of the use of the GLUE REQUESTOR:

```
IProxy proxy = Registry.bind(
  "http://localhost:8015/glue/helloworld.wsdl" );
String result = (String) proxy.invoke("hello", null);
```

The method invoke receives the method name and an array of arguments. An interesting feature is that GLUE converts string-based arguments to the correct types in the WSDL INTERFACE DESCRIPTION automatically.

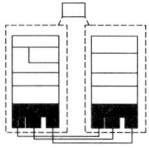

GLUE supports PROTOCOL PLUG-INS for HTTP, HTTP over SSL, and JMS. JMS has to be used to support client asynchrony. These PROTOCOL PLUG-INS are realized by instantiating one or more SERVER REQUEST HANDLER classes. The Servers class, the common superclass of these classes, contains static methods for manipulating a number of SERVER REQUEST HANDLER objects. This allows multiple PROTOCOL PLUG-INS to co-exist in one application.

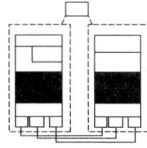

The client-side INVOCATION CONTEXT is provided by the ProxyContext class, while the server-side INVOCATION CONTEXT is provided by the ServiceContext class. These classes contain all the basic invocation information, such as endpoint, HTTP information such as HTTP proxy, proxy password, and so on, XML namespace, XML encoding, and so on, as well as authentication information and other add-on context information.

GLUE supports only so-called SOAPInterceptors, which are INVOCATION INTERCEPTORS at the level of SOAP message handling. A remote object can throw a REMOTING ERROR by raising a SOAP exception in one of its methods. An alternative is to use INVOCATION INTERCEPTORS to set the REMOTING ERROR properties.

GLUE supports three activation modes. STATIC INSTANCES are used by default. A Web Service can be configured as a PER-REQUEST INSTANCE, or as a CLIENT-DEPENDENT INSTANCE by using a session abstraction.

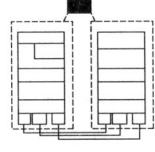

Providing automatically-generated WSDL files is a limited form of LOOKUP. By knowing only the remote location of a WSDL file, one can look up a Web Service and its supported protocols. This mechanism can also be used as a simple variant of LOCATION FORWARDER: GLUE allows the endpoint in the context object of a Web Service to be overridden. This can be used to route a Web Services invocation through an HTTP Proxy or a firewall.

UDDI is supported as a sophisticated form of LOOKUP.

In summary, many of GLUE's design decisions and pattern variants are similar to Axis. However, GLUE offers greater ease of use by providing a more simple invocation model. This is reached by generating an INTERFACE DESCRIPTION automatically and providing it remotely. GLUE also offers high performance, because it uses a simple invocation architecture without many indirections or other overheads. The REQUEST HANDLERS, PROTOCOL PLUG-INS, and the INVOKER are generally configured in a simple way. Axis, in contrast, offers a more generic, more flexible, and more extensible architecture. While GLUE uses a programmatic deployment model by default, the XML-based deployment model of Axis is more complex, incurring an overhead in processing XML files.

Microsoft's .NET Web Services

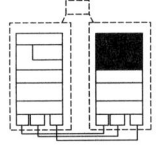

The .NET Framework offers two mechanisms for distributed application development and integration: .NET Remoting and ASP.NET Web Services. We have already looked at .NET Remoting in detail, so let's first consider a simple 'Hello World!' Web Services example in ASP.NET:

```
<%@ WebService Language="C#" Class="RemotingBook.HelloWorld" %>
namespace RemotingBook {
  using System;
  using System.Web.Services;
  public class HelloWorld : WebService {
    [WebMethod]
    public string hello() {
      return "Hello World!";
    }
  }
}
```

The above code is deployed by storing it in a file and copying it into a directory served by Microsoft's IIS Web Server. That is, the ASP.NET approach also has a runtime deployment model, similar to Axis. In contrast to Axis, however, which uses an XML-based deployment descriptor, ASP.NET stores the deployment information within the program code of the Web Service. Note that the first line of the code contains a WebService directive, an ASP.NET statement declaring that the code that follows is a Web Service. The in-line code [WebMethod] corresponds a declaration of the allowed methods of a Web Service in Axis – that is, those operations which are dispatched by the INVOKER as a Web Service. Another typical characteristic of Web Services is that the actual service providers can vary: in ASP.NET all the programming languages supported by .NET can be used to implement the service.

Even though the concepts are similar, we can see that an ASP.NET Web Service has to be prepared specifically by making the service class inherit from the class WebService, and by adding in-line code such as the [WebMethod] statement. This is in major contrast to Axis, where we use an ordinary Java class as a remote object.

ASP.NET Web Services rely on the System.Xml.Serialization.XmlSerializer class as a MARSHALLER for marshaling data to and from SOAP messages at runtime. These can generate WSDL descriptions containing XSD type definitions. As ASP.NET is relying on Web Services standards, ASP.NET Web Services can be used to interoperate with other (non-Microsoft) Web Services platforms. This also means that you can only marshal types that can be expressed in XSD – in other words, .NET-specific types cannot be exposed as interoperable ASP.NET Web Services.

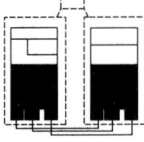

To a certain extent .NET Remoting can also be used to expose Web Services by choosing the SOAP formatter and the HTTP channel of .NET Remoting. But there are two problems with this approach. First, the generated WSDL files always describe messages in terms of SOAP encoding rules, instead of literal XSD. Second, the generated WSDL files (might) include extensions that are specific to .NET Remoting. This is legal in WSDL, as it supports extensions, but other Web Services frameworks, including ASP.NET, have to ignore these types. This is problematic, as some .NET data types, such as the .NET type DataSet, have a special meaning. If you need interoperability with other Web Services frameworks, you must restrict parameters to the built-in simple types and your own data types, but should not expose .NET data types.

IONA's Artix

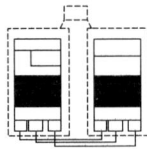

Artix is a Web Services framework implemented in C++ that focusses on high performance and middleware integration. The framework is built on Adaptive Runtime Technology (ART) [Vin02b], an efficient and scalable INVOCATION INTERCEPTOR architecture that is also the foundation of IONA's Orbix CORBA implementation. Artix extends the basic concept of Web Services to include transparent conversions between different data encoding schemas and/or transport protocols. Besides the C++ implementation, an additional Java API is offered. The Java solution is not a native Java implementation, but instead is a wrapper around the C++ libraries.

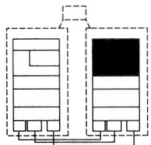

For developing simple Web Services in Artix, the developer of a Web Service needs to write a WSDL INTERFACE DESCRIPTION file. From this file, code for the client and server side is generated by a tool – both a command-line and a GUI version of this are provided. Developers of Web Services need to add the method bodies of the Web Services implementation, while client developers need to add invocation code, such as the input parameters of an invocation.

A REMOTING ERROR can be triggered by the Artix runtime library, by an Artix service (such as the locator described below), or by user-defined code. The client code needs to catch the C++ exception and handle it.

New REMOTING ERRORS can be specified in WSDL as WSDL faults. The WSDL generation tool generates an exception class for each fault. Optionally, WSDL code can be specified that causes a class containing user-defined details of the REMOTING ERROR to be generated.

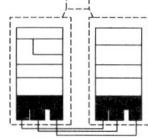

A key difference between Artix and other Web Services frameworks is that it supports integration with other middleware without requiring the developer to write complex wrapper or other integration code. Artix supports a number of PROTOCOL PLUG-INS, namely HTTP, BEA Tuxedo, IBM WebSphere MQ (formerly MQSeries), TIBCO Rendezvous, IIOP, IIOP Tunnel, and Java Messaging Service (JMS). In addition, Artix can transform automatically between different payload formats, including SOAP, CORBA's GIOP, Tuxedo's FML, and many others. Artix supports transparent transformations for these protocols and formats. These are performed using one-to-one converters to support high-performance message transformations.

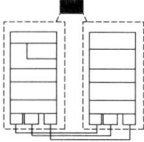

The Artix locator provides LOOKUP for Artix services by providing a repository of endpoint references. The locator also implements a LOCATION FORWARDER, which is used for load balancing: if multiple ports are registered for a single service name, the locator load balances over the service's ports using a round-robin algorithm. Artix's locator is a remote object that exposes its interface using a WSDL INTERFACE DESCRIPTION.

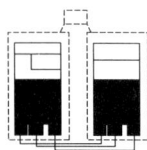

Artix implements a number of other orthogonal services for Web Services, including security, sessions, transactions, and others. These are provided as ART plug-ins, INVOCATION INTERCEPTORS that extend the CLIENT REQUEST HANDLER and SERVER REQUEST HANDLER. Configuration of these services and other properties are transported using an INVOCATION CONTEXT called the 'message attributes'. The INVOCATION CONTEXT is extensible with key/value pairs.

For example, the Artix session manager is realized by a number of ART plug-ins that provide control over the number of concurrent clients. Services are registered as part of a CONFIGURATION GROUP, and sessions are handed out for the group. The session manager also controls how long each client can use the services in the group through the use of LEASING. Clients that are going to use a session for longer than the duration the session was granted need to renew the session's lease at the appropriate time.

Leela – loosely coupled Web Services federations

Leela [Zdu04b, Zdu04c] is an infrastructure for loosely-coupled services that is built on top of a Web Services infrastructure. In addition to a Web Services infrastructure, as provided by the Web Services frameworks discussed before, Leela implements higher-level concepts from the areas of P2P systems [CV02], coordination and cooperation technologies [GCCC85, CTV+98], and spontaneous networking [Jin04].

Leela integrates and extends these concepts by providing a *federated* remote object architecture. Each federation controls its peers. Peers cannot be accessed from outside the federation without the permission of the federation. Within a federation, each peer offers Web Services (and possibly other kinds of services) and can connect spontaneously to other peers and to the federation. Each remote object potentially can be part of more than one federation as a peer, and each peer decides which services it provides to which federation. To allow peers to connect to a federation, the federation itself must be accessible remotely. Thus the federation itself is a special peer. Peers can be dynamically added and removed from a federation.

Leela is implemented using the patterns presented in this book. Its goal is to provide a powerful remoting infrastructure that is extremely flexible and easy to use. Currently Leela is implemented in the object-oriented Tcl variant XOTcl [NZ00], but an equally powerful and easy-to-use implementation in Java is also under development. For the Java port, the pattern-based design of the Leela framework helps to reuse large parts of the design presented briefly in this section.

As its basic communication resource each Leela application uses two classes that implement a CLIENT REQUEST HANDLER and a SERVER REQUEST HANDLER. Each Leela application acts as client and server application at the same time. The request handlers contain PROTOCOL PLUG-INS for the various protocols that transport the message across the network. Currently, Leela supports PROTOCOL PLUG-INS for various SOAP implementations. However, virtually any other communication protocol can be used as well, because Leela's MARSHALLER uses a simple string-based format as a message payload, and (re-)uses Tcl's automatic type converter to convert the string representations to native types and vice versa.

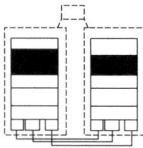Remote invocations are abstracted by REQUESTOR and INVOKER. Leela also supports peer and federation proxies that act as CLIENT PROXIES, offering the interfaces of a remote peer or federation. The following figure illustrates the basic architecture:

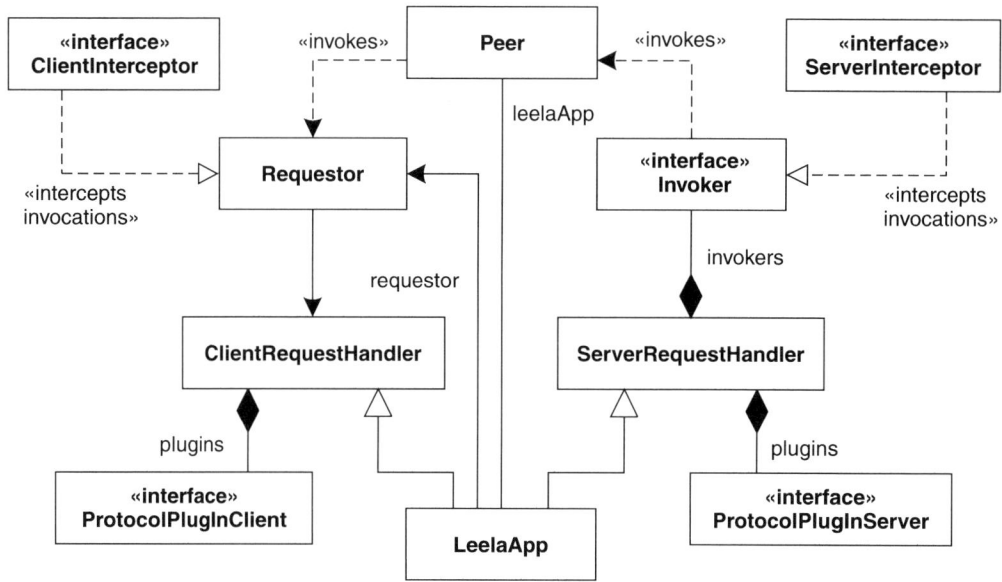

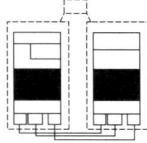The Leela invocation chain on the client side and the server side is based on INVOCATION INTERCEPTORS. That is, the invocation on both sides can be extended transparently with new behavior. The most prominent task of the INVOCATION INTERCEPTORS in Leela is control of remote federation access. On the client side, an INVOCATION INTERCEPTOR intercepts the construction of the remote invocation and adds all federation information for a peer into the INVOCATION CONTEXT. On the server side this information is read by another INVOCATION INTERCEPTOR. If the remote peer is not allowed to access the invoked peer, the INVOCATION INTERCEPTOR stops the invocation and sends a REMOTING ERROR to the client, otherwise access is granted.

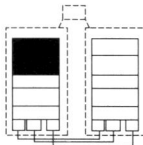On the client side different styles of asynchronous invocations and result handling are supported, which follow the patterns FIRE AND FORGET, POLL OBJECT, and RESULT CALLBACK. Because in Leela each client is also a server, synchronous invocations, those that let the client process block for the result, are not an option, because if the Leela application

blocks it can no longer service incoming requests. Leela instead implements asynchronous invocation patterns with a common callback model. The REQUEST HANDLERS work using an event loop that queues incoming and outgoing requests in a message queue, both on the client and the server side. Invocations and handling of results are performed in separate threads. Events in these threads, such as 'result is ready for sending', are placed into the event loop, which serves as a simple synchronization mechanism. This approach is also used for handling events for multiple PROTOCOL PLUG-INS.

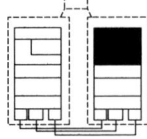

On the server side the remote object is registered for use with a particular INVOKER. There is one INVOKER per lifecycle management pattern: one for STATIC INSTANCES, using synchronized access, PER-REQUEST INSTANCES, using POOLING, and CLIENT-DEPENDENT INSTANCES. The CLIENT-DEPENDENT INSTANCES are created using a special factory operation of the federation peer, and managed using LEASING. LIFECYCLE MANAGER is thus implemented by all these components of the Leela framework.

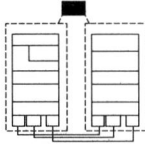

A semantic lookup service allows peers to be found using metadata, which is exposed by the peers according to some ontology. This enables loosely-coupled services and simple self-adaptations, for example to cope with interface or version changes. Peers can perform lookups in all lookup services of their federations. Leela uses the Resource Description Framework (RDF) [W3C04] to describe peers. RDF supports semantic metadata about Web resources, described in some ontology or schema. The federation provides metadata about all its peers, such as a list of ABSOLUTE OBJECT REFERENCES, supported protocols, and OBJECT IDS (the service names). Each peer adds information for its exported methods, their interfaces, and their activation strategy. This information can be seen as a dynamic and remotely-introspective INTERFACE DESCRIPTION, together with location information and semantic metadata. Users can define their own custom ontologies to provide semantic domain knowledge for peers.

Consequences of the pattern variants used in Web Services

Now that we have also discussed a few other Web Services frameworks, let's briefly revisit the consequences of applying our patterns to the implementation of Web Services. As we have seen, there are differences between the different Web Services implementations, yet these basic consequences are essentially the same.

First, let us summarize some characteristics of the pattern variants used in Web Services frameworks. The client-side invocation architecture is quite flexible, and involves dynamic invocations using a REQUESTOR, as well as runtime CLIENT PROXY generation from a WSDL INTERFACE DESCRIPTION. The INVOKER can be (re-)configured at runtime using various means, such as XML configuration files, scripting, meta-information, or programmatic APIs.

URLs are used as ABSOLUTE OBJECT REFERENCES, at least in the supported Web protocols, a simple but not ideal format because they do not stay stable over time. An advantage is that it is quite simple to implement a LOCATION FORWARDER for URLs (which might even be supported already, for example by HTTP Redirect). As Web Services are used mainly as an integration architecture, large parts of the lower-level patterns, such as REQUEST HANDLERS and PROTOCOL PLUG-INS, are not implemented by the Web Services framework itself, but by reusing existing implementations. The MARSHALLER might support some kinds of automatic type conversion, for example to and from strings or other generic types.

Note that many of these properties are similar to the inherent language properties of scripting languages. For example, using WSDL for dynamic CLIENT PROXY generation is similar to introspection and runtime class generation in scripting languages. Automatic type conversion is language-supported in most scripting languages. In fact, scripting is used in many integration scenarios in other middleware as well. Steve Vinoski refers to such scripting code as the 'dark matter of middleware' [Vin02a]. Web Services can be seen as a standardized form of implementing some of the integration tasks that typically are performed using scripting in other middlewares.

A central advantage of Web Services is that they provide a means for interoperability in a heterogeneous environment. They are also relatively easy to use and understand, due to simple APIs. Because Web Services allow for integration of other, different, middleware and component platforms as PROTOCOL PLUG-INS or backends, Web Services can be used for integration of different platforms. Web Services offer standards for process flow orchestration, long-running business transactions, and other higher-level tasks – thus they can be used to advantage in enterprise application integration (EAI) scenarios, where we are typically faced with a number of different platforms.

In the spirit of the original design ideas of XML [BPS98] and XML-RPC [Win99] as the predecessor of today's standard Web Services message format SOAP, XML encoding was expected to promote simplicity and understandability as central advantages. Today's XML-based formats used in Web Services frameworks, however, such as XML Namespaces, XML Schema, SOAP, and WSDL, are quite complex and thus not easy to read or understand.

XML, as a string-based transport format, is bloated compared to more compact binary transport formats. This results in larger messages, as well as a more extensive use of network bandwidth. XML consists of strings for identifiers, attributes, and data elements. String parsing is more expensive in terms of processing power than parsing binary data.

In many cases, stateless communication, as imposed by HTTP and SOAP, causes overheads, because it may result in repeated transmission of the same data – for example, for authentication or identifying the current session.

Unfortunately the lookup protocol UDDI is – at the moment – viewed rather negatively. For example, no standardization of the tModels is going on, making it difficult to find services with the same properties. Currently there is no real integration of WSDL and UDDI functionalities, and no automated way for programs to use the information. Some frameworks, for example GLUE, Artix, and Leela, (also) support other non-standardized lookup services to get around these problems.

In summary, Web Services serve a different purpose than conventional object-oriented middleware. Even though Web Services can only be used for RPC communication, the liabilities incurred in this area indicate that they should not be used for this purpose. Web Services are much more about loosely-coupled exchange of messages. Thus their strength lies in the complex, service-based integration in heterogeneous environments, such as integrating other middleware, orchestrating processes, or enterprise application integration.

12 CORBA Technology Projection

CORBA is the 'old man' among the distributed object middleware technologies used in today's IT world. CORBA stands for Common Object Request Broker Architecture. It defines distributed object middleware by its interfaces, their semantics and the protocols used for communication. The communication paradigm used adheres strongly to the client/server model. For the programming language in our examples, we use C++.

A brief history of CORBA

CORBA is represented by the OMG (Object Management Group), which is a consortium of over 600 companies, among them almost all big players in the IT world.

An Object Request Broker (ORB) is the core of CORBA: what it is, and how it works, is described in this chapter. The OMG issues specifications that are in turn implemented by various ORB vendors. A series of Common Object Services exist around that core, such as the Naming Service, Event Service, Notification Service, and Logging Service.

The first version of CORBA was finalized in 1991. Since then many ORBs have been implemented, both commercial and open-source ORBs. Since approximately 1998 an increasing number of open-source implementations, such as TAO, OmniORB, and JacORB have appeared. Today open-source and commercial ORBs, such as those from IONA and Borland, exist side by side.

CORBA allows objects to be accessed in a distributed environment very similarly to the way in which they are accessed locally. Some explicit setup and configuration work is necessary, burdening the programmer, but also allowing full control of behavior.

Component frameworks such as EJB [Sun04d] or CCM [Sev04] hide this code by doing all the set-up and configuration internally. CORBA is an important part of the J2EE standard – every Java Development Kit

(JDK) ships with CORBA support and a default implementation provided by Sun. CORBA has become a working tier inside modern component platforms, leading to people becoming oblivious to it, believing it to be outdated and no longer necessary in today's IT world. This view is incorrect, as CORBA is used as distributed object middleware within such component and integration platforms.

In the past few years CORBA has gained increasing acceptance in distributed real-time and embedded systems development. In this, CORBA has followed the classic Technology Adoption Life Cycle [Rog95], in which successful systems eventually start to appeal to conservative users, because they become convinced over time that the technology is well proven, solid, and reliable.

Real-time and embedded systems developers tend to be very conservative, so it's no surprise that it has taken this long for CORBA to appeal to them. Increases in available processing power and lower memory prices have also helped. In the past this domain used to rely on proprietary middleware, but now uses CORBA as standardized middleware. The OMG has tried to adapt to this domain explicitly with its Real-Time CORBA and Minimum CORBA specifications.

CORBA pattern map

The following diagram illustrates the use of the Remoting Patterns in this book when aligned to CORBA's architecture. Patterns that cover

CORBA pattern map

only dynamics, such as those in the *Client Asynchrony* or the *Lifecycle Management* chapters, are therefore not included.

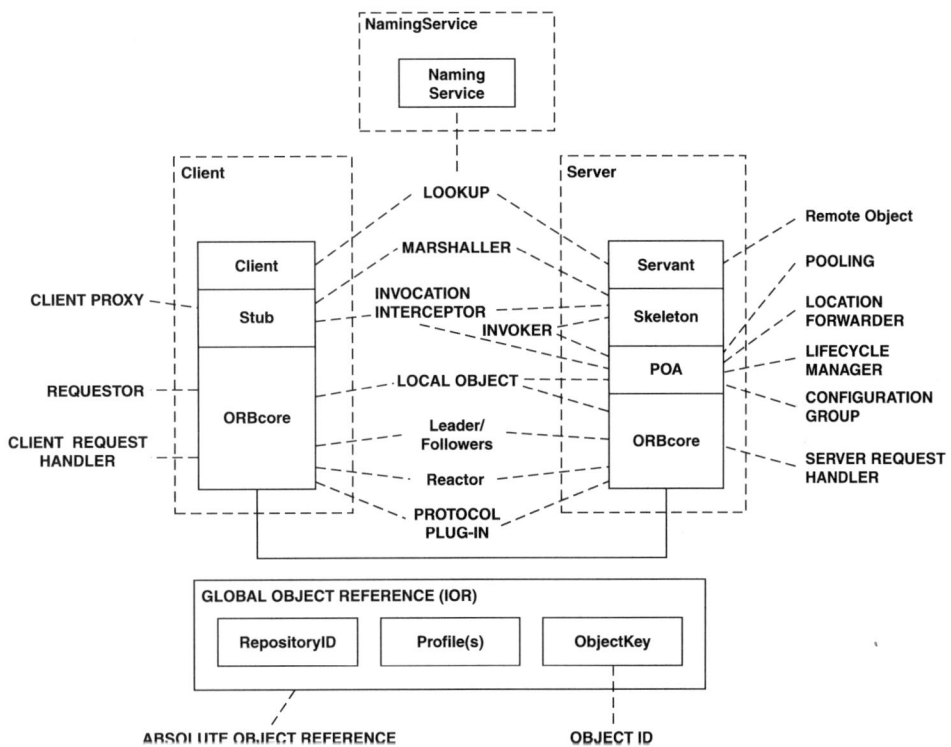

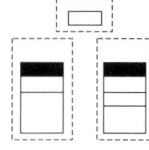

An initial example with CORBA

As in many other distributed object middleware architectures, CORBA relies on interface specifications in separate files. The syntax used in those files is called IDL (Interface Definition Language). The following code snippet shows the IDL file of a simple example.

```
interface Foo {
  void bar ();
};
```

An IDL compiler generates code from this, namely *stubs* and *skeletons* – these are explained later in this chapter. The IDL compiler also generates an abstract class to be completed as the implementation of the remote object, the POA_Foo class in the example below. The following fragment of code represents one of the simplest possible server implementations for the above IDL interface.

```
#include "FooS.h"
class Foo_Impl : public POA_Foo {
  void bar () { cout << "Hello world!" << endl; }
}
int main (int argc, char *argv[])
{
  CORBA::ORB_var orb = CORBA::ORB_init (argc, argv);
  CORBA::Object_var poa_obj =
    orb->resolve_initial_references ("RootPOA");
  PortableServer::POA_var poa =
    PortableServer::POA::_narrow (poa_obj);
  Foo_Impl foo;
  poa->activate_object (&foo);
  PortableServer::POAManager_var poa_manager =
    poa->the_POAManager ();
  poa_manager->activate ();
  orb->run ();
  poa->destroy (1,0); // parameters are explained later
  orb->destroy ();
}
```

The main routine contains the set-up and configuration information necessary to:

- Create and initialize the ORB (`ORB_init`)
- Create an object adapter (`resolve_initial_references`)
- Register the remote object implementation (`activate_object`)

An initial example with CORBA

- Activate the dispatching of requests to the remote object (`activate`)
- Run the event loop to actually dispatch requests (`run`)

A client that wants to invoke operations on the remote object looks like the following:

```
#include "FooC.h"
int main (int argc, char *argv[])
{
  // ...
  CORBA::ORB_var orb = CORBA::ORB_init (argc, argv);
  // read the object reference to the remote object from the
  // arguments list in position 1
  CORBA::Object_var obj =
    orb->string_to_object (argv[1]);
  Foo_var foo = Foo::_narrow (obj);
  // do the actual invocation
  foo->bar ();
  orb->destroy ();
}
```

The client creates an ORB instance in the same way that the server does. It then creates a local proxy for the remote object, by converting the stringified object reference – handed over as `argv[1]` in this case – to a CORBA object reference. To finally create a proxy of the correct type, it performs a `narrow` operation on the object reference. The proxy, represented by the variable `foo`, is now ready for use, and operations can be invoked on it. The proxy follows the CLIENT PROXY pattern, but we discuss more about its responsibilities later.

CORBA basics

The CORBA architecture consists of multiple components. Those used in most applications are:

- Object Request Broker core (ORB core), responsible for basic communication mechanisms
- Portable Object Adapter (POA), responsible for dispatching requests to registered remote objects
- Naming Service, responsible for the central distribution of references to remote objects

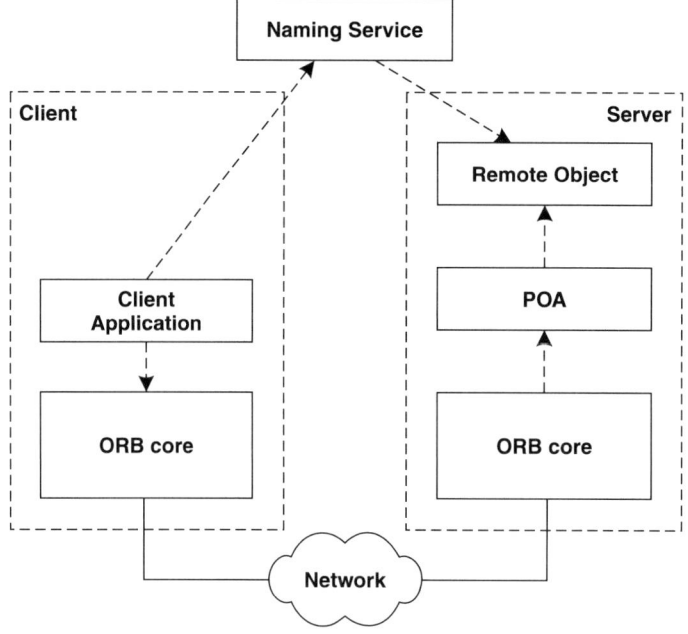

Looking at CORBA's constituent parts from a deployment perspective, the POA and ORB core are often represented as libraries. Applications implementing remote objects are mostly executables that link with the POA and the ORB library. The reason for this separation is footprint optimization, minimizing the amount of memory used. Separate libraries have two advantages:

- Different implementations can be provided, customized to the use cases in which the ORB is employed

- An application can include only those components that it really needs, keeping the overall footprint at a minimum

For example, some ORB vendors provide a minimum POA implementation specialized for embedded systems with fixed requirements, as well as the complete POA implementation needed for enterprise systems. The savings in footprint when using a minimum POA over a full-featured POA can be quite significant. Further, pure client-side ORBs can reduce the memory footprint by not including the POA, which is not needed if they do not serve remote objects.

Our technology projection of how CORBA is built on the patterns is independent of a specific ORB implementation, but the way in which the patterns are implemented is ORB vendor-dependent. ORB vendors are free to implement the ORB as they see fit, as long as they adhere to the standardized interfaces, semantics, and separation between responsibilities.

The ORB core itself is designed to be compact. It implements the essentials of connection and request handling: SERVER REQUEST HANDLER and CLIENT REQUEST HANDLER. Actual request dispatch functionality is kept in the POA, using INVOKER. This *Microkernel* [BMR+96] architecture has proved successful in many other architectures, and has proved useful not only in ORB design, but also in operating systems. Microkernel architectures are built on a core that provides the most basic functionality, and uses layers around that to extend this functionality. They are especially useful in situations in which future usage scenarios and extensions cannot be foreseen.

This design principle has been followed until today, with the current CORBA 3 specification. Most ORB vendors are able to extend their ORBs with shells of functionality through the use of add-on libraries to implement extra features, such as RT-CORBA or Portable Interceptors.

Basic connection and message handling

For managing network connections and for basic send and receive of messages, the ORB implements SERVER REQUEST HANDLER and CLIENT REQUEST HANDLER. Both patterns implement basic request handling functionality. On an initial request from a client to a server, the client-side ORB checks the connection pool for existing connections to the server. If none is available, it creates one and adds it to the connection pool [KJ04]. It then associates a message handler, implementing CLIENT REQUEST HANDLER, with that connection to send and receive bytes of marshaled requests and replies.

On the server side a new message handler, implementing SERVER REQUEST HANDLER, is created when a new connection is accepted, and is associated with the connection to receive and send bytes of marshaled requests and replies. The POA, which implements part of the INVOKER pattern, finally dispatches the request.

A *Reactor* [SSRB00] helps to avoid blocking on a single connection establishment or on send and receive operations. It allows events to be demultiplexed and dispatched efficiently to corresponding message handlers, such as connection establishment, send and receive. On the client side the reactor dispatches replies, while on the server side it dispatches requests.

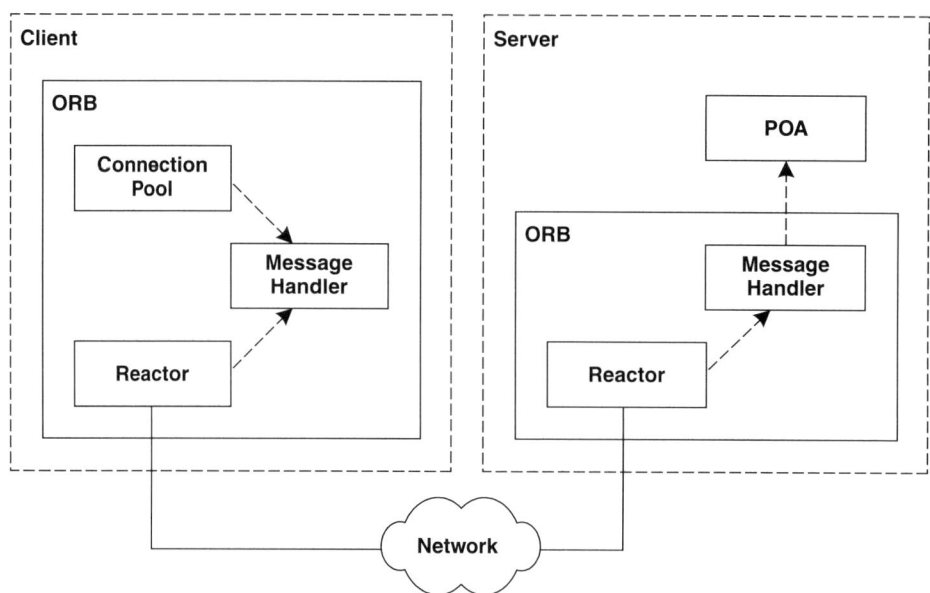

It should have become clear that client- and server-side ORBs are not that different. Both use much of the same infrastructure, such as the reactor. We will discover in the remainder of this chapter that the reactor is not the only shared component.

References to ORB extensions, such as the POA[1] and the *Current* object, representing the current thread, are bootstrapped by an invocation to `ORB::resolve_initial_references`.

The `ORB::resolve_initial_references` operation looks up an internal table for the reference. In the sample code for the server on page 296, we showed the following code:

```
CORBA::Object_var poa_obj =
  orb->resolve_initial_references ("RootPOA");
PortableServer::POA_var poa =
  PortableServer::POA::_narrow (poa_obj);
```

This code essentially provides the server application with a reference to the root POA. The root POA is, as its name implies, the root of the POA hierarchy: other POAs can be created and retrieved via the reference to the root POA. More about the POA hierarchy and the INVOKER later.

The ORB extensions themselves are represented as LOCAL OBJECTS, and their creation is typically triggered by the creation of the ORB core. LOCAL OBJECTS are represented by instances of regular C++ classes that have the same reference-passing semantics as remote objects, with the difference that they are not accessible remotely. They are registered internally to the ORB, so that CORBA applications can query for references to them in order to configure and use them.

To avoid creating and initializing a POA in client applications that do not need one, the POA component can be created and initialized on the first lookup. Thus when a server application does the lookup of the root POA via `ORB::resolve_initial_references`, the POA is created lazily using the LAZY ACQUISITION pattern. The *Component Configurator* [SSRB00] pattern documents how components such as the POA can be loaded on demand.

As the name 'Object Request Broker' indicates, the ORB is responsible for brokering requests between object, as described in the BROKER pattern. There has always been some confusion around the term ORB:

---

1. For a CORBA server, the POA is not an extension, but a necessary component. From a purely architectural perspective, however, the POA extends the ORB core with customizable dispatching functionality. For real-time systems, specialized POA implementations exist.

some think of it as one big conglomerate – a big communication bus – of many ORB instances running all over the world, while others separate the ORB instances and view them as inter-operating, self-contained ORBs, sometimes even differentiating between client- and server-side ORBs. As reality is closer to the latter variant, we prefer to think of it in that way.

Even on a local host there is no single ORB process through which all requests and replies flow, but rather many ORB instances: one or several per inter-communicating operating system process.

Client and server adaptation layers

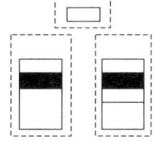

Many distributed object middleware implementations represent remote objects to clients by means of CLIENT PROXIES. In CORBA such proxies are called *stubs*. The stub provides the same interface as the remote object it represents, while it also acts as REQUESTOR, and so is also responsible for marshaling request parameters. The MARSHALLER is either contained in the stub, or in a separate component. The client stub and its server-side equivalent use compatible MARSHALLERS.

References to CLIENT PROXIES and LOCAL OBJECTS are reference-counted, which means that they destroy themselves as soon as all reference holders have given up their references to them. The implementations follow the *Counted Handler* [Hen98] pattern.

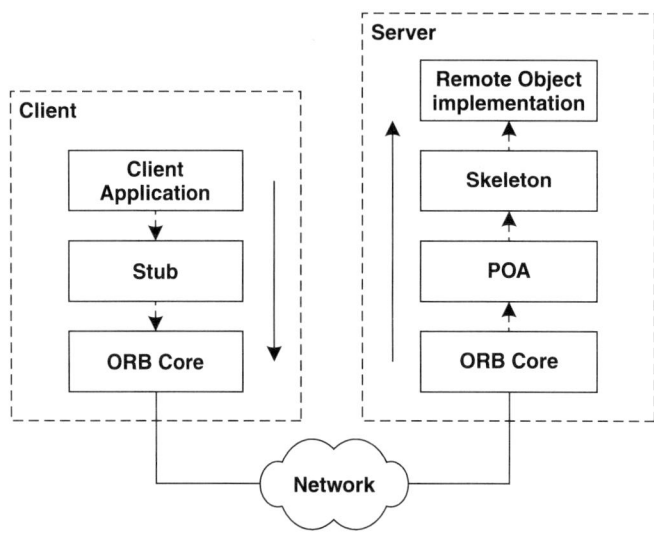

The server-side equivalent to the stub is the *skeleton*. The skeleton implements INVOKER, together with the POA. The skeleton is responsible for the actual dispatch of invocations to the target remote object. It has to demarshal in and in/out parameters before the invocation of the remote object, and marshal out and in/out parameters and results after the invocation. As before, MARSHALLER is applied for marshaling and demarshaling.

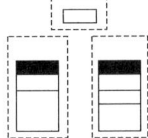

Interface Description

The interfaces of remote objects are described in CORBA using a separate language that is different than any programming language. The reason for this lies in the mission of CORBA to be platform and programming language independent. This language is the *Interface Definition Language* (IDL), and follows the INTERFACE DESCRIPTION pattern. Descriptions in IDL define the interface and the data types used by a remote object. An IDL compiler, which is always part of an CORBA implementation, uses the IDL descriptions to create the client-side stub and server-side skeleton.

The IDL also allows definition of the exceptions an operation can throw – to be exact, the user exceptions that can be thrown: CORBA system exceptions can be thrown by every operation of an interface, even though they are not mentioned in the INTERFACE DESCRIPTION. The user exceptions supported have to be declared in IDL just like every other data type. The REMOTING ERROR pattern describes how they are used by remote objects, and the respective server-side ORB required to communicate execution errors back to the client.

```
exception FooError { string reason; };

interface Foo
{
   void bar () raises (FooError);
};
```

This example declares a user exception `FooError` that can be thrown by the `bar` operation of the `Foo` interface. In C++ and Java, the language mapping allows CORBA exceptions to be thrown as native exceptions.

The following code fragment illustrates this:

```
try {
  foo->bar ();
}
catch (FooError &ex) {
  cout << ex.reason << endl;
}
catch (CORBA::SystemException &ex) {
  cout << "Critical CORBA system exception" << endl;
}
```

Server-side dispatching

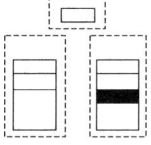

The Portable Object Adapter (POA) also implements the CONFIGURATION GROUP pattern. The POA is the glue between ORB and skeleton, as shown in the figure on page 302. Remote objects are registered with the POA by the server application, which allows the POA to apply configuration parameters to the remote objects. Invocations of remote objects are forwarded by the ORB core to the POA, which then dispatches them to the skeletons of remote objects. To find the correct POA, the ORB core has to demarshal parts of the request. The POA then continues demarshaling the request, retrieving the OBJECT ID to find the correct remote object. The POA invokes the skeleton with a reference to the servant – the implementation of the remote object – and passes the remaining parts of the request, including the in and in/out parameters. The skeleton demarshals the parameters and executes the invocation of the referenced servant. When the invocation returns, the skeleton marshals the out parameters, in/out parameters, and result, and passes them back to the POA as the reply to be sent back to the client.

```
// Install a persistent POA to achieve a persistent IOR
// for our object.
CORBA::PolicyList policies;
policies.length (1);
policies[0] =
  root_poa->create_lifespan_policy(PortableServer::PERSISTENT);
PortableServer::POA_var persistent_poa =
  root_poa->create_POA("persistent", poa_manager, policies);
policies[0]->destroy ();
```

As the POA realizes a CONFIGURATION GROUP and has to support many configurations, a single POA is not enough. CORBA supports the nesting of POAs, allowing them to be arranged on a hierarchy. At the root of the tree the root POA is configured with default policies. All child POAs, with their own sets of configuration policies, are grouped below the root POA directly, or nested as a hierarchy.

It should be clear that the responsibilities between ORB core, POA, and skeleton are clearly separated into basic request handling, retrieval and configuration of the remote objects, and actual request dispatching, respectively. While ORB core and POA are generic, the skeleton is remote object specific.

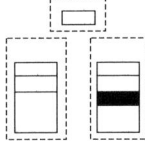

Lifecycle management in CORBA

The LIFECYCLE MANAGER pattern is implemented by *POA managers* in combination with *servant managers*. A POA manager is responsible for activation and deactivation of the request flow in the POA to the remote objects, whereas a servant manger is responsible for the actual activation and deactivation of the remote objects. A servant manager is invoked by the POA instead of the actual remote object. Note that even though POA managers and servant managers extend each other's range of influence, they are separate concepts and can be applied independently.

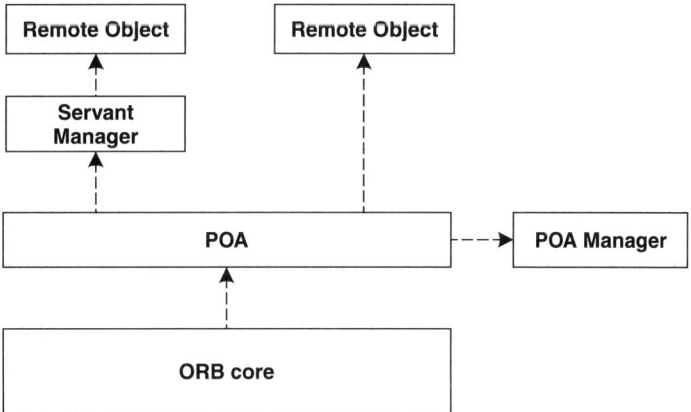

A POA manager is invoked in the call chain before any servant manager, and has no influence on the selection of the remote object. POA managers are optionally created on the call to `Porta-bleServer::POA::create_POA` and are associated with one or more POAs.

The following state diagram shows the various states in which the POA manager can exist.

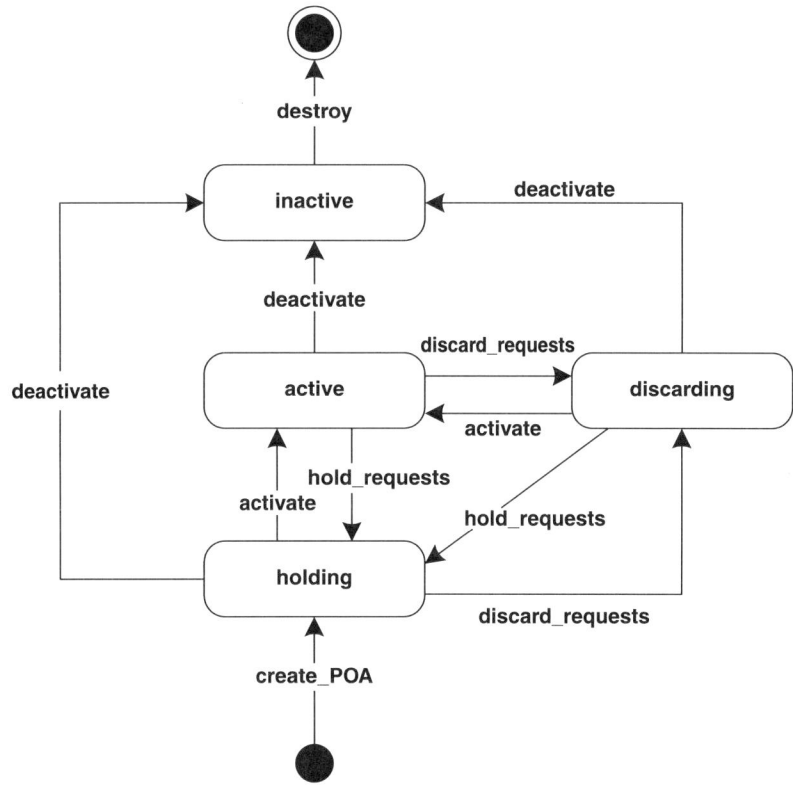

Servant managers are an ORB extension: they are not implemented by the ORB vendor, but only provisioned as an interface. The application can implement custom activation and deactivation of remote objects by implementing the interface and registering the implementation with the POA. We discuss this in more detail later.

Returning to the parameters used on the destroy operation of the POA, we saw in the introductory 'Hello World!' example on page 296:

```
poa->destroy (1, 0);
```

The first parameter tells the POA to notify the servant manager that the POA is going to be shut down. The second parameter tells the POA not to wait for pending requests to be completed before shut-down. Not waiting for pending requests has the advantage that such requests cannot block the ORB, and so the application, from being destroyed.

Object references

Remote objects have to be identified at different levels, which means that the respective ID must be unique at each level. Inside the POA, remote objects are identified by an OBJECT ID. This OBJECT ID can be chosen by the server application, or generated by the POA when activating the remote object. CORBA identifies remote objects via object references. Object references always contain an OBJECT ID.

Additional information is needed for unique identification when object references are passed outside the local process. The generation of process-external unique object references follows the ABSOLUTE OBJECT REFERENCE pattern – in CORBA ABSOLUTE OBJECT REFERENCES are called *Interoperable Object References* (IORs). To make the IOR globally unique, the ORB adds information about ORB endpoints and the POA with which the remote object is registered. Endpoint information is described in the form of *profiles*, which contain the host IP address and port number. The following figure illustrates the structure of the IOR.

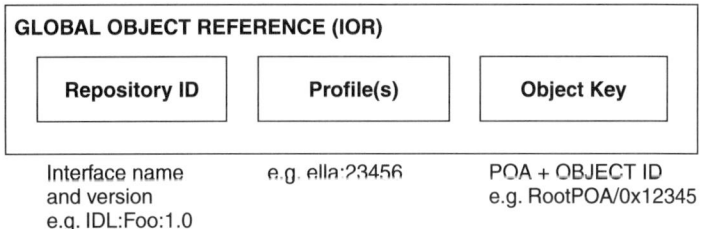

A specific servant can only be registered with one POA, and therefore with one ORB. This restriction ensures that the servant is exposed only to intentional concurrency configured via the POA policies. As a POA can be configured to serialize requests to a remote object, the server application can ensure that the servant, alias the remote object, is protected from concurrent access. If it was registered with two ORBs, and therefore with two POAs, unintended concurrent access could occur, possibly leading to data corruption.

There is an interesting story about how CORBA were first used in real-time systems. The problem was that servants were required to serve requests at different priorities. Neither the client nor the server side of an ORB distinguished between different request properties when sending or receiving requests, nor when dispatching them. The work-around was to install multiple server-side ORBs, each running in a thread with a different priority. The servant was registered with each ORB, so of course the servant had to be thread-safe. IORs were generated for each remote object, identifying the same servant in multiple ORBs. In this way clients were able to distinguish between priorities by using either the IOR of the remote object served by an ORB running at higher or lower priority. Later we describe how this is done in a standardized way today using Real-Time CORBA.

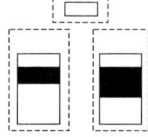

Invocation extensions

We have already mentioned that CORBA was designed to be highly extensible. In situations in which transparent services such as security or transactions need to be supported, low-level control is needed during the actual dispatch of requests. Adding just another wrapper around the microkernel is insufficient, as requests and replies would have to be demarshaled and marshaled again to make any changes or additions to invocations.

The INVOCATION INTERCEPTOR pattern allows such transparent services to be integrated. In CORBA, the instantiation of this pattern is represented by *portable interceptors*. Interceptors can be used at different levels of request processing. The following figure shows the possible interception points.

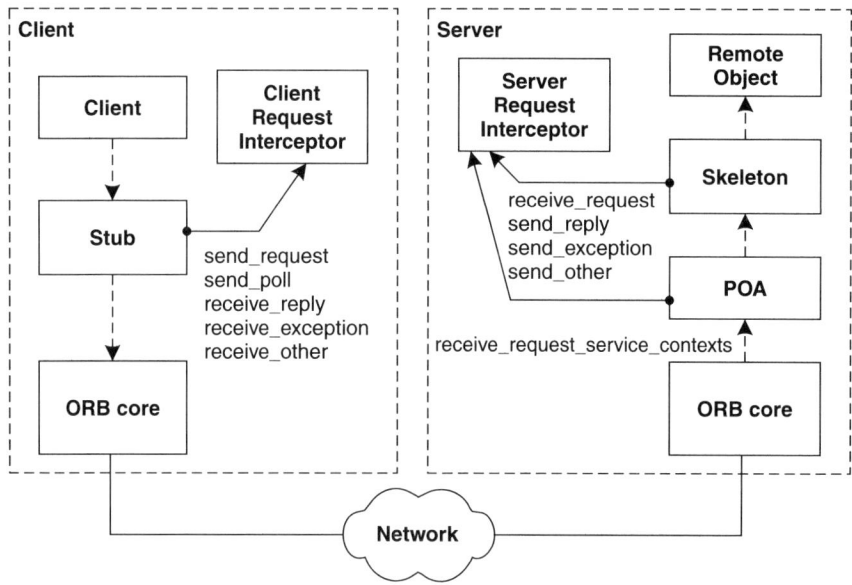

Additional services often need context information about the request or reply. For example, a transaction service needs to carry the transaction ID from the client to the server and back, so that the request can be associated with the corresponding transaction. An INVOCATION CONTEXT is the common solution, which in CORBA is called a *service context*, and which can contain any value including binary data. Service context information can be modified via Portable Interceptors.

Portable interceptors in CORBA are separated into *client request interceptors* and *server request interceptors*. The following class declaration shows an empty implementation of a client request interceptor. The method implementations can access any request information via the *client request information*.

```
class Foo_ClientRequestInterceptor
  : public virtual PortableInterceptor::ClientRequestInterceptor
{
public:
  virtual char * name () throw (CORBA::SystemException)
  {
    return CORBA::string_dup ("Foo");
  }
  virtual void destroy () throw (CORBA::SystemException) {}
  virtual void send_request (
      PortableInterceptor::ClientRequestInfo_ptr)
    throw (CORBA::SystemException,
         PortableInterceptor::ForwardRequest)
  {
    cout << "send_request invoked" << endl;
  }
  virtual void receive_reply (
      PortableInterceptor::ClientRequestInfo_ptr)
    throw(CORBA::SystemException) {}
  // ...
};
```

Client and server request interceptors must be registered inside an *ORB initializer*. For this purpose the ORB initializer is separated into two methods, a `pre_init` and a `post_init` method, which are invoked before and after the initialization of the ORB respectively.

```
class Client_ORBInitializer :
  public virtual PortableInterceptor::ORBInitializer
{
public:
  void pre_init (PortableInterceptor::ORBInitInfo_ptr)
    throw (CORBA::SystemException)
  {}

  void post_init (PortableInterceptor::ORBInitInfo_ptr info)
    throw(CORBA::SystemException)
  {
    PortableInterceptor::ClientRequestInterceptor_var
      interceptor (new Foo_ClientRequestInterceptor);
    info->add_client_request_interceptor (interceptor);
  }
};
```

The ORB initializer is registered with the ORB library before a actual ORB instance is created by `CORBA::ORB_init`.

```
PortableInterceptor::ORBInitializer_var
  initializer (new Client_ORBInitializer);
PortableInterceptor::register_orb_initializer (initializer.in());

CORBA::ORB_var orb = CORBA::ORB_init (argc, argv, "");
```

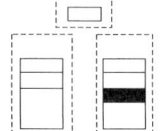

Activation strategies

The simplest and most straightforward usage of the POA is that for STATIC INSTANCES: activation of remote objects at server application start-up time.

CORBA servant managers have already been mentioned above in the context of the POA. They are used when the trivial activation of servants at start-up time, such as the case of STATIC INSTANCES, is not sufficient. This happens typically in servers that have to deal with a huge number of remote object instances. Servant managers are a separate concept of interception when compared with portable interceptors: they are specialized for servant activation and deactivation, and are historically a much older concept than portable interceptors.

CORBA basics

LAZY ACQUISITION allows the activation of remote objects to be deferred to the time when the first request reaches the remote object. The activation is done by a *servant activator*, representing one kind of CORBA servant manager. The servant activator is registered with the POA that issued the object reference to the as-yet not activated remote object. The servant activator is activated via the `incarnate` operation by the POA. Further requests are dispatched directly to the now active remote object.

To use a servant activator, the POA has to be configured in the following way:

```
CORBA::PolicyList policies;
policies.length (3);
policies[0] =
  poa->create_request_processing_policy(
                        PortableServer::USE_SERVANT_MANAGER);
policies[1] =
  poa->create_servant_retention_policy (PortableServer::RETAIN);
policies[2] =
  poa->create_id_assignment_policy (PortableServer::USER_ID);
PortableServer::POA_var servant_manager_poa =
  poa->create_POA("servant activator", poa_manager, policies);
policies[0]->destroy ();
policies[1]->destroy ();
policies[2]->destroy ();
```

For servant activators, the RETAIN policy has to be used, so that the active object map of the POA keeps track of activated servants. The servant activator can now be registered with the newly-created POA, as follows:

```
MyActivator activator;
PortableServer::ServantManager_var servant_manager = &activator;
servant_manager_poa->set_servant_manager (servant_manager);
```

At this point, an object reference to the as-yet inactive remote object is created with a user-defined OBJECT ID, which allows us to identify requests for a specific servant.

```
PortableServer::ObjectId_var object_id =
  PortableServer::string_to_ObjectId ("Foo");

CORBA::Object_var object =
  servant_manager_poa->create_reference_with_id (object_id,
                                      "IDL:Foo:1.0");
```

Once activated it is hard to monitor the further lifecycle of the servant by using servant activators, because activators are only involved in the first invocation on a remote object, not on any later invocation. *Servant locators* are more flexible. A servant locator is invoked on every invocation of the remote object. This has the advantage of better and more fine-grained control, but obviously also influences performance negatively, as the servant locator needs additional CPU cycles on every invocation of the remote object.

The `PortableServer::ServantLocator` has two operations, `preinvoke` and `postinvoke`. `preinvoke` is invoked before every invocation of the remote object identified by the OBJECT ID, while `postinvoke` is invoked after every invocation. The following servant locator implements PER-REQUEST INSTANCE: it trivially creates a new servant on every invocation. In this example the servant locator destroys the servant after the invocation has been executed, although it could also recycle servants.

```
class MyLocator : public virtual PortableServer::ServantLocator
{
public:
  virtual PortableServer::Servant preinvoke (
      const PortableServer::ObjectId & oid,
      PortableServer::POA_ptr poa,
      const char * operation,
      void * & cookie)
    throw (CORBA::SystemException,
           PortableServer::ForwardRequest)
  {
    PortableServer::Servant servant = 0;
    servant = new Foo_Impl;
    return servant;
  }

  virtual void postinvoke (
      const PortableServer::ObjectId & oid,
      PortableServer::POA_ptr poa,
      const char * operation,
      void * cookie,
      PortableServer::Servant servant)
    throw (CORBA::SystemException)
  {
    delete servant;
  }
};
```

To be able to register the servant locator with the POA, the POA has to configured as follows:

```
CORBA::PolicyList policies;
policies.length (3);
policies[0] =
  poa->create_request_processing_policy(
                         PortableServer::USE_SERVANT_MANAGER);
policies[1] =
  poa->create_servant_retention_policy (
                                 PortableServer::NON_RETAIN);
policies[2] =
  poa->create_id_assignment_policy (PortableServer::USER_ID);
PortableServer::POA_var servant_manager_poa =
  poa->create_POA("servant locator", poa_manager, policies);
policies[0]->destroy ();
policies[1]->destroy ();
policies[2]->destroy ();
```

Note that we use the NON_RETAIN policy, which tells the POA not to maintain an active object map for the mapping between OBJECT ID and servant: this differentiates the servant locator from the servant activator, as the servant locator has to keep track of the OBJECT ID-to-servant mapping itself. The servant locator registration and object reference creation is similar to that for the servant activator.

One way to apply servant managers is to perform POOLING, meaning the servant manager manages a pool of servants. A servant locator looks up a servant from the pool in `preinvoke` and hands it to the POA.

On postinvoke it returns the servant into the pool, avoiding the repetitious creation and destruction of servants.

```
class ObjectPoolLocator :
  public virtual PortableServer::ServantLocator
{
public:
  virtual PortableServer::Servant preinvoke (
      const PortableServer::ObjectId & oid,
      PortableServer::POA_ptr poa,
      const char * operation,
      void * & cookie)
    throw (CORBA::SystemException,
           PortableServer::ForwardRequest)
  {
    PortableServer::Servant servant = 0;
    servant = list.get ();
    if (!servant) {
      throw CORBA::TRANSIENT (CORBA::OMGVMCID,
                              CORBA::COMPLETED_NO);
    // throw an transient system exception if no servant
    // is availble
    return servant;
  }

  virtual void postinvoke (
      const PortableServer::ObjectId & oid,
      PortableServer::POA_ptr poa,
      const char * operation,
      void * cookie,
      PortableServer::Servant servant)
    throw (CORBA::SystemException)
  {
    list.put (servant);
  }

  List<PortableServer::Servant> list;
};
```

The way CORBA is designed prevents it from being directly possible for servers to identify clients: remote objects, the POA and the servant locator, have no way to identify the client performing the invocation. CLIENT-DEPENDENT INSTANCES have to be supported at the application layer, which means that CLIENT-DEPENDENT INSTANCES are not supported transparently by CORBA. Of course, INVOCATION INTERCEPTORS implemented as part of the application layer could integrate this functionality transparently, while the rest of the application layer could remain oblivious to it.

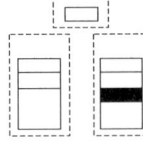
Location forwarding

Location forwarding is another interesting use case of servant managers. Location forwarding means that a server receiving a request for a remote object can forward the request to another remote object, possibly located on another server. The client-side ORB is informed about forwarding, and it is responsible for resending the original request to the new remote object. Resending is transparent to the client. Location forwarding can be triggered by applications, but also internally inside the ORB.

To trigger a location forward, applications need to throw a Forward-Request exception configured with the object reference of the remote object to which to forward requests. Servant managers (servant locators and servant activators) can be used for this task via their preinvoke and incarnate operations respectively. In that role, servant managers implement LOCATION FORWARDER. For example, a servant locator could implement the preinvoke operation as follows:

```
virtual PortableServer::Servant preinvoke (
    const PortableServer::ObjectId & oid,
    PortableServer::POA_ptr poa,
    const char * operation,
    void * & cookie)
  throw (CORBA::SystemException, PortableServer::ForwardRequest)
{
  // get the object reference of the remote object to forward to
  CORBA::Object_var my_forwarding_target = //...

  // forward the requests to forwarding target
  throw PortableServer::ForwardRequest (
    CORBA::Object::_duplicate (forwarding_target.in ()));

  return 0;
}
```

Servant managers are not the only means by which requests can be forwarded at the application level, as this can also be done by the client and server request interceptors mentioned above. If you look for PortableInterceptor::ForwardRequest exceptions in the throw definitions of the operation signatures, you can quickly identify which operations of the interceptors can be used to implement a LOCATION FORWARDER. Inside the ORB, the ForwardRequest exception is translated into a LOCATION_FORWARD status in the reply to the client.

To implement LOCATION FORWARDER at the ORB level, the ORB has to decide when to return a location forward reply. This is particularly appealing in the case of scalability: the ORB could balance load between several remote objects by forwarding requests to remote objects on other servers.

One disadvantage of using the LOCATION_FORWARD status is that the transmission of the request parameters is lost when the request is forwarded. In this case, the client has to re-transmit the complete request to the new remote object. Client-side ORBs can avoid this by sending a *LocateRequest* before the actual request. The request will be answered with a *LocateReply*, one of:

- The object does not exist.
- The object exists and is accessible.
- The object is somewhere else, and here is the object reference to it.

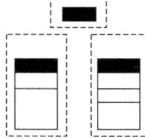

Initial access to remote objects

Initial access to remote objects can be gained in several ways. When the desired remote object X is known to any other remote object Y, Y can pass X's reference to the client. If no other remote object can be queried, the stringified ABSOLUTE OBJECT REFERENCE, the IOR, needs to be passed to the client by some means. When exchanged manually, this is usually done via a file, but it can also be exchanged by e-mail, or by cut and paste by application users using a remote shell. This is a typical problem for the application of LOOKUP.

In CORBA LOOKUP is implemented by the CORBA Naming Service. The Naming Service is a special remote object whose only purpose is the mediation of ABSOLUTE OBJECT REFERENCES. Server applications register object references of remote objects at the Naming Service with a unique name. These names can be hierarchically organized in *name contexts*. The object reference to the Naming Service itself is made available to clients via pre-configured IORs or a multicast-based protocol.

CORBA basics

Before a client or server can use the Naming Service, it needs to obtain a reference to its *initial name context*. The initial naming context can be obtained from the ORB via the `resolve_initial_reference` operation on the `CORBA::ORB` interface. To get the initial naming context object reference, the operation must be used with the argument `NameService`. The returned object reference must be narrowed to `CosNaming::NamingContext` before it can be used.

```
CORBA::Object_var object =
  orb->resolve_initial_reference ("NameService");
CosNaming::NamingContext_var naming_context =
  CosNaming::NamingContext::_narrow (object.in());
```

The ORB offers the start-up option `'-ORBInitRef'` which can be used to specify the initial object reference for a service. This initial object reference is returned when the `resolve_initial_reference` operation is called on the ORB. For the Naming Service an entry like `'-ORBInitRef NameService=IOR:0d3e42...'` configures the ORB so that `resolve_initial_reference` returns the proper object reference to the Naming Service. Alternatively, some ORB vendors implement a multicast-based protocol that allows a call to `resolve_initial_reference` to find a Naming Service instance. The multicast-based lookup is often prone to errors, and is therefore the last choice for today's designs of distributed applications.

The object references of remote objects can be bound to a naming context. As naming contexts can be nested, the naming context interface contains two operations to create bindings: one for regular objects (the `bind` operation) and one for contexts (the `bind_context` operation).

A regular remote object can be bound to a naming context in the following way:

```
CosNaming::Name name;
name.length (1);
name[0].id = CORBA::string_dup ("Foo");
naming_context->bind (name, foo);
```

If a binding already exists under that name, an exception is thrown. To override an existing binding, the `rebind` operation can be used instead of the `bind` operation.

A client has to use the `resolve` operation on a naming context of the Naming Service to look up an object reference. Because the returned object reference is of the general type `CORBA::Object`, the client has to narrow the reference to its correct type.

```
CosNaming::Name name;
name.length (1);
name[0].id = CORBA::string_dup ("Foo");
CORBA::Object_var obj = naming_context->resolve (name);
foo = Foo::_narrow (obj);
foo->bar (...); // actual invocation
```

Messaging in CORBA

For a long time CORBA only supported synchronous communication between client and server. By defining operations as *oneway* in the IDL, this was somewhat relaxed, but oneway operations are not guaranteed to be asynchronous, and they were not defined to be reliable operations. As a result, application programmers could never decide whether to use them or not. When they did, it sometimes led to unexpected results, such as situations in which the sending of requests blocked because TCP flow control kicked in, or in which users expected oneways to be received at the server in the same order the client sent them, but ORB implementations discarded or reordered messages – which is actually permitted by the specification.

The Event and Notification CORBA Common Object Services also provide asynchronous behavior, but only at high cost. The event and notification services are represented as remote objects that are accessed synchronously via two-way operations, and act as a relatively heavyweight *Mediator* [GHJV95]. They are mainly applicable to scenarios in which producers and consumers need to be decoupled. When filtering of events is important, the notification service offers a valuable solution out of the box.

The Messaging specification as part of CORBA 2.4 changed things. *Asynchronous Method Invocations* (AMI) were introduced in two variants: the *callback* and the *polling* model. The following three sections on client-side asynchrony, oneway invocations, and timeouts present the core features of that specification.

Client-side asynchrony

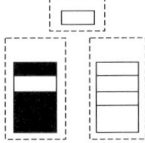

In practice the callback model, which implements RESULT CALLBACK, turned out to be more practical than the polling model, which implements POLL OBJECT. For this reason only the callback model is implemented by most ORB vendors. The callback model relies on *reply handlers*, which are implemented by the client and registered with the client-side ORB. The reply handlers receive replies to asynchronously invoked requests. It is important to note that AMI is a pure client-side functionality, the server-side ORB does not notice the difference between asynchronous and synchronous invocations.

To explain how AMI works, we define a new example:

```
exception MyException { string reason; };
interface Foo
{
  long bar (in long in_1,
            inout long inout_1,
            out long out_1)
    raises (MyException);
};
```

To send invocations asynchronously, a new operation is introduced for every original operation. This additional operations always has the prefix `sendc_`, followed by the name of the original operation.

The `sendc_` operations and the reply handler interface do not have to be specified in IDL, as the IDL compiler can be instructed to generate them. For this, the IDL compiler typically creates intermediate code internally, adding a `sendc_` operation to every interface and adding a corresponding reply handler interface. For the example above, the following additional IDL definitions are generated internally in the IDL compiler:

```
interface Foo
{
  // ..
  void sendc_bar (out long out_1, in long inout_1);
};

valuetype AMI_HelloWorldExceptionHolder
  : Messaging::ExceptionHolder
{
  void raise_foo ()
    raises (MyException);
};

interface AMI_HelloWorldHandler : Messaging::ReplyHandler
{
  void foo (in long result,
            in long inout_1,
            in long out_1);
  void foo_excep (in AMI_HelloWorldExceptionHolder excep_holder);
};
```

All the application programmer sees from this are the extended stubs of the original interfaces and the skeletons for the reply handlers.

The client has to implement the reply handler interface and register the implementation with its POA. Note that the reply handler servant forces the client be a server as well – a server for the replies of the Foo servant. For some applications this can increase the memory footprint and execution overhead significantly. as there is an additional thread running ORB::run.

```
class Foo_Handler_Impl : public POA_AMI_FooHandler
{
public:
  void bar (CORBA::Long result,
            CORBA::Long inout_1,
            CORBA::Long out_1)
    throw (CORBA::SystemException)
  { cout << "bar result arrived" << endl; }

  void bar_excep (AMI_FooExceptionHolder * excep_holder)
    throw (CORBA::SystemException)
  {}
};
```

The client uses the sendc_ operation to invoke an operation asynchronously on the server. For an asynchronous invocation the client only

Messaging in CORBA

has to supply the `in` and `inout` arguments, as no variables need be provided for `out` arguments or results. The object reference to the reply handler has to be passed as the first argument.

```
foo->sendc_bar (reply_handler, in_number, inout_number);
```

When the server sends the reply back to the client-side ORB, the ORB dispatches the reply as a request to the reply handler, invoking the `bar` operation on it with `inout`, `out` arguments and the return value. If the reply contains an exception, it will invoke the `foo_excep` operation.

The following figure shows how requests from the client are sent to the server-side ORB via the message handler. The ORB memorizes the request ID used and associates the reply handler with it. As soon as the asynchronous reply arrives at the message handler, the ORB dispatches it to the responsible reply handler via its POA.

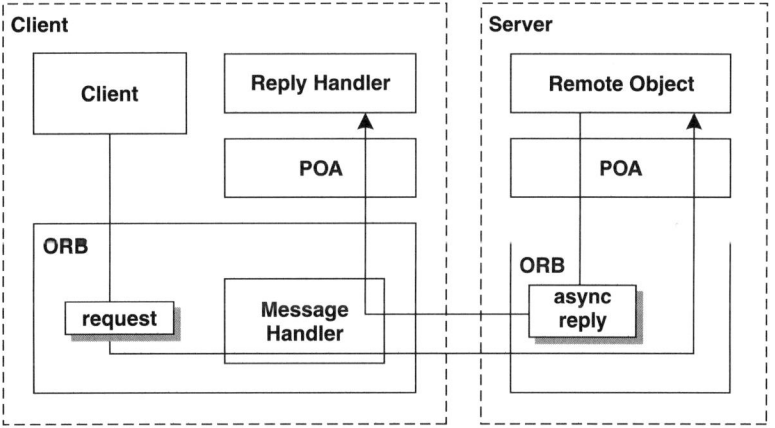

Oneway invocations

Before CORBA version 2.4, oneways were unreliable. This has changed with the appearance of the Messaging specification: CORBA now defines 'reliable oneways'.

To set the reliability of a oneway operation, the client must set a policy. The policies from which the client can choose are:

- SYNC_NONE. The client is guaranteed not to block, and the ORB returns control before it passes the request message to the transport protocol. This policy implements FIRE AND FORGET.
- SYNC_WITH_TRANSPORT. The ORB returns control to the client only after the transport protocol has accepted the request message. This policy results in a slightly more reliable invocation style than FIRE AND FORGET.
- SYNC_WITH_SERVER. The ORB returns control to the client only after the server-side ORB has accepted the request message. For this, the server-side ORB sends a reply before invoking the remote object. This policy implements SYNC WITH SERVER.
- SYNC_WITH_TARGET. The ORB returns control to the client only after the remote object has been invoked. This policy is equivalent to a synchronous invocation with no inout, out arguments or return value.

The policy can be set in various ways: at the ORB level, the PolicyCurrent (thread) level, or at the proxy level. In the following code extract the policy is set at the PolicyCurrent level – that is, at the thread level:

```
CORBA::Object_var object =
  orb->resolve_initial_references ("PolicyCurrent");
CORBA::PolicyCurrent_var policy_current =
  CORBA::PolicyCurrent::_narrow (object.in ());
CORBA::Any scope_as_any;
scope_as_any <<= Messaging::SYNC_WITH_SERVER;
CORBA::PolicyList policies(1); policies.length (1);
policies[0] =
  orb->create_policy (Messaging::SYNC_SCOPE_POLICY_TYPE,
                      scope_as_any);
policy_current->set_policy_overrides (policies,
                                      CORBA::ADD_OVERRIDE);
```

Timeouts

Besides asynchronous method invocations and oneways, the Messaging specification also standardizes how timeouts are set. The same policy framework as before is used to set the round-trip timeout of operations. Timeouts can be applied to synchronous, as well as asynchronous, operations. When an operation exceeds the timeout set, a REMOTING ERROR, a CORBA::TIMEOUT exception, is raised by the client-side ORB, while the operation may or may not have been executed by the server. The following code shows how a timeout is set for the current thread:

```
// Put timeout in an Any.
TimeBase::TimeT timeOut = requestTimeOut;
CORBA::Any timeOutAny;
timeOutAny <<= 50000; // 5 ms = 50000*100ns

// Create policy object.
CORBA::PolicyList policies (1); policies.length (1);
// Create the policy.
policies[0] = orb->create_policy (
        Messaging::RELATIVE_RT_TIMEOUT_POLICY_TYPE,
        timeOutAny);

// Add the policy to the ORBs policies.
policy_current->set_policy_overrides (orbPolicies,
                                      CORBA::ADD_OVERRIDE);
```

Real-Time CORBA

In the distributed, real-time, and embedded (DRE) domain, the QoS of invocations on remote objects must often be controlled. As most connection management and dispatching behavior is transparent to CORBA applications, stringent predictability and performance requirements cannot be met by 'plain' CORBA, which lacks explicit control of QoS properties.

This has changed with the advent of the RT-CORBA specification. The main areas RT-CORBA addresses are:

- *Portable priorities*. These ensure that priorities, which are different on each operating system, are mapped properly between client and server.
- *End-to-end priority preservation*. This ensures that priorities are observed end-to-end between client and server inside the ORBs involved.
- *Explicit connection management*. This allows the server application to determine the time at which connections are established, and to define priority ranges for individual connections.

- *Thread pooling.* This standardizes the support and configuration of thread pools by ORBs.

Introducing new features to the existing and widely-used CORBA API is a problem. How can the ORB be extended with RT-CORBA features without changing the CORBA::ORB API? The solution is to use the *Extension Interface* pattern [SSRB00], which allows transitioning between interfaces of the same component. This allows components to be extended with additional interfaces while retaining existing interfaces: lookup of extended interfaces is done via a special operation.

The aforementioned resolve_initial_references on the CORBA::ORB interface is used to obtain a reference to the RTCORBA::RTORB extension, implementing the *Extension Interface*. Thus, non-real-time ORBs and applications are not affected by RT-CORBA extensions.

```
CORBA::ORB_var orb = CORBA::ORB_init (argc, argv);
CORBA::Object_var obj =
  orb->resolve_initial_references ("RTORB");
RTCORBA::RTORB_var rtorb = RTCORBA::RTORB::_narrow (obj);
```

End-to-end priority preservation

In order to enable end-to-end preservation of QoS, priorities need to be mapped between various operating systems, as every operating system defines its own range of priorities. For example, when invocations of a client running on VxWorks in a thread with a certain priority are invoked on a server running LynxOS, the priority of the dispatching and executing thread should be aligned with that client priority.

The way in which priorities are handled end-to-end follows two different models.

A client-propagated model. The client thread's priority gets sent to the server using the INVOCATION CONTEXT, as illustrated in the figure below.

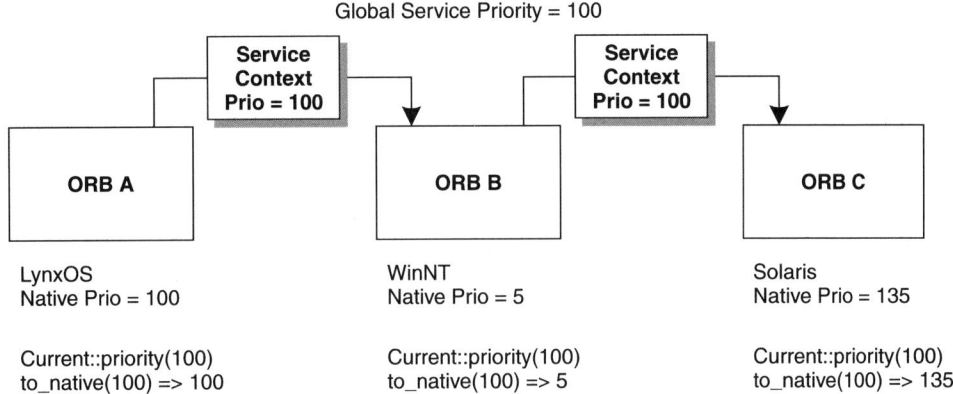

A server-declared model. The priority is set in the POA and sent to clients as part of the ABSOLUTE OBJECT REFERENCE. The following figure illustrates this.

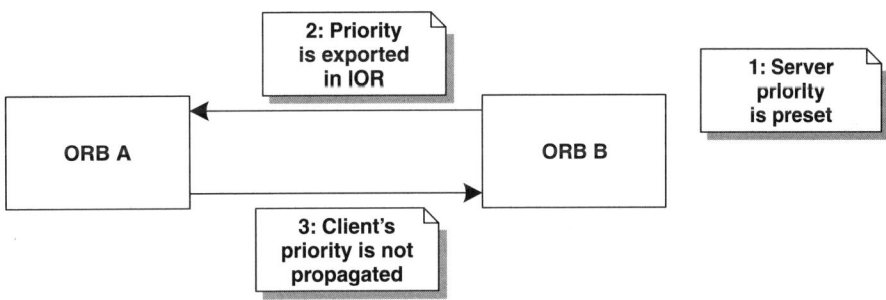

In the following code example we register a CORBA object with the POA for the client-propagated model. Operations are invoked with the

client's current priority. This means that different operations on the same remote object can subsequently be invoked at different priorities.

```
CORBA::PolicyList policies (1); policies.length (1);
policies[0] = rtorb->create_priority_model_policy (
        RTCORBA::CLIENT_PROPAGATED,
        DEFAULT_PRIORITY /* For non-RT ORBs */);

PortableServer::POA_var my_poa =
root_poa->create_POA ("My_POA",
                      PortableServer::POAManager::_nil (),
                      policies);

// Activate a servant
my_poa->activate_object (my_servant);
```

Note that the CLIENT_PROPAGATED policy is set on the server and exported to the client as part of the ABSOLUTE OBJECT REFERENCE.

Knowing how to configure for end-to-end priorities, we also need to know how to change CORBA priorities at the client. How can RT-CORBA client applications change the priority of operations? The solution is to use the RTCurrent LOCAL OBJECT to change the priority of the current thread explicitly, which is accessed in a similar way to the Current LOCAL OBJECT mentioned on page 301 and page 322. As the Current LOCAL OBJECT represents the current thread logically in regular CORBA, the RTCurrent LOCAL OBJECT represents the current thread logically in RT-CORBA. An RTCurrent can also be used to query the priority. The values are expressed in the CORBA priority range and the behavior of RTCurrent is thread-specific.

```
CORBA::Object_var obj =
  orb->resolve_initial_references ("RTCurrent");
RTCORBA::RTCurrent_var rt_current =
  RTCORBA::RTCurrent::_narrow (obj);
rt_current->the_priority (10/*VERY_HIGH_PRIORITY*/);

// Invoke the request at <VERY_HIGH_PRIORITY> priority
foo->bar ();
```

The implementation of client-propagated policies uses the underlying prioritized connection management system of the client-side ORB, which is described below. It also transfers the client's thread priority, via the INVOCATION CONTEXT, to the server-side ORB, so that it can set the correct priority of the server thread.

Real-Time CORBA

When operations must always be invoked on the remote object at the same priority, the server-declared priority model is recommended. Priorities are set at the POA level and published to clients via the ABSOLUTE OBJECT REFERENCE. The client-side ORB will already ensure that the marshaling, sending, and selection of the connection happen at the correct priority.

```
CORBA::PolicyList policies (1); policies.length (1);
policies[0] = rtorb->create_priority_model_policy (
       RTCORBA::SERVER_DECLARED, LOW_PRIORITY);
PortableServer::POA_var base_station_poa =
  root_poa->create_POA ("My_POA",
                        PortableServer::POAManager::_nil (),
                        policies);
my_poa->activate_object (my_servant);
```

Server-declared objects inherit the priority of their RT-POA by default. However, it is possible to override this priority on a per-object basis.

The priority of the client thread, when invoking an operation of a remote object that has an associated server-declared policy, is set to the correct priority in the CLIENT PROXY. Marshaling and sending therefore happen at the expected priority.

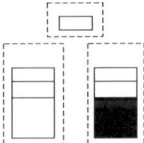

Thread pools

Embedded systems are often highly concurrent. For example, many sensors and actuators in such systems are driven by individual threads. As they often depend on each other in a client-server relationship, many clients can invoke requests on the same remote object. POOLING is used to cope with such situations, in which multiple clients invoke the same server applications. Thread pools, as an implementation of POOLING, have existed for a long time in CORBA, but the API to use them was not standardized. This has changed with RT-CORBA.

It is now possible to configure thread pools using a standardized API. Instances of thread pools are registered with the POA and are therefore available to all remote objects registered with it. Thread pools are not only groupings of threads, but also have priorities associated with them. Using a concept called *lanes*, threads can be grouped by priority inside a thread pool. This ensures that enough threads of a specific priority are available. The API of the RT-ORB used to create thread pools is shown below.

```
interface RTCORBA::RTORB {
  typedef unsigned long ThreadpoolId;
  ThreadpoolId create_threadpool (
        in unsigned long stacksize,
        in unsigned long static_threads,
        in unsigned long dynamic_threads,
        in Priority default_priority,
        in boolean allow_request_buffering,
        in unsigned long max_buffered_requests,
        in unsigned long max_request_buffer_size);

  void destroy_threadpool (in ThreadpoolId threadpool)
    raises (InvalidThreadpool);
};
```

The RT-CORBA specification also provided the API to support request buffering, a topic that has existed as long as CORBA itself has done, but which has never really been settled. It seems like a good idea to have buffers, to prevent lost requests and increase availability to clients: ideally no requests would be discarded. But when you consider the problems caused by temporary unavailability of server resources, it is fruitless to introduce buffering, as this only delays the problem and can never really solve it. If resources such as threads or CPU cycles are scarce, buffering only delays the denial of services and cannot avoid it. Request buffering also introduces significant overheads and timing jitter, by allocating memory on the heap that would otherwise be allocated from the stack. In summary, buffering is very seldom implemented in ORBs.

The management of threads within a thread pool is typically implemented using the *Leader/Followers* [SSRB00] pattern. This means that the threads manage amongst themselves which thread dispatches the next message to come, whether it is a request or a reply to a previously-sent request.

When a thread pool has lanes, every thread that implements SERVER REQUEST HANDLER functionality has its own *Reactor* [SSRB00] associated with it to avoid the risk of dispatching incoming requests and replies at the wrong priority, which could happen if the priority of the dispatching thread were set after the request was read from the socket.

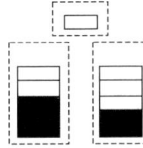

Explicit connection management

Proper connection management is crucial for predictable invocations. RT-CORBA allows for explicit connection management in three ways, which are represented as distinct policies:

- *Pre-allocating connections.* This avoids the initial delay on the first invocation.
- *Priority-banded connections.* This allocates connections to specific priority ranges.
- *Private connections.* This reserves private connections between a client and a remote object.

Note that the policies can be applied in combination. For example, you can pre-allocate all priority-banded connections to a specific object.

In the following we go into detail for each of the three policies. Pre-allocated network connections are the solution to the problem of *Lazy Acquisition* [KJ04] of connections, as it is typically done by ORB implementations, resulting in unacceptable jitter, which is detrimental to time-critical applications. Pre-allocated connections follow the *Eager Acquisition* [KJ04] pattern. The time at which the connection is acquired eagerly can be determined by the call to Object::_validate_connection, which is defined in the CORBA Messaging specification. This will cause the client-side ORB to establish a new connection internally and tell the server which priority the connection should have.

```
Foo_var foo=  ...; // Obtain reference to the remote object
CORBA::PolicyList_var policies;
CORBA::Boolean successful =
  foo->_validate_connection (policies);
```

Priority-banded connections are useful in situations in which requests of various priorities are invoked on the same server application. As a high-priority request might be delayed by a previous low-priority request, priority inversions can occur: high-priority tasks are delayed in favor of low-priority tasks, an inversion of priorities. Using different connections for different priority ranges, set up via the RT CORBA PriorityBandedConnectionPolicy, decouples invocations of different priorities.

Priority-banded connections allow the sharing of connections between a client-side and a server-side ORB for a range of priorities and multiple remote objects. The priority bands are defined at the ORB level. The following code fragment shows how two priority bands are set for requests to a remote object. As you can see, when policies are set on a CLIENT PROXY, a new CLIENT PROXY is returned:

```
RTCORBA::PriorityBands bands;
bands.length (2);
bands[0].low = 10000;
bands[0].high = 10005;
bands[1].low = 26000;
bands[1].high = 30000;
CORBA::PolicyList policies; policies.length (1);
policies[0] =
  rt_orb->create_priority_banded_connection_policy (bands);
Foo_var new_foo =
  foo->_set_policy_overrides (policies,
                              CORBA::SET_OVERRIDE);
```

When requests to a remote object are so important that they should never be queued behind any request to other remote objects in the same server application, *private connections* offer a way to guarantee non-multiplexed connections between a client and a remote object. Private connections are set via the RT-CORBA `PrivateConnectionPolicy` policy. The code to set the policy is quite simple. This time we set the policy at the thread level:

```
CORBA::PolicyList policy_list; policy_list.length (1);
policy_list[0] = rt_orb->create_private_connection_policy ();
policy_current->set_policy_overrides (policy_list,
        CORBA::SET_OVERRIDE);
```

Protocol Plug-ins

Besides the explicit management of connections, many applications in the DRE domain need to configure protocol properties. The protocol properties influence the sizes of the send and receive buffer as well as specific protocol attributes. The RT-CORBA specification incorporates this as follows:

```
RTCORBA::ProtocolProperties_var tcp_properties =
  rtorb->create_tcp_protocol_properties (
      64 * 1024, /* send buffer */
      64 * 1024, /* recv buffer */
      false, /* keep alive */
      true, /* dont_route */
      true /* no_delay */);
```

Next, we configure the list of protocols to use.

```
//First, we create the protocol properties
RTCORBA::ProtocolList plist; plist.length (1);
plist[0].protocol_type = IOP::TAG_INTERNET_IOP; // IIOP
plist[0].trans_protocol_props = tcp_properties;

RTCORBA::ClientProtocolPolicy_ptr policy =
  rtorb->create_client_protocol_policy (plist);
```

Unfortunately the configuration of protocol properties is only defined for TCP. This is mostly due to the lack of standardized PROTOCOL PLUG-INS to allow the exchange of the protocol layer underneath the GIOP (General-Inter-ORB-Protocol). The GIOP defines the messages between a client and server and how they are marshaled. Besides the widely-used TCP PROTOCOL PLUG-IN (IIOP – Internet-Inter-ORB-Protocol), other plug-ins supporting UDP or ATM are feasible. The Extensible Transport Framework specification, adopted in January 2004, addresses this. As soon as standardized PROTOCOL PLUG-INS are available, the standardization of protocol properties for such plug-ins becomes possible.

Neither CORBA nor RT-CORBA make use of any reflection techniques to track QoS properties. This is left to the application layers above CORBA. Frameworks such as Quality Objects [Bbn02] implement QOS OBSERVER functionality: in Quality Objects the QOS OBSERVER is called QoS Tracker.

13 Related Concepts, Technologies, and Patterns

The patterns in this book do not stand alone. There are several related technologies, concepts, and domains concerned with building distributed object middleware. Many of the best practices in these areas have already been captured in the form of patterns and pattern languages. While the detailed explanation of these is beyond the scope of this book, this chapter gives a brief overview of some of the important areas. We reference existing pattern material wherever possible.

The figure on the next page shows the relationships of the Remoting Patterns to patterns from other domains, and acts as a guide to this chapter. Many of the related fields are already well captured by other pattern languages, so the Remoting Patterns act as 'glue' to fill missing links between these patterns and pattern languages when applied to distributed object middleware or distributed application development. Specifically, the patterns for the internals of communication middleware, such as network communication, concurrency, and resource management, are fairly complete. Many patterns for orthogonal extensions, such as messaging, fault tolerance, scalability, and session management are currently documented by other authors. However, some domains, such as security or transactions in distributed systems, are not yet as well captured by patterns, though a security patterns book is in preparation, but was not available at the time of writing. Similarly, there is still work to be done regarding pattern languages for systems built on top of distributed object middleware. For example, so far only a few patterns are available for P2P systems, Grid computing, or aspect-oriented programming (AOP). It is quite natural for mature patterns to be missing in the latter cases, because patterns describe established knowledge, and fields like P2P, Grid, or AOP are still emergent. We expect patterns for these fields to appear in the future.

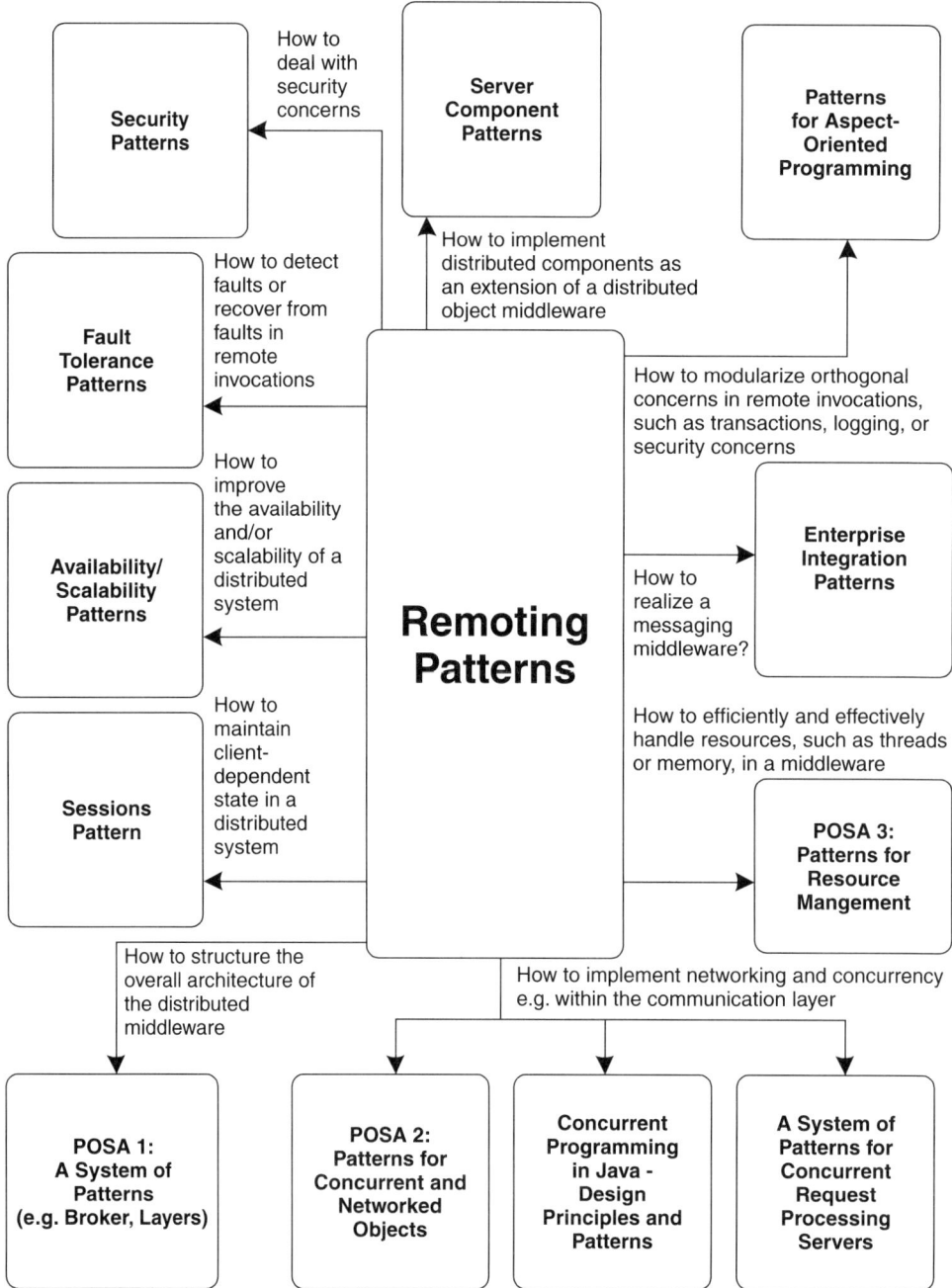

Related patterns

In this section we provide a brief overview of patterns and pattern languages that are directly related to patterns in this book.

Patterns for networking and concurrency

Distributed object middleware follows two architectural patterns documented in POSA1 [BMR+96]: *Broker*, in terms of mediating object invocations between communication participants, and *Layers*, regarding the separation of responsibilities such as connection handling, marshaling, decomposition, and dispatching of invocations. Distributed object middleware operates on top of network protocols, such as TCP/IP. It does not reinvent the wheel for this, but handles network connections and the inherent concurrency of networked communication using existing implementations and concepts. A number of patterns for networking and concurrency are documented in the following literature:

- POSA2 [SSRB00] contains many patterns that are used to implement distributed systems. The book describes many patterns that are relevant when applying the patterns in this pattern language. For example to implement CLIENT REQUEST HANDLERS and SERVER REQUEST HANDLERS, the following patterns should be considered: *Reactor, Half-sync/Half-async, Leader/Followers, Monitor Object*, and *Active Object*.

- Doug Lea's book *Concurrent Programming in Java – Design Principles and Patterns* [Lea99] describes several concurrency patterns with a special focus on Java. *Guarded Suspension* serializes access to shared objects whose methods can only be executed when certain conditions hold true: the pattern can be used to serialize access to remote objects and other resources that are concurrently accessed. The *Future* pattern provides a generalized form of POLL OBJECT: it provides a *Proxy* that can be used to query for results that are computed asynchronously.

- The patterns in the paper *A System of Patterns for Concurrent Request Processing Servers* [GT03] documents several patterns for concurrent request handling in high-performance servers. *Forking Server* the typical structure of a SERVER REQUEST HANDLER in which one listener process/thread listens to the network port and forks a worker process/thread for each incoming request. The worker thread may be obtained from a *Worker Pool*. *Job Queue* applies queueing between listener and worker threads.

Patterns for resource management

POSA3 [KJ04] deals with patterns for resource management and optimization. It documents a pattern language that describes how to acquire, access, and release resources efficiently and effectively at different layers of abstraction. That is, the book looks at the management of any kind of resource, ranging from typical operating system resources, such as threads or connections, to remote objects or application services.

Acquisition patterns, such as *Lazy Acquisition*, *Eager Acquisition*, and *Partial Acquisition*, document best practices and strategies for resource acquisition. They address non-functional properties, such as scalability, availability, and predictability. The patterns are used in distributed object middleware in several places: *Lazy Acquisition* for remote object instances, *Eager Acquisition* for memory connection and thread resources, *Partial Acquisition* for byte streams of large invocations.

Lookup documents how a system can be made flexible by decoupling its elements from each other. It is used to announce and find instances of remote objects.

Patterns for managing the lifecycle of resources, such as *Caching*, *Pooling*, and *Resource Lifecycle Manager*, elaborate methods for increasing system performance while saving the developer from tedious resource management activities. *Caching* is typically used in distributed object middleware, when connections to servers are kept available to avoid re-acquisition overhead. *Pooling* is used for managing remote object instances, but it is also applied at lower levels, for example for thread and connection management inside CLIENT and SERVER REQUEST HANDLERS.

The *Coordinator* pattern explains how to ensure consistency among any kind of resource. It is used only in advanced implementations of distributed object middleware, for example when transactions have to be supported as an additional service.

The resource release patterns, *Leasing* and *Evictor*, illustrate how resources can be released without manual intervention from a resource user. *Leasing* is regularly applied to manage resource release of remote objects by clients, whereas *Evictor* is typically used for thread and connection resources inside CLIENT and SERVER REQUEST HANDLERS.

In the LOOKUP, LAZY ACQUISITION, POOLING, and LEASING patterns described in this book, we focus on the application of resource management to remote objects, even though the patterns are not limited to these issues, as discussed above.

Sessions

Sessions deal with a common problem in the context of distributed object middleware: client-dependent state must be maintained in the distributed object middleware between individual accesses of the same client. While sessions can exist at any protocol level, they are mostly independent of lower-level communication tasks, for example when multiple client objects share the same physical network connection.

The *Sessions* pattern [Sor02] provides a solution to this problem: state is maintained in sessions, which are themselves maintained between individual client requests, so that new requests can access previously-accumulated data. A session identifier allows clients and remote objects to refer to a session.

Generally, sessions can be maintained in the server or in the client. If the session is maintained in the server, the session identifier is sent with each reply to the client, and the client refers to it in the next invocation. If it is maintained in the client, the client has to send it to the server, which refers to it in its replies. In distributed object middleware, however, sessions are typically maintained in the server. Clients and remote objects use the same session identifier in requests and replies as part of the INVOCATION CONTEXT.

On the server, sessions can be implemented either at an application level, in the form of CLIENT-DEPENDENT INSTANCES, or as part of the distributed object middleware, in the form of actual session objects.

Such session objects must be accessible through the INVOCATION CONTEXT, which is maintained by the INVOKER, transparently to the remote object. The interactions section of Chapter 6, *Extension Patterns* shows an example of its use.

The lifecycle of session objects and CLIENT-DEPENDENT INSTANCES must be managed by LEASING to dispose of sessions that are no longer needed, because the respective client has terminated.

Distribution infrastructures

There are many distribution infrastructures that are implemented on top of distributed object middleware. This section looks at prominent examples, such as transaction processing monitors, component infrastructures, peer-to-peer computing, grid computing, code mobility, and messaging.

Transaction processing monitors

Transaction processing monitors (TP monitors) are one of the oldest kinds of middleware. They provide the infrastructure to develop, run, and manage distributed transaction applications efficiently and reliably. For many decades, TP monitors were the dominant form of middleware, and many other middleware products available today have some link to a TP monitor product. One of the earliest TP monitors was IBM's Customer Information Control System (CICS) [Ibm04b], developed in the late 1960s and still in use today.

The main purpose of TP monitors is to extend a distributed application with the concept of *transactions*. Transactions were developed in the context of databases, and describe a series of operations that have so-called ACID properties. ACID is an abbreviation that stands for a number of desirable properties of a transaction:

- *Atomicity*. A transaction is treated as an indivisible unit, and is entirely either completed (committed) or undone (rolled back).
- *Consistency*. When the transaction terminates, the system must be in a consistent state.
- *Isolation*. A transaction's behavior must not be affected by other transactions.
- *Durability*. Changes are permanent after a transaction successfully terminates, and these changes must survive system failures (also referred to as *persistence*).

A distributed transaction involves more than one transactional resource, such as a database, and is usually located on more than one machine. Conventional RPC does not support the transactions, so RPC treats all invocations as if they are independent of each other. This makes it hard to recover from partial failure and enforce consistent, complete changes to distributed data. TP monitors, in contrast, allow developers to wrap a series of invocations as a transaction. They can thus guarantee either 'at most once', 'at least once', or 'exactly once' semantics for an invocation.

Transactional invocations are realized typically by marking the beginning and the end of a transaction in the client code. At the beginning of the transaction, the client contacts the TP monitor to acquire a transaction ID and context to be used throughout the transaction for the respective remote invocation. At the end of the transaction, the client notifies the TP monitor again, and the TP monitor then runs a commit protocol to determine the outcome of the transaction.

All transactional invocations must be marked as belonging to a specific transaction by using the transaction ID. This can be done by the INVOKER and REQUESTOR/CLIENT PROXY. A more elegant way is to use interceptors: INVOCATION INTERCEPTORS allow the transaction ID to be added on the client side and read it on the server side transparently. The transaction ID can be stored in an INVOCATION CONTEXT.

In a distributed transaction, a two-phase commit protocol (2PC [Gra78]) can be used for distributed transaction processing. Two-phase commit guarantees the ACID properties and supports distributed synchronization of multiple transactional resources. Finally, the client is informed whether or not the transaction was successfully committed.

TP monitors map the requests of numerous clients to server applications and/or backend resources. An important goal of commercial TP monitors is to improve the distributed system's performance. In addition, TP monitors include management features, such as process recovery by restarting, dynamic load balancing, and enforcing consistency of distributed data. Many TP monitors support a number of different communication interfaces to be used by clients and servers, such as RPC, conversational peer-to-peer communication, message queues, and publish/subscribe.

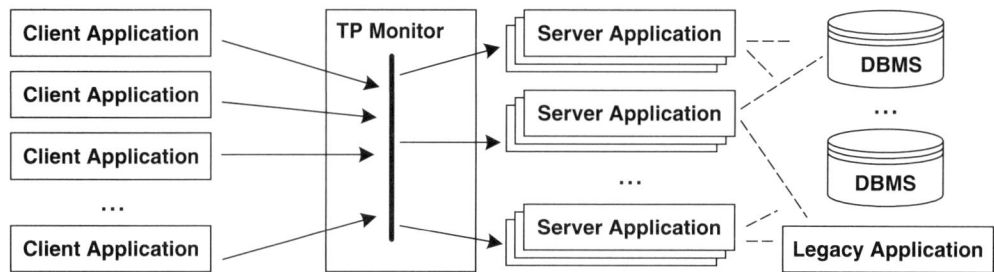

As shown in the figure above, the TP monitor breaks the direct connection between a potentially huge number of clients and application servers/back-end resources. It orchestrates the actions of all the participants and makes them act as part of a distributed transaction.

Early TP monitors were monolithic single-process systems. Today almost all TP monitor products support a 3-tier architecture. There are many commercial TP monitor products, including IBM's CICS [Ibm04b], BEA's Tuxedo [Bea04], Transarc's Encina [Tra00], and Microsoft's MTS [Mic04e]. There are also many standards in this area, such as the X/Open (Open Group) Distributed Transaction Processing (DTP) model [Ope03] or OMG's Object Transaction Service (OTS) [OMG04b].

Server components

Server-side component infrastructures [VSW02] provide a distributed execution environment for software components. The execution environment is called a component container, or *Container* for short. *Components* cannot be executed alone, they require the container to provide essential services to them. These services handle the technical issues of an application. Technical issues here are typically cross-cutting concern spanning several modules that are not related directly to the application functionality implemented within the components. What exactly constitutes such technical issues depends on the application domain. In an enterprise environment (where EJB [Sun04d], CCM [Sev04], or COM+ [Mic04d] are typically used), the technical issues are things like transaction management, resource access restrictions, fail-over, replication, and persistence.

In embedded systems, technical issues include scheduling, energy management, and diagnostics [Voe03].

The main benefit of a component-based approach is that the component developer does not need to implement technical issues over and over again. The developer only specifies the container services required by a component, by using declarative *Annotations*, and the container makes sure these services are available to the deployed components.

Many containers are implemented according to component standards, such as EJB [Sun04d], CCM [Sev04] or COM+ [Mic04d], by professional container vendors such as Microsoft, IBM, BEA, Oracle, or by open source projects such as JBoss. Application developers use the container as supplied, for non-trivial technical issues, and typically do not have to be experts on the (non-trivial) technical issues. The following paragraph lists essential building blocks for component infrastructures. For a more detailed explanation [VSW02]. For domain-specific and project specific component infrastructures, see [Voe03].

Component infrastructures are often built on top of distributed object middleware as an extension. Using INVOCATION INTERCEPTORS, INVOCATION CONTEXTS, as well as suitable LIFECYCLE MANAGERS, most of the functionality of component infrastructures can be built.

The advantage of using component infrastructures is that they already provide useful default implementations of important, recurring features. They also provide easy access and simple configuration for the developers of a specific domain through the use of *Annotations*.

If you want to build your own component infrastructure, starting with distributed object middleware as a basis is certainly a good idea. The current mainstream component infrastructures are built on top of distributed object middleware systems: EJB is based on Java RMI, CORBA Components are based on CORBA, and COM+ uses DCOM as a communications mechanism. Using distributed systems as a basis for component infrastructures is an example of reuse.

Peer-To-Peer computing

Peer-To-Peer (P2P) systems are different from other distributed systems, as they are not based on a client/server or *n*-tier model. Instead of using centralized servers to offer services, a set of equal peers communicate and coordinate themselves in fulfilling user services. Many P2P systems use remote objects internally for communication between peers.

The most popular P2P system is certainly the original Napster [Rox04]. This is a distributed music-sharing system that uses a centralized search index. There are several more or less direct clones, such as OpenNap [Ope01] or Gnutella [Gnu04], which are not all limited to sharing MP3 files. JXTA [Sun04e] provides a Java implementation of a P2P infrastructure. Jini [Jin04] and UPnP [Upn04] are architectures for spontaneous networking and can be used for building P2P networks.

In pure P2P networks, there is no central server. Each participating node can provide and consume services, and the overall state is distributed across the nodes. In other distributed object middleware, LOOKUP is implemented as a centrally-provided lookup service with a well-known ABSOLUTE OBJECT REFERENCE. In contrast, in a P2P network, the lookup service is itself provided by each node or by many nodes of the P2P network. Different techniques are applied to obtain an initial ABSOLUTE OBJECT REFERENCE to another node, or to a number of nodes already linked to the P2P network. Examples of this are broadcast messages and server lists that can be downloaded from dedicated servers. Once a link to the P2P network is established, the lookup service of any node can be queried for resources or services available by the network.

A service can be offered or withdrawn by a peer at any time. Clients have to discover whether, and where, a service is provided. A consequence of this is a need for client-side invocations. For example, Jini allows a remote object to publish its CLIENT PROXY in the lookup service. Clients can download CLIENT PROXIES from the lookup service. Thus a remote object can publish code that is later used from within clients to access the remote object. Another option for realizing flexible client access is to use just the REQUESTOR pattern, instead of using CLIENT PROXIES, because REQUESTORS allow invocations to be constructed dynamically.

In practice, the systems use hybrid approaches of centralized databases, search indexes, and 'work coordinators', acting as *Coordinator* [KJ04].

Grid computing

Grid computing [Gri04, FKT01] is about sharing and aggregation of distributed resources such as processing time, storage, and information. A Grid consists of multiple computers linked to one system. Grid computing makes extensive use of remote communication, as the distributed resources need to be managed [KJ04] and computing requests and results need to be transmitted. Distributed object middleware plays an important role here.

To find distributed resources, which are typically represented as remote objects, Grids use LOOKUP. Depending on the Grid, the role of the lookup service in the system is often referred to as 'resource broker', 'resource manager', or 'lookup service'.

The architectures of available Grid computing projects [BBL02] and toolkits vary, but some of the underlying concepts are the same in most of them. In fact, large parts of their architectures are very similar to those of ad hoc networks and P2P system – see the discussion above.

Code mobility and agents

As we discuss in several places in this book, remote invocations can exhibit a variety of limitations and drawbacks when compared to local invocations, for example in performance, configurability, and scalability. Developers cannot easily get around these problems, because they are often faced with applications that inherently need distribution. Consider a simple example: a client requests data from remote objects and evaluates this data locally. Even though the client logic might be quite simple, it cannot be placed on the server, because different clients need different information processing, and the server application developers cannot foresee all possible requirements. As a consequence, the client needs to fetch the data from the server and process it on the client side. The client therefore must send out a network request every time it needs to access data located on the server and the data needs to be sent across the network. This can become slow and consume much network bandwidth, especially if the data volume is large. Code mobility resolves such problems by providing the ability to move code between the nodes of a network. The client code can then migrate to the server, execute within the server context, and return with the result to the client. The custom client code thus executes at the same site at which the data is located, removing the need for costly data transfer.

The ability to relocate code is a powerful concept, but the field is still immature. Fuggetta, Picco, and Vigna provide a conceptual framework for understanding code mobility [FPV98]. They distinguish different code mobility paradigms:

- *Remote evaluation.* Code is sent to the server and executed in the server context using the data located at the server.
- *Code on demand.* Code is downloaded by a client and executed in the client context using data located at the client.
- *Mobile agents.* Code and associated data, and possibly also the execution state, migrates from host *A* to host *B* and executes in the context of host *B*.

These code mobility paradigms extend the client/server paradigm used in distributed object middleware concepts. Similarly to other high-level remoting paradigms, code mobility can be realized on top of almost any existing distributed object middleware. For example, in many existing mobile code systems distributed object middleware, such as CORBA or RMI, or their protocols, such as IIOP, are used actually to send the code across the network.

The ability of mobile code to change its location means that it is hard to locate the mobile code with a location-dependent ABSOLUTE OBJECT REFERENCE. LOOKUP and LOCATION FORWARDER therefore play a central role in mobile code scenarios, because some entity is needed to inform a client of the new location of mobile code.

An extension to the MARSHALLER is required for all code mobility approaches, because the mobile code must be transferred with the messages in a format appropriate for network transmission. In some approaches native machine-code is transferred. This has the disadvantage that the code can only execute on the platform for which it is compiled. As an alternative, byte-code such as compiled Java classes can be transferred, which can execute on any platform for which the byte-code's virtual machine (such as the Java Virtual Machine) is implemented. These variants – machine-code or byte-code – are often used in statically-compiled languages. In dynamic languages – those that allow for behavioral modifications at runtime – a *Serializer*

[RSB+97] and/or *Introspection Options* [Zdu03] are required to obtain the definition of the mobile code that is current at runtime. That is, the program code to be transmitted is serialized, then transferred to the remote host, where it is interpreted and/or compiled at runtime.

Scenarios in which only code can migrate are called *weak mobility* approaches [FPV98]. In contrast, *strong mobility* [FPV98] is used to describe the ability to migrate both the code and the execution state of an object. Strong mobility requires a MARSHALLER that is able to serialize the callstack state relevant to the code to be migrated, as well as the current state of the mobile code.

Mobile code approaches can exploit the security measures taken in most other distributed object middleware, such as encrypted connections and authentication, which they handle typically with PROTOCOL PLUG-INS or INVOCATION INTERCEPTORS. There are, however, further security requirements that cannot simply be handled by PROTOCOL PLUG-INS and INVOCATION INTERCEPTORS. If code can migrate between hosts, you must secure the host environment and other mobile code from malicious mobile code. A solution is to execute the mobile code in a restricted environment, such as a 'sandbox' interpreter, as in Safe Tcl [OLW98], or to use the security mechanisms of a virtual machine, such those of the Java Virtual Machine. A more complex problem – not solved well yet – is how to secure mobile code from attacks by a malicious host. A simple approach is to establish a net of trusted sites, for example by using with a third party that acts as a certification authority.

There are numerous implementations of weak code mobility without the transfer of data, such as Java applets or Jini Proxies (as explained in the P2P section above). In most scripting languages weak mobility with data transfer is frequently used, due to the *Introspection Options* [Zdu03] provided by those languages and the ability to evaluate code on the fly. Weak mobility with data transfer is also supported by a few mobile code frameworks, including Aglets [LO98], Grasshopper [BM98], and Voyager [Obj97]. Strong mobility is supported by D'Agents [GCK+02] and Ara [PS97], for example.

The *agent* concept, in which a computer program executes actions autonomously on behalf of a user, is often used with code mobility. However, not all agents are mobile agents – some agent concepts only support stationary agents. In all agent approaches there is the need for an agent to communicate with other agents. Many agents can therefore access other agents in the same server context, and, at the same time, are remote objects, which means that they can be reached by agents running in other hosts via RPC invocations. Many agent frameworks support PROTOCOL PLUG-INS for communicating with other agents, using existing distributed object middleware and protocols such as CORBA or RMI.

If agents need to exchange semantic information or multiple agent platforms need to inter-operate, the use of standardized RPC invocations might not be sufficient. In such cases, agent communication languages (ACL), such as FIPA ACL [Fip04] or KQML [Arp93], provide INTERFACE DESCRIPTIONS for sophisticated agent communication. ACLs stand a level above any INTERFACE DESCRIPTIONS provided by distributed object middleware such as CORBA or RMI. This is because they handle semantic rules and actions instead of merely remote object invocations, and also because ACL messages describe a desired state in a declarative language, rather than the invocations used to obtain the desired state.

Messaging

Message queues are the key concept for messaging systems, such as IBM's WebSphere MQ (formerly MQ Series) [Ibm04c], JMS [Sun04c], Microsoft's MSMQ [Mic04a], and Tibco [Tib04]. Patterns that describe how to implement such systems are documented in *Enterprise Integration Patterns* [HW03]. Messaging systems are related to distributed object middleware: messaging systems can be implemented by extending distributed object middleware, and distributed object middleware may use existing messaging systems inside PROTOCOL PLUG-INS. PROTOCOL PLUG-INS that integrate messaging systems are described briefly in the technology projections chapters, 9–12.

Messaging is inherently asynchronous. The messaging concepts of *Polling Consumer* [HW03] and *Event-Driven Consumer* [HW03] directly relate to POLL OBJECT and RESULT CALLBACK. In our pattern description, we have referred to the *Asynchronous Completion Token* pattern to correlate a reply with a request: in [HW03] it is named *Correlation Identifier*.

Messaging systems use the abstraction of a *Message Channel* [HW03] as their connection between a particular sender (client) and a particular receiver (server). When a client sends a message, it puts the message into a specific *Message Channel*, and the server application also receives messages from a specific *Message Channel*. To build a *Message Channel* on top of a distributed object middleware system, the REQUEST HANDLERS can be extended in one of the following ways:

- *Message Channels* can be implemented on top of the 'send' and 'receive' message queues that are part of all REQUEST HANDLERS.
- Each *Message Channel* might have its own message queue.
- Message queues are instantiated by the respective REQUEST HANDLERS for each connection between two network endpoints.

Client and server applications usually do not directly interact with the low-level details of message queues and *Message Channels*. Instead the the sender and receiver instantiate a *Message Endpoint* [HW03] that is used to connect to a *Message Channel*. The *Message Endpoint* abstraction handles all interaction with the messaging system. Client and remote object implementations only interact with the *Message Endpoint,* not with the low-level details of messaging.

Messaging extends distributed object middleware in a number of ways. Specifically, it provides for reliable message transport, order of messages, dealing with duplicated messages, expiration of messages, and different kinds of *Message Channels*. See *Enterprise Integration Patterns* [HW03] for more details on messaging systems and their related patterns.

Quality attributes

A number of measures are available for improving the quality attributes of distributed object middleware. In the following section we discuss security, availability and scalability, and fault tolerance as important examples to be considered in distributed object middleware.

Security

When clients access remote objects over a public network such as the Internet, they are vulnerable to security threats. The book *Distributed Systems* by Coulouris, Dollimore, and Kindberg [CDK94] details the following main security threats in the context of a distributed system:

- The *leakage* or disclosure of information to non-authorized parties.
- The unauthorized *modification* of information in a distributed system.

- The unauthorized *use of resources* of the distributed system.
- The *destruction* of information or parts of the distributed system.

Attacks are performed by attackers to exercise a threat. Typical attacks include *masquerading* to obtain the identity of legitimate users, *eavesdropping* to listen to request messages, *interception* and *modification* of request messages, or *replaying* of messages. A number of measures can be used to protect a distributed system against these and other attacks, ranging from organizational to technical measures (see [TS02, Emm00] for a longer discussion).

Technical security measures are pervasive, meaning that they can be applied at all layers of the distributed object middleware, from the REQUEST HANDLERS to the actual application layer.

A typical measure is encryption of request messages or message parts, which can be done using a PROTOCOL PLUG-IN based on a secure transport protocol such as SSL. Encryption, like most other security measures, can also be handled at higher-level layers of the distributed object middleware. Higher-level layers often provide and require the keys for encryption and decryption and other security information.

Authentication techniques are used to establish trust in remote invocations. This is done using so-called 'credentials', a number of security attributes that determine what a client (or server) is allowed to do. Important examples of credentials are user IDs and passwords. Authentication has to be implemented using encryption to avoid sending such credentials over the network as plain text. Encryption and decryption of messages is handled typically by the respective PROTOCOL PLUG-IN. Encryption and decryption of further security information, typically contained in the INVOCATION CONTEXT, can be done by an INVOCATION INTERCEPTOR.

Access control techniques decide whether or not access to a resource such as a remote object can be granted to a client. The parameters for the server-side access decision consist typically of the credentials, OBJECT ID, operation name, and parameters. The access control decision can be implemented in a specialized INVOCATION INTERCEPTOR or in the INVOKER. To make this possible, the credentials, or at least some kind of client authentication token, needs to be made available to the server-side distributed object middleware. An INVOCATION CONTEXT is typically used to transfer this. If access is not granted, a REMOTING ERROR containing the reason for the security error can be sent to the client to signal the fact.

Users responsible for a client (or remote object) can be made accountable for their actions through the use of digital signatures. If possible, digital signatures and other additional security information are placed in an extensible INVOCATION CONTEXT, to allow this information to be transmitted in a transparent fashion.

Security-relevant events should be logged to persistent storage so that security violations can be monitored and analyzed. Auditing policies determine which security information needs to be logged in a persistent storage. To perform this transparently in clients and servers, INVOCATION INTERCEPTORS are used.

Some technical security measures are handled outside the distributed object middleware. For example, firewalls allow tight control of message traffic between a private and a public network. If the invocations between client and server have to pass the firewalls, the firewall must decode and encode requests and replies in either direction. Virtual Private Networks (VPNs) can be used to provide a security channel on lower levels.

Note that technical measures for security are not enough: it is also necessary to take organizational measures, such as providing security policies and emergency response plans, and updating them regularly.

Improving availability and scalability

Availability and scalability can become problematic when the services of a distributed application are deployed only on one machine. If the machine fails, the whole distributed system will fail. Also, under increased load conditions, one machine alone might not be able to provide enough performance. To deal with such situations, Dyson and Longshaw introduce patterns for building highly-available and scalable distributed systems, especially Internet systems [DL04]. The targeted Internet systems cover a broad range, from a small personal Web site to multinational e-commerce sites.

The problem of availability can be resolved by introducing two or more *Functionally Identical Servers* that are configured as *Active Redundant Servers.* The two servers offer the same functionality, even though they might have different non-functional characteristics. One of the two servers is deployed as a redundant back-up that is only used in the event of failure of or the need to maintain the active server. A switch is used to redirect traffic to the redundant server, if required. Thus clients can still access the same ABSOLUTE OBJECT REFERENCES, even if the main machine serving them is down. The switch in this example uses the pattern LOCATION FORWARDER in its simple form, to forward invocations to one of the redundant servers.

Replication is simple for interaction with stateless remote objects. However, for stateful interactions (for example, *Sessions* [Sor02]), the ongoing interaction needs to be maintained. *Session Fail-over* introduces a persistent session information store that is available to both of the redundant servers. When the roles of the servers are switched, the redundant server starts using the session information that the previously-active server persisted, and continues the user interaction. The user does not notice any interruption in its interaction with the server.

Remote objects that read and write persistent state also require data consistency. *Data Replication* lets the active server write the dynamic data into an associated database, but when one server writes dynamic data, the transaction is not completed until the data is available on the other server as well. If one server is unavailable, the data will be written by the available server. When the previously-unavailable server restarts, it needs to first synchronize its state.

The measures mentioned so far primarily improve availability. How though can you balanced loads, even when some servers are unavailable? *Load Balanced Servers* are *Functionally Identical Servers* with a load balancer that forwards requests to the servers, instead of using a simple switch. The task of the load balancer can be implemented using the LOCATION FORWARDER pattern, but instead of mapping the ABSOLUTE OBJECT REFERENCE to only one server at a time, the load balancer distributes remote invocations to all machines at the same time. The load balancer ensures that performance remains reasonably consistent when a server fails or needs to be maintained.

Many systems use dedicated hardware for switches and load balancers that are proven, simple, fast, and easy to replace.

Fault tolerance

Fault tolerance techniques are applied to detect and recover from errors in a system, or to mask errors them. To apply fault tolerance techniques, it is important to understand the terminology, the underlying assumptions [Lap85, ALR01], and the kinds of faults tolerated by a specific technique. Saridakis presents basic fault tolerance techniques as a system of patterns [Sar02]. These are explained in this section.

Kopetz uses the following terminology [Kop97]:

- A *failure* is an event in which the actual function deviates from the specified function.
- An *error* is an unintended, incorrect state of a system with regard to its specified function.
- A *fault* is the cause of an error and therefore the indirect cause of a failure.

Many fault tolerant systems are inherently distributed systems, because the main means for fault tolerance is replication. A computation that should be made fault tolerant is mapped to a number of different units of failure. These units are usually located on different hardware, such as different machines or processors. In other words, fault tolerance techniques primarily tolerate hardware failures – not software bugs. There are however fault-tolerant techniques for tolerating software faults [Lyu95], such as recovery blocks or *n*-version programming.

Before a fault can be tolerated, it needs to be detected. There are a number of patterns for the detection of faults. Two important patterns are:

- The pattern *Fail-Stop Processor* replicates an input using a distributor and lets two or more processors perform the same computations. The distributor can be implemented as a simple kind of LOCATION FORWARDER that maps ABSOLUTE OBJECT REFERENCES to two or more replicated remote objects running on different machines. The results are then compared. If not the same, a fault has occurred in one of the processors (or during transmission of the message).
- Another way to detect faults is through the use of the *Acknowledgement* pattern. This is implemented by applying the pattern SYNC WITH SERVER additionally, which invokes a remote object asynchronously and only receives an *Acknowledgement*. Of course, a result is

also implicitly an *Acknowledgement* – thus synchronous invocations contain an acknowledgement implicitly.

A number of patterns are used to detect faults and support fault tolerance. There are two classes: those that recover from a fault and those that mask a fault.

Saridakis introduces the recovery pattern *Rollback* [Sar02]. This pattern assumes that there is some kind of test that can determine whether or not a fault has occurred. If a fault occurs, a replica of the system is used to repeat the computation. *Rollback* stores the state of the system in a persistent storage at specified checkpoints. This pattern can be implemented by a remote object that knows how to split an invocation into a number of steps. This remote object acts as a LOCATION FORWARDER for each of these steps, and forwards the invocation to another remote object that is located in the active replica. For each step, it tests the result. When all steps are completed, the result of the invocation is sent back to the client. Should a fault occur, it triggers another replica.

Recovery solutions like *Rollback* assume that it is possible to test for a fault. This is not possible for all kinds of computations. In some cases, such as real-time decisions, loss of the computation result and a re-computation is unacceptable. Consider a computation in the flight control system of an aircraft, for example, must produce a immediate and correct result. To cope with this problem, we can use error masking.

The most prominent error masking pattern is *Active Replication*. This extends the configuration of a *Fail-Stop Processor*. To apply error masking, the computation must produce a deterministic result. The idea is to compare a number of different results produced by an uneven number of processor units. A distributor sends the input to all processors that perform the same computation. A comparator unit compares the results and decides on the correct output using a majority vote. In this fashion N simultaneous errors of $2N+1$ processors can be tolerated.

The pattern LOCATION FORWARDER can be used to realize the distributor unit of *Active Replication*, in the same way as we outlined for *Fail-Stop Processor*. A similar configuration of replicated remote objects with a LOCATION FORWARDER is described by the pattern *Object Group* [Maf96].

So far we have introduced a number of separate fault-tolerant measures. Many highly-reliability systems, such as aircraft, however, use a combination of different fault tolerance measures, including redundancy, fail-stop processors, *n*-version programming, and others. For distributors, voters, and comparators, simple hardware units are used to minimize the risk of faults.

Aspect-orientation and Remoting

Aspect-oriented programming (AOP) [KLM+97] allows otherwise tangled cross-cutting design concerns to modularize. By this AOP becomes an important future trend in the domain of object-oriented remoting.

As an example in the area of remoting, consider the situation in which you want to expose a remote object in a server application, but you are faced with multiple, orthogonal extensions or adaptations of your original task. In the course of this book we have already discussed a number of such extension or adaptation issues, such as logging, security, activation, lifecycle management, leasing, or QoS monitoring. Simple implementations hard-code these tasks directly in the distributed object middleware, tangling them with the rest of the code and scattering them across many locations. The result of such tangling and scattering is code that is hard to maintain and evolve.

AOP solves this problem by encapsulating the extension or adaptation issue in a separate design unit called an *aspect*. The classes or components to which the aspect is applied do not have to be concerned about the aspect's existence, and can remain oblivious to it [FF00]. The term *non-invasiveness* is used to describe the situation in which an artefact to which the aspect is applied does not have to change due to its application.

Many distributed object middleware systems use INVOCATION INTERCEPTORS to support extension issues. Interceptors are conceptually close to AOP and can be used to implement AOP solutions. A major difference between INVOCATION INTERCEPTOR architectures and AOP solutions is that INVOCATION INTERCEPTORS do not support non-invasiveness. That is, the application has to provide interception points or hooks, but does not have to care what is done inside them.

AOP can be implemented in different ways. The term 'AOP' in fact denotes a number of different adaptation techniques, and a number of different aspect composition frameworks and languages exist. [Zdu03] describes a pattern language that explains how such aspect composition frameworks can be realized internally. In [Zdu04a] a projection of this pattern language to a number of popular aspect composition frameworks can be found, including AspectJ [KHH+01], Hyper/J [Tar04], JAC [PSDF01], JBoss AOP [Bur03], XOTcl [NZ00], Axis [Apa04b], Demeter/DJ [OL01], and others. These patterns for aspect composition frameworks can also be used to implement aspect solutions for distributed object middleware. Note that JAC and JBoss AOP provide aspect-orientation specifically in the context of distributed object middleware and server-side components. For a more detailed discussion of AOP and Remoting, see Appendix A, *Extending AOP Frameworks for Remoting*.

A   Extending AOP Frameworks for Remoting

Aspect-oriented programming (AOP) [KLM+97] is an important future trend for distributed object middleware. We have already provided a brief discussion of AOP in the remoting context in Chapter 13, *Related Concepts, Technologies, and Patterns*. In this appendix we explain the relationship in more detail.

In [Zdu03] a pattern language is described that explains how aspect composition frameworks are realized internally. In [Zdu04a] a projection of this pattern language to a number of popular aspect composition frameworks can be found, including AspectJ [KHH+01], Hyper/J [Tar04], JAC [PSDF01], JBoss AOP [Bur03], XOTcl [NZ00], Axis [Apa04b], Demeter/DJ [OL01], and others. In this appendix we explain how these patterns can be combined with distributed object middleware.

Let us briefly introduce a few terms that have become accepted in the AOP community and that we use in the subsequent discussion. These terms originate from the AspectJ [KHH+01] terminology. They describe the constituents of an *aspect* in a number of AOP approaches. (Note that other kinds of aspects also exist.)

- *Joinpoints* are specific, well-defined events in the control flow of the executed program.
- An *advice* is a behavior that is triggered by a specific event and that can be inserted into the control flow when a specific joinpoint is reached. Advices allow one to apply some behavior to a given control flow transparently.
- *Pointcuts* are the glue between joinpoints and advices. A pointcut is a declaration of a number of joinpoints. These declarations are used by developers to tell the aspect composition framework at which joinpoints to apply the advices.
- *Introductions* change the structure of an object system. Typical introductions add methods or fields to an existing class, or change the interfaces of an existing class. Introductions are not supported by all aspect composition frameworks.

Distributed object middleware systems are an important application area for AOP, especially when used for distributed component infrastructures. Compared with general-purpose aspect composition frameworks, in which the aspect can be applied potentially to all invocations within a system (as well as other things, such as field accesses, class structures, and so on), aspects for distributed object middleware have a more limited scope: aspects are applied only to remote invocations and remote objects. Thus when we want to adopt an AOP solution within distributed object middleware, we have the following options:

- We can use a general-purpose aspect composition framework, such as AspectJ or Hyper/J, for adapting the respective invocations to the classes of the distributed object middleware and to remote objects.

- We can use an aspect composition framework specifically designed for remoting purposes. Existing examples are JAC or JBoss AOP. Both are also examples of server component infrastructures.

- We can extend distributed object middleware to support AOP. This is not as much work as it sounds, as much distributed object middleware already supports adaptation techniques that can be used in an aspect-oriented fashion. For example, the systems in our technology projections, .NET Remoting, CORBA, and Web Services frameworks, as well as many other distributed object middleware systems, offer some support for INVOCATION INTERCEPTORS. We can use INVOCATION INTERCEPTORS as a basic infrastructure to support AOP.

Below we show examples for these three options, using the patterns from [Zdu03, Zdu04a]. First, let us briefly explain the most important patterns from this pattern language.

A pattern language for implementing aspect composition frameworks

All popular aspect composition frameworks implement the pattern *Indirection Layer*. Obviously an aspect composition framework requires some way to trace the joinpoints specified by the pointcuts. An *Indirection Layer* traces invocation and structure information of a (sub-)system at runtime. It is a *Layer* [BMR+96] between the application logic and the instructions of the (sub-)system that need to be traced. The general term 'instructions' can refer to a whole programming language, but it can also refer to a more specific instruction set, such as those instruction required to invoke remote objects. The *Indirection Layer* wraps all accesses to the relevant subsystem and should not be bypassed. It provides hooks to trace and manipulate the relevant information. Note that distributed object middleware is already one variant of this pattern, as it indirects all remote invocations to remote objects and cannot be bypassed by remote clients.

There are two popular ways to add an *Indirection Layer* to an existing system:

- The program representation (for example the source code or byte-code) can be instrumented using the *Hook Injector* pattern. That is, a semantically-equivalent program variant is produced that sends all relevant invocations through the *Indirection Layer* where the invocations can be manipulated at runtime. Except for programming languages with a dynamic object system, this variant requires static instrumentation of the 'aspectized' classes. The *Parse Tree Interpreter* pattern can be used to manipulate the source code of the classes to be 'aspectized'. A *Parse Tree Interpreter* is applied at compile time. Alternatively, a *Byte Code Manipulator* can be used to manipulate a byte code representation of the program. The latter alternative has the advantage that it can be applied to third-party code (where the source code is not available), and that it can be applied at load time. Both *Parse Tree Interpreter* and *Byte Code Manipulator* patterns are relatively easy to apply in compiled languages.

- Alternatively, the invocations can be intercepted at runtime and then manipulated, using a *Message Redirector*. A *Message Redirector* is a *Facade* [GHJV95] to the *Indirection Layer*. Clients do not access the *Indirection Layer* objects directly, but send symbolic (for example string-based) invocations to the *Message Redirector*. The *Message Redirector* dispatches these invocations to the respective method and object. This variant has the benefit that it allows for dynamic aspectization at runtime. A further advantage in the context of distributed object middleware is that the *Message Redirector* infrastructure is already present. The marshaled invocations can be used as symbolic invocation information, and the INVOKER (or sometimes the SERVER REQUEST HANDLER) can be used as a *Message Redirector*.

In most aspect composition frameworks the *Message Redirector* or *Hook Injector* is used to insert invocations to *Message Interceptors* (a general purpose variant of INVOCATION INTERCEPTOR). Because many distributed object middleware systems support INVOCATION INTERCEPTORS, we can reuse this architecture to realize AOP on top of it.

For an aspect, and for the *Indirection Layer* of an aspect composition framework, it is important to find out about the context of an invocation. This context is passed in an *Invocation Context*. Note that the *Invocation Context* required for an aspect framework is different to a remote INVOCATION CONTEXT. For aspects we require information about the caller and callee scope, as well as the order of aspects. A remote INVOCATION CONTEXT, in contrast, carries extra information, such as authentication information or session IDs. However, the remote INVOCATION CONTEXT can be extended to carry information for the AOP *Invocation Context*.

For the specification of pointcuts and their application to joinpoints at runtime, we require information about the structures and relationships of the system. This information can be provided by the pattern *Introspection Options*. In the context of remoting, this means that the distributed object middleware (or its programming language) should provide *Introspection Options* for the remote objects and their classes. Reflective information about the interface is required – something that is usually present on the INVOKER of distributed object middleware.

If aspects cannot be added using a regular programming language, the patterns *Metadata Tags* and *Command Language* can be used to configure aspects, using either metadata or a programmatic configuration language. These patterns are used especially for pointcut definition and aspect configuration.

In the remainder of this appendix we explain how these patterns are used to introduce AOP into distributed object middleware.

Using AspectJ to introduce Remoting aspects

AspectJ is a popular general-purpose aspect language. In AspectJ, the aspects are described in an extension of the Java language that consists of a set of additional instructions. AspectJ introduces the `aspect` statement, as well as pointcuts such as `call`, `target`, `args`, and advices such as `before`, `after`, `around`. Advices are *Message Interceptors* that are executed when the pointcut condition applies to a particular joinpoint. AspectJ uses a dynamic joinpoint model, but composes the aspects statically using a *Parse Tree Interpreter* or a *Byte Code Manipulator* using its aspect weaver (a kind of program generator for aspect composition).

To manipulate user-defined remote objects for which the source code is available, we can apply AspectJ aspects in a similar way as for other local objects. However, this makes it hard to define generic aspects that can be applied to the complete distributed object middleware or to all remote objects. If the code of the distributed object middleware is available, we can define aspects for its elements. For example, the following simplified aspect intercepts all invocations by an INVOKER class, and forwards them to an authentication class before they reach the INVOKER:

```
public aspect AuthenticationAspect {
  public pointcut requiresAuthenticationInfo():
    call(* Invoker.invoke(..));
    before() : requiresAuthenticationInfo(...) {
      Authentication.authenticate(...);
    }
}
```

AspectJ has potential problems in the area of remoting, as it uses static weaving. In some usage scenarios, server applications cannot be shut down to allow instrumentation of their classes. Other solutions, which we describe below, allow load time or runtime aspect weaving. In AspectJ, runtime elements of aspects can be expressed using the dynamic joinpoint model (that is, using the thisJoinPoint *Invocation Context*). However, the classes must be 'aspectized' statically at compile time. Note that this is mainly a problem for long-running server applications – for many client applications, static instrumentation is not a problem.

Java Aspect Components: JAC

JAC [PSDF01] is a framework for distributed aspect components in Java. JAC allows aspects to be deployed and undeployed at runtime. To prepare the Java classes for use with aspects, BCEL [Dah03] is used as *Byte Code Manipulator* to support 'aspectization' at load time. BCEL offers an API to access and manipulate the Java byte-code. This *Byte Code Manipulator* is used by the *Hook Injector* of JAC. The inserted hooks have the responsibility for indirecting invocations into the JAC *Indirection Layer* that implements the JAC AOP features. Three main features support dynamic aspects in JAC: aspect components, dynamic wrappers, and domain-specific languages.

- *Aspect components* are classes for which pointcuts can be defined to add before, after, or around behavior for base methods. In contrast to AspectJ, *methods* in JAC are specified with strings and looked up using *Introspection Options*. The pointcuts of the aspect components are used to invoke *Message Interceptors*, which are defined by dynamic wrappers.
- *Dynamic wrappers* can be seen as generic advice. Wrappers are ordered in *wrapping chains*. The methods of the wrapper have the aspect's *Invocation Context* as a parameter. This contains information about the wrapped object, method, arguments, and wrapping chain of the invocation.
- The aspects can define a *Command Language* – called a *domain-specific language* in JAC – to configure the pointcuts of the aspects. In the context of remoting, this feature can be used to configure the INVOCATION CONTEXT and the INVOKER, for example for access rights and authentication data.

JBoss aspect-oriented programming

The JBoss Java application server contains a stand-alone aspect composition framework [Bur03]. It is similar to JAC, but has some interesting differences in its design decisions.

The *Hook Injector* of the JBoss AOP also allows for load time instrumentation of 'advisable' classes. Internally, Javassist [Chi03] is used as a *Byte Code Manipulator*. In contrast to BCEL, this provides a source-level abstraction of the byte-code. An advice is implemented as a *Message Interceptor*. All *Message Interceptors* must implement the following interface:

```
public interface Interceptor {
  public String getName();
  public InvocationResponse invoke(Invocation invocation)
    throws Throwable;
}
```

The name returned by getName is a symbolic interceptor name. invoke is a callback method to be called whenever the advice is to be executed.

The parameter of the type Invocation and the return type InvocationResponse implement the *Invocation Context*. All pointcut definitions are given using XML-based *Metadata Tags*, for example:

```
<interceptor-pointcut class="mypackage.MyClass">
    <interceptors>
        <interceptor class="TracingInterceptor" />
    </interceptors>
</interceptor-pointcut>
```

This allows the class loader to know which classes it has to instrument at load time, and the aspects can be configured easily. JBoss AOP also offers a programmatic API to compose the interceptors for instrumented classes at runtime.

Extending Axis handler chains for AOP

Many distributed object middleware systems implement some form of INVOCATION INTERCEPTORS. For example, some support was available in all three technology projections: .NET Remoting, CORBA, and Web Services. This infrastructure can be used to build a simple aspect framework from scratch. Consider the Axis handler chains that we have discussed already in the Web Services technology projection. These can be used as *Message Interceptors* for the aspect framework.

Besides the *Message Interceptors*, Axis provides an *Invocation Context* (in Axis this is called the MessageContext) which is usable for AOP purposes. Aspect configuration is also possible in a way similar to that in JBoss AOP, because handler chains can be configured flexibly using *Metadata Tags* in the XML deployment descriptors. In contrast to the solutions explained before, Axis uses a *Message Redirector*-based architecture. The remote object classes are not instrumented at runtime, but instead the *Message Redirector* (here located in the SERVER REQUEST HANDLER) indirects the invocation into the handler chain, and finally to the INVOKER.

Note that this infrastructure alone is not an AOP framework. What's missing is a way to specify and apply pointcuts. This can be done quite easily by hand, because all necessary information is provided to the *Message Interceptors* in the *Invocation Context*. Of course, only one type of joinpoints can be specified with this information: remote invocations.

A simple implementation variant is to make `invoke` a *Template Method* [GHJV95] defined for an abstract class `AspectHandler`. All aspect handlers inherit from this class and implement the method `applyAspect`. This method is only called if there is a pointcut for the current aspect and the `MessageContext`.

```
public abstract class AspectHandler extends BasicHandler {
  public boolean checkPointcuts(MessageContext msgContext) {
    // check whether pointcuts apply and return true/false
    ...
  }
  public void invoke(MessageContext msgContext) throws AxisFault {
    if (checkPointcuts(msgContext) == true) {
      applyAspect(msgContext);
    }
  }
  abstract public void applyAspect(MessageContext msgContext);
}
```

Note that the pointcuts are defined at two levels, similar to the instrumentation in JAC and JBoss: the aspectized classes are defined as CONFIGURATION GROUPS by the Axis handler chains. The implementation of the `checkPointcuts` method determines which joinpoints are intercepted. Using the Java Reflection API, we can further implement *Introspection Options* for the remote objects to support non-invasive pointcuts. We also need some way to express the pointcuts. If we do not want to implement pointcuts programmatically, we can define XML-based *Metadata Tags*, for example.

References

[ABB+02]   S. Anderson, J. Bohren, T. Boubez, M. Chanliau, G. Della-Libera, B. Dixon, P. Garg, E. Gravengaard, M. Gudgin, P. Hallam-Baker, M. Hondo, C. Kaler (ed.), H. Lockhart, R. Martherus, H. Maruyama, P. Mishra, A. Nadalin, N. Nagaratnam, A. Nash, R. Philpott, D. Platt, H. Prafullchandra, M. Sahu, J. Shewchuk, D. Simon, D. Srinivas, E. Waingold, D. Waite, and R. Zolfonoon: *Web Services Trust Language (WS-Trust)*, 2002
http://msdn.microsoft.com/library/default.asp?url=/library/en-us/dnglobspec/html/ws-trust.asp

[ACD+03]   T. Andrews, F. Curbera, H. Dholakia, Y. Goland, J. Klein, F. Leymann, K. Liu, D. Roller, D. Smith, S. Thatte, I. Trickovic, and S. Weerawarana: *Business Process Execution Language for Web Services, Version 1.0.* 2003
http://www.ibm.com/developerworks/webservices/library/ws-bpel

[ADH+02]   B. Atkinson, G. Della-Libera, S. Hada, M. Hondo, P. Hallam-Baker, J. Klein, B. LaMacchia, P. Leach, J. Manferdelli, H. Maruyama, A. Nadalin, N. Nagaratnam, H. Prafullchandra, J. Shewchuk, and D. Simon: *Web Services Security (WS-Security)*, 2002
http://www-106.ibm.com/developerworks/webservices/library/ws-secure/

[AIS+77]   C. Alexander, S. Ishikawa, and M. Silverstein: *A Pattern Language – Towns • Buildings • Construction*, Oxford University Press, 1977

[ALR01]   A. Avizienis, J.-C. Laprie, and B. Randell: *Fundamental Concepts of Dependability.* Research Report N01145, LAAS-CNRS, April 2001

[Ans04]   ANSI Accredited Standards Committee: (ASC) X12, *EDI*, 2004
http://www.x12.org/

[Apa04a]   Apache Software Foundation: *Web Services Invocation Framework (WSIF)*, 2004
http://ws.apache.org/wsif/

[Apa04b]   Apache Software Foundation: *Web Services – Axis*, 2004
http://xml.apache.org/axis/

[Apa04c]   Apache Software Foundation: *Apache Jakarta Tomcat*, 2004
            http://jakarta.apache.org/tomcat/

[Arp93]   ARPA Knowledge Sharing Initiative: *Specification of the KQML Agent-Communication Language*, ARPA Knowledge Sharing Initiative, External Interfaces Working Group, July 1993

[Aut04]   The Autosar Consortium: *Autosar – Automotive Open System Architecture*, 2004
            http://www.autosar.org

[Bar02]   T. Barnaby: *Distributed .NET Programming in C#*, APress, 2002

[BBF+02]   M. Bartel, J. Boyer, B. Fox, B. LaMacchia, and E. Simon: *XML-Signature Syntax and Processing*, W3C Recommendations, 2002
            http://www.w3.org/TR/xmldsig-core/

[BBL02]   M. Baker, R. Buyya, and D. Laforenza: *Grids and Grid Technologies for Wide-Area Distributed Computing*, Software: Practice and Experience, 32 (15), John Wiley & Sons, December 2002

[Bbn02]   BBN Technologies: *Quality Objects (QuO)*, 2002
            http://quo.bbn.com/

[BCH+03]   D. Box, F. Curbera, M. Hondo, C. Kale, D. Langworthy, A. Nadalin, N. Nagaratnam, M. Nottingham, C. von Riegen, J. Shewchuk: *Web Services Policy Framework (WS-Policy)*, 2003
            http://www-106.ibm.com/developerworks/library/ws-polfram/

[BCK03]   L. Bass, P. Clements, and R. Kazman: *Software Architecture in Practice*, Addison-Wesley, Second edition, 2003

[Bea04]   BEA: *BEA Tuxedo 8.1*, 2004
            http://www.bea.com/products/tuxedo/index.shtml

[BEK+00]   D. Box, D. Ehnebuske, G. Kakivaya, A. Layman, N. Mendelsohn, H. F. Nielsen, S. Thatte, and D. Winer: *Simple Object Access Protocol (SOAP) 1.1*, 2000
            http://www.w3.org/TR/2000/NOTE-SOAP-20000508/

[BHM+03]   D. Booth, H. Haas, F. McCabe, E. Newcomer, M. Champion, C. Ferris, and D. Orchard: *Web Services Architecture*, W3C Working Draft 8, August 2003
            http://www.w3.org/TR/2003/WD-ws-arch-20030808/

[BM98] M. Breugst and T. Magedanz: *Mobile agents – Enabling Technology for Active Intelligent Network Implementation*, IEEE Network Magazine, 12 (3): 53–60, May–June 1998

[BMR+96] F. Buschmann, R. Meunier, H. Rohnert, P. Sommerlad, and M. Stal: *Pattern-Oriented Software Architecture – A System of Patterns*, John Wiley & Sons, 1996

[BN84] A. Birrell and B. Nelson: *Implementing Remote Procedure Calls*, ACM Transactions on Computer Systems, 2 (1), February 1984

[Bor04] Borland Inc.: *Janeva – Platform Interoperability for the Enterprise*, 2004

http://www.borland.com/janeva/

[Bpm02] Business Process Management Initiative: *Business Process Modeling Language (BPML)*, November 2002

http://www.bpmi.org

[BPS98] T. Bray, J. Paoli, C.M. Sperberg-McQueen: *Extensible Markup Language (XML) 1.0*, 1998

http://www.w3.org/TR/1998/REC-xml-19980210

[Bur03] B. Burke: *JBoss Aspect Oriented Programming*, 2003

http://www.jboss.org/developers/projects/jboss/aop.jsp

[CCC+02] F. Cabrera, G. Copeland, B. Cox, T. Freund, J. Klein, T. Storey, and S. Thatte: *Web Services Transaction (WS-Transaction)*, August 2002

http://www.ibm.com/developerworks/library/ws-transpec/

[CCC+03] L. Cabrera, G. Copeland, W. Cox, M. Feingold, T. Freund, J. Johnson, C. Kaler, J. Klein, D. Langworthy, A. Nadalin, D. Orchard, I. Robinson, J. Shewchuk, and T. Storey: *Web Services Coordination (WS-Coordination)*, September 2003

http://www-106.ibm.com/developerworks/library/ws-coor/

[CCM+01] E. Christensen, F. Curbera, G. Meredith, and S. Weerawarana: *Web Services Description Language (WSDL) 1.1*, 2001

http://www.w3.org/TR/wsdl

[CDK94] G. Coulouris, J. Dollimore, and T. Kindberg: *Distributed Systems – Concepts and Design*, Addison-Wesley, Reading, MA, 1994

[CFH+02]   M. Clark, P. Fletcher, J. J. Hanson, R. Irani, M. Waterhouse, and J. Thelin: *Web Services Business Strategies and Architectures*, Wrox Press, August 2002

[Chi03]   S. Chiba: *Javassist*, 2003

http://www.csg.is.titech.ac.jp/~chiba/javassist/

[Cia04]   CAN in Automation (CiA): *Controller Area Network*, 2004

http://www.can-cia.de

[Cop04]   James O. Coplien: *A Pattern Definition*, 2004

http://hillside.net/patterns/definition.html

[CTV+98]   P. Ciancarini, R. Tolksdorf, F. Vitali, D. Rossi, A. Knoche: *Coordinating Multiagent Applications on the WWW: A Reference Architecture*, IEEE Transactions on Software Engineering, 24 (5): 362–375, 1998

[CV02]   E. Chtcherbina and M. Völter: *Peer to Peer Systems – EuroPLoP 2002 Focus Group Results*, Proceedings of the 7th European Conference on Pattern Languages of Programs (EuroPLoP 2002), Irsee, Germany, July 2002

http://www.voelter.de/data/pub/P2PSystems.pdf

[Dah03]   M. Dahm: *The Byte Code Engineering Library (BCEL)*, 2003

http://jakarta.apache.org/bcel/

[DHH+02]   G. Della-Libera, P. Hallam-Baker, M. Hondo, T. Janczuk, C. Kaler, H. Maruyama, N. Nagaratnam, A. Nash, R. Philpott, H. Prafullchandra, J. Shewchuk, E. Waingold, and R. Zolfonoon: *Web Services Security Policy (WS-Security Policy)*, 2002

http://www.ibm.com/developerworks/library/ws-secpol/index.html

[DL04]   P. Dyson and A. Longshaw: *Architecting Enterprise Solutions: Patterns for High-Capability Internet-based Systems*, John Wiley & Sons, 2004

[Dub00]   O. Dubuisson: *ASN.1 – Communication Between Heterogeneous Systems*, Morgan Kaufmann, 2000

[Emm00]   W. Emmerich: *Engineering Distributed Objects*, John Wiley & Sons, 2000

[ERI+02]   D. Eastlake (ed.), J. Reagle (ed.), T. Imamura, B. Dillaway, and E. Simon: *XML Encryption Syntax and Processing*, W3C Recommendation, 10 December 2002

http://www.w3.org/TR/xmlenc-core/

[FF00]   R. Filman and D. P. Friedman: *Aspect-Oriented Programming is Quantification and Obliviousness*, OOPSLA Workshop on Advanced Separation of Concerns, Minneapolis, USA, October 2000

http://ic.arc.nasa.gov/people/filman/text/oif/aop-is.pdf

[FGM+97]   R. Fielding, J. Gettys, J. Mogul, H. Frystyk, T. Berners-Lee: *Hypertext Transfer Protocol — HTTP/1.1*, RFC 2068, January 1997

http://www.ietf.org/rfc/rfc2068.txt

[FHA99]   E. Freeman, S. Hupfer, and K. Arnold: *JavaSpaces – Principles, Patterns, and Practice*, Addison-Wesley, 1999

[FHF+01]   W. Ford, P. Hallam-Baker, B. Fox, B. Dillaway, B. LaMacchia, J. Epstein, and J. Lapp: *XML Key Management Specification (XKMS)*, W3C Note, 30 March 2001

http://www.w3.org/TR/xkms/

[Fip04]   FIPA: *Agent Communication Language Specifications*, 2004

http://www.fipa.org/repository/aclspecs.html

[FKT01]   I. Foster, C. Kesselman, and S. Tuecke: *The Anatomy of the Grid: Enabling Scalable Virtual Organizations*, International Journal of Supercomputer Applications, 15 (3), 2001

[Fow96]   M. Fowler: *Analysis Patterns: Reusable Object Models*, Addison-Wesley, 1996

[Fow03]   M. Fowler: *Patterns of Enterprise Application Architecture*, Addison-Wesley, 2003

[FPV98]   A. Fuggetta, G. P. Picco, and G. Vigna: *Understanding code mobility*, IEEE Transactions on Software Engineering, 24 (5): 342–361, May 1998

[FV00]   A. Fricke and M. Völter: *SEMINARS – A Pedagogical Pattern Language on how to Teach Seminars Efficiently*, 2000

http://www.voelter.de/publications/seminars.html

[GCCC85]   D. Gelernter, N. Carriero, S. Chandran, and S. Chang: *Parallel programming in Linda*, Proceedings of the 1985 International Conference on Parallel Processing, 255–263, 1985

[GCK+02]   R. S. Gray, G. Cybenko, D. Kotz, R. A. Peterson, and D. Rus: *D'Agents: Applications and Performance of a Mobile-Agent System*, Software – Practice and Experience, 32 (6): 543–573, May 2002

[Gel99]	D. H. Gelernter: *Machine Beauty: Elegance and the Heart of Technology*, Basic Books, 1999
[GHJV95]	E. Gamma, R. Helm, R. Johnson, and J. Vlissides: *Design Patterns*, Addison-Wesley, 1995
[Gnu04]	Gnutella home page, 2004 http://www.gnutella.com
[GNZ01]	M. Goedicke, G. Neumann, U. Zdun: *Message Redirector*, Proceedings of the 6th European Conference on Pattern Languages of Programs (EuroPLoP 2001), Irsee, Germany, July 2001
[Gra78]	J. N. Gray: *Notes on Database Operating Systems*: Operating Systems: An Advanced Course, Lecture Notes in Computer Science, 60: 393–481, Springer-Verlag, 1978
[Gri97]	R. Grimes: *Professional DCOM Programming*, Wrox Press Inc., 1997
[Gri04]	Grid Computing Info Centre, 2004 http://www.gridcomputing.com
[Gro01]	W. Grosso: *Java RMI*, O'Reilly & Associates, 2001
[GT03]	B. Gröne and P. Tabeling: *A System of Patterns for Concurrent Request Processing Servers*, Proceedings of the Second Nordic Conference on Pattern Languages of Programs (VikingPLoP 2003), Bergen, Norway, 2003
[Hen98]	K. Henney: *Counted Body Techniques*, Overload 25, April 1998 http://boost.org/more/count_bdy.htm
[Hen01]	K. Henney: *C++ Patterns: Reference Accounting*, Proceedings of the 6th European Conference on Pattern Languages of Programs (EuroPLoP 2001), Irsee, Germany, July 2001
[HV99]	M. Henning and S. Vinoski: *Advanced CORBA Programming with C++*, Addison-Wesley, 1999
[HW03]	G. Hohpe, B. Woolf, K. Brown, C. F. D'Cruz, M. Fowler, S. Neville, M. J. Rettig, J. Simon: *Enterprise Integration Patterns*, Addison-Wesley, October 2003
[Ibm04a]	IBM: *TSpaces*, 2004 http://www.almaden.ibm.com/cs/TSpaces/

References

[Ibm04b]   IBM: *CICS (Customer Information Control System) Family*, 2004
           http://www.ibm.com/software/htp/cics/

[Ibm04c]   IBM: *WebSphere MQ Family*, 2004
           http://www-306.ibm.com/software/integration/mqfamily/

[Jen02]   R. Jennings: *Monitor Web Service Performance*, XML & Web Services Magazine, 10, 2002
           http://www.fawcette.com/xmlmag/2002_10/online/webservices_rjennings_10_30_02/

[Jin04]   The Jini Community: *Jini Community Home Page*, 2004
           http://www.jini.org/

[KHH+01]   G. Kiczales, E. Hilsdale, J. Hugunin, M. Kersten, J. Palm, G. Griswold: *Getting Started with AspectJ*, Communications of the ACM, 44 (10): 59–65, October 2001

[KJ04]   M. Kircher and P. Jain: *Pattern-Oriented Software Architecture – Patterns for Resource Management*, John Wiley & Sons, 2004

[KLM+97]   G. Kiczales, J. Lamping, A. Mendhekar, C. Maeda, C. V. Lopes, J. M. Loingtier, J. Irwin: *Aspect-Oriented Programming*, Proceedings of the 11th European Conference on Object-Oriented Programming (ECOOP 97), Jyväskylä, Finland, LCNS 1241, Springer-Verlag, June 1997

[Kop97]   H. Kopetz: *Real-Time Systems – Design Principles for Distributed Embedded Applications*, Kluwer Academic Publishers, Boston, Dordrecht, London, 1997

[Lap85]   J.-C. Laprie: *Dependability: Basic Concepts and Terminology*, Proceedings of the 15th International Symposium on Fault-Tolerant Computing (FTCS-15), Michigan, USA, June 1985

[Lea99]   D. Lea: *Concurrent Programming in Java – Design Principles and Patterns*, Addison-Wesley, Second edition, 1999

[LO98]   D. B. Lange and M. Oshima: *Programming and Deploying Java Mobile Agents with Aglets*, Addison Wesley, 1998

[Low03]   J. Lowy: *Decouple Components by Injecting Custom Services into Your Object's Interception Chain*, MSDN Magazine, March 2003
           http://msdn.microsoft.com/msdnmag/issues/03/03/ContextsinNET/default.aspx

[Lyu95]   M.R. Lyu (ed.): *Software Fault Tolerance*, John Wiley & Sons, 1995

[Mae87]   P. Maes: *Computational Reflection*, Technical Report TR-87-2, VUB AILAB, 1987

[Maf96]   S. Maffeis: *The Object Group Design Pattern*, Proceedings of the 2nd Conference on Object-Oriented Technologies and Systems (COOTS 96), Toronto, Canada, June 1996

[Mic04a]   Microsoft: *MSMQ Microsoft Message Queue Server*, 2004

http://www.microsoft.com/windows2000/technologies/communications/msmq/default.asp

[Mic04b]   Microsoft: *Indigo*, 2004

http://msdn.microsoft.com/Longhorn/understanding/pillars/Indigo/default.aspx

[Mic04c]   Microsoft: *Data Transfer Object*, 2004

http://msdn.microsoft.com/library/default.asp?url=/library/en-us/dnpatterns/html/DesDTO.asp

[Mic04d]   Microsoft: *Information on Microsoft COM+ technologies*, 2004

http://www.microsoft.com/com/tech/COMPlus.asp

[Mic04e]   Microsoft: *Microsoft Transaction Server (MTS)*, 2004

http://www.microsoft.com/com/tech/MTS.asp

[Min04]   The Mind Electric: *GLUE*, 2004

http://www.webmethods.com/Solutions/Glue

[Moc87]   P. V. Mockapetris: *RFC 1035: Domain Names – Implementation and Specification*, November 1987

[Nob97]   James Noble: *Basic Relationship Patterns*, Proceedings of the Second European Conference on Pattern Languages of Programs (EuroPLoP 1997), Irsee, Germany, 1997

[NZ00]   G. Neumann and U. Zdun: *XOTcl, An Object-oriented Scripting Language*, Proceedings of Tcl2k, The 7th USENIX Tcl/Tk Conference, pages 163–174, Austin, Texas, USA, February 2000

http://www.xotcl.org

References

[Oas02]   Organization for the Advancement of Structured Information Standards (OASIS): *UDDI Version 3.0*, October 2002

http://www.uddi.org/specification.html

[Oas03a] Organization for the Advancement of Structured Information Standards (OASIS): *Security Assertion Markup Language (SAML), Version 1.1*, September 2003

http://www.oasis-open.org/committees/security/

[Oas03b] Organization for the Advancement of Structured Information Standards (OASIS): *eXtensible Access Control Markup Language Security Assertion Markup (XACML)*, Version 1.0, February 2003

http://www.oasis-open.org/committees/xacml

[Obj97]   ObjectSpace: *Voyager Core Package Technical Overview*, Version 1.0, ObjectSpace, Inc., December 1997

[OG03]   J. Oberleitner and T. Gschwind: *Transparent Integration of CORBA and the .NET Framework*, in *On The Move to Meaningful Internet Systems 2003*, CoopIS, DOA, and ODBASE, Springer LNCS, Volume 2888, 2003

http://www.springerlink.com/index/KHLAA764JFM640RX.pdf

[OL01]   D. Orleans and K. Lieberherr: *DJ: Dynamic Adaptive Programming in Java*, in *Reflection 2001: Meta-level Architectures and Separation of Crosscutting Concerns*, pages 73–80, Kyoto, Japan, September 2001.

[OLW98]   J. Ousterhout, J. Levy, B. Welch: *The Safe-Tcl Security Model*, in *Mobile Agents and Security*, G. Vigna (ed.), LNCS Volume 1419. Springer, 1998

[OMG04a] Object Management Group: *Common Object Request Broker Architecture (CORBA/IIOP)*, 2004

http://www.omg.org/technology

[OMG04b] Object Management Group: *Object Transaction Service*, 2004

http://www.omg.org/technology

[Ope91]   Open Software Foundation: *DCE Application Development Guide*, Revision 1.0, Cambridge, MA, 1991

[Ope97]   The Open Group: *Universal Unique Identifier*, 1997

http://www.opengroup.org/onlinepubs/9629399/apdxa.htm

[Ope01]   OpenNap: *The Open Source Napster Server*, 2001
            http://opennap.sourceforge.net/

[Ope03]   The Open Group: *Transaction Processing*, 2003
            http://www.opengroup.org/products/publications/catalog/tp.htm

[Ped04]   The Pedagogical Patterns Project, 2004
            http://www.pedagogicalpatterns.org

[PS97]   H. Peine and T. Stolpmann: *The Architecture of the Ara Platform for Mobile Agents*, Proceedings of the First International Workshop on Mobile Agents, Volume 1219, Lecture Notes in Computer Science, pages 50–61, Springer-Verlag, Berlin, Germany, April 1997

[PSDF01]   R. Pawlak, L. Seinturier, L. Duchien, G. Florin: *JAC: A Flexible Framework for AOP in Java*, in *Reflection 2001: Meta-level Architectures and Separation of Crosscutting Concerns*, pages 1–24, Kyoto, Japan, Sep 2001

[Qui03]   M. Quinn: *Parallel Programming in C with MPI and OpenMP*, McGraw-Hill, 2003

[Ram02]   I. Rammer: *Advanced .NET Remoting*, APress, 2002

[Rie97]   D. Riehle: *Bureaucracy*, in *Pattern Languages of Program Design 3*, Eds. R. Martin, D. Riehle, F. Buschmann, Addison-Wesley, 1997

[Rog95]   E. M. Rogers: *Diffusion of Innovations*, 4th Edition, Free Press, 1995

[Rox04]   Roxio, Inc.: *The Napster Homepage*, 2004
            http://www.napster.com

[RSB+97]   D. Riehle, W. Siberski, D. Bäumer, D. Megert, H. Züllighoven: *Serializer*, in *Pattern Languages of Program Design 3*, Eds. R. Martin, D. Riehle, F. Buschmann, Addison-Wesley, 1997

[Sar02]   T. Saridakis: *A System of Patterns for Fault Tolerance*, Proceedings of the 7th European Conference on Pattern Languages of Programs (EuroPLoP 2002), Irsee, Germany, July 2002

[Sar03]   T. Saridakis: *Design Patterns for Fault Containment*, Proceedings of the 8th European Conference on Pattern Languages of Programs (EuroPLoP 2003), Irsee, Germany, June 2003

[Set04]	Seti@Home: *The Search for Extraterrestrial Intelligence*, 2004 http://setiathome.ssl.berkeley.edu/
[Sev04]	D. Sevilla: *The CORBA & CORBA Component Model (CCM) Page*, 2004 http://ditec.um.es/~dsevilla/ccm/
[Sor02]	K. E. Sorensen: *Sessions*, Proceedings of the 7th European Conference on Pattern Languages of Programs (EuroPLoP 2002), Irsee, Germany, July 2002
[SSRB00]	D. C. Schmidt, M. Stal, H. Rohnert, F. Buschmann: *Pattern-Oriented Software Architecture – Patterns for Concurrent and Networked Objects*, John Wiley & Sons, 2000
[Sta00]	M. Stal: *The Activator Pattern*, 2000 http://www.stal.de/articles.html
[Sta03]	M. Stal: *Distributed .NET Tutorial*, 2003 http://www.stal.de/Downloads/OOP2003/oop_distrnet.pdf
[Ste98]	R. Stevens: *UNIX Network Programming*, Prentice Hall, 1998
[Sun88]	Sun Microsystems: *RPC: Remote Procedure Call Protocol Specification*, Technical Report RFC-1057, Sun Microsystems, Inc., June 1988
[Sun04a]	Sun Microsystems: *Core J2EE Patterns – Transfer Object*. 2004 http://java.sun.com/blueprints/corej2eepatterns/Patterns/TransferObject.html
[Sun04b]	Sun Microsystems: *Java API for XML-Based RPC (JAX-RPC)*, 2004 http://java.sun.com/xml/jaxrpc/
[Sun04c]	Sun Microsystems: *Java Message Service (JMS)*, 2004 http://java.sun.com/products/jms/
[Sun04d]	Sun Microsystems: *Enterprise Java Beans Technology*, 2004 http://java.sun.com/products/ejb/
[Sun04e]	Sun Microsystems: *Project JXTA*, 2004 http://www.jxta.org

[Swi02]   SWIFT: *Annual Report 2002*, La Hulpe, Belgium, 2002
           http://www.swift.com/

[Tar04]   P. Tarr: *HyperJ*, 2004
           http://www.research.ibm.com/hyperspace/HyperJ/HyperJ.htm

[Tib04]   Tibco: *Messaging Solutions*, 2004
           http://www.tibco.com/software/enterprise_backbone/messaging.jsp

[Tra00]   Transarc: *Encina*, 2000
           http://www-306.ibm.com/software/htp/txseries/library/techsheets/encina/

[TS02]   A. Tanenbaum and M. van Steen: *Distributed Systems: Principles and Paradigms*, Prentice Hall, 2002

[Upn04]   UPNP Forum: *Universal Plug and Play*, 2004
           http://upnp.org/

[Vin02a]   S. Vinoski: *Middleware "Dark Matter"*, Toward Integration column, IEEE Internet Computing, September–October 2002

[Vin02b]   S. Vinoski: *Chain of Responsibility*, Toward Integration column, IEEE Internet Computing, November–December 2002

[Vin03]   S. Vinoski: *Integration with Web Services IEEE Internet Computing, Toward Integration* column, IEEE Internet Computing, November–December 2003

[Voe03]   M. Völter: *Small Components – A Generative Component Infrastructure for Embedded Systems*, 2003
           http://www.voelter.de/data/pub/SmallComponents.pdf

[VSW02]   M. Völter, A. Schmid, E. Wolff: *Server Component Patterns*, John Wiley & Sons, 2002

[Win99]   D. Winer: *XML-RPC Specification*, 1999
           http://www.xmlrpc.com/spec

[W3C04]   W3C: *Resource Description Framework (RDF)*, 2004
           http://www.w3.org/RDF/

[Zdu03]	U. Zdun: *Patterns of Tracing Software Structures and Dependencies*, Proceedings of the 8th European Conference on Pattern Languages of Programs (EuroPLoP 2003), Irsee, Germany, June 2003
[Zdu04a]	U. Zdun: *Pattern Language for the Design of Aspect Languages and Aspect Composition Frameworks*, IEE Proceedings Software. 151 (2): 67–83, 2004
[Zdu04b]	U. Zdun: *Loosely Coupled Web Services in Remote Object Federations*, Proceedings of 4th International Conference on Web Engineering (ICWE 2004). Munich, Germany, 2004
[Zdu04c]	U. Zdun: *Leela*, 2004 http://sourceforge.net/projects/leela
[Zer04]	ZeroC Software: *The Internet Communications Engine*, 2004 http://www.zeroc.com/ice.html
[ZVK03]	U. Zdun, M. Völter, M. Kircher: *Design and Implementation of an Asynchronous Invocation Framework for Web Services*, Proceedings of International Conference on Web Services Europe (ICWS-Europe 2003), Erfurt, Germany, pages 64–78, 2003

Index

A
Absolute Object Reference 23, 28, 31, 73,
  77–80, 142, 342, 344, 349, 350
  in .NET Remoting 193, 198, 237
  in Client-Dependent Instance 97
  in CORBA 307, 316, 325, 326, 327
  in Invoker 45
  in Lazy Acquisition 101
  in Lifecycle Manager 143
  in Location Forwarder 154, 155
  in Lookup 81, 82
  in Marshaller 56
  in Object Id 75
  in Requestor 37, 39
  in Result Callback 181
  interactions 85, 183
Abstract Factory 84
Acceptor/Connector 49, 52, 128
Access to remote objects,
  CORBA 316
ACID properties 338
Acknowledgement 351
Activation 88
  in .NET Remoting 208
Activation strategy, in CORBA 310
Activator 145
Active Object 184, 335
Active redundant server 349
Active Replication 156, 352
Adaptation layer, in CORBA 302
Adapter 62, 263
Adaptive Runtime Technology 136, 262,
  285, 286
Administration Module
  See Aspect-Oriented Programming
Agent 343, 345

Agent Communication Languages 346
Aglets 345
AMI
  See Asynchronous Method Invocation
Annotations 341
AOP
  See Aspect-Oriented Programming
Application domain, in .NET
  189, 196
Application layer 127
Ara 345
Artix 185, 239, 280, 291
  support for Web Services 285
ASMX 235
ASN.1 57
ASP.NET 283
Aspect 353
Aspect orientation,
  and Remoting 353
AspectJ 132, 353
Aspect-Oriented Programming 132,
  333, 353
Assembly 188
  implementation in .NET 195
Asynchronous communication, in .NET
  Remoting 228
Asynchronous Completion Token 172,
  180, 271, 272, 346
  in .NET Remoting 233
Asynchronous Method Invocations 318,
  319
ATM 331
Atomicity 338
Attribute, in .NET 189
AUTOSAR 2
Availability, improving 349

Axis 136, 185, 239, 245, 253, 256, 258, 259, 263, 270, 281, 354
 as example in Web Services 245
 asynchrony support 270
 building asynchrony patterns 271

B
B2B
 See Business-to-business
Basic Remoting patterns, interactions 66
Big endian 55
Binding 82
Bootstrapping, in .NET Remoting 208
Borland 293
BPEL4WS 278
Broker 19, 335
Broker **20–26**, 27, 30
 in .NET Remoting 198
 in CORBA 301
 in Web Services 262
Business object 216
Business Process Execution Language for Web Services 242
Business Process Modelling Language 243
Business-to-business 240

C
C# 188
C++ 188, 197
C++.NET 187
Caching 50, 336
`CallContext` 225
CAN 136
CCM 112, 293, 340, 341
CDR 57
Channel 221
 in .NET 193, 198
 in Indigo 235
Channel sink 223
CICS 340
Client Proxy 35, **40–42**, 127, 234, 249, 290, 339, 342
 example using WSDL 251
 in .NET Remoting 197, 218, 219
 in Absolute Object Reference 77, 79
 in Client Request Handler 48
 in CORBA 297, 327, 330
 in Interface Description 59, 60, 61, 62
 in Leasing 108
 in Object Id 74, 76
 in Remoting Error 64
 in Web Services 244, 245, 251, 253, 254, 255, 256, 257, 258, 264, 270, 281
 interactions 67, 70, 181
Client Request Handler 22, 30, 35, **48–50**, 99, 127, 129, 335, 336, 337
 in .NET Remoting 198, 217, 236
 in Absolute Object Reference 77, 78
 in CORBA 299, 300
 in Invocation Interceptor 132
 in Object Id 76
 in Poll Object 172
 in Protocol Plug-in 135, 136, 137
 in Qos Observer 152
 in Remoting Error 64, 65
 in Requestor 38
 in Web Services 256, 258, 259, 266, 286, 287
 interactions 67, 69, 86, 177, 178
Client request interceptor 309
Client state 29, 96
Client-Dependent Instance 29, 87, 88, **96–98**, 337
 in .NET Remoting 199, 208, 209, 215
 in Leasing 106, 107
 in Object Id 75
 in Web Services 269, 283
 interactions 111, 115, 119, 120, 121, 124
Client-side asynchrony
 in CORBA 319
 in Web Services 270
CLR
 See Common Language Runtime
Code mobility 9, 343
Code on demand 344
COM+ 112, 187, 215, 235, 340, 341

Index

Command 257, 273
Common Language Runtime 188, 204
    instance 217, 220
Common Object Request Broker Architecture 12, 185, 217, 219, 237, 239, 240, 241, 272, 341, 344
    access to remote objects 316
    activation strategies 310
    adaptation layer 302
    basics 298
    client-side asynchrony 319
    connection handling 299
    example of Remoting patterns 296
    history 293
    lifecycle management 305
    location forwarding 315
    messaging 318
    Naming Service 316
    object references 307
    pattern map 294
    provider 258
    system exception 303
    technology projection 293–331
    Version 2.4 specification 318
    Version 3 specification 299
Communication layer 128
Communication Middleware 7
Concurrency 5
Configuration Group 129, 141, **146–148**
    in CORBA 304
    in Local Object 149
    in Qos Observer 151, 152
    in Web Services 286
    interactions 119, 160
Connection handling, in CORBA 299
Connection management, in RT-CORBA 329
Consistency 338
Context 82
    in .NET 196, 197
Coordinator 336

CORBA
    See Common Object Request Broker Architecture
corbaloc 79
Correlation Identifier 346
Counted Handler 302
CRM systems 240

D
D'Agents 345
Data Replication 350
Data Transfer Object 24, 192
Database Management System 15
DCE
    See Distributed Computing Environment
DCOM 12, 187, 239, 241, 341
Deactivation 88
Debugger 198
Delegate, in .NET Remoting 229
Demeter/DJ 354
Deployment descriptor 246
Dispatcher, in .NET 197
Distributed Computing Environment 12
Distributed systems
    application areas 1
    challenges 1
    design challenges 5
    overview 1–17
    reasons for use 3
Distributed Transaction Processing model 340
Distributed, Real-time, and Embedded domain 323, 330, 340
Distribution infrastructure 338
Domain Name System 247, 279
.NET Enterprise 187
.NET 57, 186, 240
    concepts 188
    error handling 198
    Remoting boundaries 195
    Remoting framework 193
.NET framework 215, 217

.NET Remoting 12, 185, 187, 196, 241
    basic internals 197
    example 190
    extensibility 221
    history 187
    internals 217
    outlook 235
    pattern map 189
.NET Web Service 239, 280, 283
DRE domain
    See Distributed real-time
        and embedded domain
Durability 338
Dynamically Loaded Library,
    in .NET 195

E
Eager Acquisition 91, 104, 202, 329, 336
EAI
    See Enterprise Application
        Integration
Eavesdropping, in security threat 347
EDI
    See Electronic Data Interchange
EJB
    See Enterprise Java Beans
Eiffel 188
Embedded system 2, 5, 58, 76, 101, 146,
    294, 299, 327
Encina 340
Enterprise Application Integration
    4, 239
Enterprise Java Beans 112, 293, 340, 341
    provider 258
Entity Components 113
Error 351
Error handling, in .NET 198
Event-Driven Consumer 346
Evictor 102, 145, 336
Extended infrastructure patterns 141–161
    interactions 158
Extension Interface 62, 324
Extension patterns 127–140
    interactions 138

F
Facade 24, 138
Factory 97
Factory Method 84, 269
Fail-over 340
Fail-Stop Processor 156, 351, 352
Failure 351
Fault 351
Fault tolerance 350
Fire And Forget 32, 163, 164, **165–167**, 168,
    169, 288
    in .NET Remoting 233
    in CORBA 322
    in Web Services 270, 274
    interactions 176, 177
Firewall 135, 136, 175, 283, 349
Forking Server 335
Forwarder-Receiver 50, 54
Framework, setting up in .NET 194
FTP 242
Functionally identical server 349
Future 184, 335
Futures 171

G
General-Inter-ORB-Protocol (GIOP) 331
GLUE 185, 239, 253, 291
    support for Web Services 281
Grasshopper 345
Grid computing 2, 3, 9, 333, 342
Guarded Suspension 335

H
Half-sync/Half-async 50, 53, 335
HTTP over SSL 282
HTTPAuth 259
Hyper/J 353

I
Ice 79
Identification pattern interactions 85
IDL
    See Interface Definition Language

Index **381**

IIOP
    See Internet-Inter-ORB-Protocol
Indigo 187
    pattern mapping 236
    structure 235
Instance, lifetime in .NET Remoting 206
Interception, in security threat 347
Interceptor 129
Interface
    description language 60
Interface Definition Language 296, 303
Interface Description 35, **59–62**,
  289, 346
    in .NET Remoting 218, 224
    in Broker 21
    in Client Proxy 41, 42
    in CORBA 303
    in Invoker 45
    in Local Object 150
    in Marshaller 57
    in Requestor 39
    in Web Services 240, 242, 245, 249,
      250, 251, 256, 274, 280, 281, 282,
      283, 285
Internet system 349
Internet-Inter-ORB-Protocol 331, 344
    reflective 61
    repository 61
Interoperable Object References 307
Introspection Options 344
Invocation asynchrony 163–184
Invocation Context 129, **133–134**, 225, 268,
  288, 337, 339, 341, 348
    in .NET Remoting 221, 226
    in CORBA 309, 325, 326
    in Invocation Interceptor 131, 132
    in Local Object 149
    in Marshaller 55
    in Web Services 257, 259, 260, 261,
      264, 265, 266, 268, 282, 286
    interactions 138
Invocation extension 308
Invocation interception, using contexts 224

Invocation Interceptor 31, **130–132**, 147,
  288, 341, 345, 348, 353
    in .NET Remoting 221, 226
    in Configuration Group 146, 147
    in CORBA 308
    in Lifecycle Manager 145
    in Local Object 149
    in Web Services 257, 259, 261, 262,
      266, 278, 285
    interactions 138, 139, 140, 159
Invocation layer 127
Invocation stream, intercepting in .NET
  Remoting 221
Invoker 21, 27, 30, 31, 35, **43–47**, 52, 56, 88,
  94, 127, 129, 131, 141, 154, 160, 288, 289,
  290, 337, 339, 348
    example using WSDL 251
    in .NET Remoting 197, 236
    in Absolute Object Reference 77,
      78, 80
    in Broker 20, 22
    in Client Proxy 42
    in Configuration Group 147
    in CORBA 299, 300, 301, 303
    in Fire And Forget 166
    in Interface Description 59,
      60, 61
    in Invocation Context 134
    in Invocation Interceptor 130, 132
    in Lazy Acquisition 100, 101
    in Lifecycle Manager 144, 145
    in Location Forwarder 155
    in Lookup 81, 83
    in Marshaller 55
    in Object Id 74, 75
    in Passivation 109, 110
    in Per-request Instance 95
    in Pooling 104
    in Qos Observer 152
    in Remoting Error 63, 64
    in Server Request Handler 51
    in Static Instance 92
    in Sync With Server 169

Invoker (*Continued*)
    in Web Services 244, 245, 246, 247, 249, 251, 253, 254, 256, 257, 259, 264, 283
    interactions 68, 85, 114, 121, 126, 179, 184
IONA 293
IOR
    See Interoperable Object Reference 316
IP routing 157
Isolation 338

J
J2EE 240, 293
JAC 354
JacORB 293
Java 57, 185, 256
    applets 345
    Java Virtual Machine 344
    object 172
    RMI 12, 341
Java Messaging Service 14, 242, 264, 271, 346
    messaging provider 258
Java Remote Method Invocation 239, 344, 346
    provider 258
Java RMI
    See Java Remote Method Invocation
Java2WSDL 251
JavaSpaces 16
JAX-RPC handler 263
JBoss 341
    Aspect-Oriented Programming 354
Jini Proxy 345
Job Queue 336

K
KQML 346

L
Lane, in RT-CORBA 327
Latency 5, 22
Layer
    application 127
    architecture 127, 128
    communication 128
    invocation 127
    request handling 127
Layers 244, 335
Lazy Acquisition 29, 87, 89, 99, **100–102**, 118, 336, 337
    in Per-request Instance 94
    in .NET Remoting 194, 200, 203, 204, 206, 212
    in CORBA 301, 311, 329
    in Object Id 75
    in Static Instance 91
    interactions 111, 112
Leader/Followers 50, 53, 328, 335
Lease 89, 98, 99, 108
    management 123
    renewal 107
    role of sponsor 214
    time-based 106
Leasing 29, 87, 89, 99, **106–108**, 289, 336, 337, 338
    in .NET Remoting 204, 206, 208, 212
    in Client-Dependent Instance 98
    in Lazy Acquisition 102
    in Lifecycle Manager 144
    in Lookup 83
    in Web Services 269, 270, 286
    interactions 111, 112, 113, 120
Leela 239, 291
    support for Web Services 287
Lifecycle Callback 104, 110, 143, 144
Lifecycle management
    advanced in .NET Remoting 215
    in CORBA 305
    in Web Services 269
Lifecycle management patterns 87–126
    interactions 111
Lifecycle Manager 31, 87, 88, 89, 99, 141, **143–145**, 289, 341
    in .NET Remoting 217
    in Client-Dependent Instance 98

Index

in Configuration Group 146, 147
in CORBA 305
in Invoker 45, 47
in Lazy Acquisition 100, 101
in Leasing 106, 107
in Local Object 149
in Object Id 75
in Passivation 109, 110
in Per-request Instance 94, 95
in Pooling 104
in Qos Observer 152
in Web Services 270
interactions 113, 115, 116, 117, 118, 119, 120, 121, 124, 125, 158, 159, 160, 161
Lifecycle Operation 118, 145
Lifecycle, pattern interactions 114
Lifetime, of instance in .NET Remoting 206
Linda 16
Little endian 55
Load balanced server 350
Local Object 31, 142, **149–150**
in CORBA 326
interactions 180
Location Forwarder 142, **154–157**, 290, 344, 350, 351, 352
in .NET Remoting 228
in CORBA 315, 316
in Invoker 45
in Static Instance 92
in Web Services 247, 277, 283, 286
Location forwarding, in CORBA 315
Lookup 28, 73, **81–84**, 316, 336, 337, 342, 343, 344
in .NET Remoting 193
in Absolute Object Reference 79, 80
in Broker 22
in Client Proxy 41
in Client-Dependent Instance 97
in CORBA 316
in Local Object 149
in Remoting Error 65
in Static Instance 91, 92

in Web Services 240, 247, 279, 283, 286
interactions 85

M
Managed Resource 95
Marshaling, using SOAP XML encoding 266
Marshaller 35, **55–58**, 268, 287, 290, 344, 345
in .NET Remoting 221, 226, 228
in Absolute Object Reference 79
in Broker 20, 21
in Configuration Group 146, 147
in CORBA 302, 303
in Invocation Context 134
in Invoker 45
in Protocol Plug-in 135, 137
in Qos Observer 151, 152
in Requestor 38
in Web Services 257, 259, 266, 284
interactions 67, 68, 85
Masquerade, in security threat 347
Mean Time Between Failure 3
Mediator 318
Message
channel 346
modification, in security threat 347
replay, in security threat 348
Message handling
in CORBA 299
in Indigo 235
Message passing 12
Message Passing Interface 14
Message processing, in Web Services 256
Message queue 346
Message Redirector 46
Message sink 223
Message-Oriented Middleware 14
Messaging 346
in CORBA 318
Microkernel 299
Microsoft Foundation Classes 187
Microsoft Intermediate Language 188, 189, 196

Mobile agent 344
Model-View-Controller 165
MOM
   See Message-Oriented Middleware
Monitor Object 335
MPI
   See Message Passing Interface
MQ Series 14, 240, 346
MSIL
   See Microsoft Intermediate Language
MSMQ 14, 346
MTBF
   See Mean Time Between Failure
MTS 340

N
n-tier model 341
Name, persistent 80
Namespace
   in .NET 188
Naming service 82
Network
   latency 22
   unreliability 22
Non-invasiveness 353
n-version programming 352

O
Object
   activation 88
   business 216
   deactivation 88
   state 11, 79
   well-known 82
Object Group 156, 352
Object Id 23, 28, 73, **74–76**, 116, 348
   in .NET Remoting 198
   in Absolute Object Reference 77, 78, 79
   in CORBA 304, 307, 311, 313
   in Interface Description 62
   in Invocation Context 133
   in Invocation Interceptor 131
   in Invoker 44
   in Lifecycle Manager 145
   in Location Forwarder 155
   in Lookup 81
   in Marshaller 55
   in Per-request Instance 94
   in Web Services 246
   interactions 68, 69, 85, 115, 121, 158
Object invocation, from client 247
Object lifecycle 114
Object Management Group 293
Object reference, in CORBA 307
Object Request Broker 293, 315, 317, 318, 321
   client-side 329
   core 298, 299
   extension 301
   in connection handling 299
   in message handling 299
   initializer 309
   instance 297
   role 301
   server-side 329
Object state
   See State
Object Transaction Service 340
Observer 165
OmniORB 293
On the fly
   class generation 197
   code evaluation 345
   code generation 220
   compilation 62
   creation of .NET types 188
   object construction 79
   proxy generation 219, 251, 254
   WSDL generation 251
Oneway 233, 318, 321
   reliable 321
Open Software Foundation 12
ORB
   See Object Request Broker

P
P2P
   See Peer-to-peer

Index

PageSpace 16
Partial Acquisition 101
Partial failure 6
Passivation 29, 87, 88, 89, 99,
   109–110
   in .NET Remoting 216, 217
   in Client-Dependent Instance 98
   in Lazy Acquisition 102
   in Lifecycle Manager 144
   in Static Instance 91
   interactions 111, 112, 113, 124, 159
Pattern
   basic remoting 35–71
   basic remoting, interactions 66
   building asynchronous on Axis 271
   chapter overview 27–33
   consequences in Web Services 289
   extended infrastructure 141–161
   extended infrastructure,
      interactions 158
   extension 127–140
   extension, interactions 138
   general resource
      management 99–110
   identification 73–86
   identification, interactions 85
   invocation asynchrony 163–184
   lifecycle management 87–126
   lifecycle management,
      interactions 111
   related concepts, technologies 333–354
   roles 66
   thumbprint 186
Pattern language
   overview 19–33
Pattern map 186
   in CORBA 294
   in .NET Remoting 189
   in Web Services 244
   .NET Remoting 189
   for Web Services 244
Pattern mapping, in Indigo 236
Peer-to-Peer 9, 10, 287, 333, 341, 343

Per-request Instance 29, 87, 88, **93–95**,
   113, 118
   in .NET Remoting 200, 206, 209
   in Client-Dependent Instance 97
   in CORBA 312
   in Lazy Acquisition 102
   in Object Id 75
   in Web Services 246, 269, 283
   interactions 111, 115, 116, 117
Persistence 338, 340
Persistent name 80
Pivot point 260
POA
   See Portable Object Adapter
Poll Object 32, 163, 164, **170–172**, 175, 274,
   288, 335, 346
   in .NET Remoting 230, 231
   in Client Request Handler 50
   in CORBA 319
   in Result Callback 174
   in Web Services 271, 274, 275
   interactions 176, 180, 181, 182, 184
Polling Consumer 346
Pooling 29, 87, 88, 89, 99, **103–105**, 159,
   289, 336, 337
   in .NET Remoting 201, 215, 216, 217
   in Broker 24
   in Client Request Handler 50
   in CORBA 313, 327
   in Invoker 45
   in Lazy Acquisition 102
   in Lifecycle Manager 143, 144
   in Object Id 75
   in Per-request Instance 93, 95
   in Server Request Handler 53
   in Web Services 269, 270, 277
   interactions 111, 112, 113, 117, 119, 158
Port, in Indigo 235
Portable Interceptor 299
Portable Object Adapter 298, 299, 304, 320
Predictability 5
Priority, preservation in RT-CORBA 324
Protocol integration, in Web Services 264

Protocol Plug-in 31, 129, **135–137**, 345, 348
  in .NET Remoting 221, 226, 228
  in Client Request Handler 49
  in Configuration Group 146, 147
  in CORBA 331
  in Local Object 149
  in Qos Observer 151, 152
  in RT-CORBA 330
  in Web Services 250, 264, 265, 271, 278
Proxy 42, 95, 335
  generation using WSDL 249
  real 218
  transparent 218

Q
QoS
  see Quality of Service
Qos Observer 141, **151–153**
  in .NET Remoting 228
  in CORBA 331
  in Web Services 276
Quality Objects 331
Quality of Service 17, 135, 137, 142, 146, 151, 152, 153, 271
  attributes 347
  in RT-CORBA 323
  in Web Services 276
  monitoring 353

R
RDF
  See Resource Description Framework
Reactor 49, 52, 128, 265, 300, 328, 335
Real proxy 218
Real Time-CORBA 185, 299, 308, 323–331
Receiver 54
Reflection 57, 61
Remote evaluation 9, 344
Remote object 22
  dynamic invocation on server 245
  state 80, 90, 91, 93, 96, 103, 109, 111, 144, 198, 203
  stateless 104

Remote Procedure Call 10, 11, 12, 244, 253, 339, 345
Remoting
  and aspect orientation 353
  styles of operation 9
Remoting boundary
  in .NET 195
Remoting Error 22, 36, 40, **63–65**, 71, 124, 167, 288, 348
  in .NET Remoting 198
  in Broker 24
  in Client Request Handler 50
  in CORBA 303, 323
  in Interface Description 62
  in Invocation Interceptor 131
  in Invoker 46
  in Leasing 108
  in Per-request Instance 95
  in Requestor 38, 39
  in Web Services 246, 254, 258, 283, 285
  interactions 69, 70, 121, 138
Remoting framework 192
Remoting Proxy 42
Replication 340
Reply handler, in CORBA 319
Request Handler 348
  in Marshaller 56
  in Qos Observer 151
  in Remoting Error 63
Request handler, in .NET Remoting 217
Request handling layer 127
Requestor 35, **37–39**, 127, 129, 288, 290, 339, 342
  in .NET Remoting 218, 236
  in Absolute Object Reference 77, 78, 80
  in Broker 22
  in Client Proxy 40, 41, 42
  in Client Request Handler 48, 50
  in CORBA 302
  in Fire And Forget 165, 166
  in Interface Description 61, 62
  in Invocation Context 134

Index   387

    in Invocation Interceptor 130, 131, 132
    in Invoker 43, 44, 46
    in Marshaller 55, 56
    in Object Id 74, 76
    in Poll Object 171
    in Qos Observer 152
    in Remoting Error 63, 64, 65
    in Result Callback 173, 174
    in Sync With Server 168, 169
    in Web Services 244, 247, 248, 249, 256, 257, 259, 270, 272, 274, 282
    interactions 67, 69, 70, 86, 138, 177, 182
Resource access restriction 340
Resource Description Framework 289
Resource Lifecycle Manager 145, 336
Resource management patterns 99–110
Result Callback 33, 163, 164, **173–175**, 288, 346
    in .NET Remoting 232
    in Client Request Handler 50
    in CORBA 319
    in Poll Object 172
    in Web Services 271, 274, 275
    interactions 176, 180, 181, 182, 183, 184
Role, pattern 66
Rollback 352
RPC
    See Remote procedure call
RT-CORBA
    See Real-time CORBA
RT-ORB 328
RT-POA 327

S
Safe Tcl 345
SAIWS
  See Simple Asynchronous Invocation Framework for Web Services
SAML 278
Sandbox interpreter, 345
Scalability 6
    improving 349
Security 347
    in Web Services 278

Separation of concerns 43, 61
Serializer 58, 344
Servant locator 312
Server application, in Broker 25
Server component 340
Server Request Handler 22, 30, 31, 35, **51–54**, 76, 99, 127, 129, 136, 142, 287, 335, 336, 337
    in .NET Remoting 198, 217, 236
    in Absolute Object Reference 77
    in Client Request Handler 50
    in Configuration Group 147
    in CORBA 299, 300, 328
    in Invocation Interceptor 132
    in Invoker 44, 45, 47
    in Object Id 74
    in Protocol Plug-in 135, 137
    in Remoting Error 64
    in Sync With Server 169
    in Web Services 257, 259, 264, 265, 282, 286
    interactions 68, 179, 183
Server request interceptor 309
Server-activated instance, in .NET 199
Server-side dispatching, in CORBA 304
Service Components 113
Service Configurator 301
Service context 309
Service-Oriented Architecture 240
Session 337, 350
Session Components 113
Session Fail-over 350
Shared repositories 14
Simple Asynchronous Invocation Framework for Web Services 272
Simple Object Access Protocol 235, 241, 242, 253, 257, 264, 266, 278, 291
    envelope 266
    messages 244
Singleton 204, 216

Sink
    channel 223
    formatter 223
    in .NET Remoting 222
    message 223
SMTP 242, 264, 266
SOA
    See Service-Oriented Architecture
SOAP
    See Simple Object Access Protocol
Society of Worldwide Interbank Financial Telecommunication 2
Sponsor, last hope in lease expiry 214
SSL 348
State
    client 29, 96
    client-dependent 337
    conversational 208
    described by messages 346
    diagram, CORBA
        Portable Object Adapter Manager 306
    distribution across nodes 342
    execution 344, 345
    finite-state machine 243
    in session 139
    maintenance of 269
    management 29, 87, 99
    non-trivial 144
    object 11, 79
    passivated 113
    persisted 109, 158, 350, 352
    remote object 80, 90, 91, 93, 96, 103, 109, 111, 144, 198, 203
    session 270
    storage 352
    transient 88
Static instance 90
Static Instance 29, 87, 88, **90–92**
    in .NET Remoting 200, 201, 209
    in Client-Dependent Instance 96, 97
    in CORBA 310
    in Object Id 75
    in Per-request Instance 93
    in Web Services 240, 269
    interactions 111, 115, 118
Strategy 53, 115, 176
Stream
    asynchronous 16
    intercepting in .NET Remoting 221
    isochronous 17
    synchronous 16
Streaming 16
Streaming server 16
Strong mobility 345
Studio.NET 198
Sun RPC 12
SWIFT
    See Society of Worldwide Interbank Financial Telecommunication
Sync With Server 32, 163, 164, **168–169**, 351
    in .NET Remoting 234
    in CORBA 322
    in Web Services 271, 274, 275
    interactions 176, 178, 180, 183

T
TAO 293
Technology adoption life cycle 294
Technology projection 185–331
Thread pool
    in RT-CORBA 327
Tibco 14, 346
Time To Live 212
Timeout, in CORBA 322
tModels 279
Total cost of ownership 4
TP monitor
    See Transaction processing monitor
Transaction management 340
Transaction processing monitor 338, 339
Transparent proxy 218
TSpaces 16
TTL
    See Time To Live

Index

Tuxedo 340
Two-phase commit protocol 339

U
UBR See Universal Business Registry
UDDI 241, 242, 256
    in Web Services lookup 279
    support in GLUE 283
UDP 166, 229, 331
Universal Business Registry 279

V
VB.NET 187, 188
Virtual Instance 87
Virtual Private Network 349
Virtual Shared Memory 16
Visual Studio 216
Voyager 345
VSM
    See Virtual Shared Memory
VxWorks 324

W
W3C 241
Weak mobility 345
Web Server 284
Web Services 2, 12, 185, 187, 235, 237
    and QoS 276
    consequence of patterns 289
    definition 240
    history 239
    Lookup 279
    security 278
    technology projection 239–291
Web Services Description Language 241, 242, 249, 254, 256, 281, 285, 291
    structure 249
Web Services Invocation Framework 270
    asynchrony support 270
WebSphere MQ 14, 346
Well-known object 82
Worker Pool 336
WSDL
    See Web Services Description Language
WSDL2Java 251, 253, 255, 281
WSIF
    See Web Services Invocation Framework
WS-Coordination 278
WS-Policy 279
WS-Security 278
WS-SecurityPolicy 279
WS-Transaction 278

X
XACML 279
XLANG 242
XM 242
XML 57, 170, 185, 194, 223, 227, 240, 247, 254, 256, 291
    deployment descriptor 284
    key management specification 278
    parser 276
    schema 267
    validation 276
    signature 278
XML-RPC 241, 291
XOTcl 354
XSD 285